TCP/IP For Dummies, 3rd Edition

Nifty Web Sites and Pages with Security Information

✔ **Netsurfer Focus on Computer and Network Security:** A document by a private company that develops technologies for the Internet and intranets. `www.netsurf.com/nsf`

✔ **The WWW Security FAQ:** Frequently asked questions about security on the World Wide Web. `www-genome.wi.mit.edu/WWW/faqs/www-security-faq.html`

✔ **COAST (Computer Operations and Security Technology) and CERIAS (Center for Education and Research in Information Assurance and Security), both at Purdue University:** A huge archive of computer security resources, including documents and about 200 tools for various operating systems, such as DOS, Macintosh, and UNIX. `www.cs.purdue.edu/coast` and `www.cerias.purdue.edu`

✔ **Site Security Handbook — RFC 2196:** A security bible. `info.internet.isi.edu/in-notes/rfc/files/rfc2196.txt`

✔ **Electronic Privacy Information Center Home Page:** The latest news about security and privacy, and links to security resources. Check out the Online Guides to Practical Privacy Tools and Privacy Resources. `www.epic.org`

✔ **Computer Emergency Response Teams (CERT) around the world:**

- AUSCERT — Australia, `www.auscert.org.au`
- CERT — United States, `www.cert.org`
- CERT/NL — Netherlands, `www.nic.surfnet.nl/surfnet/security/cert-nl.html`
- DFN/CERT — Germany, `www.cert.dfn.de/eng`

✔ **Computer Incident Advisory Capability:** U.S. Department of Energy. `ciac.llnl.gov`

✔ **U.S. National Institute of Health Unix Security Page:** Security issues and advisories, programs, patches, and a directory of other security sites. `www.alw.nih.gov/Security`

✔ **U.S. National Institute of Standards and Technology Computer Security Resource Clearinghouse:** Includes security publications, alerts, and news, including the U.S. Department of Defense's documents on security architecture and trusted systems. `csrc.nist.gov`

✔ **E-commerce and security issues and products:**

- Secure Electronic Transactions: MasterCard International and Visa. `www.mastercard.com/set/set.html` and `www.visa.com/cgi-bin/vee/nt/main.html?2+0`
- Electronic Commerce and Cash: Payment technology products, online shopping, and online bill paying. `www.cybercash.com`

For Dummies®: Bestselling Book Series for Beginners

TCP/IP For Dummies, 3rd Edition

Cheat Sheet

TCP/IP Definitions

- **Protocol:** A formal description of the rules that computers on a network must follow to communicate. Protocols define communications rules that range from the order of bits and bytes to how two programs transfer files across an internet.

- **Protocol stack:** A layered set of protocols that work together so that computers can communicate across a network.

- **TCP/IP (Transmission Control Protocol/Internet Protocol):** A set of protocols, services, and applications for linking computers of all kinds. Intranets, private internets, and the Internet are built on TCP/IP.

- **IP address:** The 32-bit (IPv4) or 128-bit (IPv6) numeric address for a computer. You must have an IP address to be connected to an intranet or the Internet.

- **internet:** Any network of networks connected by TCP/IP.

- **the Internet:** The largest international network of networks connected by TCP/IP. The Internet includes the World Wide Web.

- **World Wide Web (WWW, the Web):** An information system (mostly graphical) that runs on the Internet. The WWW uses TCP/IP's HTTP (hypertext transfer protocol) to access Web pages. You use a computer program called a browser to navigate the Web and to see the information provided by Web servers.

- **InterNIC:** The organization that registers and maintains IP addresses for the .com, .net, .edu, and .org Internet domains. Visit the InterNIC Web site at `www.internic.net`.

- **intranet:** An organization's private network that uses TCP/IP protocols, applications, and services.

Acronym challenged? If you don't know what a particular acronym means, try `www.ucc.ie/info/net/acronyms`, the WorldWideWeb Acronym and Abbreviation Server. You may get a laugh out of some of the translations.

IDG BOOKS WORLDWIDE

Copyright © 1999 IDG Books Worldwide, Inc. All rights reserved.
Cheat Sheet $2.95 value. Item 0473-8.
For more information about IDG Books, call 1-800-762-2974.

For Dummies®: Bestselling Book Series for Beginners

TM

References for the Rest of Us! ®

BESTSELLING BOOK SERIES

Are you intimidated and confused by computers? Do you find that traditional manuals are overloaded with technical details you'll never use? Do your friends and family always call you to fix simple problems on their PCs? Then the *...For Dummies*® computer book series from IDG Books Worldwide is for you.

...For Dummies books are written for those frustrated computer users who know they aren't really dumb but find that PC hardware, software, and indeed the unique vocabulary of computing make them feel helpless. *...For Dummies* books use a lighthearted approach, a down-to-earth style, and even cartoons and humorous icons to dispel computer novices' fears and build their confidence. Lighthearted but not lightweight, these books are a perfect survival guide for anyone forced to use a computer.

> *"I like my copy so much I told friends; now they bought copies."*
>
> — Irene C., Orwell, Ohio

> *"Quick, concise, nontechnical, and humorous."*
>
> — Jay A., Elburn, Illinois

> *"Thanks, I needed this book. Now I can sleep at night."*
>
> — Robin F., British Columbia, Canada

Already, millions of satisfied readers agree. They have made *...For Dummies* books the #1 introductory level computer book series and have written asking for more. So, if you're looking for the most fun and easy way to learn about computers, look to *...For Dummies* books to give you a helping hand.

IDG BOOKS WORLDWIDE ®

1/99

by Candace Leiden and Marshall Wilensky

Foreword by John Landry

IDG
BOOKS
WORLDWIDE

IDG Books Worldwide, Inc.
An International Data Group Company

Foster City, CA ♦ Chicago, IL ♦ Indianapolis, IN ♦ New York, NY

TCP/IP For Dummies®, 3rd Edition

Published by
IDG Books Worldwide, Inc.
An International Data Group Company
919 E. Hillsdale Blvd.
Suite 400
Foster City, CA 94404
www.idgbooks.com (IDG Books Worldwide Web site)
www.dummies.com (Dummies Press Web site)

Library of Congress Catalog Card No.: 98-89938

ISBN: 0-7645-0473-8

Printed in the United States of America

10 9 8 7 6 5 4 3

3O/SR/QR/QQ/IN

Distributed in the United States by IDG Books Worldwide, Inc.

Distributed by CDG Books Canada Inc. for Canada; by Transworld Publishers Limited in the United Kingdom; by IDG Norge Books for Norway; by IDG Sweden Books for Sweden; by IDG Books Australia Publishing Corporation Pty. Ltd. for Australia and New Zealand; by TransQuest Publishers Pte Ltd. for Singapore, Malaysia, Thailand, Indonesia, and Hong Kong; by Gotop Information Inc. for Taiwan; by ICG Muse, Inc. for Japan; by Intersoft for South Africa; by Eyrolles for France; by International Thomson Publishing for Germany, Austria and Switzerland; by Distribuidora Cuspide for Argentina; by LR International for Brazil; by Galileo Libros for Chile; by Ediciones ZETA S.C.R. Ltda. for Peru; by WS Computer Publishing Corporation, Inc., for the Philippines; by Contemporanea de Ediciones for Venezuela; by Express Computer Distributors for the Caribbean and West Indies; by Micronesia Media Distributor, Inc. for Micronesia; by Chips Computadoras S.A. de C.V. for Mexico; by Editorial Norma de Panama S.A. for Panama; by American Bookshops for Finland.

For general information on IDG Books Worldwide's books in the U.S., please call our Consumer Customer Service department at 800-762-2974. For reseller information, including discounts and premium sales, please call our Reseller Customer Service department at 800-434-3422.

For information on where to purchase IDG Books Worldwide's books outside the U.S., please contact our International Sales department at 317-596-5530 or fax 317-572-4002.

For consumer information on foreign language translations, please contact our Customer Service department at 1-800-434-3422, fax 317-572-4002, or e-mail rights@idgbooks.com.

For information on licensing foreign or domestic rights, please phone +1-650-653-7098.

For sales inquiries and special prices for bulk quantities, please contact our Sales department at 800-762-2974 or write to the address above.

For information on using IDG Books Worldwide's books in the classroom or for ordering examination copies, please contact our Educational Sales department at 800-434-2086 or fax 317-572-4005.

For press review copies, author interviews, or other publicity information, please contact our Public Relations department at 650-653-7000 or fax 650-653-7500.

For authorization to photocopy items for corporate, personal, or educational use, please contact Copyright Clearance Center, 222 Rosewood Drive, Danvers, MA 01923, or fax 978-750-4470.

is a registered trademark under exclusive license to IDG Books Worldwide, Inc. from International Data Group, Inc.

IDG
BOOKS
WORLDWIDE

About the Authors

Candace Leiden is currently the Chief Technical Officer at Cardinal Consulting. Forced to learn about computers because she was afraid of slide rules, Candace has been a software developer, a system administrator, and a database designer and administrator. When she is not worrying about Emily (her 10-year-old niece) knowing more about computers than she does, Candace teaches computer classes worldwide and writes courseware for major international software companies. She is an internationally recognized speaker on client/server computing, databases, and the UNIX and Microsoft Windows NT operating systems. Candace met Marshall Wilensky in 1981 when they both worked at the same company. She taught him everything he knows.

Marshall Wilensky has been working with computers for more than 20 years (and still has fewer wrinkles than Candace and less gray hair). He has been a programmer, a system administrator, and has managed large multivendor and multiprotocol networks, including those at Harvard University's Graduate School of Business Administration. He is currently a technical consultant for Lotus Notes and Domino in the Worldwide Partners Programs at Lotus Development Corporation. He is in demand worldwide as a speaker on UNIX, Windows NT, networking, and Lotus Notes. Marshall met Candace Leiden in 1981 when they both worked at the same company. He taught her everything she knows.

Candace and Marshall are both members of the Internet Society and the Internet Engineering Task Force.

ABOUT IDG BOOKS WORLDWIDE

Welcome to the world of IDG Books Worldwide.

IDG Books Worldwide, Inc., is a subsidiary of International Data Group, the world's largest publisher of computer-related information and the leading global provider of information services on information technology. IDG was founded more than 30 years ago by Patrick J. McGovern and now employs more than 9,000 people worldwide. IDG publishes more than 290 computer publications in over 75 countries. More than 90 million people read one or more IDG publications each month.

Launched in 1990, IDG Books Worldwide is today the #1 publisher of best-selling computer books in the United States. We are proud to have received eight awards from the Computer Press Association in recognition of editorial excellence and three from Computer Currents' First Annual Readers' Choice Awards. Our best-selling ...For Dummies® series has more than 50 million copies in print with translations in 31 languages. IDG Books Worldwide, through a joint venture with IDG's Hi-Tech Beijing, became the first U.S. publisher to publish a computer book in the People's Republic of China. In record time, IDG Books Worldwide has become the first choice for millions of readers around the world who want to learn how to better manage their businesses.

Our mission is simple: Every one of our books is designed to bring extra value and skill-building instructions to the reader. Our books are written by experts who understand and care about our readers. The knowledge base of our editorial staff comes from years of experience in publishing, education, and journalism — experience we use to produce books to carry us into the new millennium. In short, we care about books, so we attract the best people. We devote special attention to details such as audience, interior design, use of icons, and illustrations. And because we use an efficient process of authoring, editing, and desktop publishing our books electronically, we can spend more time ensuring superior content and less time on the technicalities of making books.

You can count on our commitment to deliver high-quality books at competitive prices on topics you want to read about. At IDG Books Worldwide, we continue in the IDG tradition of delivering quality for more than 30 years. You'll find no better book on a subject than one from IDG Books Worldwide.

John Kilcullen
Chairman and CEO
IDG Books Worldwide, Inc.

Steven Berkowitz
President and Publisher
IDG Books Worldwide, Inc.

**Eighth Annual
Computer Press
Awards ≥1992**

**Ninth Annual
Computer Press
Awards ≥1993**

**Tenth Annual
Computer Press
Awards ≥1994**

**Eleventh Annual
Computer Press
Awards ≥1995**

IDG is the world's leading IT media, research and exposition company. Founded in 1964, IDG had 1997 revenues of $2.05 billion and has more than 9,000 employees worldwide. IDG offers the widest range of media options that reach IT buyers in 75 countries representing 95% of worldwide IT spending. IDG's diverse product and services portfolio spans six key areas including print publishing, online publishing, expositions and conferences, market research, education and training, and global marketing services. More than 90 million people read one or more of IDG's 290 magazines and newspapers, including IDG's leading global brands — Computerworld, PC World, Network World, Macworld and the Channel World family of publications. IDG Books Worldwide is one of the fastest-growing computer book publishers in the world, with more than 700 titles in 36 languages. The "...For Dummies®" series alone has more than 50 million copies in print. IDG offers online users the largest network of technology-specific Web sites around the world through IDG.net (http://www.idg.net), which comprises more than 225 targeted Web sites in 55 countries worldwide. International Data Corporation (IDC) is the world's largest provider of information technology data, analysis and consulting, with research centers in over 41 countries and more than 400 research analysts worldwide. IDG World Expo is a leading producer of more than 168 globally branded conferences and expositions in 35 countries including E3 (Electronic Entertainment Expo), Macworld Expo, ComNet, Windows World Expo, ICE (Internet Commerce Expo), Agenda, DEMO, and Spotlight. IDG's training subsidiary, ExecuTrain, is the world's largest computer training company, with more than 230 locations worldwide and 785 training courses. IDG Marketing Services helps industry-leading IT companies build international brand recognition by developing global integrated marketing programs via IDG's print, online and exposition products worldwide. Further information about the company can be found at www.idg.com.   1/24/99

Dedication

To Emily Duncan, who is wise beyond her years. Emily taught us an important lesson that got us through the times we thought this book would never be finished: "Be brave, be brave, be brave." Use this as your mantra when it seems like you will never be able to keep up with changing technologies. It really helps.

Candace would like to dedicate this book to her mother, who knows what the most important thing is in life and has proven that you can do anything if you have to. (I don't know how she ever managed.)

Marshall would like to dedicate this book to his father, who passed on the work ethic that made it possible for Marshall to finish the book nights and weekends and still keep his cool.

Authors' Acknowledgments

We were astounded at how many people it takes to create a book. We'd like to thank the team at IDG Books for putting up with us. Special thanks go to Tere Drenth. Her patience, good humor, and positive reinforcement never flagged. Thanks also go to Mary Bednarek for convincing us to update the first edition (and also for lunch) and to Sherri Morningstar, our acquisitions editor. Thanks to all the people behind the scenes at IDG Books who helped make our documents a real book.

We'd like to thank all the people who helped us out with software for the examples in this book. L. Stuart Vance provided the basis for the interesting network devices in Chapter 22. When we heard of networked cola machines years ago at one of his presentations, we were hooked on weird stuff. Dave Kurtzer and FTP Software, Inc. provided our IPv6 client, Secure Client for Windows 95. Bob Watson from Digital Equipment Corporation at the Centre Technique Europe in Sophia Antipolis, France, was extremely generous in providing examples from an IPv6 server running Digital UNIX. Thanks also to John M. Wobus for permission to use parts of the DHCP FAQ.

Ken Duncan's technical comments in the first edition were always brief and so precisely on target that we think he might be clairvoyant. He actually took the time to check our binary arithmetic, and the work he did still stands.

Katherine Duncan's technical editing on this recent edition has been really helpful. Besides checking for technical boo-boos, she was kind enough to double check our Web references, which is a time consuming and tedious job. She saved us a lot of time.

Publisher's Acknowledgments

We're proud of this book; please register your comments through our IDG Books Worldwide Online Registration Form located at http://my2cents.dummies.com.

Some of the people who helped bring this book to market include the following:

Acquisitions, Editorial, and Media Development

Project Editor: Tere Drenth

Acquisitions Editor: Sherry Morningstar

Technical Editors: Katharine Duncan, Cardinal Consulting, Inc.

Associate Permissions Editor: Carmen Krikorian

Editorial Manager: Mary C. Corder

Production

Project Coordinator: Karen York

Layout and Graphics: Kelly Hardesty, Angela F. Hunckler, Jane E. Martin, Brent Savage, Jacque Schneider, Janet Seib, Brian Torwelle

Proofreaders: Kelli Botta, Christine Berman, Rebecca Senninger, Kathleen Sparrow, Janet M. Withers

Indexer: Lori Lathrop

Special Help

David Mehring, Michelle Vukas

General and Administrative

IDG Books Worldwide, Inc.: John Kilcullen, CEO; Steven Berkowitz, President and Publisher

IDG Books Technology Publishing Group: Richard Swadley, Senior Vice President and Publisher; Walter Bruce III, Vice President and Associate Publisher; Joseph Wikert, Associate Publisher; Mary Bednarek, Branded Product Development Director; Mary Corder, Editorial Director; Barry Pruett, Publishing Manager; Michelle Baxter, Publishing Manager

IDG Books Consumer Publishing Group: Roland Elgey, Senior Vice President and Publisher; Kathleen A. Welton, Vice President and Publisher; Kevin Thornton, Acquisitions Manager; Kristin A. Cocks, Editorial Director

IDG Books Internet Publishing Group: Brenda McLaughlin, Senior Vice President and Publisher; Diane Graves Steele, Vice President and Associate Publisher; Sofia Marchant, Online Marketing Manager

IDG Books Production for Dummies Press: Debbie Stailey, Associate Director of Production; Cindy L. Phipps, Manager of Project Coordination, Production Proofreading, and Indexing; Tony Augsburger, Manager of Prepress, Reprints, and Systems; Laura Carpenter, Production Control Manager; Shelley Lea, Supervisor of Graphics and Design; Debbie J. Gates, Production Systems Specialist; Robert Springer, Supervisor of Proofreading; Kathie Schutte, Production Supervisor

Dummies Packaging and Book Design: Patty Page, Manager, Promotions Marketing

♦

The publisher would like to give special thanks to Patrick J. McGovern, without whom this book would not have been possible.

♦

Contents at a Glance

Cartoons at a Glance

By Rich Tennant

page 7

page 317

page 5

page 55

page 173

Fax: 978-546-7747
E-mail: richtennant@the5thwave.com
World Wide Web: www.the5thwave.com

Table of Contents

Foreword

· ·

*I*f you're looking for a buzzword to capture the essence of the next great leap forward in the computerization of society, "TCP/IP" just doesn't seem to hack it. Few would have guessed even a few years ago — even those of use who have been toiling away in the computer industry for years — that this tongue-twister acronym would come to represent what it does today. For many, TCP/IP means the dawning of the golden age of computing: universal access to the increasingly rich information resources of the Internet.

Now boasting millions of users, with more rushing to get online every day, the Internet and the graphical World Wide Web may foretell the most significant impact on commerce and society since the development of the assembly line. Today, businesses can target marketing efforts as mass groups of consumers, interactively fine-tuning the content to meet each group's own specific needs and desires. New channels of sales and product distribution that have been impossible until now, or at least astronomically expensive, can be deployed on the Internet rapidly and economically. Large corporations can create virtual organizations nimble enough to quickly take advantage of rapidly changing opportunities. Small entrepreneurs can develop virtual infrastructures to compete with the titans of industry, without having to raise huge amounts of capital.

So what's driving all of this? The answer to that question is unimportant to most of the millions who will be influenced by online technology. Most consumers aren't interested in exactly how the video and sound make their way from network broadcasters into the television set; these folks only want to enjoy and learn what they watch and hear. Similarly, you don't need to know exactly how the Internet operates in order to get on line and surf the Web. But if you're the kind of person who likes to be more familiar with what's behind the screen, then *TCP/IP For Dummies,* 3rd Edition is the book for you.

This book takes you past the command lines and graphical user interfaces of Internet tools. In plain language, this volume tells you what really happens to create the illusion of magic. It's a guide for normal people who want to know what forces are driving their lives. It's for those of you who want straightforward information, without the technobabble that so often cloaks the wonders being created by the computer industry today.

John Landry
Chief Technology Officer and Senior Vice President
Lotus Development Corporation

Introduction

*T*CP/IP is a hot topic these days, because it's the glue that holds the Internet (and the World Wide Web) together. In order to be well connected (network-wise, that is), sooner or later you have to get familiar with what it is and what it does. So if you want to understand what TCP/IP is, why you need it, and what to do with it, but you just don't know where to start, this book is for you.

This book takes an irreverent approach to TCP/IP. We've taken the mystery out of it by giving you down-to-earth explanations for all the buzzwords and technical jargon that TCP/IP loves.

This isn't a formal tutorial; you can skip around and read as much or as little as you want. If you need to impress your boss and colleagues with buzzwords, you can find out just enough to toss them around intelligently at meetings and cocktail parties. On the other hand, you can go all the way and discover TCP/IP's most important features and tools and the role that TCP/IP plays in the Internet. It's all right here in your hands.

About This Book

TCP/IP For Dummies, 3rd Edition is really two books in one. First, this book is an introduction to the basics — it tells you exactly what TCP/IP is and what it's for. Second, if you already understand these fundamentals, you can use this book as a reference to help you use TCP/IP applications on all kinds of computers connected to networks. This book also helps you understand the many tools associated with TCP/IP.

Here are some of the subjects that we cover:

- Understanding the relationship between TCP/IP and the Internet
- Understanding the relationship between the Internet and the World Wide Web (WWW)
- Discovering who owns TCP/IP and how you get it
- Exploring client/server and how it's the foundation of TCP/IP
- Realizing that TCP/IP isn't just for UNIX

- ✔ Understanding intranets and extranets
- ✔ Uncovering tools and applications for getting around the Internet
- ✔ Building and enforcing security
- ✔ Boldly going to the next generation of TCP/IP

Conventions Used in This Book

This book is loaded with information. But don't try to read it cover-to-cover. You may hurt yourself. If your head explodes, don't call or send e-mail. Instead of reading cover-to-cover, we recommend using this book as a reference. Each topic stands alone, so you don't need a lot of prerequisite information. Look up the topic you want in the Index or Table of Contents, and you find helpful facts and instructional information as well as some detailed techie stuff.

All commands that you need to enter yourself appear like this:

COMMAND to type

To enter this command, you type **COMMAND to type** exactly as you see it here, using the same upper- and lowercase letters, and then press the Enter key.

When you type commands, be careful to use the same upper- and lowercase letters that we show (some computer systems are fussy about this).

Whenever we show you something that's displayed on the screen (such as an error message or a response to your input), it looks like this:

```
A TCP/IP message on your screen
```

Foolish Assumptions

We have made some assumptions about you and what you're looking to get from this book:

- ✔ You use some kind of computer. It doesn't matter what kind — that's part of the beauty of TCP/IP.
- ✔ Your computer's already connected to (or would like to be connected to) some kind of network.
- ✔ You have TCP/IP or you're considering TCP/IP as the protocol for that network.

✔ You may know something about TCP/IP and want to know more.

✔ You may have heard that TCP/IP is the protocol to use for your network, but you're not sure how to get started.

✔ You may be worried that future changes in TCP/IP protocols will wreck your network.

Most of all, we know that you're not really a dummy. You're just trying something new. Good for you!

How This Book Is Organized

This book contains four parts. Each part contains several chapters, and the chapters are divided into smaller sections. Here's the layout and a quick look at what you can find in each major part:

Part I: Basics and Buzzwords

This part explains why TCP/IP is such a hot topic. You read about the relationship between TCP/IP and the Internet, how TCP/IP got started, and where TCP/IP is going. We also include some important background information about networks in case you don't have a clue about network terminology. You find out about all the major buzzwords of the day, including ones that should go far into the 21st century, "where no one has gone before...."

Part II: TCP/IP from Soup to Nuts to Dessert

This part contains the heavy-duty technical information about the protocols that make up the TCP/IP suite. You may want to skip over many of the topics here, depending on how deeply you want to get into theory. But don't skip this whole part! It describes all the services TCP/IP provides for you and how the network finds you by name and address. We help you explore TCP/IP tools and commands and provide the how-to information so that you can make them work for you. We also examine some of the system files on your computer that support TCP/IP and what you have to do to manage them.

Part III: TCP/IP Stew — a Little of This, a Pinch of That

This part covers various topics, including security and hardware. Don't get all excited about the hardware topics, though. We know that hardware decisions are made in highly private, agonizing sessions between you and your computer salesperson. We wouldn't dream of interfering with that relationship, so we won't recommend specific hardware or how to configure it. Instead, we give you general information about when you need a certain type of hardware — for example, when you need to get a computer to function as a gateway for e-mail (see Chapter 7).

Part IV: The Part of Tens

You may already know that every ...*For Dummies* book has one of these parts. Here, you can find frequently asked questions, tips, and also some silly but true TCP/IP factoids — roughly in sets of ten.

Icons Used in This Book

This icon highlights buzzwords in the text, so that you can find them more easily. You can build your own Cheat Sheet from these icons.

This icon signals nerdy techno-facts that you can easily skip without hurting your TCP/IP education. But if you're a technoid, you'll probably eat this stuff up.

This icon marks TCP/IP security issues and advises you on how to manage them.

This icon indicates nifty shortcuts or pieces of information that make your life easier.

This icon marks pointers for you to remember — chances are, they'll come up again.

This icon lets you know that there's a loaded gun pointed directly at your foot. Watch out!

Each time that we use this icon, we're highlighting an RFC (Request for Comments). RFCs are the documentation for the Internet and include:

- Standards for the protocols.
- For Your Information (FYI) reference materials.
- Humorous articles, such as "The Twelve Days of Technology Before Christmas" (RFC1822).

Where to Go from Here

Check out the Table of Contents or the Index and decide where you want to start. If you're an Information Technology manager, you're probably interested in the buzzwords and why everyone seems to be getting on the TCP/IP bandwagon. If you have no idea what a network is, you may want to start with Chapter 3, just to get a little background. If you're a network manager, Chapter 6 lists the major protocols and what they do. Chapter 19, about security, is for everyone who is concerned that his or her data is at risk on an internet.

Part I
Basics and
Buzzwords

The 5th Wave   By Rich Tennant

"EXCUSE ME — IS ANYONE HERE NOT TALKING ABOUT TCP/IP?"

In this part . . .

You can't play the game if you don't know the rules. And TCP/IP is the rules — called *protocols* — for networks. Protocols are the software underpinnings of networks, and the TCP/IP protocols are the software underpinnings of all internet technology, including the Internet and its World Wide Web. So, before we get into the hairy details of the protocols themselves, we give you some background about the Internet and the World Wide Web, networks in general, and TCP/IP's relationship to them. We also discuss some of the hottest buzzwords in the computer business.

Bear in mind that TCP/IP stays alive by morphing regularly, almost daily, sometimes. So, in this part, we also describe how TCP/IP got to where it is today and what you should expect in the next year and the next millennium.

Chapter 1

Understanding TCP/IP Basics

. . . .

In This Chapter

▶ Pronouncing TCP/IP

▶ Defining a protocol and a transport

▶ Understanding how TCP/IP fits with open systems

. . . .

You bought this book (or maybe you're just flipping through it) to find out about TCP/IP. TCP/IP stands for

Transmission Control Protocol / Internet Protocol

As you work through this book, you discover all kinds of cool stuff about TCP/IP — including what the terms *Transmission Control Protocol* and *Internet Protocol* mean. But we start with something simple: how to pronounce it!

Pronunciation Guide

You wouldn't believe how some people say "TCP/IP," but pronouncing this acronym correctly is easy — you just say the name of each letter. Oh yeah, ignore the slash (/). Ready? Go. Say

T C P I P

Good! That didn't hurt, did it? What you said should have sounded like this:

Tee See Pee Eye Pee

(Now, now, none of those off-color jokes.) And don't emphasize any of the letters, unless you're commenting about your bathroom habits. Got it? You're off to a great start. Occasionally you may hear someone cut corners and say just

Tee See Pee

That's okay. The computer industry uses lots of three-letter acronyms, or TLAs. You may also hear someone say simply

Eye Pee

(Here, too, you want to refrain from making any silly jokes. Really. Please.) As you find out in later chapters, sometimes it's technically correct to say just "TCP" or just "IP."

Dear Emily Post: What's a Protocol?

A *protocol* is basically a set of rules for behavior. These rules may be unwritten, but the people using them accept them as correct. For example, in the 1970s, when friends met on the street they gave each other the peace sign and said "Right on!" When Siamese citizens met their King, (at least in *The King and I*), everyone kneeled and bowed, and they spoke Siamese (but only when spoken to). And when Scarlett O'Hara insisted on that off-the-shoulder green and white gown for the barbecue at Twelve Oaks, Mammy said no — "It ain't fittin'! It just ain't fittin'!"

Where do these behavior rules come from? How is it that they are so well known and understood? They aren't always written down, yet we standardize on certain acceptable behaviors. You can find some minor differences due to circumstances and cultures, but here are some examples of situations when certain behavior is expected:

- When a commoner meets royalty
- When people meet and greet, as in "Enchanté de faire votre conaissance" or "Hey dude!"
- On the Titanic, as in "Ladies first" or "Women and children first" (or is it "Every man for himself" nowadays?)

These examples are parts of the formality of communication.

Sometimes the rules are written down — the rules for driving, for example. Still, they can vary widely from country to country or region to region. The United States consists of 50 states, each with its own driving laws. For example, you can turn right at a red light almost everywhere in the U.S., but not in New York City. In the United States, a yellow traffic light means "Caution, prepare to stop," but in Germany, that same yellow light means "Get ready — the light is going to turn green."

Similarly, when two or more computers need to communicate, they need rules of behavior and conventions for both writing and sending their messages. ("After you." "No, after you.") Just as the people of the world speak different languages in different regions, computers may need to "speak" particular network protocols. (When in Rome . . . .) If a computer isn't able to speak a certain protocol, it can't communicate with the computers that speak only that protocol.

Thus, in the world of computers, a protocol is the collection of designated practices, policies, and procedures — often unwritten but agreed upon between its users — that facilitates electronic communication between those users. So, if computers that are linked into a network are the basis of the Information Superhighway, the TCP/IP protocols are the rules of the road.

The Protocol of Open Systems

TCP/IP is often called the protocol of *open systems.* Here's the world's shortest definition of open systems:

> *Open systems provide a standards-based computing environment.*

These standards for open systems normally include the following:

- ✔ Application programming interfaces (APIs) such as MAPI (the Microsoft Messaging API specification)
- ✔ Networking protocols such as TCP/IP
- ✔ Database access methods such as SQL

The term *open systems* is one of those computer-industry buzzwords. Many of the concepts of open systems began with the UNIX operating system, and some people still believe that UNIX means "open." That's because when you move from one vendor's implementation of UNIX to another vendor's implementation of UNIX, most of the commands are the same.

Remember the scene in *Jurassic Park* when Lex realizes she's looking at a UNIX system? "I know this!" she hollers, staring at the monitor and beginning to press some keys. It's the beginning of the end for the raptors! Thank goodness it was a UNIX system. Otherwise, Lex would be lunch. UNIX exists on all major hardware platforms, even the PC and the Macintosh. A PC UNIX user can move to a mainframe and get around with ease because the basic commands are the same. UNIX is like the McDonald's of operating systems — wherever you are in the world, you have a good idea of what you're going to get.

When you extend this concept to network protocols, you can understand why TCP/IP is the industry standard for open networking. With TCP/IP networks, users perform the Big Four network tasks — electronic mail, file transfer, signing on to remote computers, and browsing the World Wide

Web — in the same way, regardless of the computer hardware. And if your company gets you a brand-new computer system that you've never even heard of, the mail, file transfer, Web browsing, and remote logon all still work in familiar ways, compliments of TCP/IP.

The fact that TCP/IP is an internationally-accepted standard for networking makes it an excellent choice for building the network piece of open systems. However, although TCP/IP is the most widely used, it isn't the only protocol that is considered a standard. In Chapter 2, you see how TCP/IP grew into a standard and take a look at TCP/IP's competition.

What's a Transport?

When you need to travel from Boston to New York for a business meeting, it doesn't really matter how you travel, as long as you get there on time. You may choose to go by car, taxi, bus, plane, train, bicycle, foot, or snowmobile. Certainly, you will notice differences in the length of the trip, the cost, your comfort level, and the exact route. But you really just want to get there, and for that you need transportation.

Depending on your destination and your personal requirements, some transportation choices may be unwise, illegal, or impossible. If you need to get to the moon, would you ride your bicycle? If you had $1 million dollars and a hot date in the middle of the Golden Gate Bridge in 30 days, how would you proceed? If you had one French franc and needed to get to the observation level of the Eiffel Tower in ten minutes during rush hour, could you make it?

Now, consider transporting *information*. For example, how many different ways can you tell your mother that you'll be home for the holidays?

- ✔ Telephone call.
- ✔ Postcard or letter.
- ✔ Telegram.
- ✔ Fax (if she has a fax machine).
- ✔ E-mail (if she has an account somewhere).
- ✔ Homing pigeon.
- ✔ Tell your father and let him tell her.
- ✔ Tie a note to a rock and throw it through the front window.
- ✔ Rely on mother's radar to know that you're coming.

Did you think of others? Does the method matter as long as she gets the message? Probably not.

You may be used to thinking of a *transport* as the way you move yourself or your things around. But computer networks move *information* from one place to another. Many times you don't care exactly how the data gets where it's going, as long as it arrives

- ✔ On time
- ✔ Safely
- ✔ Intelligibly
- ✔ Affordably
- ✔ Intact
- ✔ Uncorrupted

TCP/IP is both a transport for carrying your data and a protocol with rules for how your data should move. And there's one more piece: TCP/IP also has a set of applications, or programs, for chatting with other people on a network, for sharing files, for signing on to other computers, and more. The chapters in Part II explore these services and applications.

Chapter 2

TCP/IP and Internets, Intranets, and Extranets

In This Chapter

▶ Looking into the Internet and an internet

▶ Investigating intranets, extranets, and Virtual Private Networks (VPNs)

▶ Checking who's in charge of TCP/IP and the Internet

▶ Questioning whether you need IPv6, the new version of TCP/IP

This chapter gives you facts about the origin of the species (TCP/IP species, that is), and a look into its future. It's also loaded with buzzwords.

The Internet versus an internet

The Internet is the worldwide collection of interconnected computer networks that use the TCP/IP protocol. These networks reach every continent — even Antarctica — and nearly every country. So, if your favorite penguin has an Internet address, you can invite him to your formal dinner party via electronic mail! (He'll already have a black tie.)

The Internet is also much more than its network connections. It's all of the individual computers connected to those individual networks, plus all of the users of those computers, all of the information accessible to those users, and all of the knowledge those people possess. The Internet is just as much about people and information as it is about computers and computer networks.

The Internet links universities, companies, governments, cities, countries, organizations, students, researchers, parents, kids, personal computers, supercomputers, weather stations — even candy and soda machines (see Chapter 22)!

The Internet is a hot topic these days, so you may hear people refer to it using other names. The terms *Information Superhighway, the Net,* and *the Web* are some of the most popular. The network hardware is the road surface itself. And the rules of the road are TCP/IP.

When you look up the word "internet" in the dictionary, you find that

- *inter* means between, among, or in the midst of
- *net* is a group of communications stations operating under unified control

So, an internet is what goes on between, among, and within communications stations that are on a network. Many organizations (companies, universities, and so forth) have their own internets. An internet is also how you link one network to another — for example, to extend a local area network (LAN) so that it becomes a wide area network (WAN) — see Chapter 3.

One way we distinguish "the Internet" from "an internet" is by capitalizing the "I" in "Internet."

The Internet is

- The one and only international network of networks using TCP/IP, and the home of the World Wide Web.
- A network that has evolved over the last 30 years.
- Public (not free, but open to everyone).
- A carrier of your electronic mail (e-mail) to people all over the world, including the President of the United States and fictional characters, such as Sherlock Holmes.
- A place to get free software.
- A place where the U.S. government published sexually-explicit material (the Starr Report).
- Where you can hear a live Webcast of the Spice Girls.
- Thousands of networks, hundred of thousands of computers, millions of people, and enough information to fill your hard disk (and ours) thousands of times over.
- Where you can write to Santa Claus (at santa@northpole.net) and he'll send you a button that says "I e-mailed Santa."
- Tens of millions of users with too much time on their hands.

Is the Internet free?

Yes, the Internet is free, in the sense that you don't pay any of the Internet committees to access the Internet. If you want to register an organization or a private citizen for an Internet address though, the InterNIC (see the section "Who's in charge of TCP/IP and the Internet, Anyway?") charges a fee.

On the other hand, to connect to the Internet you need:

🗸 A computer or a terminal, or even a television set (read about WebTV in Chapter 12).

🗸 TCP/IP software (for full access to the Internet, including the World Wide Web).

🗸 A network connection of some kind: Ethernet, token ring (flip to Chapter 3 for more on those), or a modem and a telephone line. It can be a simple voice line or a special line for data.

🗸 A connection to a network that connects to the Internet or an account with an Internet Service Provider (ISP) or online service, such as America Online (AOL), which provides Internet access. Shop around. If you plan to use the Internet frequently, you want a provider who charges a monthly flat rate for full service.

Most ISPs and regional networks connect to larger networks that make up the Internet backbone. The backbone carries data around the world and even into space. The backbone networks lease the wiring for the backbone from telephone companies. The backbone networks then connect the wires together with special computers called *routers*. (If you find this interesting, you'll love Chapter 18.)

An internet is

🗸 A network of networks, normally set up for one organization.

🗸 A network that uses TCP/IP protocols. It may or may not run other network protocols.

🗸 Private. Only you and the other members of your organization are allowed to use it. It works like a private version of the Internet.

🗸 A carrier of your e-mail to the other people in your organization.

🗸 Perhaps connected to the Internet, perhaps not. If your organization has an internet that's not connected to the Internet, you can't send e-mail to Marshall and Candace, your authors, because we don't have access to your private internet and you don't have access to the Internet, where we are.

🗸 A system that runs TCP/IP, if it's connected to the Internet.

Nets, Nets, and More Nets

An *intranet* is a private network within an organization or department — a university on the East coast, for example, may have an intranet for its medical school, another one for its college of liberal arts, and a different one for the business school. That university may also network those intranets together into an internet so that people from different academic areas can share data. When that university needs to share data with a different university on the West coast, the two universities can link their respective internets together to create an *extranet*. *Virtual Private Networks,* defined in this section, are used for both intranets and extranets.

An intranet is

✔ A kind of internet.

✔ A cool name for your organization's private network. Purists say that an intranet must use TCP/IP networking. If it uses some other network protocol, it's just a plain old network.

✔ Perhaps connected to the Internet (or even an internet). If part of your intranet is available to people outside your company (such as customers and suppliers), that part is called an extranet.

✔ Behind your *firewall,* if the intranet is connected to the Internet or an internet. At least we *hope* that it's behind a firewall. See Chapter 19, which is all about security, to find out what a firewall is and how it protects your intranet.

An extranet is

✔ Multiple, interconnected intranets and internets.

✔ The organization's extended family of business partners, vendors, suppliers, customers, and research partners that all collaborate electronically.

✔ Something that may not exist physically — it's a virtual network.

A Virtual Private Network is

✔ A private network that runs over public facilities, such as the Internet.

✔ Safe and secure because it

- • Uses a special tunneling protocol on the public network — see Chapter 17 for more information.

- • Can scramble data before sending on the public lines.

✔ A money-saver for large organization's networks, because sharing public telecommunications lines is usually cheaper than leasing private lines.

✔ Used for both intranets and extranets.

The TCP/IP Declaration of Independence

When in the course of network events . . . to form a more perfect union . . . .

You can find many different kinds of network designs and hardware technologies, ranging from circles to stars, from telephone wire to signals bounced off satellites into the ether. (If you're interested — and you don't have to be — Chapter 3 explains some of the characteristics of these technologies.) And new technologies are emerging to enhance or replace the existing ones. One of the biggest strengths of TCP/IP is that it's independent of all the available alternatives:

✔ The network design. Circles or stars — TCP/IP doesn't care.

✔ The transmission medium. Wire or satellite — no problem.

✔ Specific vendors. Take your choice.

✔ The operating system and computer hardware. Pick your favorite.

TCP/IP ties networks and the Internet together, regardless of the hardware and software used to build those networks. TCP/IP runs on and connects just about everything. You may have heard about other network protocols, such as IBM's SNA or Novell's SPX/IPX. But no protocol connects as many different hardware and software platforms as TCP/IP. This versatility is the reason that TCP/IP is the world's most popular network protocol.

Dedicated to the proposition that all vendors are created equal

From the beginning, TCP/IP was designed to link computers from different vendors, such as IBM and Hewlett Packard, to name just two. Other network protocols aren't this flexible. With TCP/IP, you can buy the computer that you want or need and know that it can communicate with all of the others.

TCP/IP — child of the Cold War

In the 1960s, the United States government agency DARPA (Defense Advanced Research Projects Agency) funded research on how to connect computers in order to exchange data among them. The purpose of this research was to build command and control functions that would survive a nuclear "incident."

This first network was called the ARPANET, and it connected academic and military research centers. As the ARPANET continued to grow, people began to use it for purposes quite different from the original military uses. The major users were still universities and military and government installations, but they began using the network to share all kinds of nonmilitary information, files, and documents.

DARPA funded the development of a whole set of protocols for communication on the ARPANET. These internetworking protocols are known by two of its parts, TCP and IP, yielding TCP/IP. In the early 1980s, the Secretary of Defense mandated that all computers connected to the ARPANET had to use TCP/IP. That's when the Internet came into being.

TCP/IP was — and still is — the protocol of choice because it enables transparent communication using a common packet protocol for getting data around and between many different network types.

Because all implementations of TCP/IP must work together, or *interoperate*, regardless of who created them, you may have several implementations from which to choose. The various products may differ in price, number of features, performance, or in any number of other ways. Investigate your options carefully and make the right choice for your circumstances.

Dedicated to the proposition that all operating systems are created equal

Some computers are capable of running several operating systems. For example, you can install Microsoft Windows 98, Microsoft Windows NT, and UNIX, all on one PC. Not to worry — you can run any or all of these operating systems and still have TCP/IP working for you — just use the operating system that best meets your needs.

In fact, although the UNIX operating system was the first to come with TCP/IP "built in," most operating systems come with TCP/IP these days.

This widespread incorporation of TCP/IP is one indication of its popularity. Other vendors' TCP/IP implementations are still important, though, because they may have features that the bundled implementations don't have. For example, the TCP/IP that Microsoft includes in Windows 95 and Windows 98

Is TCP/IP free?

With the TCP/IP specs conveniently at hand on the Internet, anyone can take them and implement TCP/IP. In fact, many people have. Some of those people and their companies can sell their implementations or just give the products away. TCP/IP is usually included with the operating systems sold with computers.

Because no one really "owns" TCP/IP, the developers of products that implement or include it don't have to pay royalties to anyone. That helps keep down the cost of the products made available to you — and keeps the profit margins fairly high, as well. If no one owns TCP/IP, though, who keeps house for it? Today, TCP/IP is an international standard, watched over by the Internet Society, described in the section "Who's in Charge of TCP/IP and the Internet, Anyway?".

---

only contains network client capabilities. If you need server capabilities, you must buy a TCP/IP product with more features. (See Chapter 4 for definitions of client and server.)

Today, more than 25 million computers run TCP/IP. From this statistic, you can see that, although TCP/IP is bundled on many operating systems, individudal TCP/IP vendors have plenty of business.

Who's in Charge of TCP/IP and the Internet, Anyway?

"The only thing constant is change," as the saying goes, and TCP/IP is no exception. New capabilities are regularly added. Additional organizations connect every day, bringing more users on line every minute. Here are a few important members of the team watching over this rapid growth:

✔ **InterNIC:** Network Services, Inc. (NSI) is responsible for the Internet Network Information Center, known as *the InterNIC* (pronounced "inter nick"). The InterNIC assigns IP addresses to computers and networks. Your organization must register with the InterNIC in order to connect to the Internet. NSI plans to offer WorldNIC Services, a new set of Internet registration services for businesses. You can contact the InterNIC at `www.internic.net`.

- **The Internet Assigned Numbers Authority (IANA):** The Internet Assigned Numbers Authority (IANA, pronounced by saying the letters I A N A) has been the central control for Internet addresses, domain names, and protocol parameters. The IANA has been run by the University of Southern California's Information Sciences Institute and was funded by the U.S. government. Contact the IANA at www.iana.org.

- **The Internet Corporation for Assigned Names and Numbers (ICANN):** The Internet Corporation for Assigned Names and Numbers (ICANN), (ICANN, pronounced by saying the letters I C A N N, or as "eye can") is a nonprofit corporation run by an international board of directors and funded by the Internet community. ICANN was incorporated on September 30, 1998, and is taking over IANA's work. You can contact the ICANN at www.icann.org.

- **Internet Activities Board (IAB):** The Internet Activities Board (IAB, pronounced by saying the letters I A B) oversees the Internet and its protocols (TCP/IP). The IAB has subcommittees of volunteers who set standards and work on new solutions to Internet growth problems. The IAB works with the following committees to set the direction for research and development of the Internet. Contact the IAB at www.iab.org.

- **Internet Engineering Task Force (IETF):** The Internet Engineering Task Force (IETF, pronounced by saying the letters I E T F) is responsible for keeping the Internet up and running every day. Over 70 working groups make up the IETF. Members of these groups draft and develop standards for TCP/IP. One of these standards is the new generation of IP protocols, IPv6 (discussed in the "IPv6, the Next Generation of TCP/IP" section, later in this chapter).

  IETF meetings are open to anyone willing to pay the reasonable fee. If you want to participate in guiding the Internet and TCP/IP, this is the place to start. Nonjoiners can subscribe to free monthly reports about the Internet by sending an e-mail to imr-request@isi.edu. If you're interested in participating in discussions of cosmic importance to the IETF, send an e-mail to ietf-request@cnri.reston.va.us. You'll receive information about how the IETF is run and a schedule of upcoming meetings. Contact the IETF at www.ietf.org.

  Check out RFC 1718, The Tao of the IETF — A Guide for New Attendees of the IETF.

- **Internet Engineering Steering Group (IESG):** The Internet Engineering Steering Group (IESG, pronounced by saying the letters I E S G) sets strategic directions and goals for the Internet. The IESG coordinates creating a much larger TCP/IP addressing scheme so that the Internet won't become "full." The IETF makes recommendations to the IESG about standardizing TCP/IP protocols for the Internet. You can contact the IESG at www.ietf.org/iesg.html.

RFCs, FYIs, and STDs

When someone comes up with an idea for a new or improved capability for TCP/IP, he or she writes the proposal as a Request for Comments (RFC, pronounced R F C) and publishes it on the Internet. You can depend on one thing about RFCs: As long as we have TCP/IP and the Internet, people will write new RFCs.

RFC authors are volunteers and aren't compensated for their creations. Each RFC is assigned a number by which it is known forever after. Reviewers (more volunteers) respond with comments and constructive criticism. RFC authors then revise and update the documents. If everything goes smoothly, the RFC becomes a *draft standard.* Programmers use the draft standard as they design and build software that implements the functionality described by the RFC. Until there is real working code, the RFC isn't considered documentation of an official standard.

RFCs are categorized. For example, an RFC that documents a technical standards is labeled "STD." RFCs that are on the way to being adopted as standards are called "Draft Standards and Proposed Standards". RFCs that provide general information are labeled "FYI. "

- ✔ **Internet Research Task Force (IRTF):** The Internet Research Task Force (IRTF) manages research into network protocols, such as TCP/IP. (This group's name, too, is pronounced by saying the letters I R T F.) The IETF moves the IRTF's research into the practical world of TCP/IP and the Internet. Contact the IRTF at www.irtf.org.

- ✔ **The Internet Society:** The IAB, IETF, and IRTF are part of the Internet Society, which guides the future of the Internet. The Internet Society publishes two electronic magazines: the *ISOC Forum* (www.isoc.org/in forum) and *On The Internet* (www.isoc.org/isoc/publications/oti/interim.html), which are included with your membership. Contact the ISOC at www.isoc.org.

IPv6, the Next Generation of TCP/IP

The Internet is close to reaching the limits of the current address numbering system. How close is close? Well, although the estimates vary depending on the panic level of the estimator, addresses for small networks will probably run out sometime around 2010. That's not far away.

If the Internet is close to running out of addresses, does that mean that soon it won't be able to accept new companies or individuals? Not at all. The IESG created a task force to determine how best to enhance TCP/IP to deal with this problem. IPv6 to the rescue! (You pronounce IPv6 by saying the individual letters and the number — I P V 6 — or by saying "IP version 6.")

IPv6 is the next generation version of IP. It offers millions more addresses than we have now, which ought to satisfy the world for the foreseeable future. Software vendors must develop products that understand the new addressing scheme — a few products are already in place, but as of this writing, most people still use version 4 (called *v4*) of TCP/IP.

The current version of IP is known as IPv4. So what happened to IP version 5? It was a research version that never made it to production.

In order to offer more addresses on the Internet, IPv6 changes the address format. Does this mean that all travelers on the Internet have to figure out a new way to access the Internet or that network hardware and operating systems have to change to accommodate IPv6? The IPv6 task force mandates that old-style IP addresses and new IPv6 addresses must coexist. Stay tuned — and check out Chapters 13 and 15 for more information about addresses today and tomorrow.

If you're worried about these future events in cyberspace, don't be. We're just trying to get you thinking about possible future directions for your network. The transition from IPv4 to IPv6 will be slow and gradual, phased in over the next few years. And you can be sure that the Internet will understand both forms of IP addresses for years to come.

Besides increasing the address space on the Internet, IPv6 has additional goodies:

✔ If you manage a network, IPv6 makes it easier to assign addresses, leaving time for long lunches.

For everyone concerned with security (and who isn't these days?), IPv6 provides new ways to *encrypt* data (use a secret code) so that the bad guys can't snatch your stuff off a network.

✔ If you want lots of technical detail about IPv6, read RFC 1883, the IPv6 specification. Chapter 24 shows how to get an RFC.

Now the down side: While IPv6 solves the Internet addressing problem, this version is more complicated to implement, and in real life, people tend to put off hard work that's not absolutely necessary — the way your authors put off writing this chapter until we absolutely had to. Classless InterDomain Routing (CIDR) technology and the Dynamic Host Configuration Protocol (DHCP) make existing IP addresses go further without converting to IPv6. Read Chapter 13 to find out how to use CIDR and DHCP to work around limited IP address space.

Chapter 3

What You Need to Know about Networks

- -

In This Chapter

▶ Figuring out what makes up a network

▶ Understanding the advantages of being connected to a network

▶ Watching out for problems if you're sharing resources across a network

▶ Finding out whether TCP/IP works better on a LAN or a WAN

▶ Understanding what you need to know about Ethernet or token ring network technologies to use TCP/IP

▶ Discovering TCP/IP's relationship to network services

- -

Computer networking is rapidly becoming a part of life — not just at work, but at home, too. So, we think you should understand some basic terminology and fundamental concepts concerning this important technology.

TCP/IP provides connectivity for networked computers. (*Connectivity* is just a fancy way of saying *communication*.) Because it's hard to describe just the TCP/IP piece without introducing how the machines are organized and cabled together in the network, this chapter discusses just that.

What's a Network?

A *network* is a combination of computers (and other devices) along with the cabling, the network interface controllers that are inside the computer, and the network software (such as TCP/IP protocols). Figure 3-1 illustrates some of the pieces that make up a network. (You can find out more about net-worked toasters in Chapter 22.)

The protocol software governs how information moves around on the network hardware, and TCP/IP is the most widely used protocol on the largest variety of hardware.

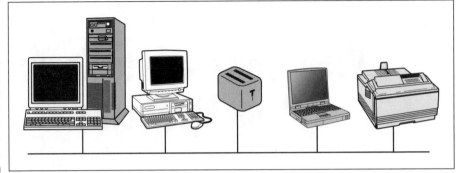

Figure 3-1:
A network
and a few
of its
compo-
nents.

What kinds of devices can be on a network?

Any device that sends or receives data can be part of a network. Here are some typical components:

- **Computers:** This includes PCs, Net PCs, palmtops, workstations, computers acting as clients (that is, borrowing resources from other computers), and computers acting as servers (that is, lending resources to other computers). Chapter 4 tells you much more about clients and servers.

- **Printers:** Most people think of printers as being attached to computers, but you can also put certain kinds of printers directly on the network.

- **Cash registers and those fancy point-of-sale (POS) devices:** These devices help retail stores with inventory control. The bar code scanners in modern grocery stores are good examples.

- **Connection media:** This includes cables and wires, fiber-optics, microwaves, even signals beamed to or from a satellite.

- **Other hardware:** This category is quite broad and includes hubs, routers, gateways, terminal servers, and modems (some special modems can be attached directly to the network). You can find more information about these devices in Chapter 18.

- **Things you may not expect to find on a network:** You won't believe what some people have connected to a network — we've seen soda and candy machines and toilets, to name a few. Your next new car may be a network device. Read Chapter 22 if you're interested in weird and wild things that people have turned into network devices.

How does TCP/IP fit into the network?

With all these hardware possibilities for a network, you can see why you need a set of rules for how data should be transmitted across the connection media among all those components. These rules are the network protocols, such as TCP/IP. Some of the other network protocols available are IPX from Novell and SNA from IBM.

Networks and protocols are inseparable: Without networks, protocols have no reason to exist. Without protocols, a network would be a useless collection of expensive machinery. And without TCP/IP, the Internet would be an idea in search of an implementation — kind of like the wall before Humpty Dumpty decided to sit down.

The pieces of the TCP/IP protocol "suite" are described in terrifically techie detail in Chapter 6.

What a Network Does for You (Oooh! Ahhh! More Stuff!)

A network provides many conveniences and services to its users.

- ✔ You can move information and files from one computer to another.

- ✔ Without copying them, you can access shared objects such as directories and files on other computers. (You must pay a price to share resources, however — more about this in the "What a Network Does to You" section.)

- ✔ You can share a printer attached to some other computer.

- ✔ You can use applications that take advantage of the network. For example, groupware applications run across networks, letting coworkers communicate and share data — a salesperson can create expense reports and forward them across the network to a manager for an electronic signature. The network's users may never hear of network protocols, but TCP/IP provides the network communications part of these applications.

- ✔ You can send e-mail to other people who are also connected to your network. Via the Internet, you can send mail to famous people, including Santa Claus and the President of the United States, or to not-yet-famous people — including your authors! In Chapter 2, we give you a couple of Internet addresses for sending mail to Internet committees, and you can find others as you read this book.

- ✔ You can participate in electronic discussion groups. For example, are you thinking of going to Disney World? You can go to a discussion group on the Internet at `rec.arts.disney` and get hotel and restaurant recommendations and find out about the rides and attractions in the park. If you're planning to spend your vacation finding out more about TCP/IP, check out `comp.protocols.tcp-ip`. For more details on discussion groups, read about Usenet news in Chapter 7.

What a Network Does to You (There's No Such Thing as a Free Lunch)

So you want to take advantage of shared resources? Okay, but keep in mind that to share resources across the network, you must make sure you have enough resources to share. (By the way, when we say *resources,* we're talking about things on your computer that network users can share, such as hard disks, printers, and even the internal processing power of your computer.)

A network can consume your resources. For example, if you allow other users on the network to use the hard disks connected to your computer, will you still have enough room for your own files? Or if you have a printer connected to your machine, will someone else from across the network always be using it when you want to print?

If you plan to share your disk and printer resources, you should decide who can share with you and how much of your resources they can share. After all, you wouldn't hand your entire paycheck over to your friendly government tax service every month, would you? Hmmm, bad example. How about this example: You parents out there wouldn't hand over your entire paycheck to your child week after week, would you? Although it may seem like you do, most likely your child gets an allowance, which is a piece of your paycheck resource.

On the other hand, if you're thinking, "Well, I won't get into trouble if I don't share my resources with other users. I'll just use their disks and printers," think again. That would make you dependent on resources that are beyond your control. For example, if another computer on the network lets you store some of your files there (called *remote file-sharing*), what happens if that computer is offline for a while? Your files are incommunicado. You'd better hope that the system administrator for that machine has plans in place to guarantee its availability, before problems arise. Or, if you use a printer that's connected to another computer and the computer's owner turns it off and goes on vacation, how do you print your stuff? (We hope you have access to another printer!)

You have to decide your level of network participation. If you choose not to use or provide network resources, you have complete control of your environment, but you have to live with limited resources and will have difficulty working and playing well with others. If you choose to use or to provide network resources, you're codependent with others on the network. Either way, you pay a price.

How to make it work

To make resource-sharing useful and reliable, your organization should install special computers that are dedicated wholly to sharing disks or printers with many other users. These computers are managed so that they're always available unless there's a hardware problem. These computers are called *file servers* or *print servers* or simply *servers.*

For more information about using servers to share disks and printers across the network, take a look at Chapter 4 on client/server computing, as well as the section on the Network File System in Chapter 10.

Figure 3-2 shows people sharing disks and files located on a file server somewhere on the network. Depending on how the file server is set up, users may not even know that they are getting files from the network.

Figure 3-2:
Using a file
server to
share disks
among
networked
users.

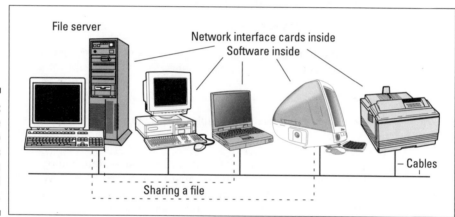

Watch out for viruses!

In addition to all those files, a network can also transport a virus to your computer. Of course, floppy disks can, too. Think carefully about accessing a file server that's unfamiliar to you. We strongly recommend that you regularly and faithfully scan your computer's disks and diskettes for viruses. And always scan any software that you copy — before you use it.

Protocols and Packets and Humpty Dumpty's Fall off the Wall

Protocols aren't really tangible "things" on the network. Instead, they specify how tangible things (the network devices and computers) talk to one another. King TCP/IP tells the network devices what to do with Humpty Dumpty — your data. Each time a network device manipulates your data, it obeys the rules set down by TCP/IP.

One rule stipulates that your data may have to be transferred in smaller chunks — Humpty Dumpty may get pushed off his wall. TCP/IP makes sure your data doesn't get ruined in the process of getting put back together again.

All the King's horses and all the King's men . . .

The data that you send and receive over the network is packaged into one or more packets. Each packet holds

- The data that it has to transmit
- Control information, which tells the network what to do with the packets

The network protocol — TCP/IP in this case — determines the format for each packet. And all of this is transparent to the user. If we hadn't told you, you may never have known that your messages are split into pieces for transmission and then reassembled, just like Mr. Dumpty.

. . . can put your packets together again (with the help of TCP/IP)

After the packets are sent, they may not arrive at their destination in order. In Figure 3-3, an e-mail message is split into packets. If your data gets spread over several packets, King TCP/IP tells his horses and soldiers how to put it together again so that the message makes sense.

Figure 3-3:
TCP/IP
sequences
packets
correctly.

What's a LAN?

LAN stands for *local area network*. (It's usually pronounced as a word, LAN, not as the letters L A N.) The computers and other devices in a LAN communicate over small geographical areas, such as the following:

✔ One wing of one floor in a building

✔ Maybe the whole floor, if it's a small building

✔ Several buildings on a small campus

LANs can run over various network architectures, such as Ethernet and token ring. These network architectures are ways for data to move across wires and cables. The following sections describe Ethernet and token ring.

How Ethernet works — would you send me a packet of pastrami?

With Ethernet, any device on the network, from the mainframe computer at the company headquarters to a cash register in the local delicatessen, can send data in a packet to any other location on the network, at any time. Often lots of machines are on a network, and they'll undoubtedly be sending data at the same time. When the packets of data collide, Ethernet makes the devices stop transmitting, wait a little while, and try again. The wait time interval is random and is different each time that a collision happens.

The Ethernet architecture is called *CSMA/CD* (Carrier Sense Multiple Access/Collision Detection), meaning that the devices realize when a collision has occurred, so they wait and retry. With Ethernet, the data from the small deli's cash register is equal to anything that the headquarters' mainframe has to send. All of the devices on the network are peers. Figure 3-4 illustrates an Ethernet LAN.

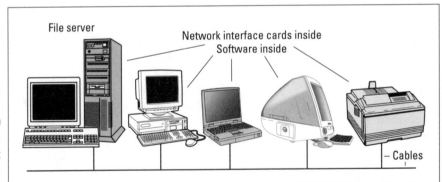

Figure 3-4:
An Ethernet
LAN.

With this ring . . .

In a token ring network, the network devices are connected in a circle (ring), and a token is passed among the devices on the ring. When a device has data to send, it must first wait to get the token. Possession of the token ensures that the sending device will not compete with any other device. If a device has nothing to send, or when it is finished sending, it passes the token. In a token ring, everyone gets an equal turn, unimpeded. Figure 3-5 shows a token ring LAN.

Token ring versus Ethernet

Whether your network runs on token ring or Ethernet technology, your data will go where it's supposed to go. The advantage of token ring is that Ethernet-style collisions don't occur, no matter how busy the network gets. On the other hand, all devices must take a turn with the token, even if they have nothing to send. So, on a not-so-busy network, the devices with data to send have to wait for devices that aren't doing much besides taking the token and passing it on.

TCP/IP has nothing to do with Ethernet or token ring. In addition to all the good features of TCP/IP that are described in Chapter 2, here's another one: TCP/IP runs on both of these popular network schemes. Ethernet and token ring are all about hardware. But TCP/IP is mostly about software, and works on almost all hardware.

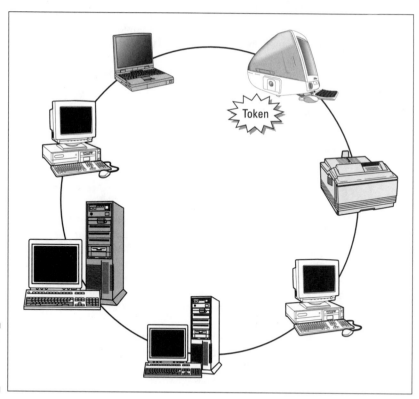

Figure 3-5:
A token
ring LAN.

So if TCP/IP isn't the issue, how do you pick between Ethernet and token ring?

Geez, do you really have to bother us with such a complicated question? Network design practically has its own encyclopedia, for Pete's sake. Okay, okay, if you insist. When you're trying to choose between Ethernet and token ring, you need to consider many factors, including the following:

✔ **Amount of traffic on your network.** How big is your network? In a high-traffic network, collisions may slow down your Ethernet considerably.

✔ **Geographical area spanned by the network.** How BIG is your network? Token ring has fewer distance limitations than Ethernet.

✔ **Likelihood of network failures such as broken cables.** When an Ethernet cable is cut, you may still have other working networks in place of the original network. When a token ring cable is cut, you probably just have one disabled token curve.

✔ **Availability of network interface cards for the particular computers you're using.** In general, Ethernet cards are more common, but for the most popular computers, both Ethernet and token ring cards are available.

When all else fails, choose Ethernet. Or choose the technology that seems to make sense for the current problem. Who said you have to choose only one or the other? In any case, be sure to link together all of your networks!

Fast Ethernet and Faster Ethernet satisfy the need for speed

Information moves at a *theoretical* rate of 10 Mbps (mega, or million, bits per second) on Ethernet. Each character you type is usually 8 or 16 bits. Do the math — 10,000,000 ÷ 8 — and that seems like a lot of data speeding over your network. We use the term "theoretical rate," because plenty of things happen on Ethernet that slow down your data.

A new version of Ethernet, called *Fast Ethernet,* moves data at a rate of 100 Mbps, ten times faster than regular Ethernet! Still, collisions act like electronic friction — they keep your data from reaching top theoretical speed. At 100 Mbps, even slowed down, your data will burn rubber.

Imagine your data whizzing by on the net at 1 Gbps. The "G" stands for giga, so 1 Gbps is 1 billion bits per second. That's *Gigabit Ethernet*. Be prepared to spend giga-units of money if your information craves this kind of speed.

The Institute of Electrical and Electronics Engineers (IEEE), another group that designs and champions standards, is currently developing the standard for how Gigabit Ethernet devices should work. The final standard is due sometime in 1998. Equipment you purchase today (such as switches, hubs, and network cards) to run Gigabit Ethernet, may not to conform to the standard's final requirements.

What's a WAN?

What if your company has several buildings in different towns and states, or even in different countries? Does that mean that all the people who work in the company can't be on the same network because a LAN is limited by distance? Of course not. The Internet is worldwide, so you can even space out with your network by bouncing data off satellites in outer space.

A WAN (*wide area network*) spans geographical distances that are too large for LANs. LANs can be joined together by special-purpose hardware, such as routers, hubs, and gateways (see Chapter 18), to form a WAN. See Figure 3-6.

LAN versus WAN — which one for TCP/IP?

It doesn't matter — TCP/IP works for both. It can be the protocol that connects various computers on LANs as well as WANs. Your choice of network depends on the distance between the computers that you want to network, not on which protocol you want to use. Remember, an internet is two or more interconnected networks, and the individual networks can be WANs, LANs, or a combination.

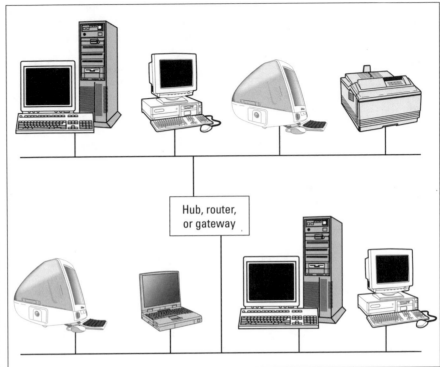

Figure 3-6:
Using a
router, hub,
or gateway
to connect
two LANs
into a WAN.

Hub, router,
or gateway

Mother Goose Network Services, Inc.

A *network service* is a special function that is available to people on the network and their computers. (You may already be familiar with typical network services, such as shared printers and e-mail.) The original design of TCP/IP defined three categories of services that operate at specific levels of the network hierarchy. (You can find out more about this hierarchy in Chapter 5.)

  ✔ **Connection services.** These services, operating at the lowest level of the network's hierarchy, determine how information gets from one computer onto the network cable (or other connection medium) and how that information moves from the network cable to the next computer. The connection services don't guarantee that the information will arrive at the destination in the right order or that it will even arrive at all. As strange as it seems, this unreliable communication between the computers is perfectly adequate for some applications.

✔ **Transport services.** These services, operating at the middle level of the network's hierarchy, augment the connection services to provide completely reliable communication between the computers. The packets are numbered to make sure that the data can be placed in the right order even when the packets arrive out of sequence. The computers then perform error checking to make sure that no packets are lost or damaged.

✔ **Application services.** These services are the functions that you're probably most interested in. Application services let an application on one computer talk to a similar application on another computer in order to perform tasks, such as copying files. Application services, operating at the highest level of the network hierarchy, depend on connection services and transport services for reliable, efficient communication.

Protocols define network services. We use e-mail as an example: When Ms. L. Bo Peep sends her message to Humpty Dumpty, TCP/IP has to tell the network devices how to do all of the following:

1. **Translate Mr. Dumpty's name (actually, the name of Humpty's computer, but we're trying to keep this simple) to a TCP/IP format address. This is the connection service at work.**

2. **Create the packets and mark them "From L. Bo Peep to Humpty Dumpty." This is the transport service at work.**

3. **Send the packets across the network. This is the connection service at work.**

4. **Make sure that the message gets to Humpty ungarbled and in one piece (well, it's not really one piece until after the packets are reassembled into the message). This is the transport service at work.**

5. **Deliver the mail message to Mr. Dumpty himself. This is the application service at work.**

Even in our elementary Mother Goose example, you can see that TCP/IP is responsible for many different network activities. That's why TCP/IP is actually a collection of many protocols, each with a specialized task to perform. You can find out more about these tasks in Part II.

Chapter 4

Client/Server — Buzzword of the Century (The 20th or the 21st?)

. . . .

In This Chapter

▶ Looking into client/server computing

▶ Exploring how TCP/IP enables client/server computing and takes advantage of it

▶ Finding out how client/server interacts with the Internet and the World Wide Web

▶ Investigating server "push" technology

. . . .

Client/server may be the computer industry buzzword of the century (although "Web" is giving it a run for its money). Only time will tell whether it's the buzzword for the 20th century or the 21st! We may not see really successful client/server solutions for a few more years, or client/server computing may turn out to be just a fad and fizzle out. So far, though, client/server has provided a lot of activity with a lot of promise.

As you take a look at what client/server means to a network computer user, you see that TCP/IP is an excellent protocol choice for client/server computing. That's because TCP/IP allows so many different computers and network devices to communicate as both clients and servers.

What Exactly Is Client/Server, Anyway?

You won't find one single, straightforward definition of client/server. The computer industry has wavered here, and client/server has come to mean different things to different people in different situations and at different times.

To some organizations, client/server is part of a hardware "rightsizing" plan. But does that mean downsizing from mainframe computers to smaller computers or upsizing from personal computers to larger computers? To some other organizations, client/server is part of a software engineering plan. But is it for building applications or buying them?

Client/server computing combines traditional styles of computing into a different, distributed way of working. These traditional styles include mainframe computers and departmental minicomputers located in a central data center, non-networked PCs on people's desks, enterprise-wide databases, application programs, networking, and more.

Client/server is defined by software, not hardware. In the client/server game, a client application on one computer requests services from a computer running server software. (You can find definitions of these players later in the "The Server Part of Client/Server" section, later in this chapter.) The client and server can be any kind of hardware. You may even use a gigantic Cray supercomputer client to request services from a tiny little PC via some network protocol, such as TCP/IP.

So the key element in client/server computing isn't hardware or even software — it's figuring out how to divide up your work and information across the network in the most appropriate way.

What client/server is

- ✔ **A style of computing.** To be more specific, it comprises various separate technologies working together to provide a solution. These technologies include the applications, the hardware, the operating systems, and the network technologies that provide communication between the clients and the servers.

- ✔ **Very popular right now.** Every day, organizations are building, deploying, and evaluating client/server solutions.

- ✔ **Something that people think they have to have, even though they don't know what it is.** That's one of the curious things about fads — the excitement is catching. (Gee, where did we put our Pet Rock? It was here a minute ago.)

What client/server isn't

- ✔ **The only style of computing.** Individual, stand-alone computers still have their uses. Just because client/server is popular doesn't mean that older styles are extinct.

- ✔ **The best solution for everything.** Sometimes people get so excited about a hot trend that they fail to determine whether the trend suits their needs. (Remember leisure suits? Back in the 1970s, most men — regardless of height, weight, or dignity — simply had to have a pastel polyester leisure suit.)

Don't let this happen to you

Here's a real-life example of a company that tried a client/server solution without thinking it through — and now has it stored in the back of a closet. An Information Systems manager read that client/server was the way to go, so he bought PCs to connect to his IBM mainframe that held a large database. Then he had an application developed in client/server style. Each time a user ran the client application to generate reports, the database was downloaded from the mainframe to the user's PC. The server application on the mainframe only stored the database and repeatedly downloaded it to the personal computers.

The end result was that each PC had to have enough disk space to hold the database, and all report processing was done there, on the PCs, while the mainframe sat idle. Was it really client/server? Yes, hardware played the roles of both the server and the clients. Yes, the application had a client part (the report

generator) and a server part (the downloadable database). Maybe it conformed to the letter of client/server, but it certainly did not conform to the spirit. Three factors conspired to prevent this application from being a true client/server environment:

✔ The considerable network traffic generated by all the downloads

✔ The large disk space requirements for downloading the data

✔ The lengthy report-generation time on the small PCs

The moral of this story? Stop and think before implementing new technologies. In this example, a client/server solution would have worked if the PC client requested a report and if the mainframe server generated the report and sent it (not the whole database) back to the user at the PC.

✔ **Dead.** Some industry analysts are planning the funeral for client/server computing. They grieve, "It never fulfilled its potential. It used too many computer resources. RIP." Don't believe it. What's one of the hottest applications in use today? Web browsing. And what do you need to browse the Web? A Web CLIENT that accesses Web SERVER software.

The Server Part of Client/Server

Even though the word *client* comes first in client/server, we need to start with the definition of the server.

In a client/server system, a *server* is a computer that has a resource it can share with other computers or a service it can perform on behalf of other computers and their users.

Often a server is dedicated to one task only. In some explicit configurations, the server must be dedicated for that purpose, either for performance or security reasons or because certain software requires it. For example, if you install Novell NetWare server software on a PC, that PC becomes a dedicated file server.

Web servers — spun across the Internet

A *web server* accepts requests from browser clients to deliver web objects, such as home pages and documents. The World Wide Web server finds the requested information on the Internet and ships it back to the browser for you to see. Flip to Chapter 12 for more on the World Wide Web. (Note that a web server on a private intranet is called an *internal information server.*)

Web application servers — collaboration across space and time

Most web servers simply deliver information and files to browsers, a function that can be incredibly useful and has become amazingly popular. But there's more to life than just raw information. A *web application server,* such as Lotus Domino, lets groups of users interact through browsers to generate collaborative results that aren't possible otherwise. The applications are in all kinds of industries including banking and financial services, healthcare, customer service, advertising, and entertainment.

Commerce servers — may I please have your credit card information?

A *commerce server* is a type of web application server that lets you conduct business over the Web. The server software includes security features such as the Secure Socket Layer (SSL) so that you can use your credit card without worrying about security. You still have to worry about your bills, though. Check out Chapter 19 for information on commerce servers.

File servers — from Timbuktu to Kalamazoo

A *file server* shares its disk space with other computers. One advantage of having a file server, besides being able to borrow another computer's disk space, is that the shared files still look like they're on your own computer. You don't have to do anything special or different to use the files stored on a file server in your network — even if that file server is thousands of miles away in Timbuktu. Most users don't even realize that they use files that aren't on their own computers.

The computers that borrow the file server's disk space are the clients. These clients may use an operating system that's different from the server's and from one another's. And when you have various operating systems, you have various file formats. The server's job is to hide those format differences from the clients.

Print servers — closer to home

Theoretically, you can use the printer on a print server that's set up in Kalamazoo, but unless you like long commutes, it would be a pretty long walk to retrieve your printed documents. So it makes sense that print servers are most convenient if they are located geographically close to the people who use them. The *print servers* on a network allow many people to share a printer, as opposed to each user's computer having its own dedicated printer.

In many offices, the printer on a print server is a fancy and powerful laser printer. The quality of personal printers, on the other hand, may range from the CEO's laser to your pathetic dot-matrix printer that jams and prints reports too faint to read even under 1,000 watts of halogen light.

Compute servers — both near and far

The idea behind compute servers has actually been with us since the development of the first computers, but the term itself has only been in use a short time. A *compute server* is a computer that runs a program for you.

When computers were dinosaurs that filled an entire room and ran only one program at a time, you requested an appointment and physically went to the computer to run your program. Even though today's computers come in a wide variety of sizes and capabilities and most of us have one at our disposal 24 hours a day, sometimes you still need to use a computer with special capabilities.

The compute server may have that expensive program you can't afford or those secret data that you must not copy, or it may simply have more disk space and power to run your program more efficiently. Traveling to the compute server is still necessary, but nowadays you can do that over the network. See Chapter 8 for more information on compute servers and "cycle stealing."

File servers and all those formats — how do they do it?

Software is what makes it all work. Suppose you're on a PC, where your files are in the FAT (File Allocation Table) format, and you want to use some files on a UNIX server that uses the UNIX File System. If your PC doesn't understand UNIX, how can you make any sense of the files over on the server? Easy! Software on the server translates the files from the server's UNIX file format to your PC's (the client) FAT format. And you never see it happen. As far as you, the client, are concerned, your file is automatically in the appropriate format for you to use. This translation is part of what's called *transparent file access* in a client/ server environment.

The Client Part of Client/Server

It's this simple: A *client* is a computer that borrows a resource or service from another computer.

Clients do all sorts of work — anything they want. It's not the type of work done that makes a computer a client; it's the fact that the computer is borrowing some sort of resource.

Thin clients

The question often comes up: Can you run that cool new client application on your current computer system or do you need to add more memory and another disk drive, or do you have to get a whole new computer?

Before you spend a lot of money on a new computer, though, see if a thin client may help. A *thin client* is the smallest, simplest, least expensive combination of hardware and software configured to perform the exact tasks that you need — and nothing else. Users of thin clients run their applications on servers across the network.

The new Net PCs are examples of hardware that run thin client software. (Some people joke that the VT100 and 3270 fixed-function terminals attached to minicomputers and mainframes are thin clients. Who's to say that they're wrong?) See Chapter 8 for information on a new thin technology, called Microsoft Windows NT Terminal Server Edition.

Thin clients mean fat servers. Don't forget to increase the processing power of the servers that support thin clients — you need more power on servers because most of the work occurs there. Using thin clients also can increase network utilization. Don't forget to upgrade the network so that it can handle the heavier usage. If you need your network to go faster, check out Chapter 18 for some tips on network wiring and hardware.

Browsers

A *browser* is client software that receives services from a web server. The browser lets you navigate the files and information on a web, including the World Wide Web. For a full-function browser, you need a graphical browser. Text-based browsers, however, usually work faster than graphical ones and provide access to web data for people who don't have a graphical interface the way that a Windows or the Macintosh operating system does. To see examples of browsers, check out Chapter 12.

Are You Being Served?

Any computer can be

- ✔ Either a client or a server
- ✔ Both a client and a server
- ✔ Neither a client nor a server

and can change as often as necessary to provide and access any number of services.

Figure 4-1 shows an example of multiple roles. One computer provides a shared printer and is thus a print server. The same computer also shares some of its disk space and files and is thus a file server, and it's also a client of a file server because it accesses some files from another computer.

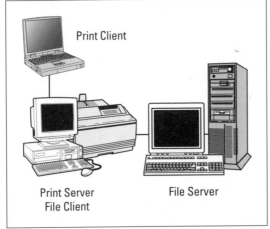

Figure 4-1:
A computer
can be a
client and a
server at
the same
time.

What Does All This Have to Do with TCP/IP?

Client/server and TCP/IP may seem unrelated to you — after all, client/server is a style and TCP/IP is a technology, right? Why, then, does the computer industry link the two together? Because TCP/IP is a key element of many, but not all, client/server solutions.

TCP/IP is one of the major enablers of client/server computing, and also one of the biggest users of it. TCP/IP's layered and modular design makes it easy to design and implement new network services. But one of the biggest advantages of TCP/IP compared to some other network protocols is that all of the computers on the network are peers.

In a *peer-to-peer network*, no computer is better than any other, or different from any other, at least until the system managers and users make them different. A peer-to-peer network doesn't require dedicated servers; however, a peer-to-peer network does benefit from having dedicated servers.

The Microsoft Windows NT Workstation is an excellent example of peer-to-peer networking — all of the machines on the workgroup network are equals. They all may (and probably do) function as either clients or servers. In fact, most computers in a peer-to-peer network work simultaneously as both client and server. While this environment is convenient, you may find that it's not practical. What happens when your colleagues are using so much of your computer's shared disk space that there's no space left for you? Do you turn off disk sharing or disconnect the network cable? You could. It's your computer, right? Before your group disintegrates into a collection of separate PCs, though, your group should look into getting a dedicated file server.

Server Push

When you're browsing the Web, your browser (the client) pulls information down from the server. *Server push technology* (often called *push technology*) is just the opposite — the server initiates information delivery to the client. Pointcast, an example of server push, is an Internet news service that broadcasts news to your client. You need to download a Pointcast client (it's free!), that shows you how to push information based on your interests. One neat Pointcast feature is that it displays news headlines as a screen saver.

Here's the difference between push and pull: With pull technology, you must ask for the news. With push technology, you get the news as it happens.

Oh ... Now I Get It!

In the other chapters in this book, you investigate many more client/server topics — including TCP/IP's own components and some popular services, and the basics of programming your own applications. Until then, remember that client/server is like sex:

- ✔ It's on everyone's mind most of the time.
- ✔ Everyone's talking about it.
- ✔ Everyone thinks that everyone else is doing it.
- ✔ Everyone thinks that he or she is the only one not getting any.
- ✔ Everyone brags about his or her success.

TCP/IP — size doesn't matter

TCP/IP is accepted as *the* protocol that links computers not just to each other but to all of the different computers and servers in the world, from the smallest palmtop to the mightiest mainframe. TCP/IP makes all of them candidates for clients or servers.

Chapter 5

Luscious Layers

· ·

In This Chapter

▶ Introducing OSI — the International Standards Organization's protocols for open systems interconnection

▶ Exploring the OSI protocol's layered architecture

▶ Comparing OSI and TCP/IP layers

▶ Understanding why TCP/IP beat OSI in the standards race

· ·

*B*efore you can really understand the components of TCP/IP, we need to show you the basis for their design. To do this, we compare them with the components of another standard for network architecture and protocols: OSI.

ISO OSI — More Than a Palindrome?

ISO, the International Standards Organization, specifies worldwide standards for different types of computing. (ISO is pronounced eyeso — eyesore without the ore.) ISO sets standards for networking, database access, and character sets, among other things.

In order to support the idea of open systems, the products of major hardware and software vendors must comply with standards. As far as networks and protocols are concerned, ISO wants all vendors to use a standard network architecture for their hardware and software products, thereby making all network users able to communicate happily and easily with each other, regardless of what computer products they happen to use.

ISO's most visible effort in this network and protocol compatibility dream is *OSI,* Open Systems Interconnect, which defines a network architecture and a full set of protocols. (OSI is pronounced as the letters O S I. Often, it's referred to as ISO OSI, pronounced eyeso O S I. We know it's not consistent, but don't blame us.)

The ImpOSIble Dream?

Not surprisingly, attaining this dream of overall compatibility has been somewhat difficult to bring about. Maybe ISO should have named itself ParadISO, after its goal!

ISO isn't the first organization to define a network architecture — sometimes called a *model* — and protocols to go with it. Table 5-1 lists three proprietary network models and protocols.

Table 5-1	Some Vendor-Defined Protocols
Vendor	*Architecture/Protocol*
IBM	System Network Architecture (SNA)
IPX/SPX	Novell Corporation
Apple Computer	AppleTalk

The difference between the vendor-defined models in Table 5-1 and those of the ISO is that the ISO OSI (have your eyes crossed yet?) enables interoperability between vendors. ISO's interoperability standards have been designed to allow all parts of your network to work together, regardless of which suppliers you bought them from. Toward this goal, OSI divides network functions into layers and specifies how those layers should interact. Theoretically, then, OSI is blissful paradise for network users.

Okay. So far this makes sense. Even the United States government liked OSI. (Maybe we should have worried when we heard that.) In fact, the U.S. government first became interested in using OSI to connect government installations.

But in the late 1970s, when ISO was just beginning to recommend the development of OSI as a standard for multivendor networking, TCP/IP had already been in use for years (for the federal government as well as others) as a standard on the ARPANET and the other networks around the world that evolved into the Internet.

Today, little of OSI is in production, as compared to TCP/IP. One reason is that the OSI specification is extremely complicated and it's taking too long to implement all the functionality. Another reason is that TCP/IP is already here and in use. During the long (and seemingly never-ending) trip to ParadISO, people realized that their computers could work together by using TCP/IP's set of already existing protocols.

The United States government was one of the last groups to figure this out, but now — having communicated via TCP/IP for years — the government recommends TCP/IP as an alternative to the OSI network protocols. The government has decided to let TCP/IP be a standard as well.

Taking a Modular Approach to Networking

The best things to come out of OSI, so far, are its aim to support large networks without running out of addresses and the idea of a structured, layered network model. We can thank ISO for clearly delineating network layers and services through which applications, especially client/server applications, can communicate. When the OSI model was born, it defined the "right" way to design network protocols and applications, and in this case, "right" meant modular.

TCP/IP, as well, uses the concept of layers. Actually, the TCP/IP notion of five layers predates the ISO OSI Reference Model (see the next section) by nearly ten years, but TCP/IP's concept wasn't firmly entrenched. Today, new developments in TCP/IP follow the OSI example of modular layers and clean interfaces. Internet committees that direct the evolution of TCP/IP watch ISO's efforts and the OSI Reference Model's layered approach. IPv6 borrows some of OSI's goals and plans.

The ISO OSI seven-layer cake

There are seven layers in what's officially called the *ISO OSI Reference Model*. We, however, are predisposed to more satisfying things like desserts and snacks, so we call it a seven-layer cake.

Each layer of the cake depends on the layers below it; that is, each layer provides services to the layer above it. When two peer computers are communicating, each computer has its own set of layers. When you send a message to another computer on the network, your information starts at the top layer of your computer, travels down all the layers to the bottom of the cake, and jumps across to the other computer. When your information gets to the other computer, it starts at the bottom layer and moves up the cake to the application in the top layer. Technically, the seven layers are called a *stack*. Figure 5-1 illustrates these layers.

Creamy white cake, raspberry filling, sugary frosting — mmmmmm — er, sorry. You want to know what the layers are for, don't you? Here we go: Each layer has a special function. The lower layers are hardware oriented. The highest layer does user stuff, such as e-mail and file transfers. Starting with Layer 1 at the bottom of the cake, we examine each layer.

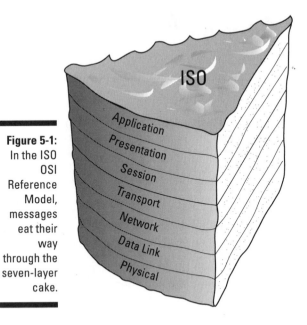

Figure 5-1:
In the ISO
OSI
Reference
Model,
messages
eat their
way
through the
seven-layer
cake.

Layer 1: The physical layer

The physical layer is pure hardware, including the cable, satellite, or other connection medium and the network interface card. This is where electrical signals move around, and we try not to think too hard about how it works.

Layer 2: The data link layer

This is another layer we don't want to strain our brains trying to figure out. Again, hardware is involved. This is the layer that splits your data into packets to be sent across the connection medium. Here's where wiring, such as Ethernet or token ring (see Chapter 3), gets involved. After the information is on the wire, the data link layer handles any interference. If there is heavy sunspot activity, the data link layer works hard to make sure the interference doesn't garble the electric signals.

Sunspot activity and solar flares tend to disturb all sorts of transmissions, not just network signals. Your cellular telephone and television reception, for example, can degrade during solar episodes. Even cable TV is affected. Wouldn't it be nice if television broadcasts had a data link layer like ISO OSI's and TCP/IP's to fix poor reception?

Layer 3: The network layer

Here's the first place on the OSI Model where a TCP/IP protocol fits into the equation. IP is the TCP/IP protocol that works at this layer. This layer gets packets from the data link layer (Layer 2) and sends them to the correct network address. If more than one possible route is available for your data to travel, the network layer figures out the best route. Without this layer, your data would never get to the right place.

Layer 4: The transport layer

Although the network layer routes your information to its destination, it can't guarantee that the packets holding your data will arrive in the correct order or that they won't have picked up any errors during transmission. That's the transport layer's job. TCP is one of the TCP/IP protocols that work at the transport layer; UDP is another one. (Chapter 6 explains what these protocols do.) The transport layer makes sure that your packets have no errors and that all the packets arrive and are reassembled in the correct order. Without this layer, you couldn't trust your network.

Layer 5: The session layer

The other protocols that make up TCP/IP sit on Layer 5 and above. This layer establishes and coordinates a *session*, which is simply the name for a connection between two computers. You have to have a session before two computers can even think about actually moving data between themselves.

Layer 6: The presentation layer

The presentation layer works with the operating system and file system. Here's where files get converted from one format to another, if the server and client use different formats. Without the presentation layer, file transfer would be restricted to computers with the same file format.

Layer 7: The application layer

This is the layer where you do your work, such as sending e-mail or requesting to transfer a file across the network. Without the application layer, you couldn't create any messages or data to send, there would be no Web browsers, and your computer wouldn't know what to do with any data that someone else sent you.

Fitting TCP/IP into the Seven-Layer Cake

The protocols of TCP/IP stack up in layers, too, similar to the OSI Reference Model. But TCP/IP has fewer layers. As you can see in Figure 5-2, the TCP/IP cake is five layers high. Notice that the fifth (top) layer is a rich one. Although it's called the application layer, it combines OSI's session, presentation, and application layers. TCP/IP's third layer is the Internet layer — it's analogous to OSI's network layer.

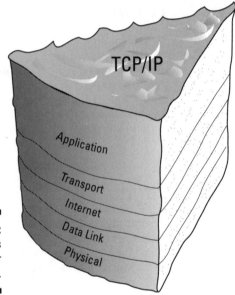

Figure 5-2:
TCP/IP's
five-layer
cake.

The ISO OSI's physical and data link layers are included in the TCP/IP layer cake in Figure 5-2, even though they are hardware and have nothing to do with TCP/IP. TCP/IP is software that's independent of the underlying hardware, but we don't want you to forget that the hardware is still part of the total solution.

We know that cake alone is yummy but not very nutritious. For the main course, from soup to nuts, read Part II, where we explain the set of TCP/IP protocols and show the many applications that run over those protocols. That way you'll have a healthy, balanced meal.

Part II
TCP/IP from Soup to Nuts to Dessert

The 5th Wave   By Rich Tennant

LARRY'S
LUNCH TRUCK
MENU

SAY HI!

"Can someone please tell me how long 'Larry's Lunch Truck' has had his own page on the intranet?"

In this part . . .

Hold on to your forks! Part II delves into the ingredients of the TCP/IP suite: the protocols themselves. You see how the protocols fit into the network layer cake and you get a chance to become familiar with most of them. Using TCP/IP "dinnerware," you can serve up the Internet's goodies. With TCP/IP applications and protocols, you can take advantage of everything from reading news to exchanging e-mail and online conversations with other users to copying good stuff like games, technical articles, and even TCP/IP itself.

(TCP/IP is called a *suite* because it consists of more protocols than the two it is named for, plus a set of services and applications. The TCP/IP protocols, services, and applications in the suite work together just like the rooms in a hotel suite or the pieces in a furniture suite work together. The protocols are also referred to as a *stack,* a term we particularly like because it makes us think of a stack of pancakes.)

Is your computer underpowered? In this part, we help you figure out how you can "borrow" processing power from across the network. It's a piece of cake!

Last, but not least, in this part, you find out how the Internet uses TCP/IP to organize its own client/server structure — here's where you get to examine Web browser clients and Web servers.

Chapter 6

Do You Have a Complete Set of TCP/IP Dinnerware?

In This Chapter

▶ Discovering that TCP/IP is so much more than two protocols

▶ Finding out the difference between TCP/IP protocols, services, and applications

▶ Investigating the major protocols that make up TCP/IP (and what they do)

▶ Discovering some of TCP/IP's newest protocols, including security protocols

*I*f you read Chapter 1, you know that a protocol is the set of agreed-upon practices, policies, and procedures used for communication. In this book, we're concerned with TCP/IP as the protocol for communication between two or more computers. Remember that TCP/IP is actually a large suite of pieces that work together.

The TCP/IP Protocol Suite

What's a suite, you ask? In a hotel, a suite is a collection of rooms that are treated as a single unit. Similarly, the TCP/IP suite is a collection of protocols, named after two of the original pieces, TCP and IP.

Now you may say, "A suite is too big. Can I just rent a room?" Nope. Sorry. The protocols in the TCP/IP suite move the data from one network layer to another and interact with one another. You can't really have a functional network with just one of the TCP/IP protocols.

In Chapter 5, we talk about layer cakes — Figure 6-1 shows the TCP/IP five-layer cake with some of the protocols drawn on the layers. You don't need every protocol on the cake to run a network application, but you need at least a taste from each layer. So even though you may not use all the rooms in the suite, you definitely need more than one.

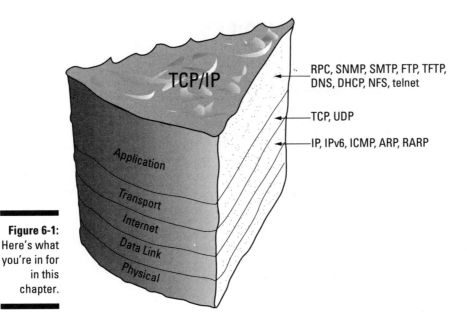

Figure 6-1:
Here's what
you're in for
in this
chapter.

Getting the picture? Good, but this is as far as we're going in comparing TCP/IP to a hotel room. That's because you need to know that there's more to TCP/IP than just TCP and IP. To help you understand, we're going for an analogy that lets you compare all the pieces to something more familiar. Read on.

Many people try to compare the TCP/IP protocol to a Swiss Army knife, which has cutting blades of various sizes, a corkscrew, scissors, a nail file, and so on. The analogy works pretty well except for one thing. The really cool Swiss Army knives, with all those clever and handy pieces, are too big to have with you all the time. They'll poke a hole in your pocket!

So we have a different analogy for you. TCP/IP is like a complete set of dinnerware: plates, bowls, glasses, forks, spoons, and yes, even knives. And TCP/IP continues to expand, which means we can also include cups and saucers, wine glasses, the cream pitcher, finger bowls, and matching salt and pepper shakers. When we say complete, we mean complete! Okay, okay. We're getting carried away with the dinnerware idea, maybe. We suspect you probably eat off paper plates as often as we do. But TCP/IP doesn't know or care whether your plates are paper, stoneware, or bone china. A plate is a plate.

TCP/IP bowls you over

Many pieces of the TCP/IP suite function as protocols, applications, and services. In this and the next six chapters, as we talk about all the great things you can do with TCP/IP, we'll keep you well informed of whether you're using a TCP/IP protocol, a network service, or an application — and highlight the places where the same name applies to one or more of these things.

To kick off the TCP/IP dinnerware analogy, imagine a large bowl. You can use that one bowl in various roles, in more than one room:

- To mix a cake batter (a mixing bowl in the kitchen)
- To hold Seinfeld-sized portions of your favorite cereal, or tonight's soup, or the dog's breakfast (a serving bowl in the dining room)
- To hold flowers (when you don't have a vase in the living room)

TCP/IP's modular, layered design makes it easy to innovate and add new components. If you envision a new network service, as you go about designing the server and client applications you can simultaneously design a new protocol to add to the TCP/IP suite. The protocol enables the server application to offer the service and lets the client application consume that service. This simplicity is a key advantage of TCP/IP.

If you create a new protocol/application/service combination for the Internet, be sure to follow the RFC (Request For Comments) process described in Chapter 2. Follow the instructions in Chapter 24, and get a copy of RFC 1543, "Instructions to RFC Authors."

Protocol, application, or service?

In the fabric of a network, you find the protocol/application/service relationship so tightly woven together that it may be very difficult to distinguish the threads in the cloth. We use FTP as an example. FTP stands for *file transfer protocol,* but it's not only a protocol — FTP is also a service and an application. (Don't worry about FTP itself at this point — it's just an example. If you need to find out how to use FTP, check out Chapter 9.) In this section, we show you how the FTP service, application, and protocol work together to move files around the network.

- FTP is a service for copying files. You connect to a remote computer offering this service, and you can "pull" or "push" files from or to that computer.

✔ FTP is also an application for copying files. You run a client application on your local computer to contact the FTP server application on the remote computer. Your client application is either FTP, the *file transfer program,* or your Web browser, which uses the FTP protocol behind-the-scenes for downloads. The server application is often called FTPD, the *file transfer protocol daemon.* (The term "daemon" comes from UNIX. Think of friendly demons haunting the computer to act on your behalf.) You tell the client what you want to do — pull or push files — and it works with the server to copy the files.

✔ Finally, FTP is a protocol for copying files. The client and server applications both use it for communication to ensure that the new copy of the file is, bit for bit and byte for byte, identical to the original.

FTP is three, three, three things at once — application, service, and protocol. Suppose you need to copy a file from a remote computer. Without the application, your computer doesn't know that you want to copy. Without the service, you don't get a connection to the remote computer that has the files you need. Without the protocol, the client and server can't communicate.

Most of the time, you know from the context whether someone is referring to the service, the application, or the protocol. If you can't quite tell, maybe it doesn't really matter.

And now, on to the protocols!

The Protocols (And You Thought There Were Only Two!)

Hold on tight — here come the pieces in the TCP/IP protocol suite, listed in no particular order.

IP: Internet Protocol

The Internet Protocol, IP, is responsible for basic network connectivity. IP is the plate in a basic place setting. When you're eating, you need a plate to hold your food. When you're networking, you need a place to put (send and receive) data — that place is a network address.

The core of IP works with Internet addresses (you can find the details about these addresses in Chapters 13 and 16). Every computer on a TCP/IP network must have a numeric address. The IP on your computer understands how and where to send messages to these addresses.

While IP can take care of addressing, it can't do everything to make sure that your information gets to where it's going correctly and in one piece. IP doesn't know or care when a packet gets lost and doesn't arrive. So you need some other protocols to ensure that no packets and data are lost and that the packets are in the right order.

All of this is true for both IP version 4 and the new version 6 (IPv6, originally called *IPng* for "next generation"). IPv6 is just bigger and better. So if IP is a plate, IPv6 is a serving platter.

Refer to RFCs 791 and 1883 for more information.

TCP: Transmission Control Protocol

After the food is on your plate, you need something to get it into your mouth without dropping it all over your lap. In your place setting, this is the spoon. Yeah, sure, you could use a fork, and some of you can probably even eat your peas from a knife without losing any, but a spoon is the most reliable implement for most foods. Try eating soup with a fork!

TCP, the Transmission Control Protocol, is our network spoon. No matter what kind of data you have, TCP makes sure that nothing is dropped. TCP uses IP to deliver packets to those upper-layer applications and provides a reliable stream of data among computers on the network. Error checking and sequence numbering are two of TCP's more important functions. After a packet arrives at the correct IP address, TCP goes to work. On both the sending and receiving computers, it establishes a dialog to communicate about the data that's being transmitted. TCP is said to be "connection oriented" because it tells the network to resend lost data.

Theoretically, you can have TCP without IP. Some other network mechanism besides IP can deliver the data to an address, and TCP can still verify and sequence that data. But in practice, TCP is always used with IP.

Check out RFC 793 for TCP information.

UDP: User Datagram Protocol

As just mentioned, your TCP network spoon does the best job on that homemade cream of mushroom soup. In contrast, the User Datagram Protocol, UDP, is like your fork. You can do a pretty good job of cleaning your plate with a fork, and although it's not as reliable as TCP, UDP nevertheless gets a lot of data across the network.

UDP uses IP to deliver packets to upper-layer applications and provides a flow of data among computers. UDP provides neither error checking nor sequence numbering, although these features can be added by the application that has chosen to use UDP. This protocol is said to be "connectionless" because it doesn't provide for resending data in case of error.

NFS (Network File System), DNS (Domain Name System), and RPC (Remote Procedure Call) application programming interfaces use UDP. The protocols, applications, and services for NFS and DNS are discussed in detail in Chapters 10 and 11 respectively.

Figure 6-2 shows the relationship between IP, TCP, and UDP, and the applications at the upper layers. All the applications shown are provided with TCP/IP. If you write your own TCP/IP applications, you can draw those in on the picture, too.

See RFC 768 for more information on UDP.

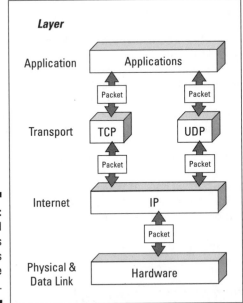

Figure 6-2:
TCP and UDP pass IP packets to the applications.

ARP: Address Resolution Protocol

When all you know is the TCP/IP address of the remote computer, the Address Resolution Protocol, ARP, finds that computer's network interface card hardware address. ARP is like your salad plate. With its load of addresses for the devices on the network, ARP is closely allied with IP, the dinner plate. (See Chapter 13 for more on TCP/IP addresses.)

You have to have connections — or do you?

TCP/IP communicates among the layers in different ways. These methods are either *connectionless* or *connection oriented*.

Connection-oriented communication is reliable and pretty easy to understand. When two computers are communicating with each other, they "connect." Each understands what the other one is doing. The sending computer lets the receiving computer know that data is on the way. The recipient acknowledges receipt of the data (called *ACKs* for short) or denies receipt of the data (negatively acknowledges, or NACKs). This ACKing and NACKing is called *handshaking*.

Suppose you send a fax to your friend Ken in Tokyo. If you want to be sure he gets it, you might call and say, "I'm faxing you the baseball results now. Call me when you get it." After the fax comes in and Ken checks it over to make sure it is readable, he calls you and says, "Thanks. I'm thrilled to hear that the Sox finally won the World Series." That's connection-oriented communication.

But suppose you send the fax without first notifying your friend. And, for some reason, it never gets there. Ken doesn't know to expect anything, so he doesn't know that anything is lost. That's connectionless communication. When connectionless data are sent, the computers involved know nothing about each other or the data being sent. If you're on the receiving end, no one tells you that you're about to get anything. If you're sending data, no one bothers to mention whether or not they got it or if it was totally garbled.

With this in mind, you may wonder why any data communications would be done in connectionless mode. But there's a time and place for everything. First, communication is faster without the ACKs and NACKs. Second, not every network message needs to be as accurate as your e-mail. Finally, some applications do their own error checking and reliability processing, so they don't need the connection-oriented overhead of TCP.

Refer to RFC 826 for more on ARP.

RARP: Reverse Address Resolution Protocol

When all you know is the network interface card (NIC) hardware address of a remote computer, the Reverse Address Resolution Protocol, RARP, finds the computer's TCP/IP address. RARP is your salad fork because it goes with your salad plate. We don't mean to suggest any relationship to the UDP dinner fork, however. Hey, there are places where we have to stretch the analogy a little, okay?

Check out RFC 903 for more on RARP.

ICMP: Internet Control Message Protocol

The Internet Control Message Protocol, ICMP, reports problems and relays other network specific information, such as an error status, from some network device. IP detects the error and passes it to ICMP. A very common use of ICMP is the echo request generated by the ping command. ICMP is like your crystal water glass, the one that "pings" so nicely when you accidentally hit it with the fork you're waving around to emphasize your point in that argument about the greenhouse effect.

See RFCs 1256 and 1885 for the scoop on ICMP.

FTP: File Transfer Protocol

The File Transfer Protocol, FTP, is like your knife. Not a special steak knife or a little butter knife, just the regular dinner knife. It's FTP that helps you copy files between two computers. You use your FTP knife to either "pull" the files from the remote computer (known as *downloading*) or "push" them to the remote computer (known as *uploading*). As described earlier in this chapter, FTP is also the name of an application and a service, so we'll be looking at it again (and again). (Check out Chapter 9 for lots more on FTP.)

See RFC 959 for more on FTP.

Telnet

The telnet protocol lets you connect to a remote computer and work as if you were sitting in front of that computer, no matter how far away that computer may be. With telnet, you can lounge around in Tahiti and work on a remote computer in Antarctica as if you were there surrounded by penguins — without even a shiver. Besides being a protocol, telnet is also a service and an application — three for the price of one. Telnet is the "lazy Susan" that helps you reach the mango chutney that would otherwise be out of reach.

Check out Chapter 8 for lots more on telnet. If you want to do more with penguins, check out www.ai.mit.edu/people/paulfitz/plank/horde.doit.

See RFCs 854 and 855 for more on telnet.

TFTP: Trivial File Transfer Protocol

The Trivial File Transfer Protocol, TFTP, is a specialized FTP. One common use of TFTP is to install a computer's operating system from a TFTP server's files. TFTP is your butter knife, a smaller version of the FTP dinner knife. You can see why we needed to be a little specific about your FTP knife.

Refer to RFC 1350 for more on TFTP.

SNMP: Simple Network Management Protocol

SNMP is the protocol that's used to monitor and manage networks and the devices connected to them, and to collect information about network performance. If you want to write a network management application, you read SNMP messages called *protocol data units* (PDUs) to see when devices connect or disconnect from the network and whether everything is okay on the network.

But wait! Don't waste your time. Why should you write a network management application that uses SNMP when you can buy one from your choice of vendors? IBM's Netview, HP's Open View, and other network management products show the state of your entire network with some neat graphics. So watch the pretty pictures and go have a long lunch on your boss.

SNMP is the head waiter who makes sure that every part of your dining experience is meeting your needs and expectations.

RFC 2272 has more on SNMP.

SMTP: Simple Mail Transfer Protocol

The Simple Mail Transfer Protocol, SMTP, is the protocol for Internet e-mail. It transfers e-mail messages among computers. The messages may go directly from the sender's computer to the recipient's, or the messages may proceed through intermediary computers in a process known as *store and forward*.

SMTP is like your wine goblet. Again, a disclaimer is in order: We don't mean to suggest any relationship to the ICMP water glass, which you managed to knock over anyway as that discussion heated up.

E-mail, of course, is one of the Big Four network applications (along with file transfer, signing on to remote computers, and Web browsing), and many vendors have their own mail protocols. SMTP is the mail transfer protocol for the Internet. UNIX mail understands SMTP, but some other operating systems don't. When users of SMTP-ignorant computers need to get out to the outside world (in other words, get to the Internet), a special SMTP gateway must be established for that communication. Chapter 7 tells you more about SMTP gateways and e-mail in general.

RFC 821 also has information on SMTP.

POP3: Post Office Protocol, v3

The latest version of the Post Office Protocol (version 3), POP3, provides basic client/server features that help you download your e-mail from a POP3 mail server to your computer. POP3 is like the corkscrew that helps you get the e-mail wine out of the bottle and into your wine goblet. If your computer has an SMTP connection to a neighboring computer, you don't need to use POP3.

POP3 was designed to allow home users to move their e-mail off their Internet Service Provider's (ISP's) computers and onto their own. You need a POP3 mail client to communicate with a POP3 mail server. See Chapter 7 for more information about POP3 clients and servers.

RCF 1939 has more on POP3.

IMAP4: Internet Message Access Protocol, v4

The latest version of the Internet Message Access Protocol (version 4, revision 1), IMAP4, provides sophisticated client/server capabilities that give you choices about how you handle your e-mail. IMAP4 provides a richer set of features than POP3. IMAP4 is like a fancy decanter that holds the wine better than the bottle does but still helps you get the e-mail wine into your wine goblet. If your computer has an SMTP connection to a neighboring computer, you don't need to use IMAP4. You still may choose to use IMAP4, however, because of its sparkling functionality. You need an IMAP4 client to communicate with an IMAP4 mail server.

POP3 and IMAP4 don't interoperate. You can't use a POP3 client with an IMAP4 server or an IMAP4 client with a POP3 server, but you can find clients and servers that speak both protocols.

See RFC 2060 for more on IMAP4.

LDAP: Lightweight Directory Access Protocol

LDAP (pronounced as L-dap, which rhymes with cap) is the way to look up information such as user names and e-mail addresses in an X.500-compatible directory service. Whew! That's a mouthful. Think of the directory service as a big set of telephone books containing all of the information you may need. The problem is, there isn't just one set of phone books. Each organization has several.

LDAP helps applications get what they need from any or all sets of phone books. LDAP reminds us of the condiment tray filled with pickles, olives, capers, relishes, a little bit of this, a little bit of that, each in its own separate compartment.

X.500, part of ISO OSI, had its own Directory Access Protocol (DAP), but neither X.500 or DAP became popular. LDAP capitalizes on the work done by X.500 and DAP's visionary designers.

Check out RFC 2251 for more on LDAP.

NTP: Network Time Protocol

The time-of-day clocks that computers maintain are synchronized by the Network Time Protocol, NTP. Time-stamping is important in all sorts of applications, providing everything from document creation dates to network routing date/time information. NTP gets the time data from a time-server computer, which gets it from an official source, such as the United States National Institute of Standards and Technology. In continental Europe, ISO provides a time service used with banking transactions and stock transfers.

NTP is like your seafood fork. You know, the tiny one you use (or try to, anyway) to get the lobster meat out. NTP is a special-purpose tool, just right for the job it's made for.

RFC 1305 has more on NTP.

HTTP: HyperText Transfer Protocol

The HyperText Transfer Protocol (HTTP) transfers HyperText Markup Language (HTML) and other components from the servers on the World Wide Web to your browser client. (You can find lots more about the World Wide Web in Chapter 12.)

HTTP is like a large pitcher filled with sangria — a lot of delicious ingredients that are combined to make something even better. (Candace makes the world's best sangria, but in a sick twist of fate she's allergic to red wine.) The HTTP pitcher brings the various Web ingredients to you. It's similar to the wonders of e-mail brought to you by the SMTP wine goblet.

See RFC 2068 for more on HTTP.

S-HTTP: Secure HTTP

S-HTTP is a secure version of HTTP that *encrypts* (codes) sensitive data, such as credit card transactions. Think of it as a hidden flask that discreetly holds your sangria. No one knows what you're drinking.

BOOTP: Boot Protocol

Not all computers come with the operating system pre-installed — sometimes you have to install the operating system yourself. If the computer has no disks for storage (horrors!, but it happens mostly in large organizations where people share resources), you can download the operating system into your computer's memory from another computer on the network. When you do, your diskless computer uses the Boot Protocol, BOOTP, to load its operating system (or other stand-alone application) via the network. *Booting* means loading the operating system.

RFC 2132 has more information on BOOTP.

If you do have disk storage on your new computer, you should install your own local operating system. Some operating system vendors let you perform a remote installation from another computer on the network. The remote installation copies all the operating system files to your computer's disk; from that point on, you can boot the operating system locally.

RIP, OSPF: Gateway (Router) Protocols

Under your network place settings are a tablecloth made of gateways and routers, which have various gateway and router protocols that allow them to exchange network topology and status information. *Routing* is the process of moving packets between networks.

Here are the some of the most popular ones, along with RFCs with more information:

✔ Routing Information Protocol (RIP) — RFCs 1723 and 2080 (for RIP with IPv6)

✔ Open Shortest Path First (OSPF) — RFC 2328

✔ Inter Domain Routing Protocol (something rescued from the OSI effort) — RFC 1479

Chapter 18 has more information on the gateways, routers, and other hardware devices that use these protocols.

PPTP: Point to Point Tunneling Protocol

The Point to Point Tunneling Protocol (PPTP) lets you create a *Virtual Private Network* (VPN) on the public Internet. Using PPTP you can have a secure link to your organization's network — as if you were inside the building and on the LAN — even though you're actually connected to the Internet via an Internet Service Provider (ISP). Your communication traffic can even be encrypted to ensure that no miscreants can see your data. You get all of the benefits of a global private network without any of the hassles of launching your own satellites, laying your own undersea cables, or working with any of the boring pieces in Chapter 3.

PPTP is like your napkin because it augments the tablecloth provided by the router protocols. The encryption is like an optional napkin ring.

DHCP: Dynamic Host Configuration Protocol

We couldn't forget about you housekeeping haters out there when putting together the TCP/IP dinnerware. We knew you'd want a recyclable paper plate. DHCP, the Dynamic Host Configuration Protocol, is that paper plate. This protocol is a client/server solution for sharing numeric IP addresses. The DHCP paper plate (a DHCP server) maintains a pool of shared addresses — and those addresses are recyclable. When a DHCP client computer wants to use a TCP/IP application, that client must first request an IP address from the DHCP server. The server checks the shared supply; if all the addresses are in use, the server notifies the client that it must wait until another client finishes its work and releases an IP address. If an address is available, the DHCP server sends a response to the client that contains the address.

This shared-supply approach makes sense in environments in which computers don't use TCP/IP applications all the time or in which there aren't enough addresses available for all the computers that want them.

Refer to RFC 2131 for more on DHCP.

SSL: Secure Sockets Layer

SSL (the Secure Sockets Layer) version 2 provides security by allowing applications to encrypt data that go from a client, such as a Web browser, to the matching server. (*Encrypting* your data means converting to a secret code. Chapter 7 discusses encrypting your e-mail.) In other words, when you buy that Lamborghini over the Web, no one but the dealer can read your credit card number. SSL version 3 allows the server to authenticate that the client is who it says it is.

SSL is like the engraved invitation you must show at the front door before you're allowed to see your glorious dining table set with all this wondrous TCP/IP dinnerware. It's the way you convince the big brute of a bouncer to let you in.

SET: Secure Electronic Transaction

When the Web-based Lamborghini dealer checks with the bank to make sure your credit card is good, you don't want any Internet snoops stealing a peek at your credit card number. SET is the protocol that protects your credit card on the dealer's end of the sale.

IPSec: IP Security Protocol

As the security protocol for VPNs (Virtual Private Networks), IPSec includes some very strong encryption (coding) techniques to protect your data in the public/private world of VPNs. IPSec also makes sure that the computer accessing your private network across the very public Internet is really a part of your network and not a pretender trying to sneak into your VPN. We describe VPNs in Chapter 17, and you can read more about IPSec in Chapter 18.

And many, many more . . .

You can find many more existing pieces of TCP/IP, and new ones are being developed this very minute! The ones described in this chapter are the most important, the most visible, and the most common. All of the protocols that use an IP address must be updated so that they understand the IPv6 address. Aren't you glad you're not a TCP/IP programmer?

The changes in IPv6 also affect services such as DNS. You can read about IPv6 details in Chapter 15.

Chapter 7

E-Mail and Beyond — Shipping and Handling Included

· ·

In This Chapter

▶ Understanding e-mail: Is it a TCP/IP application or not?

▶ Having aliases without getting your picture on the police station wall

▶ Finding out that Internet e-mail goes with SMTP (Simple Mail Transfer Protocol) like meat and potatoes

▶ Meeting the latest and greatest (at least for now) mail technologies — POP3 and IMAP4

▶ Loving MIME for making it possible to send audio, video, and lots more

▶ Getting tips on how to protect and speed up your e-mail

▶ Making toll-free telephone calls and faxes on the Internet

▶ Substituting a Web browser for a newsreader client

· ·

*A*t the restaurant at the end of the network, Web browsing, e-mail, file transfer, and remote login are the Big Four favorites on the TCP/IP plate — a high calorie meal. And of these four, e-mail is a whole banquet of choices and features. In this chapter, you sample the many courses that make up the e-mail banquet. But before you go there, you need to know the difference between a plain vanilla application and a TCP/IP application.

The Medium Is the Message (Sometimes)

When we talk about services and applications in this chapter, remember that we're talking about TCP/IP services and applications for the most part. You need to understand what is and what is not a TCP/IP application. It may be different from what you think.

Take e-mail as an example. When you start a session to compose and send an e-mail message, the program you use to create the message is an application, but not a TCP/IP application. In modern e-mail terminology, you use a *mail user agent* (MUA) to create your message. Eudora (Eudora Light is a free, public domain MUA), Lotus Notes, and Netscape Communicator's Messenger are examples of MUAs.

When you send an e-mail message, the MUA hands it to a mail transfer agent (MTA). Sendmail, with implementations for various operating systems, is the most common MTA. Lotus Domino is another widely-used MTA. The MTA is a TCP/IP application, and it uses the TCP/IP protocol SMTP (Simple Mail Transfer Protocol). The MTA delivers the message to another MTA. The message moves from MTA to MTA until it gets to the addressee's computer. The addressee then uses the MUA to read the message.

The communication between an MUA and an MTA doesn't have to be TCP/IP, but the communication between MTAs does.

POP3, IMAP4: You can't escape client/ server, even in the spirit world

Eudora and Netscape Communicator's mail use TCP/IP's POP3 (Post Office Protocol version 3) to download your mail from a POP3 server (such as the Netscape Mail Server) to your computer.

Corporate users may prefer to use TCP/IP's IMAP4 protocol between an MUA (such as Lotus Notes or Sun Microsystems' Solstice Internet Mail Client) and an IMAP4 server (such as Lotus Domino). Of course, you can use other POP3 and IMAP4 clients and servers — you must evaluate them and decide which products meet your needs.

The SMTP protocol, POP3, and IMAP4 are described in Chapter 6.

It doesn't matter whether your MUA is a UNIX application, a Microsoft Windows application, an X Window System application, a Macintosh application, or any other vendor's application. Just remember that whichever Internet e-mail application you choose can talk to the TCP/IP application and protocol. The TCP/IP applications, which you can't see, are those other agents, the MTAs.

Click here for free e-mail

If you browse the Web much, you may see advertisements saying "Click here for free e-mail." Is this for real or is it a marketing sting? Yes, it really is a free service. Yes, it really is a marketing tactic because your free e-mail accounts are subsidized by advertising. All your mail's stored on the server, and you don't need a mail client. Your Web browser is the MUA that lets you read and write e-mail.

Casper, the friendly MTA

Now don't get nervous here. It's okay that the mail transfer agents and TCP/IP are invisible to you. Your MUA can see the TCP/IP application and service, and that's what matters. Think of TCP/IP as a friendly ghost, only visible to certain beings. You can't see the ghost with your eyes, but you can communicate with it through your MUA medium.

So, e-mail is a kind of electronic seance in which you need an intermediary to get you to TCP/IP. This paranormal approach isn't true of every application. You do have direct contact with certain TCP/IP applications, such as FTP. Whether you get to talk to TCP/IP directly or have to go through a medium depends on what you're trying to do (e-mail, file transfer, or something else).

And Now — On to the Restaurant at the End of the Network

After you have e-mail — Number One of the Big Four — you wonder how you ever lived without it. You'll complain every time you have to pick up a pen and paper to write a real, old-fashioned letter. Okay, so you don't write letters anyway, but aren't those *#!*@$&% long-distance telephone charges annoying? (When will our parents get on the Internet?!)

One other thing before we dive into the e-mail banquet: Talking about TCP/IP without talking about the Internet is impossible — it would be like discussing gasoline without talking about cars. So, in this chapter, you find lots of references to the Internet as we describe the things that TCP/IP lets you do.

The E-Mail Course at the TCP/IP Banquet

Electronic mail is the first network application most people meet. (File sharing is the other contender for this prize, but sometimes people don't realize file sharing is even happening, much less that it's a network service.) E-mail has been around so long that many of us forget some folks still don't have it yet.

The following sections take a look at everything in the e-mail banquet. And wait 'til you read about MIME, a delicious dessert that TCP/IP gives you — at no extra charge.

E-mail addresses: @ marks the spot

To send or receive e-mail, you and your correspondent each need to have an e-mail address. (You can see an e-mail address in this book in Chapter 2.) These addresses take this form

```
username@address
```

The first part, username, is a username on a computer. The @ character is always there. Then comes the address: the computer name and some information about the computer's location on the network, separated by periods. Here's a sample (fictitious) e-mail address:

```
smith@abc.university.edu
```

In this address, smith is the username, abc is the computer name, university is where the computer is located, and edu is a domain name that represents educational institutions.

Don't worry yet about all the pieces of the address. Chapter 13 explains all you need to know about Internet addresses and domain names.

How can I find someone's e-mail address?

Looking up someone's e-mail address is similar to finding a home address. Wanna take a date to the e-mail banquet? You have several choices for getting hold of that person, and sometimes the simplest way is the best. Here are some ways you can find out where your favorite person lives on the Internet:

- ✔ **Use the telephone.** In spite of all the people-searching tools on the Internet, the telephone is still the best way to find an e-mail address. Sometimes the phone number is right there on the person's business card. Or you may even find it in the phone book or by calling Directory Assistance (although you have to pay for this last alternative in the United States! %!@$*#!&$!).

✔ **Get the e-mail address from e-mail you've received.** The sender's address is there. If you don't believe us, go look and see.

✔ **Look up the address in a Whois database.** The InterNIC (the Internet information center that we tell you about in Chapter 2) maintains the original Whois database. Not everyone is listed, but it may be worth checking. Figure 7-1 shows a session with the InterNIC. We connected with the `telnet` command (more on telnet in Chapter 8) and used the `whois` command to look up the addresses for a major corporation and a world leader. Notice that there is no match for the President of the United States. This shows that you may have to look in more than one place to find the e-mail address you're looking for. In this case, we had to go to a different Whois database, one for the U.S. government. Figure 7-2 shows how to look up a U.S. government e-mail address. Other Whois databases you can telnet to include:

- `whois.arin.net` — American Registry for Internet Numbers
- `whois.ripe.net` — European IP Address Allocations
- `whois.apnic.net` — Asia Pacific IP Address Allocations
- `whois.nic.mil` — U.S. Military
- `whois.nic.gov` — U.S. Government

Anybody home?

There are lots of ways to find out who or what is out there on the networks, including the Internet. Four of the tools you can use are finger, rwho, ruptime, and ping. These are explained in more detail for you in Chapter 15, but here is a brief description of what they do. (We think you'll find their names somewhere between mildly amusing and slightly perverted. Most of them come from UNIX. Need we say more?)

✔ The finger utility displays plenty of information about network users, including their current plans. Finger is good for finding out someone's e-mail address. This utility is amazingly thorough — it'll even tell you how many cold sodas are in a machine in Pittsburgh, PA.

✔ The rwho utility tells you all the users currently logged in to computers on your network. You can find out if someone is signed on before you try to talk to them electronically (see Chapter 7).

✔ The ruptime utility lists all the computers on the network. You can use ruptime to see if a computer is available before you use FTP or rcp to transfer files to or from it.

✔ The ping utility lets you find out if a specific computer is up and running on the network. When you already know the name of the computer you want, ping is a lot more efficient than ruptime.

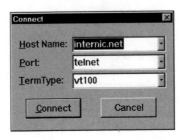

```
UNIX(r) System V Release 4.0 (rrs1)

***********************************************************
* -- InterNIC Registration Services Center   --
*
* For the *original* whois type:      WHOIS [search string] <return>
* For referral whois type:            RWHOIS [search string] <return>
*
# Questions/Updates on the whois database to HOSTMASTER@internic.net
***********************************************************
The InterNIC Registration Services database contains ONLY
non-military and non-US Government Domains and contacts.
Other associated whois servers:
        American Registry for Internet Numbers - whois.arin.net
        European IP Address Allocations        - whois.ripe.net
        Asia Pacific IP Address Allocations    - whois.apnic.net
        US Military                            - whois.nic.mil
        US Government                          - whois.nic.gov
Cmdinter Ver 1.3 Sun Nov 22 16:55:51 1998 EST
(vt100)
Whois: internic.net
Registrant:
Network Solutions, Inc. (INTERNIC-DOM)
   505 Huntmar Park Drive
   Herndon, VA 20170

   Domain Name: INTERNIC.NET

   Administrative Contact:
      Network Solutions, Inc.  (HOSTMASTER)  hostmaster@INTERNIC.NET
      (703) 742-4777 (FAX) (703) 742-9552
   Technical Contact, Zone Contact:
      Kosters, Mark A.  (MAK21)  markk@NETSOL.COM
      (703) 925-6874 (FAX) (703) 742-5427
   Billing Contact:
      Bowles, Carol  (CB2487)  billing@INTERNIC.NET
      703-742-4777 (FAX) 703-318-9125
   Record last updated on 19-May-98.
   Record created on 01-Jan-93.
   Database last updated on 22-Nov-98 06:34:34 EST.

   Domain servers in listed order:

   RS0.INTERNIC.NET           198.41.0.5
   NOC.CERF.NET               192.153.156.22
   NS.ISI.EDU                 128.9.128.127

Whois: ibm.com
IBM Corporation (IBM-DOM)
IBM.COM
International Business Machines (IBM4-HST) IBM.COM
129.34.139.30

[vt100] InterNIC > whois clinton@whitehouse.gov
Connecting to the rs Database . . . . . .
Connected to the rs Database
No match for mailbox "CLINTON@WHITEHOUSE.GOV".
Whois: whitehouse.gov
No match for "WHITEHOUSE.GOV".
```

Figure 7-1:
Finding an
e-mail
address in
the InterNIC
Whois
database.

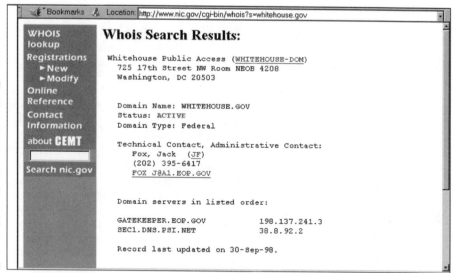

Figure 7-2:
Finding an
e-mail
address
for the
President of
the U.S. in
the U.S.
government
Whois
database.

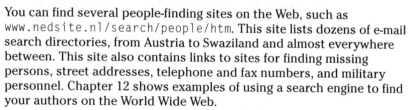

✔ **Search the World Wide Web.** You can use a *search engine* (a program that searches the Web for information that you request) to look for people. Yahoo! (www.yahoo.com) and AltaVista (www.altavista.digital.com) are two widely used search engines.

You can find several people-finding sites on the Web, such as www.nedsite.nl/search/people/htm. This site lists dozens of e-mail search directories, from Austria to Swaziland and almost everywhere between. This site also contains links to sites for finding missing persons, street addresses, telephone and fax numbers, and military personnel. Chapter 12 shows examples of using a search engine to find your authors on the World Wide Web.

When a search engine finds the person you want, the search isn't guaranteed to turn up that person's e-mail address. Many sites that collect name and address information, let you search for free. The person you're looking for may or may not be listed. Give it a try.

✔ **Use an online service's directory.** Online services, such as America Online and CompuServe, maintain directories of their users. If you subscribe to an online service, you can search its directories for other subscribers.

Ooh No! No entry for Mr. Bill (Gates or Clinton)

Whois is a TCP/IP protocol, service, and application that enables you to look up information about networks, networking organizations, domains, and the people who manage them. The information is stored in a Whois database. The InterNIC created the first Whois database, but recently, other organizations have implemented Whois and maintain their own Whois databases. For example, the American Registry for Internet Numbers (ARIN) created a Whois database in December, 1997.

The creation of multiple databases means that more information about networks is available. Multiple databases also mean more work if you're searching for someone or some group on the Internet, because now you may need to look in more than one place. You can look up

network information in the InterNIC's Whois database at `rs.internic.net/cgi-bin/whois` and in ARIN's database at `www.arin.net/whois/arinwhois.html`.

RFC 954 describes Whois.

Try looking up the name Bill with whois, and you'll find over 140 entries for various people and organizations named Bill, but not a thing for a certain bespectacled young billionaire, `bill@microsoft.com`. And nothing for Bill Clinton, either. By the way, you won't find Marshall or Candace (your authors) with whois, but you will find the networks that they use and the contact person who manages those networks.

✔ **Query an LDAP (Lightweight Directory Access Protocol) server.** An LDAP server maintains a directory of names, e-mail addresses, and more. The LDAP directory is similar to a Whois database. If your MUA uses POP3 or IMAP4, you can query an LDAP server for e-mail addresses. See Chapter 6 for a description of LDAP. Popular LDAP servers include `ldap.bigfoot.com` and `ldap.switchboard.com`.

SMTP: The Meat and Potatoes

SMTP (Simple Mail Transfer Protocol) is the part of the TCP/IP protocol suite that MTAs use to communicate. SMTP defines how messages move from one computer's MTA to another's MTA, but not what path each message takes. A message may go directly from the sender's computer to the recipient's, or it may proceed through intermediary computers via the store and forward process.

In the store and forward style, as each message travels through the network on the way to its destination, it may pass through any number of intermediate computers, where it is briefly stored before being sent on to the next computer in the path. This is sort of like a weary traveler stopping to rest occasionally before continuing the trip across the network galaxy (see Figure 7-3).

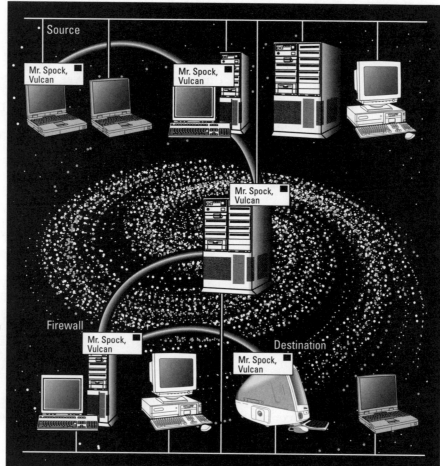

Figure 7-3:
A message
is stored
and
forwarded
across the
network
galaxy.

The SMTP protocol is strictly about moving messages from one computer to another. Although SMTP doesn't care about the content of an e-mail message, it does limit the formatting attributes of the message. SMTP can transfer only ASCII text. It can't handle fonts, colors, graphics, attachments, or any other of those fancy e-mail features that you may already know and love.

If you like to send deluxe e-mail — sounds, movies, a picture of your dog — you need to read the next section about MIME.

MIME Means a Lot More Than Marcel Marceau

To enhance the body of an e-mail message so that it can be used to carry fonts, colors, and so forth, some good-deed doers (RFC writers, as described in Chapter 2) invented MIME, Multipurpose Internet Mail Extensions. MIME is pronounced the way you may expect, as "spoken" by Marcel Marceau. If the SMTP is the meat and potatoes of e-mail, MIME is dessert. And a meal isn't complete without dessert, is it?

MIME is described in RFCs 2046 through 2049.

MIME allows the body of e-mail messages to have all those cool enhancements such as colors, sounds, and animation, while still allowing them to be delivered by SMTP (which, as explained earlier, couldn't care less about anything but ASCII text).

"How do they do that?" we hear you asking. Well, it requires that you use a *MIME-compliant* mail user agent — that is, your MUA must know how to generate MIME message bodies. When you compose your sophisticated e-mail message, your MIME-compliant MUA encodes the deluxe features into a text-only representation that SMTP can transfer. The message can then pass through the necessary intermediary computers as usual, and none of them needs anything special to process your enhanced message.

When the message arrives at its final destination, your correspondent also needs a MIME-compliant MUA in order to decode the fancy features. Without a MIME-compliant MUA, the recipient of your message may not be able to do much with it.

S/MIME secures communications between an e-mail sender and the recipient. For example, Candace and niece Emily need secrecy for sharing important Beanie Baby news. See Chapter 19 for more information about S/MIME.

How an SMTP Gateway Works

Because of the long-standing relationship between UNIX and TCP/IP, the UNIX mail system uses SMTP. The same can't be said, however, about some other e-mail products. Those other e-mail systems need an SMTP gateway.

An *SMTP gateway* is software that translates e-mail messages between RFC822/MIME format and the format of another e-mail system. For example, suppose your organization doesn't use an SMTP e-mail system. In order to exchange e-mail with people who do use one, your organization needs an

SMTP gateway. The gateway converts outbound mail messages into RFC822/MIME format and inbound mail messages into the correct format for your system.

Every SMTP gateway has to deal with the fact that no two e-mail systems are exactly alike, no matter how similar their features. Some things just won't match up when the gateway translates the message formats. The simple elegance of SMTP means that its mail system usually appears less sophisticated than other systems, although MIME does help narrow the gap.

"Alias Smith and Jones"

Mail aliases are the after-dinner drinks of the e-mail meal — they're sometimes nice to have, but definitely not required.

Mail aliases provide a handy way to forward e-mail to another address. Suppose you'll be working at a branch office for a month. Instead of connecting to the main office each day to read your e-mail, you can have your e-mail forwarded to a computer at the branch office. The postmaster at the main office creates a mail alias on the main office computer to forward your e-mail to the branch office computer.

There are two different kinds of mail aliases: private and public (although they do similar things).

- ✔ The mail aliases you create are private; no one else can use them. To find out how to create your private mail aliases, consult the manual for your MUA. (On a UNIX system, you normally define them in the file named .mailrc located in your home directory.)
- ✔ The mail aliases that a postmaster creates are public; everyone can use them. The operating system and e-mail environment dictate how public aliases are created and maintained. (On a UNIX system, the postmaster normally defines them in the file /usr/lib/aliases.)

Neat things you can do with mail aliases

Mail aliases can also provide assistance to e-mail users in the following ways.

Mailing lists

In e-mail parlance, a mailing list is one e-mail address that sends your message to multiple recipients. For example, a mailing list could translate the following alias:

```
tcpip_for_dummies_authors
```

Into these two addresses:

```
mwilensky@lotus.com
leidencci@aol.com
```

Mailing lists are sometimes called *exploders* because one e-mail message "explodes" into many more.

Friendlier or more standard addresses

It's fairly obvious that this address

```
Marshall_Wilensky@crd.lotus.com
```

takes more effort to type than this alias

```
mwilensky@lotus.com
```

By means of public aliases, a postmaster can create and implement a consistent, more user-friendly naming convention for your organization.

A way to reach people with unspellable names

A lot of people have trouble spelling Marshall's last name, so the postmaster may define this public alias

```
mwilenski@lotus.com
```

for this address

```
mwilensky@lotus.com
```

(Look closely; the *i* in Wilenski has been changed to a *y*.) Now, Marshall will get the e-mail whether or not you spell his name correctly.

Some interesting e-mail examples

Here is a message sent to a regular username, with no alias:

```
% mail marshall_wilensky@crd.lotus.com
Subject: Hello there
This message is to user marshall_wilensky. No alias. The
sender had to type a long address and know how to spell
Marshall's name (3 "l"s and a "y" at the end).
This message was written using the UNIX mail user agent,
Mail. SMTP got this message from the mail transfer agent
```

```
and delivered it across the network. Because this message
is plain text, we don't need MIME to handle any fancy stuff.
That's all. Bye for now.
.
Cc:
%
```

Here is a mail message sent to an alias. This looks the same whether the alias is public or private.

```
% mail wilenski@lotus.com
Subject: Hello there
This message is to the same person, but to his mail alias.
And I didn't even have to know how to spell his name. Hard
to tell the difference just by looking, isn't it?
That's all. Bye for now.
.
Cc:
%
```

Speed up your e-mail delivery. Many e-mail clients such as Lotus cc:Mail, Lotus Notes, Microsoft Outlook Express, and Qualcomm Eudora Pro let you dial in for automatic delivery. You can set up a schedule so that your overnight mail is waiting for you before you get to work.

Is Your E-Mail Secure?

Do you think you have nothing to hide? Maybe you don't, but e-mail security is always a personal privacy issue even if you aren't mailing credit card numbers or secret formulas for eternal youth. Don't think that using S/MIME for security can completely protect you. In the landmark court case, Microsoft had to turn over not only paper documents, but e-mail messages as evidence to the United States Department of Justice.

Don't let people eavesdrop on your mail

Imagine that you're having a wonderful time in Tahiti. But you run out of money. What do you do? Send a letter to Mum asking for money. This letter moves from the post office in Tahiti to Australia to Singapore to Bombay to Cairo and finally reaches good old Mum in Dublin. Suppose that in each post office, an employee reads your mail before forwarding it. How rude! And worse. Suppose some day a member of the Royal Family proposes marriage to you, and then an unscrupulous postal employee comes forward and reveals that you're likely to slack off and expect someone else to pay your bad debts. That's the end of the engagement. So you think, "If only I'd e-mailed to Mum, no one would have been able to read it but her." Not so.

Your mail message goes through more computers than just yours and your recipient's. Refer to Figure 7-3, which shows mail being stored briefly and forwarded through several computers on its way to its intergalactic destination. A hacker doesn't even have to be very good to snoop on your mail. All the busybody has to do is use a packet sniffer program to intercept passing mail messages. A *packet sniffer* is a tool that a network administrator uses to record and analyze network traffic.

Make your mail an enigma and foil snoopers

Cryptography isn't just for secret agents. Many e-mail products allow your messages to be encrypted (coded in a secret pattern) so that only you and your recipient can read them. Lotus Notes provides e-mail encryption. You can read more technical details about encryption in Chapter 19.

Wall up your network to keep out shady characters

If you receive mail from people outside your network, you should set up a firewall to protect your network. The *firewall* is a computer that prevents unauthorized data from reaching your network. For example, if you don't want anything from snoopers.com to penetrate your net, put your net behind a firewall. The firewall blocks out all snoopers.com messages. Refer to Figure 7-3, which shows our favorite Vulcan's network defended by a firewall. If you're interested in firewalls, Chapter 19 is for you.

Usenet News: Sharing Info over Lunch at the Network Table

If e-mail is the number one dinner choice on the TCP/IP plate, then news is number one for lunch. News via TCP/IP is known by various names, including Usenet news, netnews, and Network News. We call it Usenet news in this book.

Usenet news is a TCP/IP service consisting of a worldwide collection of online newsgroups. Each newsgroup is an electronic conversation group about a particular topic. Topics range from Disney to Star Trek, from home repair to gay and lesbian rights. Anyone on the Internet can post an article stating an opinion and/or asking for information. You've heard the stories of people meeting online through newsgroups and falling in love, sight unseen — it really happens!

There are over 20,000 different Usenet newsgroups, and new ones are being created every day. We mention `rec.arts.disney` in Chapter 3. Newsgroups are categorized by interest areas, and the pieces of a newsgroup name are the hierarchy for those interest areas, separated by dots (periods). The first part of the name is the most general topic, and each subsequent part of the name gets a little more specific. Newsgroup names look somewhat like the part of an e-mail address on the right-hand side of the @ sign, but it's just a coincidence.

Table 7-1 lists the main newsgroup hierarchies that you'll see often in newsgroup names.

Table 7-1	The Main Newsgroup Hierarchies
Hierarchy	*Subject*
`comp.`	Computers and related topics
`misc.`	Miscellaneous
`news.`	Usenet news subjects, not the evening news or the newspaper
`rec.`	Recreation and the arts
`sci.`	Science
`soc.`	Society/sociology; sometimes relevant, sometimes wildly theoretical
`talk.`	Discussion; often controversial
`alt.`	"Alternative"; weird and serious stuff, as well

Table 7-2 lists many other special or regional categories.

Table 7-2	Special Newsgroup Hierarchies
Hierarchy	*Subject*
`ne.`	New England and the northeastern United States
`biz.`	Business
`bionet.`	Biology

Newsgroups to help newcomers

If you're new to Usenet news, you can check out a few newsgroups to help you find out how to read and write articles. Here are three of the most useful ones:

✔ news.announce.newusers: The articles in this newsgroup are about Usenet news features.

✔ news.newusers.questions: You can post articles here asking questions about how Usenet news works.

✔ news.answers: The articles here list the most frequently asked questions (FAQs) from the most popular newsgroups. This newsgroup is a fascinating catchall of useful and useless trivia.

How to use newsgroups to find out more about TCP/IP

You can find several newsgroups about TCP/IP. In the following list, many of the newsgroups are categorized by operating system.

✔ comp.os.ms-windows.networking.tcp-ip

✔ comp.os.os2.networking.tcp-ip

✔ comp.os.ms-windows.nt.admin.networking

✔ comp.os.linux.networks

✔ comp.protocols.tcp-ip

✔ comp.protocols.tcp_ip.domains

✔ comp.protocols.tcp-ip.ibmpc

Newsgroups come and go, and sometimes an existing newsgroup becomes inactive (that is, no more articles are written for it). Our lists of TCP/IP-oriented newsgroups is current as of this writing, but as you look around on the Internet, you may see the list grow or shrink.

With so many interesting electronic discussions out there, you could spend all of your waking hours chit-chatting on the Internet. And you wouldn't even have to shower and dress, because no one can see or smell you.

rn tin tin: The dog's breakfast the morning after the TCP/IP banquet

The end-user application for accessing Usenet news is called a *newsreader*. It's similar to the MUA for e-mail: The newsreader passes your requests on to the TCP/IP service. You don't communicate directly with any TCP/IP components; the newsreader does it for you, invisibly. Whether news is stored on your own computer (as with older technology) or on a server (the newer client/server technology), you use a newsreader to read articles, post follow-ups or new articles, mail a response directly to the article's author, forward an article via e-mail to another person, and so on.

Newsreaders come in all shapes, sizes, and flavors. Many are free (called *public domain*). You may have several to choose from on your computer. Some of the more popular ones are

- ✔ rn
- ✔ trn (see Figure 7-4)
- ✔ tin

Every newsreader needs to keep track of which articles you've already read. A good newsreader helps you by organizing the articles by discussion thread. Sometimes this means the newsreader looks at the article's Subject: or Summary: line to see if it's similar to other articles. Without this kind of feature, you're stuck reading articles in the chronological order in which they arrived on your computer or the server.

Watch out! Reading news articles in chronological order can give you mental indigestion! For example, suppose a news user in Honolulu posts an article. As the article flows via the Internet around the world and toward you, another news user in San Francisco reads it and posts a response. The response, too, flows via the Internet around the world and toward you. It's entirely possible that the response will arrive before the original article. If the original article was a question and the response is an answer, you may see the answer before the question! This confusing situation is quite common on the Internet, so get used to it.

By the way, if you're in a network environment in which the news articles are stored on a server, that news server is running NNTP, the Network News Transfer Protocol. (NNTP is pronounced by saying the letters N N T P.) NNTP moves articles from server to server and from server to newsreader (client). NNTP is another invisible part of TCP/IP.

```
┌─Directory of unread articles
│ % trn comp.protocols.tcp-ip                                    I want to read #6
│ Group comp.protocols.tcp-ip.ibmpc ('q' to quit)...
│         1   +       228 MONEY! Try this and you won't be sorry  Look at Me
│         2   +        24 Limit of TCP sockets available on Wind  Heiko Grebien
│         3   +     5  15 Implementation of a NETSTAT-like utili  Milosch Meriac
│         4   +        33 FTP Control connection                  Alun Jones
│         5   +        14 WATTCP                                  Erick Engelke
│ > 6     +      1420 DHCP FAQ Memo (Most recent update: 5/1  John M. Wobus
│         7   +         4 DOS mailer and Winsock                  Mike Turk
│         8   +        15 PC/TCP-Kernel ABI for DOS               Ian McLean
│         9   +     2  16 Multiple listen sockets                 The Undertaker
│        10   +        29 Help me please                          ramji
│        11   +     2  32 TCP/IP, NT 4.0 Server, and Multiple NI  Mike Byrd
│        12   +        32 NT 4.0 Server and Multiple NICs with T  tcpial@austin360.com
│        13   +     2  26 TCP/IP send data hang problem           Im
│        14   +        13 WFW 3.11 TCP/IP                         Gregorio Loppi
│        15   +     7   8 Resolving IP's to country of origin     Jonathan Kidd
│        16   +     2  10 download/save pages from multiple site  Jonathan Kidd
│        17   +     2  42 Experience writing an ODI/NDIS driver   Thomas Berndes
│        18   +        13 How to setup TCP/IP, PPP between 2 NTs   nguyead@cat.com
│        19   +     2  15 TCP Port 678 ?                          Ivan.Otero@inter.net
│        20   +        63 Send Thousand of Newsgroup Postings

Reading...

Mon, 02 Jun 1997 12:24:58    comp.protocols.tcp-ip.ibmpc    Thread    6 of    20
Lines 1420    DHCP FAQ Memo (Most recent update: 5/17/97) No responses
jmwobus@spider.syr.edu  John M. Wobus at Syracuse University, Syracuse, NY (USA

Threading articles...
Select thread > 6

                                   DHCP FAQ


        Author
                    John Wobus, jmwobus@syr.edu (corrections welcome)

        Date
                    5/16/1997

        This file
                    http://web.syr.edu/~jmwobus/comfaqs/dhcp.faq.html

        Web page of other links on the subject of LANs
                    http://web.syr.edu/~jmwobus/lans/

T 6 of 20 (p 2), John M. Wobus:  DHCP FAQ Memo (Most recent update: 5/17/97)


Questions

        1. General
                1. What is DHCP?
                2. What is DHCP's purpose?
                3. Who Created It? How Was It Created?
                4. How is it different than BOOTP or RARP?
                5. What is an IP address?
                6. What is a MAC address?
                7. What is a DHCP lease?
                8. Why shouldn't clients assign IP numbers without the use of a
                   server?
                9. Can DHCP support statically defined addresses?
    Stuff deleted ──────────►
```

Reading the article

Figure 7-4:
Here's a
sample
session
with trn, a
character-
based
newsreader.

Don't like the commands? Use a Web browser and mouse your way through the newsgroup

Web browsers are providing the functions of most TCP/IP client applications. If you have a browser, you no longer need a separate FTP client, newsreader client, or mail client. If you don't know what a Web browser is, take a peek at Chapter 12. Figure 7-5 shows a browser accessing the same newsgroup article as Figure 7-4.

Here are some newsgroups   These are articles in the selected newsgroup

Let's look here   Let's read this article

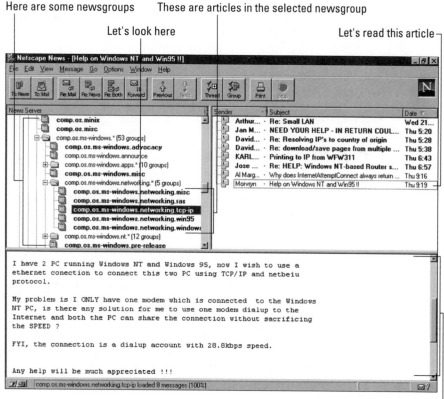

Figure 7-5:
You can read news articles with a Web browser.

This plea for help is the article. If you can solve the problem, why are you reading this book?

Just because you don't NEED separate clients doesn't mean that you don't WANT them. The Web is like dessert. As fun and delicious as it may be, it adds a lot of fat to your Internet diet. And it doesn't always taste as good as it looks. An old-fashioned newsreader gets the news to you faster than a glitzy browser. In Chapter 8, we tell you why you may prefer to use the plain FTP client instead of your fancy browser.

Talking the Talk

E-mail and Usenet news carry messages among users that are separated by space and time. Two other Internet services, talk and Internet Relay Chat (IRC), carry online messages among users that are separated only by physical space.

Talk, in this case, doesn't mean speaking out loud, unless you like to talk to yourself. The Internet talk service lets you have live, interactive keyboard conversations. If you want to speak out loud and hear voices answer over the Internet, you need Internet phone.

Private line only

Using talk, you can actually make "telephone calls" via TCP/IP. Both you and the other person (the talkee) must be online at the same time. Talk provides a private, one-to-one connection. There are no party lines or conference calls. (See the following section on IRC for multiparty conversations.)

Why use talk?

- ✔ You can't use the phone. It's broken, or your kids are using it, or maybe you have only one telephone line and you're using it for a dialup connection to the Internet or for a fax transmission. So, instead, why not use a network connection to carry your "voice" message?

- ✔ You don't want to use the phone, maybe because you don't want long-distance telephone charges to appear on your phone bill. When you use a talk session, instead, its cost is built into the cost of your network connection.

- ✔ You want to check to see if someone is actually there before you use the phone.

- ✔ One or both of you is hearing impaired.

Have you already guessed that talk involves a client, a server, and a TCP/IP protocol?

You won't find answering machines on talk, so if you want to leave a message at the tone, send e-mail instead.

When you're "talking" to someone, your screen gets split into two sections; your words appear in one half, and your talkee's words show up in the other half. What you type is sent across the network immediately. That means your talkee sees exactly what you type, including mistakes and "mistalks," so think before you type!

Internet Relay Chat (IRC): TCP/IP's version of CB radio

Internet Relay Chat (IRC) is the citizen's band (CB) radio of TCP/IP. (You pronounce IRC by saying the letters I R C.) Chatting was created to overcome the primary limitation of talk — namely, that only two people at a time can communicate. IRC provides a party-line environment.

Chatting is done on channels, which are named rather than numbered. Each channel is supposed to be for a specific topic, but you'll have to judge the situation for yourself when you're connected. Chatting is a pretty "loose" environment, although discussions can be scheduled in advance for a specific time, topic, and channel. Each channel has at least one operator, who can't moderate the discussion but can disconnect individual chatters. Because the chatters can simply sign in again, however, disconnecting them may not help keep the discussion focused and free of unruly behavior.

As you may expect, in order to chat, you use an IRC client that communicates with IRC servers via a TCP/IP protocol. The client helps you communicate with the IRC server, connect to the channel of your choice, and chat with the other users. The servers keep track of the chatters and the channels, and they exchange the messages so that all the chatters see all of the chatting.

Both talk and IRC let you communicate live with people anywhere in the world. You don't have to bathe or put on clean clothes. No one will ever know that you're in your pajamas.

ET should have used Internet phone

Can you imagine the telephone charge when that cute little alien, ET, phoned home? Internet phone is a toll-free option.

Okay — you don't incur any charges from the telephone company, but you do need the following:

✔ Internet phone software

✔ A sound card and speakers for your computer

✔ A headset or a microphone

✔ An Internet connection

After you have the equipment and software, you pay the same to talk to the Philippines for one hour as you do to talk to Podunk for one minute.

Before you become too excited about phoning your friends around the world, you should realize that you can only call people who are connected to the Internet and have Internet phone software, usually the same kind as yours.

In order to make a call with Internet phone, you need to follow these steps:

1. **Connect to the Internet.**

2. **Start your phone software.**

3. **Type in your mom's IP address, or select it from an electronic phone book that comes with your phone software.**

4. **After your mom answers, ask her for money.**

You can attach cameras to your computer and your mom's to send your picture, as well as your voice.

How else can TCP/IP help you communicate over the Internet?

You can do a lot more than phone home or send e-mail to your mom. TCP/IP and application software lets you

✔ Send faxes to her on the Internet

✔ Set up a videoconference with all the members of your family

Will someone let us know when we can send dirty laundry to Mom over the Internet?

Here's how TCP/IP makes Internet phone work

Your telephone software takes your voice and converts it into 1s and 0s (called *binary data*) and puts the 1s and 0s into files. Then your software compresses those files, squeezing them as small as possible to get them across the Internet efficiently. Next, the software breaks up the compressed files into packets to send via TCP/IP. At your mom's phone, TCP/IP makes sure that all of the packets are there and in the proper order.

The future is now

Here are some of the latest communications applications being tested on the Internet:

- You make an Internet call, and it actually rings your friend's telephone and works like a normal voice.

- You send a long distance fax through an Internet fax gateway. You pay only for the local call to the fax gateway. RFCs 2304 and 2305 describe Internet faxing.

- You make an Internet call and leave voice mail when no one answers.

You can add telephone capabilities to your computer by installing a telephony board (under $300 U.S.) that acts as your modem, sound board, speakerphone, and voicemail system, all in one. For more information on computer/telephone/fax capabilities, check out www.computertelephony.com.

Chapter 8

Over There, Over There, Do Some Stuff, Do Some Stuff, Over There

*I*s your computer working too hard? Is it hungry for power? Is it low on disk space? (Whose computer isn't at some time or other?) Well, worry no more. Thanks to TCP/IP applications such as telnet and rlogin (remote login), you can connect to another computer and work remotely. Do you need to edit files stored on that other computer? This chapter shows you how to telnet or rlogin to the remote computer to read and edit files across the network.

Still worried? If all those characters streaming over the network between the server and your client affect network performance and make reading a file too slow, take a look at Chapter 9, which shows you how to bring a file to your own computer and then read and edit the file locally.

The Crepe Place ÷ In Paris = TCP/IP?

Suppose you're hungry, craving a big, juicy burger, but for some reason, you aren't going to use your own stove to grill it. Maybe you're out of meat, or maybe your studio apartment only has a pathetic little hot plate without the necessary heat to charbroil half a pound of prime ground beef. No problem — you can get what you want from your favorite neighborhood burger place. It's not far away, and it's no big deal to walk over and place your order.

You can do that with computers, too. If you're lucky, when your computer is too weak to do what you want (not enough memory, speed, or software), you can wander down the hall and borrow a colleague's computer for a while.

But what if it's not a burger that you crave? What if you want some of those fabulous crepes suzettes that you can only get in Paris? In that case your favorite restaurant is slightly less accessible! And it's the same with computers. It's not always easy or convenient to find a computer that you can borrow to do what you need for as long as you need to do it.

So what *do* you do if the computer you need to access is in Paris, and you're in Scranton, PA? It's time to order in. And here's where TCP/IP is a lot more accommodating than the best restaurant in Paris. If you ask that restaurant to deliver your crepes to Scranton, probably the best you can do, at great expense, is overnight delivery — and you'd have to reheat them, which would ruin them, anyway.

But with TCP/IP, accessing that big, powerful computer in Paris is just as easy as if it were at your desk, and you can do it in fractions of a second. And better yet, if your colleagues need to use the Paris computer as well, lots of you can share it at the same time without even getting up from your desks.

Sharing Other People's Computers

In a network environment, the computers within your organization are often shared resources. In Chapter 4, we introduce the client/server concept of a compute server, a computer willing to share its CPU power. In this section, we look at some of the TCP/IP tools that you can use to access a compute server.

You say you want me to steal a Harley?

Sharing a computer's CPU resources is called *cycle stealing.* No, we're not talking about going out to a biker bar and committing a felony. In this case, we're talking about stealing computer processing cycles. The computer component that does the processing is called the *central processing unit* (CPU). A CPU cycle occurs each time a computer's internal clock ticks. (Those clocks tick a lot faster than your alarm clock, by the way.) So when you cycle steal, you use the CPU power of another computer.

To handle the distribution of computer power in an organized way, many businesses set up compute servers for you to steal from or share with. A compute server is a powerful computer that's configured especially for sharing among many users. When you steal CPU cycles from a compute server, you don't have to feel guilty.

In this chapter, you discover how you can cycle steal with TCP/IP, but computer etiquette requires that you always do it with permission. After all, if you cycle steal from a computer that has an underpowered CPU, you're stealing from someone who can't afford to share, and processing for both of you is slower as a result. Besides, if your victim is a techie, she knows how to detect your theft, and you may wind up in worse shape than if you had tried to steal some big biker's Harley.

You can't steal a moped

Not every computer can be a compute server. Some operating systems can't provide this service — others are set up so that they don't. Neither the Macintosh (when it runs the Macintosh operating system) nor personal computers running DOS and Microsoft Windows 95 or Windows 98 can provide compute services for other network users. They're designed to be used by only one person at a time. (Why do you think they're called "personal computers?")

A multiuser operating system, regardless of the computer running it, is designed to be used by more than one person at a time. Most multiuser timesharing systems, such as UNIX and IBM's AS/400, are capable of providing compute services, although they may not offer them. The person responsible for keeping the computers running (the system manager) may have purposely set up a particular computer in that way. You have many techniques for doing that, and the choices depend on the operating system itself.

Microsoft Windows NT is an interesting operating system example because it's a hybrid. Only one user can log in interactively to a computer running Windows NT, but many users can still share the CPU power by using TCP/IP applications.

But let's deal with the positive. You know that you have a computer somewhere on your network that you can use to steal more power. Luckily, for you to borrow some compute cycles from another computer, that computer doesn't need to have the same operating system you have. In fact, this is one of the big benefits of telnet and rlogin, two TCP/IP applications for cycle stealing. You can see them in action a bit later in this chapter.

Why did the hungry user steal cycles? To get to the restaurant on the other side of the network

You can put your stolen cycles to various uses. Suppose you have a Macintosh without much CPU power and you need to do some major calculations about weather systems. You don't want to tie up your Mac by making it grind out the calculations. Instead, you can telnet to the big supercomputer at the central office and use the remote CPU to do your math in seconds rather than minutes or hours.

Oldies but goodies

Most telnet applications emulate a Digital Equipment Corporation (DEC) VT100 terminal. In its time, starting in the early 1980s, a VT100 was the thing to have, and its fancier successor models were equally state of the art. You needed a VT100 in order to use the large, central computer shared by you and everyone near you. After personal computers became popular, VT100 terminals and their descendants virtually disappeared outside of the DEC environment. These days,

instead of a dedicated dumb terminal, most people use a terminal emulator application running on a smart computer.

Another standard in its day was the IBM 3270 terminal. A special version of telnet, called tn3270, emulates an IBM 3270. (The tn is short for telnet.) If you're connecting to an IBM mainframe computer, you probably need to use tn3270 rather than telnet.

Does your organization maintain a large database? Or even several? Say you have access to one that tracks restaurants. To use it, you don't need to install a database management system on your PC. When you're hungry, you telnet over to the computer and read through the information on restaurants in your area. (You didn't think we'd let you get away without a food example in this section, did you?)

Many people also use telnet to do research. Public telnet sites give you access to libraries around the world. Chapter 7 shows you how to telnet to the InterNIC to search for e-mail addresses.

But even if you're not interested in supercalculations or researching exotic butterflies in the rainforests, don't forget that telnet can help you with your everyday life. Instead of having your e-mail forwarded to you while you're on a business trip, you can use telnet or rlogin to connect to your home office and read your mail remotely.

Using Telnet or tn3270 to Borrow Processing Power

Telnet is both a TCP/IP application and a protocol for connecting to a remote computer and using it interactively. The computer you use — maybe you're sitting in front of it right now — is the local computer. The remote computer is the other one, the one farther away from you.

The telnet application acts as a terminal emulator, making your expensive, high-powered computer act just like an old-style computer terminal. Whatever commands you type on your local keyboard are sent across the network for execution by the remote computer.

What you need to know before starting telnet

Before using telnet to grab those cycles, you need the name of the computer to which you want to connect, or at least its numeric TCP/IP address. If you only use e-mail addresses, the computer name is the part right after the @ sign. For example, in `smith@abc.university.edu`, the computer name is `abc.university.edu`. See Chapter 13 for the full discussion of TCP/IP names and addresses.

Next, because you're connecting to a multiuser operating system, you need to know a username and password for the remote computer. A system manager can restrict access to a compute server or prevent a computer from acting as a compute server in the first place by not disclosing any valid username and password for the computer.

On the Internet, you can find public telnet sites (that is, remote sites accessible via telnet) that publish their usernames and passwords. And some really public sites (see the InterNIC example in Chapter 7) don't even require usernames and passwords.

After you have the computer name (or numeric address) and a username and password, or know that you're connecting to a public site, you're ready to start.

Whenever you're asked for a computer's name, you can supply that computer's numeric TCP/IP address instead. From now on in this book, we just say "computer name," but you can give either the name or the numeric address. (For more about computer name-and-address translation, see Chapter 11.)

Master telnet by following these steps:

1. **Run the telnet program on your local computer.**

   This usually means typing the command **telnet**, followed by the computer name that you're accessing. After you type the name, telnet opens a connection to the remote machine for you.

   Or, if you're on a Mac or running some form of Windows, click on the icon to start telnet. Connect to the remote computer by selecting other commands, for example, the Open command in the File menu. Then enter the remote computer's name.

2. **Pay attention to the telnet messages about your connection that appear on your screen.**

   You should see the numeric address of the remote computer and its name as TCP/IP tries to make your connection.

When you read the telnet connection messages, take special note of what the telnet application tells you about the Escape character (you can see examples in Figures 8-1 and 8-2). You may need to use this character later, if you want to interrupt your remote computer session temporarily and issue some additional commands to telnet itself. More on this in "The great escape" section, later in this chapter.

Let's "borrow" computer frodo   We started on bilbo

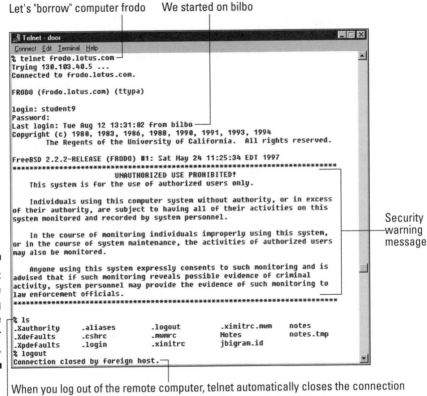

Figure 8-1:
Here, we're connecting to a remote computer using telnet.

Security warning message

When you log out of the remote computer, telnet automatically closes the connection

Frodo is a UNIX system. Use the UNIX command to list the directory

3. Log on to the remote computer using the uw mame and password that you have determined in advance.

You may then see some messages from the remote computer. In Figure 8-1, the messages are from a UNIX operating system on a Sun Microsystems computer. Here, the system manager has chosen to display a security warning message as part of the log-on process. In Figure 8-2, we use a PC running Microsoft Windows 98.

Figure 8-2:
Here, we're
connecting
to a remote
computer
using telnet
and a
graphical
user
interface.

New Connection
Hostname:
candicel   Connect
Shortcuts: Cancel
untitled
New... ⌘N
Edit... ⌘E
Remove
☐ **Highlight This Shortcut On Startup**

4. **Start typing the commands that you want to use in your remote work session.**

   In Figure 8-1, the commands appear preceded by a percent sign (%), the UNIX operating system's command prompt.

In our sample telnet session in Figure 8-1, our computer has taken care of the terminal emulation mode automatically by setting us to be a VT100. Terminal emulation tells the remote computer how we need to see data displayed on our local computer. (VT100 is the most common terminal emulation mode.) On some computers, however, you may have to set your own terminal emulation mode. If all you see on your screen when you type are nonsense characters, you're probably in an incorrect terminal emulation mode. If everything looks fine on the screen, you can enter any command that works on the remote computer's operating system.

Pay careful attention to any security messages that the remote computer displays. It is a federal offense to break ("hack") into a computer you aren't allowed to share. All kinds of law enforcement agencies will track you down — people have gone to jail for hacking.

The great escape

By pressing the key(s) that represent the Escape character in your telnet application, you can switch from issuing operating system commands to issuing telnet commands. Table 8-1 contains some useful telnet commands.

Table 8-1	Some Useful Telnet Commands
Telnet Command	*Function*
open	Initiates a connection to a remote computer.
close	Terminates your connection to a remote computer. If you started telnet with a computer address, close also quits telnet. If you used the open command to start your remote connection, the close command closes the connection, but telnet remains active so that you can open a connection to another computer.
quit	Terminates your connection and quits telnet.
set echo	If the characters you're typing aren't appearing on screen, set echo may help fix the problem.

The IBM mainframe connection

If you need to connect to an IBM 3270-type mainframe computer, tn3270 is the TCP/IP application for you. It works like telnet but sets the terminal emulation mode to work with your mainframe.

R you Ready foR moRe Remote log-ins?

An alternative to telnet is rlogin. Although it's not available on every operating system, many systems have it. Although they provide the same kind of functionality, telnet and rlogin were implemented by separate groups of people, and each works differently at the bit and byte levels.

The rlogin application is one of the *r utilities,* a group of network utilities developed at the University of California at Berkeley for accessing remote computers. The utilities in the group all start with the letter *r.*

When you rlogin to the remote computer, you may or may not be prompted for a username and password. You aren't prompted for this information if the remote computer *trusts* you or the computer from which you're logging on. The notion of trust in this discussion comes from UNIX and the TCP/IP environment that grew up with it. When two UNIX computers are set up so that they trust each other, all the users on one computer are allowed to use the other computer. The concept of trust has spread to other operating systems, such as Microsoft Windows NT Server.

Trust isn't automatically reciprocal. Just because computer A trusts computer B (and all of computer B's users) that doesn't mean that computer B trusts computer A and all its users. Nevertheless, it is quite common for trust to be defined in both directions. Figure 8-3 shows an rlogin session on an untrusted computer, so the user has to type a password. After the password is entered, the user can list the files in the remote computer's directory and send e-mail.

Figure 8-3:
Here, we're
accessing a
remote
computer
with rlogin.

```
$ rlogin max ── rlogin to computer "max"
Password: ──────────────────────────── rlogin assumes my username and asks for my password
Last login: Tue Aug 12 13:25:22 from 207.60.16.16
Copyright (c) 1980, 1983, 1986, 1988, 1990, 1991, 1993, 1994
            The Regents of the University of California. All rights reserved.

FreeBSD 2.2.2-RELEASE (SHELL2) #0: Sat May 24 11:25:34 EDT 1997
You have mail.
$ ls ──── Get a directory listing
???                        bob_watson ───────────── He helped me with IPV6
.                          cal0627.txt
.bash-rc                   dbi_pilot.txt.Z
.bash_profile              draft-ietf-pppext-pptp-00.txt
.bashrc                    ftp.example.Z
.gopherrc                  fyi3.txt.Z
.plan                      rfc1816.txt ┐
.profile                   rfc1834.txt ┘──── We've been getting RFCs

$ mail─────────────────────────────── Check my mail (still borrowing "max")
Mail version 8.1 6/6/93.  Type ? for help.
"/var/mail/leiden": 199 messages 199 unread ───── Time to read some mail
>U  1 jones@broke.ENET.dec  Wed Sep  6 20:52 126/4253  "Input ... Training co"
 U  2 espic.christian@alle  Mon Sep 11 12:17  33/1261  "Re: A: Course Hardwar"
 U  3 Marshall_Wilensky/CA  Fri Nov 10 13:51  27/1333  "Re: error in tcp/ip f"
 U 20 Marshall_Wilensky/CA  Thu Jun 27 13:53 133/5732  "Seminar abstracts"

$ mail fay@cookie.enet.dec.com ──────────── Send some mail (still borrowing "max")
Subject: Hi. This is from an rlogin session. I am stealing cycles from a
computer named max.
```

Stealing Cycles with rsh

Sometimes you need to connect to a remote computer and work interactively to perform a variety of tasks, as with rlogin or telnet. At other times, you simply have just one thing to accomplish. The University of California at Berkeley's r utilities include rsh, short for *remote shell*. With rsh, you can tell a remote computer to execute one command.

When you use rsh, the command you enter must include the following three elements, separated by spaces:

✔ The rsh command itself

✔ The name of the remote computer you want to use

✔ The command to perform on the remote computer

Here is the syntax:

```
rsh remote_computer command_to_execute_there
```

So a sample command to list files residing on the UNIX computer max looks like this:

```
rsh max ls
```

For rsh to work smoothly, the remote system must trust you. (See the description of trust in the previous section.)

If you can rlogin to a remote computer without being prompted for a username or password, you can use rsh.

What? They Don't Trust You? No Problem. It's rexec to the Rescue!

Another r application, rexec, is like rsh — it allows you to connect to a remote computer to issue one command at a time. Rexec is different from rsh because you must know a valid username and password for the remote computer.

Before it attempts to execute your command, rexec always prompts you for a username and password. Your password is encrypted before it is sent "across the wire" to the server (see Chapter 19 for more information about encryption and other security issues). Rexec uses the TCP/IP service rexecd.

Although rsh is quicker because it doesn't involve thorough log-in processing, rexec is more secure because it does. Take your pick.

Multiheaded Beast

The Microsoft Windows Terminal Server is server software that runs on the Windows NT (version 4 or 5) operating system. The Terminal Server software lets thin clients, such as low-cost Net PCs, share its 32-bit Windows applications and graphical user interface services (the Windows desktop). Just as in telnet and rlogin, you can't tell that the applications are running on some remote computer.

During development, the Windows Terminal Server was code-named "Hydra" after the mythical beast with many heads. The server software is the beast's body, and the clients connected to it are its heads. The neat thing about this Hydra is that the heads can be all over the world.

Because the Microsoft Terminal Server also services Windows 3.11 and DOS clients, you can run new Windows applications on your older PC. The Windows Terminal Server also serves clients that run UNIX and Macintosh operating systems, as well as Windows 95 and Windows 98.

Chapter 9
Share and Share Alike

- -

In This Chapter

▶Discovering various ways to get files from the Internet and Web

▶Finding good stuff on the Internet and Web, using FTP or a browser

▶ Using rcp to copy files

▶ Deciding whether or not to trust rcp — and figuring out if it trusts you

- -

*I*n Chapter 8, we show you some ways to access remote computers with telnet, rsh, or rlogin. After you sign on to a remote computer, you can look at files on that computer. But in many cases, you may not be trusted enough to sign on to the remote computer in the first place.

In this chapter, you see ways to share files on remote computers, with and without explicitly logging on across the network.

Using Web Browsers to Get Good Stuff

The World Wide Web, also called *the Web, the W3,* and *the WWW,* is the multimedia part of the Internet. (Chapter 12 has lots more about the Web.) You need software, called a *browser,* to use the Web.

All of the information on the Web is good stuff to someone, and you may want or need to copy some of it onto your very own computer by using a Web browser to copy files. It's easy. No commands to remember. Hardly any typing at all. Just direct your browser to the appropriate site, point the mouse at what you want, and click. Figure 9-1 shows your hungry authors browsing the Web for recipes. Those dog biscuits sound interesting, especially washed down with eggnog!

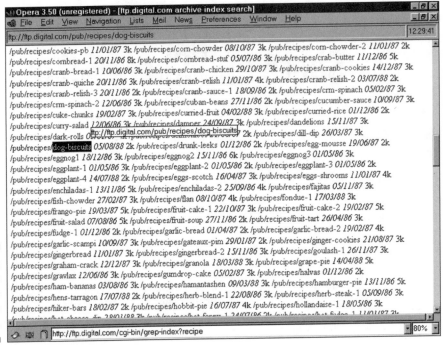

Figure 9-1:
Fido fetches
biscuits
from the
Web.

But guess what? After you click your mouse button, the Web browser uses a protocol called *FTP* (File Transfer Protocol) behind the scenes to copy the files to your computer. (This process of copying files from a server to your client computer is called *downloading*.) Figure 9-2 shows using FTP to fetch the same dog-biscuit recipe that we showed with the Web.

We prefer to use an FTP client to get files. The Web is yummy, but it's the high-fat portion of the Internet diet. It's a lot quicker and more efficient to skip the slick Web interface and go directly to FTP. So, we devote the rest of this chapter to discussing FTP.

Using FTP to Share Files across a Network

Making a copy of a file is often the simplest way to share it. With a personal computer, you can copy a file onto a floppy disk (also called a *diskette*) and easily share it that way.

After you copy the file, you can take it to any *compatible* computer anywhere in the universe. This method of sharing files is called Sneakernet. It's not very efficient and it doesn't work if you want to copy a file between two

```
`C:\WINDOWS>ftp gatekeeper.dec.com
Connected to gatekeeper.dec.com.
```
Warning from the FTP site.
```
    Gatekeeper.DEC.COM is an unsupported service of Digital Corporate Research.

    Use entirely at your own risk - no warranty is expressed or implied.
    Complaints and questions should be sent to <gw-archives@pa.dec.com>.

    EXPORT CONTROL NOTE: Non-U.S. ftp users are required by law to follow U.S.
    export control restrictions, which means that if you see some DES or
    otherwise controlled software here, you should not grab it.  Look at the
    file OOREADME-Legal-Rules-Regs (in every directory, more or less) to learn
    more.  (If the treaty between your country and the United States did not
    require you to respect U.S. export control restrictions, then you would
    not have Internet connectivity to this host.  Check with your U.S. embassy
    if you want to verify this.)
```

```
User (gatekeeper.dec.com:(none)): anonymous
```
——— Anonymous FTP
```
331 Guest login ok, send ident as password.
Password:
```
——— Type your e-mail address.
```
230 Guest login ok, access restrictions apply.
Remote system type is UNIX.
Using binary mode to transfer files.
```
——— Interesting – FTP assumes binary.
```
ftp> dir
total 54357
```
——— This is a huge site with lots of direction.

```
ftp> cd pub
```
——— Move to the public directory.
```
250 CWD command successful.
*******************************
ftp> dir
```
——— See what's in it.
```
dr-xr-xr-x  78 0        0        8192 Oct 12 13:42 DEC
lrwxrwxrwx   1 0        0           3 Apr 14  1995 Digital -> DEC
dr-xr-xr-x  14 0        0       40960 Oct 26 08:11 GNU
dr-xr-xr-x   5 0        0        8192 Apr 14  1995 Mach
dr-xr-xr-x   2 0        0        8192 Apr 14  1995 conferences
dr-xrwxr-x   4 0        0        8192 Apr 14  1995 data
dr-xr-xr-x   5 0        0        8192 Apr 14  1995 database
lrwxrwxrwx   1 0        0           3 Nov 28  1995 digital -> DEC
dr-xr-xr-x  10 0        0        8192 Oct 15  1996 doc
dr-xr-xr-x   2 0        0        8192 Apr 14  1995 editors
dr-xr-xr-x   4 0        0        8192 Apr 14  1995 forums
dr-xr-xr-x   5 0        0        8192 Oct 13  1996 games
dr-xr-xr-x   7 0        0        8192 Sep  1  1995 graphics
dr-xr-xr-x   4 0        0        8192 Oct 17  1996 linux
dr-xr-xr-x   7 0        0        8192 May  3  1995 multimedia
dr-xr-xr-x  18 0        0        8192 Apr 14  1995 net
dr-xr-xr-x  12 0        0        8192 Oct 23  1995 news
dr-xr-xr-x   3 21       8       16384 Apr 14  1995 recipes
dr-xr-xr-x   3 0        0        8192 Nov 18  1996 sysadm
dr-xr-xr-x   8 0        0        8192 Apr 14  1995 usenet
```
How about some new games?
There's a free operating system in here.
Go there.

```
ftp> cd recipes
250 CWD command successful.
ftp> dir
```
——— What recipes are available?
```
200 PORT command successful.
150 Opening ASCII mode data connection for /bin/ls.
-r--r--r--   1 21       8        2064 Mar 31  1988 advokaat
```

Figure 9-2:
You can use
FTP to get
a recipe
for dog
biscuits!

```
-r--r--r--   1 21        8           2322 Aug 21  1987 african-stew  ⌐
-r--r--r--   1 21        8           1631 Jan 28  1988 armenian-rice
-r--r--r--   1 21        8           1791 Jan 11  1987 artichoke-cass       A very
-r--r--r--   1 21        8           3361 Mar 25  1988 asparag-soup-1    ├ International
-r--r--r--   1 21        8           2652 Feb 27  1987 autumn-hens          selection.
-r--r--r--   1 21        8           3491 May 18  1986 avgolemono
-r--r--r--   1 21        8           3020 Mar  6  1988 barmi-goreng
-r--r--r--   1 21        8           2758 Feb 18  1987 basmati-rice-1
-r--r--r--   1 21        8           2015 Jun  9  1987 berlinerkranz  ⌐
-r--r--r--   1 21        8           2948 May 22  1986 berry-cobbler
-r--r--r--   1 21        8           1990 Mar 10  1988 cheese-grits
-r--r--r--   1 21        8           3287 Nov 15  1987 cheese-soup1
-r--r--r--   1 21        8           3924 Jan 11  1987 cheesecake-1
-r--r--r--   1 21        8           3164 Apr 26  1986 cheesecake-2       You can never
-r--r--r--   1 21        8           1923 Apr 26  1986 cheesecake-3    ├ have too many
-r--r--r--   1 21        8           2623 Jun  5  1986 cheesecake-4       of these.
-r--r--r--   1 21        8           2297 Feb 11  1987 cheesecake-5
-r--r--r--   1 21        8           3291 Feb 11  1987 cheesecake-6
-r--r--r--   1 21        8           4620 Mar 19  1987 cheesecake-7 ⌐
-r--r--r--   1 21        8           2682 Sep 24  1987 dandelions ── Green's, anyone?
-r--r--r--   1 21        8           2570 Nov 15  1987 dark-rolls
-r--r--r--   1 21        8           3325 Jan  3  1987 delmonicos
-r--r--r--   1 21        8           1576 Aug 21  1987 dill-dip
-r--r--r--   1 21        8           2773 Mar 26  1987 dog-biscuits ── Aha! Here's the
-r--r--r--   1 21        8           1721 Aug  4  1988 drunk-leeks      one we want.
ftp> ascii
200 Type set to A.
ftp> get dog-biscuits ─────────────────────── Nothing's too good for Fido.
200 PORT command successful.
150 Opening ASCII mode data connection for dog-biscuits (2773 bytes).
226 Transfer complete.
2853 bytes received in 1.21 seconds (2.36 Kbytes/sec)
ftp> quit
221 Goodbye.
   └─ Before we get it, let's use ascii mode.
```

different operating systems, such as IBM's OS400 and Windows 98. So, in the following sections, we take a look at the better ways TCP/IP supplies for copying files over a network.

The FTP Blue Plate Special

In Chapter 6, we first tell you about FTP, the protocol/service/application for copying files to and from a remote computer. (Keep in mind that the computer where you're sitting is the local computer. The remote computer is the other one farther away from you.) Recall that you use the FTP client application to connect to a remote computer that's providing the FTP service. The FTP protocol comes into play when you actually (finally) ask the application to transfer the files.

Suppose it's dinnertime, and you're hungry for egg rolls, Hungarian goulash, and crepes suzette, with an Alka Seltzer chaser. You have some choices:

- ✔ Travel around the world to China, Hungary, and France to assemble your meal. If the egg rolls are cold and greasy before you get to eat them, well, that's life in the multicultural world. We hope you have the Alka Seltzer to get you through the night.

- ✔ Order in. Get on the phone or fax to China, Hungary, and France and talk to the best restaurant in each country. Have everything shipped to you at the same time by the fanciest messenger service you can find. The egg rolls may even still be warm when your doorbell rings.

It works the same way with computers and files. If you want files from three different computers, you can travel to each one and get what you need. Or you can stay put and use FTP. It's the next best thing to being there.

With FTP, you don't have to care what operating system is on those remote computers, because they all have TCP/IP. This ability to transfer files to and from computers running different operating systems is one of the best benefits of FTP. For example, suppose your local computer runs DOS with Microsoft Windows, and you need a file that's on a UNIX system. No problem. Start up the FTP client application on your PC, connect to that UNIX system, and *get* or *put* your files.

"Get? Put? What are we talking about?" you ask. Relax — these are FTP commands, and you'll see them in action shortly.

Using FTP to Transfer Files

You're about to get the lowdown on using one of the handiest TCP/IP goodies around. But first, here are a few things you must have ready before you start the FTP client application:

- ✔ The name of the remote computer or its TCP/IP address.

- ✔ Your account name and password — these are what get you access to the remote computer, unless you're using Anonymous FTP, which we describe in the "Using Anonymous FTP to Get Good Stuff" section, later in this chapter.

If possible, you should also know in advance

- ✔ The names of the files that you're interested in.

- ✔ The locations of the files. If you aren't sure what directory or folder holds your files, you can always browse around to find them.

- ✔ Whether the files contain anything besides plain text. If they do, you must transfer them in binary mode rather than the default ASCII mode.

By the way, be sure to scan every file you transfer for viruses. You never know what's contagious.

You must follow six basic steps if you want to transfer files using FTP:

1. **Start your FTP client application.**

   If you have a graphical user interface, such as Microsoft Windows, this step may be as simple as clicking your mouse on an FTP icon (see Figure 9-3). Without a graphical interface, you need to type the ftp command. In Figure 9-4, someone starts an FTP session from a command line.

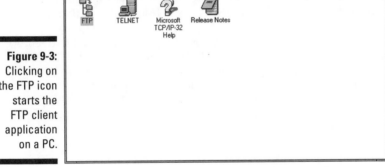

Figure 9-3:
Clicking on
the FTP icon
starts the
FTP client
application
on a PC.

2. **Tell the FTP client application the name (or numeric address) of the remote computer that's holding the files you want.**

   You can type the computer name as part of the ftp command, as shown in Figure 9-4. Or you can use the FTP open command at the ftp> prompt to connect with the remote computer, as shown here:

   ```
   ftp> open candace1
   ```

Figure 9-4:
Type **ftp**
and the
address of
the remote
computer.

```
% ftp frodo
Connected to frodo.
220 frodo FTP server (SunOS 4.1) ready.
Name (bilbo:wilensky): student9
331 Password required for student9.
Password:
230 User student9 logged in.
```

3. **When you're prompted, tell the remote computer your account name and password.**

The prompt from FTP lists your computer name followed by a colon and your username in parentheses. If you have an account on the remote system with that name, just confirm the prompt by pressing Enter. Otherwise, type a valid username. As an extra security precaution, when you type the password, nothing appears. Here's what all this looks like:

```
** Name (candy:leiden):
331 Password required for leiden.
Password:
230 User leiden logged in.
```

If you don't know a valid account name for the remote computer, you can try entering the username *anonymous*. Anonymous FTP is discussed in the "Using Anonymous FTP to Get Good Stuff" section, later in this chapter.

4. **At the ftp> prompt, type dir or ls (both commands work the same) to find the files you want:**

```
ftp> dir
```

5. **If you need to move to another directory on the server, type cd (the change directory command) followed by the name of the directory.**

If you're not sure where you're on the remote computer, use the pwd command to print the working directory on the screen.

```
ftp> cd pub
ftp> pwd
```

6. **Now you can transfer the files you want by using the get command to copy files from the remote computer to your computer.**

Use the put command to copy files from your computer to the remote computer.

```
ftp> get file1
ftp> put file2
```

If you want the new copy of the file to have a different name, add it to the end of the get or put command, like this:

```
ftp> get file1 newfile1
ftp> get file2 newfile2
```

File1, file2, newfile1, and so on, stand for the real names of the files that you enter. Be sure you enter the filenames in the correct case. Under DOS and Windows, file1, File1, FILE1, FiLe1, and fIlE1 are all the same file. But under UNIX, those are five different files!

In fact, you may have to rename files when you copy files between two different operating systems that have different file-naming capabilities. For example:

```
ftp> get pretty-long-UNIX.file.name DOSFILE.txt
```

7. Exit from FTP when you're done by entering

```
ftp> quit
```

If you've spent any time at all working on a UNIX or MS-DOS system, some of the previous commands should look familiar to you. DOS stole some commands, such as cd, from UNIX, so some of the commands are the same on both operating systems and have been used by many applications, including FTP. There are some differences; for example, dir will be familiar to you DOS folks, but only UNIX people will recognize pwd. If you're not sure what FTP command to use in any situation, type **help** or **?** at the ftp> prompt to get a list of FTP commands, as shown in Figure 9-5.

```
─ Mem: 43.0 Mb  User: 80% GDI: 63%              FTP                4/27/95 10:27 PM ▼ ▲
□  File  Edit  State  Window  Help                                                  ▲
                                                                                    ▼
ftp> ?
Commands may be abbreviated.   Commands are:

?               debug        ls           put          status
append          dir          mdelete      pwd          trace
ascii           disconnect   mdir         quit         type
bell            get          mget         quote        user
binary          glob         mkdir        recv         verbose
bye             hash         mls          remotehelp
cd              help         mput         rename
close           lcd          open         rmdir
delete          literal      prompt       send
ftp>
ftp> open frodo



Running    Input pending in Stdin/Stdout/Stderr
```

Figure 9-5:
Using the
help (?)
command
to see the
valid FTP
commands.

Beyond the Basics (Just a Little)

What if you want to move more than one file? You can always do multiple gets or puts — not too bad if you only need a couple of files, but downright painful if you want to transfer a bunch of files.

And how about specifying file types? So far, we've shown you how to transfer ASCII text files. If you want that neat new computer game, it's going to be stored as a *binary file*. Binary files are made up of 0s and 1s instead of letters so they can be executed by your computer, but to us they look like transmissions from outer space.

A file's filename extension gives you a clue as to whether the file contains ASCII text or binary code. ASCII files usually have names that end with the extension .TXT. Files in binary have names that end with various extensions such as .EXE, .DOC, .ZIP, and .TIF.

The following sections take a look at how to manage these tasks with FTP.

ASCII and ye shall receive

Unless you tell it otherwise, FTP assumes that you're moving plain old ASCII text files. But if you want to transfer something a bit more exotic, like that new game or maybe a zipped file with a special format, FTP has the binary option to take care of that. ("Zipping" is one form of file compression; see "Smart FTP Tricks," later in this chapter.)

To switch to binary mode, type **binary** at the ftp> prompt any time before you type **get** or **put**. Then, after transferring your binary file, you can easily switch back to ASCII transfer mode by typing **ascii**.

If you transfer a file in the "wrong" mode, you may not be able to use it, especially if you copy an application in ASCII mode. You'll have to redo the copying operation in the correct mode. The FTP client application doesn't warn you when you're doing it wrong because it doesn't know that something may be wrong. It can only do what you tell it to do.

Shortcuts for multiple files

If you want lots of files, you can use mget and mput (for multiple get and multiple put) to transfer groups of files. Just name the files right after the command, like this:

```
ftp> mget file1 file2
ftp> mput file3 file4
```

Here *file1, file2,* and so forth stand for the names of the files you want. The only catch is that the list of files has to fit on one line.

You can't rename the files you copy with mget and mput, so you may have to use multiple get and put commands.

If you want to copy a group of files so large that all of their names don't fit on the command line, you can use wildcard characters to condense the string of names.

For example, to copy the files that contain account records for multiple customers whose names start with smit, you would use an asterisk (*) wildcard, attached to a partial filename, like this:

```
ftp> mget smit*
```

This tells FTP to get all the files whose names start with the characters preceding the *.

If you want to copy every file in the directory, it's even easier: Just use a single * with the mget or mput command. For example, to put all the files from your local directory into the remote computer's directory, type

```
ftp> mput *
```

To see all this in action, take a look at the sample FTP session in Figure 9-6.

Just looking at a file

Want to check out the contents of a file without actually transferring it? Just specify an output filename of hyphen (-):

```
ftp> get README -
```

This command transfers the README file to your screen. It doesn't matter which operating system you're using; the hyphen always means "the screen." The file isn't saved in any way. If you like the contents of the file and want a copy of your own, get it again without the hyphen.

Using Anonymous FTP to Get Good Stuff

The Internet has a large number of publicly accessible FTP servers. These are known as *Anonymous FTP sites* or *archives,* because when you connect to them, you specify *anonymous* as the account name. When you're challenged for a password, enter your own e-mail address. Actually, you can enter anything here, except nothing (you have to enter something) — but the right thing to do is provide your e-mail address.

Companies such as Microsoft, Lotus, and IBM provide some Anonymous FTP sites. In fact, we once used Anonymous FTP to get a copy of TCP/IP from Microsoft. (The catch-22 in this was that we had to use a computer already set up with TCP/IP and connected to the Internet.) Universities and numerous other good-deed doers provide the other sites.

```
% ftp frodo
Connected to frodo.
220 frodo FTP server (SunOS 4.1) ready.
Name (bilbo:wilensky): student9
331 Password required for student9.
Password:
230 User student9 logged in.
ftp> dir
200 PORT command successful.
150 ASCII data connection for /bin/ls (130.103.40.225,1109) (0 bytes).
total 36
-rw——-  1 student9 users         0 Mar  1  1994 .Xauthority
-rw-r—r—  1 student9 users       579 Feb 18  1994 .Xdefaults
-rw-r—r—  1 student9 users     13888 Jan 26  1994 .Xpdefaults
-rw-r—r—  1 student9 users       449 Feb 18  1994 .aliases
-rw-r—r—  1 student9 users       793 Jan 26  1994 .cshrc
-rw-r—r—  1 student9 users       790 Feb 18  1994 .login
-rw-r—r—  1 student9 users         6 Dec 13  1993 .logout
-rw-r—r—  1 student9 users      4340 Dec 13  1993 .mwmrc
lrwxrwxrwx  1 student9 users        27 Feb 18  1994 .xinitrc ->
/usr1/student9/.xinitrc.twm
-rw-r—r—  1 student9 users      1221 Jan 26  1994 .xinitrc.mwm
-rw-r—r—  1 student9 users       459 Feb 18  1994 Notes
-rw-r—r—  1 student9 users      3027 Jan 27  1994 jbigram.id
drwxr-xr-x  4 student9 users      3072 Jan 27  1994 notes
-rw-r—r—  1 student9 users      1490 Jan 10  1994 notes.tmp
226 ASCII Transfer complete.
939 bytes received in 0.074 seconds (12 Kbytes/s)
ftp> bin
200 Type set to I.
ftp> get jbigram.id
200 PORT command successful.
150 Binary data connection for jbigram.id (130.103.40.225,1110) (3027 bytes).
226 Binary Transfer complete.
local: jbigram.id remote: jbigram.id
3027 bytes received in 0.0014 seconds (2.1e+03 Kbytes/s)
ftp> ascii
200 Type set to A.
ftp> put dead.letter
200 PORT command successful.
150 ASCII data connection for dead.letter (130.103.40.225,1111).
226 ASCII Transfer complete.
local: dead.letter remote: dead.letter
1097 bytes sent in 0.0022 seconds (5e+02 Kbytes/s)
ftp> quit
221 Goodbye.
%
```

You already know this signing-on part.

Your first command.

UNIX directory listing of files on the server.

Techie message from ftp.

Your command to do a binary transfer.

200 Type set to I. ——— Another FTP message.

Finally, the transfer of the file from frodo to bilbo.

More messages.

Your command to do an ASCII file transfer.

Transfer a file from bilbo to frodo.

Figure 9-6:
A user transfers files with FTP.

Anonymous FTP sites are like snowflakes — no two are identical — but ALL of the sites contain files that you can retrieve for free. Some have megabytes and megabytes of public-domain software and shareware. Others hold graphics, music, and movies, and still others contain weird and wonderful things too numerous to mention. (Did that get your interest?)

Although all Anonymous FTP sites are "publicly readable," only a very small percentage are "publicly writeable." You can connect to any of them and retrieve all the files you want, but you can't place files on most of them.

In any case, Anonymous FTP is both fun and valuable. Let's all say a great big thank you to the wonderful people who provide Anonymous FTP sites. THANK YOU!

If you're one of the people we're thanking, be sure to protect your FTP sites so that some scoundrel doesn't load it up with objectionable or even illegal content.

How to use Anonymous FTP

Start your FTP client application just as you did before for any regular FTP session. After you log in as anonymous, go ahead and use the cd and dir commands to discover what's available at the remote site. Many directories have files named README or some variation thereof, such as READMEFIRST. If you spot those files, use them as needed for help in navigating through the archives of directories and files.

If you see a directory named "pub" in an anonymous site, look there first. Many sites put the good public stuff in pub.

When you log in as anonymous, you may see a message from the site's manager asking you to copy files only during evening hours. This is because each FTP request chews up system resources on the remote computer, and if lots of people are connecting to that remote computer, it slows down the people who work there. So, be nice.

Anonymous isn't ubiquitous

Don't assume that you can copy files from just anywhere on the Internet or on your organization's internet. The system or network administrator at the remote site must have configured the system to allow the use of Anonymous FTP. If the remote system doesn't accept Anonymous FTP, you're out of luck. In that situation, you need a valid account username and password if you want to use FTP to copy files to and from that computer.

Watch out — that naked lady has no PG rating

If you're the parents of cyberkids, you need to monitor what they retrieve via Anonymous FTP. They can get great stuff, such as a copy of a U.S. Supreme Court decision to use in a school report. Dream on, you say? Okay, let's be more realistic — they can get lots of Beanie Baby information and free computer games. But watch out for those games. Some of them are more violent than what you may want your kids to see. More significantly, be aware that, although Anonymous FTP is a great source for just about anything, among that "anything" is a wide selection of pornography.

Protect your children with safety software that lets you block out Internet content that you determine is objectionable. Some of these programs, such as Net Nanny, also let you block outgoing information, such as credit card numbers, home addresses, and phone numbers.

Smart FTP Tricks

FTP, transferring files, get and put — sounds pretty basic, doesn't it? But what if you copy a compressed file — can you use it? And what about those people out there who would love to use FTP but whose connection to the outside world provides only e-mail? Are they out of luck?

You can use these smart FTP tricks to make life on the Internet easier.

- ✔ Decompress compressed files
- ✔ Work around your connectivity problems to receive files from FTP archives when you can't open an FTP connection

Disk space is nearly always a problem for almost everyone. The unwritten rule is: The more you have, the more you fill it up — and you never have enough. To save space and make even more files available to you, many FTP sites compress their files. After you find the file you want, you need to decompress it so you can use it. Here's where you have to get smart.

Unfortunately, there's no neat little utility called FTP Unzip to get you by. So, your first task is to determine what compression method was used on the file. You have literally dozens of (and maybe more) ways to compress files. That's why we think dir will become one of your favorite FTP commands — because you use dir to find the README files. We're not kidding. Read the README first, and it will probably tell you how the files were compressed and where to get the decompression utility. Most compression/decompression programs are in the public domain (which means that they're free or very cheap).

Sometimes you can tell what compression software was used by looking at the file type. The file type is represented by a period and some letters following the filename. You DOS users know this as a filename extension. Table 9-1 lists some of the most widely used file types and the compression method used.

Table 9-1	Popular File Compression/Decompression Methods	
File Type	*Operating System*	*Compression Utility*
.zip	MS-DOS	PKZIP/PKUNZIP
.z or .Z	UNIX	compress/uncompress
.tar	UNIX and many others	Actually this is a personal backup utility that groups one or more files into an archive. *Tar* stands for "tape archive," but you frequently find tar archives on disk (that's UNIX for you . . .).
.sit	Macintosh	StuffIt

Using rcp (Not Just Another Copy Program)

An alternative to FTP is rcp (pronounced by saying the letters R C P), another of the Berkeley UNIX r utilities for remote access. (rcp is available on many, but not all computers that use TCP/IP.)

The rcp utility is a little more lightweight than FTP, and therefore faster. For one thing, you don't explicitly log in with a username and password. For another, there's no Anonymous rcp variation.

Here are the three ways to use rcp, with the syntax and a sample command for each.

 ✔ To copy a file from your computer to a remote computer across the network:

```
rcp local_file remote_computer:remote_file
rcp profits1 candacel:profits1
```

✔ To copy a file from a remote computer on the network to your local computer:

```
rcp remote_computer:remote_file local_file
rcp candacel:profits2 profits2
```

✔ To copy a file from one remote computer to another:

```
rcp remotecomputer_a:remotefile remotecomputer_b:remotefile
rcp marshallcomp:profits3 candacel:profits3
```

If you haven't already read the discussion of trust in Chapter 8, you should check it out. Trust is essential for rcp.

Chapter 10

Sharing Loaves and Fishes — NIS and NFS

● ●

In This Chapter

▶ Sharing information with NIS

▶ Introducing NIS domains

▶ Understanding more about clients and servers

▶ Sharing files with NFS

▶ Moving into future file sharing technology with WebNFS

▶ Revealing NIS and NFS security tips

● ●

*I*n this chapter, we look at NIS, the Network Information Service, and then we get acquainted with NFS, the Network File System. Together, these services let you share your network's bounty. After you look through this chapter, you may want more information about how to share files and computers across a network. Chapter 9 explains how to use FTP and rcp to copy files across the network. Chapter 8 helps you log in to remote computers to share files without copying those files. Chapter 12 is about more advanced information sharing, including accessing the World Wide Web. In this chapter, we get started with some services and tools that are especially useful on an organization's private intranet. Near the end of this chapter, we describe WebNFS, a protocol that extends intranet file-sharing to the Internet.

If you're not interested in the UNIX operating system, skip the NIS section and go ahead in this chapter to the "Using NFS to Share Fishes . . . er, Files" section. While NIS is primarily for the UNIX environment, NFS runs on almost all operating systems.

Fishing for Information with NIS

NIS, the Network Information Service, is a client/server environment that lets computers — primarily UNIX systems — share system and user account information over a TCP/IP network. You pronounce NIS by saying the letters N I S. (Some people think it rhymes with *hiss,* but we don't.)

While NIS is for UNIX, it's very common because it's available on all the popular UNIX flavors.

In the NIS environment, an NIS client issues queries for information stored in NIS servers. An NIS server acts on the query and sends a response to the client. That response is either the requested information or an indication that there is no information. (Do you have any threes? Go fish!)

Because NIS is for sharing system files, it is useful mainly to system managers. Users, as well, can benefit from NIS when they have accounts on several different computers. If you're only interested in sharing user files, skip to the "Using the NFS to Share Fishes . . . er, Files" section, later in this chapter.

By the way, if you've already read Chapter 9, you may wonder how information that's shared via NIS differs from FTP-shared files. With NIS, you share the information without making extra copies of the files.

Figuring out what kind of information you can get with NIS

Nifty as NIS is, the information distributed via NIS is almost exclusively specific to the UNIX operating system. NIS organizes its information into *maps,* including the following:

- ✔ UNIX user accounts
- ✔ UNIX group definitions (a component of UNIX security)
- ✔ TCP/IP computer names and addresses (check out Chapter 13)
- ✔ Mail aliases (refer to Chapter 7)

There is one small exception to the general UNIX flavor of NIS: Some versions of TCP/IP for the Microsoft Windows operating systems (all of them except Windows CE) can query NIS servers for computer name-and-address information. But your PC can't be a full-function NIS client.

What's in a name?

NIS was developed by Sun Microsystems, Inc. The service was originally called Yellow Pages, but British Telecom owns the rights to that name, so Sun changed it to NIS. Some people and some computers may still refer to NIS by its old initials, YP. Apparently, British Telecom doesn't own the abbreviation.

Understanding why NIS is so popular on intranets

The NIS information sharing service is extremely valuable to

- ✔ **Users,** because they can easily work on more than one computer without having to remember the different usernames and passwords for every computer to which they sign on. They may not even know that NIS is running. They just know that life is easier because each user only needs to remember one username and one password.

- ✔ **System managers,** because they can more easily take care of multiple computers, and they don't have to reproduce as many files across the network. NIS can save system managers enormous amounts of time configuring and managing computers on an organization's intranet.

The technical specifications for NIS are freely available, and the source code has been licensed to almost every operating system vendor and to the third-party TCP/IP vendors. Specifications and source code are important if you're planning to write your own version of NIS, but very few people are. We're customers and we want to buy and use the tools that vendors build for us!

What's Domain Idea?

An *NIS domain* is the collection of computers in your organization that share the information contained in the maps. The domain may include all of the computers on your intranet, or only a subset. The *domain name* is the key that unlocks the data for the members of the domain.

The term *domain* is used by several networking products, including Microsoft Windows NT Server, Lotus Notes, and Novell NetWare. But be aware that *domain* has a different meaning in every product that uses it. As you work through this chapter, set aside any other domain definitions you may know and concentrate on NIS domains as defined in the preceding paragraph.

Master of your domain

In every NIS domain there is one, and only one, *master server,* which holds the data files that feed the maps. One of the computers on your intranet must be selected to fill this role. Whenever a map's data needs to be changed, the UNIX system manager edits the proper data file on the master server.

The NIS master server answers queries from NIS clients and periodically supplies the slave servers, if any, with copies of the map data.

The role of slave servers

In the NIS domain, there may be *slave servers* — they're optional, and there are no hard-and-fast rules about how many to have. Slave servers help the master server answer client queries. NIS clients don't care which server answers a query, as long as the answer is correct.

Every NIS slave server answers queries from NIS clients and periodically gets copies of the map data from the master server.

The role of the clients

In an NIS domain, there are only three roles. If a participating computer isn't the master server or a slave server, it's simply a client. The client issues queries and eagerly awaits the answers from any available server. The master server and any slave servers are technically clients too, but they normally handle their own needs.

As an end user, you can log in to the master server, a slave server, or a client computer. Your account information is available throughout the domain. The system manager may choose to limit access to the servers, because they're usually pretty busy.

NIS in Action

Take, for example, a famous fictitious fish and mollusk distributor, Odd Octopus Pies and Sushi, with the acronym OOPS. The company has an intranet of 20 computers distributed throughout its international branch offices. All of the computers run the UNIX operating system. Traveling salespeople have accounts on all 20 computers and can log in to any available computer at whatever site they happen to be visiting for the day.

How does NIS serve this company?

Behind the scenes at OOPS

On UNIX systems, user account information is stored in a file called /etc/passwd. (The directory part, /etc/, is pronounced "slash E T C slash" or "slash etsee slash." The passwd part is generally pronounced "passwid" — get a Boston native to say it for you.) This file holds usernames, passwords, home directories, and other general user information. So, if OOPS has 20 computers on the intranet, that means someone has to store and update 20 passwd files.

The OOPS problem

Employment at OOPS is volatile. After all, selling octopus products can be quite lucrative, but the demand is limited to only a few parts of the world. Clem Chowder, the system manager for the OOPS intranet, keeps plenty busy maintaining those 20 passwd files, and he never has time to do any research on toxicity studies and local dredging regulations — much less sample his company's wares. OOPS needs to find a way to share one copy of the passwd file across the entire intranet.

The OOPS solution

Ta da! It's NIS to the rescue. Because NIS is part of UNIX, Clem doesn't need to purchase or install it. He already has NIS. So Clem decides to create an NIS domain for the 20 OOPS computers. He chooses Octopussy as the domain name and picks one computer to be the master server. The other 19 computers join the Octopussy domain as NIS clients.

Clem then stores the information from all 20 computers in files on the master server. Those files feed the NIS maps. When Clem learns about new employees, he only has to update the central files. Now he has time to eat all the octopus pies he wants.

When an OOPS employee logs in to any of the computers on the company's intranet, the log-in process requests account information from the NIS domain's master server via the UDP and IP protocols (described in Chapter 6).

Okay, NIS Is Great — Are There Pitfalls?

There are three areas in which NIS sometimes is difficult:

- Configuration and administration
- Performance
- Security

We return to our fictitious fish factory's intranet to examine these challenges and some ways to meet them.

Configuration and administration

System administrator Clem Chowder may have a lot of work ahead of him when he initially sets up NIS on the OOPS intranet. He needs to change from a local file model with multiple copies of the password and system files, to a single, central set of files replacing or supplementing the local files. He can't simply delete the local files and create the central NIS files. Rather, he has to decide how much information (if any) to keep local and how much to share across the intranet. So, the initial setup to deploy NIS may take a long time, but it's worth it to gain the benefits of easier management of the intranet in the future.

Most UNIX operating system vendors provide a tool to set up NIS. These tools do all the work of editing files and configuring computers as servers or clients. If he uses a tool, Clem doesn't have to flounder <grin> around in a sea <second grin> of configuration files.

OOPS's files on the NIS master server are only as good as the most recent update, so Clem has to be careful to take care of updates immediately. Happily, with NIS, he has only to update the central files, and that's a lot less work than having to maintain 20 copies as in the pre-NIS system.

Performance

The queries from the NIS clients (the main school of OOPS's computers) to the master and slave servers result in increased intranet traffic, and the larger the NIS domain (that is, the more computers in the domain), the more a network's response may slow down.

Also, if OOPS is configured with just one master server and no slaves, the performance of the master server slows down everyone in the domain when all the clients hit on the master at the same time. Clem can use slave servers to help reduce the load on the master, but they put a different burden on the master server — keeping the slaves' maps up-to-date.

The master server, then, is a single point of failure. If the master server is out of action and there are no slave servers, the clients' queries aren't answered. The client application that issued the query waits — conceivably forever — for the answer, unless the user can abort the program's request. NIS queries are such a common part of the normal operation of the client that the computer will ultimately be incapable of completing any processing for any user. The client doesn't crash, but it seems to freeze solid, or *hang* (as in hang around doing absolutely nothing). We think you can see the value of having at least one slave server on the network.

If the master server is out of action, the slave servers answer queries, but they can't continue forever. To keep their maps up-to-date, the slave servers issue periodic queries to the master server. When these go unanswered, the slave servers eventually hang, and then the clients hang.

There is no automatic way to convert a slave server into a replacement master server. So Clem, if he's wise, keeps backup copies of the data files in safe places and maintains a plan for manually converting one of the slave servers into a temporary master server. OOPS needs at least one slave per network segment on the intranet.

Security

Using NIS may open up some holes in the security of the OOPS intranet. Clem can't restrict membership in the NIS domain — any computer can join the domain at any time and access all the information in the maps. The only piece of information that an OOPS employee needs to add a client to the domain is the domain name, Octopussy. To add a slave server, an employee needs only the domain name and the name of the master server. If the employee were to set up another master server for the Octopussy domain, the slave servers wouldn't use it because they know the name of the master server, but the clients would accept the responses from the phony server.

A malicious person could add a client to the domain, take the UNIX account information from the passwd map, and attempt to break into users' accounts. Someone really evil could add a bogus master or slave server that replies to queries with incorrect data.

What should OOPS do to prevent any of this? One option may be NIS+, which is described in the next section. Clem and his contemporaries can also check out the security information in Chapter 19.

Don't use NIS on any computer that's accessible from the outside world. What we're really saying is don't use NIS on a firewall or a gateway that connects any part of your network to someone else's network, especially the Internet. You don't want to share NIS system files — your password file, for example — with outsiders.

NIS+ is a fine kettle of fish

Sun Microsystems created NIS+, a new generation of NIS. The old NIS *maps* become NIS+ *tables,* but their function is the same — to store information about user accounts and computers, network addresses, and system configuration data in central locations.

NIS+ offers improved performance features for large domains, as well as tighter security, but the new product isn't yet available from all the UNIX vendors and third party TCP/IP vendors. Until it is, Odd Octopus Pies and Sushi must accept the security risks as the price that it pays for a useful service on its intranet.

Using NFS to Share Fishes . . . er, Files

Sharing disk space is one of the most common reasons to link computers via a network. (Sharing printers, sending e-mail, and surfing the World Wide Web are at the top of the list, too.) The previous sections in this chapter discuss NIS maps — one example of sharing system files. But what about user files, such as documents, spreadsheets, text, and word-processing documents? If Ms. Selena Sushi, a user in the OOPS domain, can log in to any computer, can she see her files there? Or will she have to copy them from her home computer to the computer at which she is logged in for the day?

In Chapter 9, you find out how you can use FTP and rcp to copy files, so if Ms. Sushi has to copy her files, she has the tools. But if she copies files, she's using twice the disk space, and if she updates any files, she has to be careful to copy those updates back to her home computer. Otherwise, her files will be out of sync. There must be an easier way for Ms. Sushi to stay in touch with her files without copying them all over the company intranet as she travels.

There is an easier way. It's called *NFS,* the Network File System (pronounced by saying the letters N F S). NFS uses the UDP and IP protocols, which are discussed in Chapter 6. NFS is extremely common on UNIX systems and is also supported on most other operating systems.

NFS means nifty file sharing

NFS is a client/server environment that allows computers to share disk space and users to see their files from multiple computers without having to copy the files to those computers.

In the NFS environment, computers that have disk space they're willing to share are *NFS servers,* and computers borrowing disk space are *NFS clients.* A given computer can be

    ✔ Either an NFS server or an NFS client.

    ✔ Both a server and a client, simultaneously.

    ✔ Neither a server nor a client.

Most operating systems provide the NFS client portion, but some don't provide the server.

Who needs NFS? The NFS disk sharing service is extremely valuable to

- ✔ **Users,** because they can access much more disk space.
- ✔ **System managers,** because they can more easily provide disk space to the users and more easily back up the users' files.
- ✔ **Everyone,** because they don't have to worry about keeping track of multiple copies of the same file.

NFS was originally developed for UNIX by Sun Microsystems, Inc. (also the creator of NIS). The technical specifications are easy to get, and the source code has been licensed to almost every operating system vendor and to the third-party TCP/IP vendors. Specifications and source code are important if you plan to write a version of NFS yourself, but you probably aren't. You're a customer, and you want to use the tools that vendors build for you.

Why is NFS so great?

One of the best things about NFS is that it's transparent. With NFS, the OOPS employees can't tell the difference between local disk space (connected directly to a particular computer) and shared disk space coming from an NFS server on the intranet.

With NFS, Selena Sushi can work at any participating computer on her intranet and still have access to her files. The files follow her from computer to computer, including laptop and notebook computers, when they're connected to the intranet. A file is a file is a file, no matter where she's logged on.

If your computer breaks, you can find out who's absent and you can use his or her computer. With NFS, your files are there. If you need to use a different operating system instead of your regular one, you can log in to a computer that's running what you need. With NFS, your files come with you.

NFS is great for sharing files across intranets. But Selena wants to share files on the Internet, NFS won't help her. Or will it? She needs to look ahead in this chapter to the "WebNFS — Technology Moves into the Future" section to see how to share files on the Internet.

Your home away from home

With NFS, your home directory may not be located on your home computer. And because file access via NFS is so transparent, you may not even know it.

What about NFS Performance?

The NFS client/server environment is very flexible in that any computer can play the role of client and server simultaneously. But system administrator Clem Chowder should think about the trade-offs between flexibility and performance when he sets up the servers.

NFS performance tips

Use fast hardware for frequently accessed files. For example, if the most frequently used file is Charlie Tuna's inventory file, Clem should place it on a fast disk on the most powerful computer for quick retrieval.

For best performance, Clem can dedicate a computer to be an NFS server and limit the other services provided by that computer. Everyone's files get stored on the NFS server, and the users' computers become clients that access the files on the server. A dedicated NFS server also makes it easier for Clem to back up all the OOPS employees' files, because all files are on one computer. Clem can and should dedicate as many computers as he needs. He's not limited to just one.

Weighing performance against security

If OOPS employees are working on a really big project, such as editing a large document, they can reduce network traffic (and therefore work faster) by logging in to the server to work on the file locally.

However, with a dedicated server, Clem may not be too happy about letting everybody log in directly to the server, and he may not even allow them to, unless they have a very good reason, such as a long edit session on that large document.

Getting in one another's way

Because NFS maintains a single copy of shared files, sometimes more than one person accesses the same file. If you're all just reading the file, there's no problem. But if two or more of you're trying to update the same file simultaneously, that's when the fun begins. Imagine three users trying to update simultaneously the file that holds the NBA all-time scoring record.

Which of the three updates wins? You can't tell. But you can be sure that in the world of NFS, just like the NBA, the winner buries the losers' updates. Unlike the NBA, however, none of the NFS users will know what happened. It will be as if two of the updates never occurred.

Some operating systems have file systems with *locking features* (also called *concurrency control*) to avoid the problem of buried updates. Here are two imaginary users to show how concurrency control and locking work: The first user who grabs the data gets a lock on it, which prevents other users from updating the data. When the first user is done, the next user gets the lock and is assured of seeing the first user's update before deciding whether to bury the updates or not. But you can't count on such file system locks in an environment of heterogeneous computers, operating systems, and file systems. Each computer on the intranet may be running a different operating system, which may or may not provide concurrency control.

We're not trying to scare you away from NFS. It really is an excellent solution for sharing files and saving disk space. Many environments never encounter the "buried update" problem because most users are reading files, not updating the same shared files at the same time. If buried updates become worrisome, Clem should make sure that the operating systems and file systems both support locking. Or, OOPS can establish policies and procedures for collaborative efforts on the intranet.

There's interoperability and then there's interoperability

TCP/IP's prized interoperability is another strength of NFS. The operating system for the server doesn't have to match the operating systems of the clients. That means Selena Sushi can use her PC or anybody else's PC to

---

Don't buy your network solutions from the trunk of someone's car

When you think about performance, you have to consider hardware, ugly as that may be. From an NFS client, you access files across the network. That means cables, packets traveling across wires, network controllers, and maybe even things like gateways and routers.

The quality and robustness of the hardware you use has a significant effect on NFS performance. If the network interface card inside your computer is old and slow, don't expect to see files as quickly as your neighbor, who has

the latest and greatest interface card. If some of the hardware on your intranet is cheap and unreliable, the NFS server may not always be up and running. And that means your files (and a lot of other people's) won't be available.

The good news is that there are reliable, redundant hardware and software solutions to performance problems. When it comes to network hardware and server/file availability, you get what you pay for.

access files stored on a UNIX server, if that's how Clem Chowder set it up. All is not what it seems, however.

There may be a few NFS surprises in a mixed operating system environment, because each operating system uses a different file format. For example, suppose Ms. Sushi's PC runs DOS, and she's trying to edit a file on the UNIX server. The UNIX file may appear to Selena's PC editor as one long sentence. That's because of the way the different file formats treat the ends of lines in a file.

On the DOS file system, the end of each line is marked by a two-character combination of a carriage return <CR> plus a line feed <LF>. On the UNIX file system, the end of line is marked by just one character, the line feed <LF>. And that difference confuses some PC editors and word-processing products, as well.

OOPS users (and you) must also be aware of the difference in filename conventions when using DOS clients. DOS only allows 8.3 file specifications — that is, 8 characters for the name, a . separator, and 3 optional characters designating the file type. UNIX, Windows 95, Windows NT, and other operating systems allow long filenames — sometimes as long as 255 characters (although, would you really want to have to type a filename that long, much less remember it?). Anyway, OOPS folks should name files stored on the server according to the lowest common denominator, which in most cases is DOS.

Automounting — It Sounds Illegal

Before you can understand the *automounter* for NFS, you need to know about *mounting* in general.

Mounting

On UNIX, files and directories flow seamlessly together in a tree structure with a root at the top, not the bottom. (Aw, c'mon, give us a break here. This is computer science, not earth science.) The system administrator mounts directories onto the tree. The users on a UNIX system don't need to know what disk device holds their files. They only need to know the files' locations in the directory tree.

Figure 10-1 shows a typical UNIX directory tree. At the top is the familiar forward slash (/) representation of the root directory, meaning the top of the tree. The UNIX help directories, man1 through man8, lie on the path named /usr/man (please excuse the UNIXism).

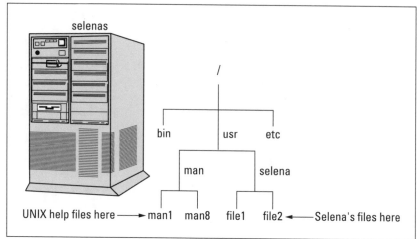

Figure 10-1:
The selenas computer has Selena's files and some UNIX help directories.

NFS mounting

Using NFS, Mr. Chowder, the system administrator, mounts remote directories on the tree. The technical term for this is *NFS mounting.* The files look local to the users, even though the files exist physically on the remote computer.

Figure 10-2 shows two computers, each with a directory tree. Although the trees look exactly the same, some of the files exist on only one of the computers. The charliet computer doesn't have very much free disk space, so the system manager NFS-mounted the UNIX help directories there, leaving the physical directories and files residing on the selenas computer. Users on the charliet computer access the help files just as if they were local. Even the directory path name is the same, /usr/man/man1. Clem then does the same with Selena's files. When Selena is logged in to the charliet computer, she can access her files in exactly the same way as when she is on the selenas computer.

Now do I get to find out what the automounter is?

Yes, now you do. Consider this: Selena usually doesn't sign on to the charliet computer; only occasionally does she need to see her files there. Keeping that in mind, Clem Chowder doesn't want to have Selena's files always mounted on charliet. Nor does he want to be at Selena's beck and call to mount the files on charliet whenever Selena decides she needs them. Clem is, after all, a busy person.

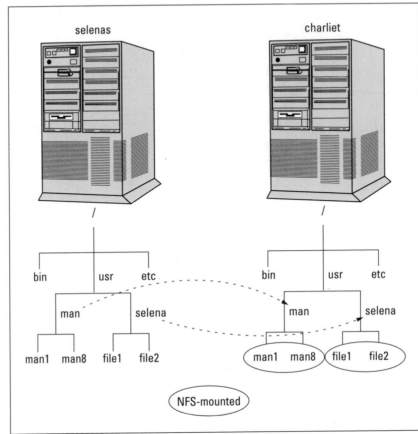

Figure 10-2:
Selena can access her NFS-mounted files just as well when she is logged in to the charliet computer.

Enter the automounter — an enhancement to NFS. It automatically mounts the disk space you need, when you need it. This is called *dynamic mounting*. Automountable disk space is registered in an NIS map (see the discussion of NIS at the beginning of this chapter), so the participating computers on the intranet know about all of that space. The automounter is very fast — you should never notice the delay in getting to the disk space. But even if you do, the benefit is worth the tiny performance penalty.

Using the automounter is a handy option for system managers like Clem Chowder, who manage file systems that are inactive for large amounts of time. The automounter keeps a timer for each of the mounted disk spaces, so it knows when you aren't using them any more. When a timer expires, the automounter dismounts the disk space. When you need the disk space again, the automounter remounts it.

How about Some NFS Security Tips?

To secure NFS files, you need to do two things:

✔ **Protect the files.** File system security helps you do this.

✔ **Protect the server from unauthorized access.** The `exports` file helps you do this.

To protect your files and server, try the following:

✔ Use the file system protection that's available on your server.

✔ Generally restrict permission for NFS files to read-only.

✔ Be cautious about allowing write access.

✔ Be selective about the hosts that you allow to access your NFS files.

(An NFS server has a file called `exports` that lists the hosts that can access the NFS files on that server.)

✔ Don't leave your file system open to access by everyone on the Internet.

Inside the guts of NFS is a client/server programming technique called *Remote Procedure Calls* (RPCs). You don't see RPCs, and you don't really need to know about them except that there is a version called *Secure RPC.* If you're concerned about NFS security, try to buy an NFS implementation that uses Secure RPC. NFS plus Secure RPC is called Secure NFS — imagine that! It isn't as readily available as plain NFS, but Secure NFS prevents the bad guys from fooling your NFS server into thinking they come from a legitimate address called *address spoofing.*

NIS and NFS Together

NFS and NIS are completely independent of each other, but they're very often used together. NIS allows the information in system files to be shared; NFS allows user files to be shared. When NIS and NFS are used together, Selena Sushi has only one username and one password that each work on every NIS client on the OOPS intranet.

Although NIS and NFS can be used in mixed operating-system environments, they're most commonly used together in UNIX environments.

When she logs on to a computer that's also an NFS client, all of Selena's files are there waiting for her. If the computer is an NIS client only, Selena has access only to the files stored on that computer. In this case, she may wind up having files stored on every computer in the NIS domain.

If the computer is an NFS client only, Selena has a separate account on every computer, and each computer has a unique username and a unique password — but at least she has to worry about only one set of files.

When NIS and NFS are used together, they hide the location details of remote files from you. As far as you're concerned, your account and files automatically follow you as you go from one computer to another on the intranet.

One computer can be both an NFS server and an NIS server (master or slave).

Are NIS and NFS Used on the Internet?

NIS isn't used to tie the Internet together, for some fairly obvious reasons. Who would control the one master server? What would happen if the master server failed? How could any number of servers handle the load from the enormous number of clients? Tough questions. Many of the organizations that are connected to the Internet, however, use NIS every day. Those organizations couldn't run their intranets without NIS. There is some use of NFS on the Internet to give public access to files and information. You can think of these offerings as fancy anonymous FTP archives.

WebNFS — Technology Moves into the Future

Until recently, the Internet has been missing one important component: a distributed file system. WebNFS allows system administrators to export files to the Internet. When you need an exported file, you don't need to know where it is on the Internet. WebNFS can automatically locate the file, check to make sure that you have the necessary file access privileges, and mount the file from anywhere on the Internet. You access the file as if it were stored on your own hard disk on your own computer.

What's WebNFS?

RFC 2055 describes the specifications for a server of WebNFS clients.

WebNFS is a proposed Internet standard protocol from Sun Microsystems that provides Web access to files on about 10,000,000 NFS servers as of this writing. Yes, those are the people who brought you the original NFS. WebNFS extends NFS to the Internet. With WebNFS, Ms. Selena Sushi can log on to any computer on the Internet, not just her OOPS intranet, and see her documents. Just as with NFS, major computing corporations are jumping on the bandwagon. IBM, Sequent Computer Systems, Netscape, Oracle, Apple, and Novell have announced support for WebNFS.

How to use WebNFS

To use WebNFS, you need the following:

- **Your Web browser needs to understand WebNFS.** Sun includes a WebSoft client with its thin-client Network Computer (NC). WebSoft is an example of a client layered on a client.

- **Your Web or FTP server needs to work with WebNFS servers.**

- **When requesting a file with WebNFS, the Uniform Resource Locator (called *URL*, see Chapter 12) must start with** nfs **instead of** http. For example:

```
nfs://mycomputer.mysite.com/mydirectory/myfile
```

WebNFS solves NFS-Internet problems

Internet Problem: Slow dial-up connections are prone to losing data.

Solution: WebNFS servers can recover from dropped lines and recover lost data. Even if your dialup connection is as slow as turtle soup, you get reliable access to information over the Internet. (One reason that WebNFS can recover from poor network connections is that WebNFS uses TCP instead of UDP.)

Internet Problem: Browsing the Web can be painfully slow.

Solution: For displaying graphics and animation, WebNFS is up to ten times faster than the traditional HTTP protocol.

Problem: Regular NFS has too many security holes to work safely on the Internet.

Solution: Besides enhanced security features, WebNFS can work with and through firewalls. Chapter 19 explains firewalls and why you need them.

Chapter 11

Fishing in a Really Big Pond

. . . .

In This Chapter

▶ Uncovering how DNS keeps the Internet's (or your intranet's) computers organized

▶ Understanding why your e-mail address has so many parts (the DNS version of domains)

▶ Finding names and addresses on the Internet using `whois` and `nslookup`

▶ Understanding why WINS, the Microsoft version of name and address translation, may be going away

. . . .

In Chapter 10, you fish for information with NIS, which lets computers that are grouped fairly close together on a network share system and user information. Well, that's small fry. That's an appetizer, a sardine, compared to the main course in this chapter.

Here you discover another service: the Domain Name System (DNS, pronounced by saying the letters D N S). But when you fish for information with the DNS rod and reel, you're fishing around not just on your own intranet but also on the Internet.

By the way, at this point in our journey writing this book, we got full. We lost our appetites. We gained 10 pounds and decided to go on a diet. Actually, we ran out of food metaphors as the technical pace of our subject matter picked up. So, although we promise to keep you entertained right on through the glossary, you won't find any more references to chocolate, cherries, cheesecake, or china — for a while anyway.

Getting to Know DNS

A *name service* translates (or *resolves*) a computer name into a numeric address. The Domain Name System, DNS, is the name service for the Internet, and it translates computer names into TCP/IP numeric addresses. (You find out more about computer names and addresses in Chapters 13 and 15.)

Do you drive a Lotus or just work there?

In Chapter 2, we tell you about the ARPANET, predecessor to the Internet. Imagine a time (long ago!) when there were only a few computers on that network. Those computers had ordinary names of just one word. A computer named lotus, for example, didn't need any other names to identify it because it was the only lotus on the network.

With millions of computers participating on the Internet, finding unique names is more difficult. Today, you'd wonder if the computer called lotus belongs to the software vendor or the car manufacturer. And if you send e-mail to user Wilensky on computer lotus, will it go to your friend at the car company or to someone you never heard of at the software company?

If your organization's network is connected to the Internet, you must use DNS. If your organization has a private internet, you may use DNS to provide the name service for your network.

DNS was created specifically to handle the requirement that each computer needs to be uniquely named on the network. By adding some pieces to your computer name to make it unique, DNS solves the problem of duplicate computer names.

People like names. Computers like numbers.

DNS = Does Nifty Searches

DNS is a way for computers to share information about computer names and addresses over a TCP/IP network. On a large network (such as the Internet), that's a lot of information.

In techie terms, DNS is the *name-and-address resolution service* used on the Internet. In more straightforward terms, DNS is a kind of directory service. It searches for and finds the numeric Internet address for a computer name, and vice versa. (Of course, if we could remember those complicated numeric addresses, we wouldn't need a name-and-address resolution service, but brain cells being what they are . . . .)

Unlike NIS, which is primarily used by computers running the UNIX operating system, DNS is used by all operating systems.

Computers on a TCP/IP network — and that includes the Internet — have both a name and a numeric address. Most of us mere mortals prefer to call our computers by name, and the network is nice enough to accept either names or numbers. When you use a name, the network translates the name into numbers behind the scenes.

To be unique, a computer name has multiple parts separated by periods —
that is, the . character. Although it looks like a period, the computer world
calls it "dot." Take the e-mail address

```
candace@max.tiac.net
```

You pronounce it "candace at max dot teeack dot net."

Remember that the first piece of this address, max, is the computer's name;
and the last piece of the computer name on the right, net, represents a
domain name — a DNS domain name. The intermediate pieces represent
things like company names.

Client/Server Again — You Can't Get Away from It

DNS is a client/server environment. Queries are issued by the clients
(application programs such as telnet, FTP, and so on), asking a *name server*
for a computer name-to-numeric address translation. If the name server can
answer the query, it responds with the requested information, and all is well.

If the name server can't supply the information, two things may occur,
based on whether the name server is or is not *responsible for* the information (more on this in the next section).

- ✔ If the name server is responsible for the information, it responds with
  message that indicates that the information doesn't exist. (Do you have
  any fives? Go fish!)

- ✔ If the name server isn't responsible for the information, it forwards the
  query to, or at least toward, the name server that's responsible. (The
  name server knows to do this based on how the system manager has
  set things up.) When the answer comes back, it travels all the way back
  down the chain to the client.

- ✔ If the client "times out" — gets tired of waiting for a response — that's
  the same as receiving a "No Information" answer from the queried name
  server.

- ✔ If at this point *you* have timed out, too, hang in there. We explain this
  "responsibility" thing next.

Who's responsible?

So what does it mean to be "responsible for" the name and address information? The DNS term for responsibility is *authority.* Several different types of name servers may be deployed in your environment. In the DNS world, there is no single master server, as there is with NIS. Instead, primary name servers know, via the DNS database, the names and addresses of the computers in your organization. These name servers are responsible for this information, and the answers they give to client queries are said to be authoritative.

Because DNS is *distributed* (that is, decentralized), no one computer has to have all the information about all the addresses. Can you imagine the size of the disk you'd need to hold the addresses of all the computers on the Internet? Not practical, even if it were possible. Therefore, multiple name servers work together to translate a name to an address.

Name servers and resolvers

The name server program that responds to queries for a resolution of a name to an address is one of the pieces of the DNS puzzle. The name server program may or may not be included in your TCP/IP product. If you need to set up and run your own name server, make sure you have the program.

Another piece of DNS is a library of programs called a *resolver,* which takes the client program's request to get address information and converts it into a query to the name server. (The resolver is part of every TCP/IP product. You need it. You have it. Don't worry.) More specifically, when a programmer writes an application that needs to know a computer's address, the application contains a call to the resolver routines. For example, this request in a program, "Open an FTP connection to computer X," generates a DNS query for the address of computer X.

Figure 11-1 shows the resolver communicating with the name server on behalf of a client application.

DNS's pieces and parts

Lots of bits and pieces that work together for DNS, including hardware, software (programs and some TCP/IP protocols), data files, and people. Here is a summary:

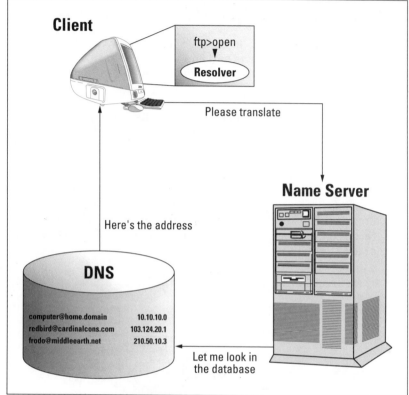

Figure 11-1:
The resolver asks the name server to answer an address query.

- ✔ **The distributed database** holds information about computers in domains on the Internet or on your internet.

- ✔ **Domains** are logical collections of computers whose requests for network address lookups are all handled by the same server(s).

- ✔ **Name servers** are programs that access information from the database and respond to client queries.

- ✔ **Clients** are programs that request network address information from the name servers.

- ✔ The **resolver** works on behalf of the client applications to get network address information from the name server.

- ✔ **System managers and network administrators** set everything up and maintain the databases.

In the next few sections, we take a closer look at these pieces.

The Internet's Definition of Domain

In the discussion of NIS in Chapter 10, we show you that the term *domain* is used by various products and applications to mean different things. Here we go with a new one. Because *domain* is the first word in the DNS name, it's a good place to start.

The Internet is so huge that it organizes its participating computers into groups of administrative units; these units are called *domains*. The domains themselves are organized hierarchically into a tree structure, as illustrated in Figure 11-2.

The Internet's tree structure has branches extending from the top-level domains. Your computer sits in the leaves, at the edge of this hierarchy of domains. The InterNIC establishes and maintains the domain at the root of this tree. Just above the root is the set of top-level domains, the kingfishes of the Internet.

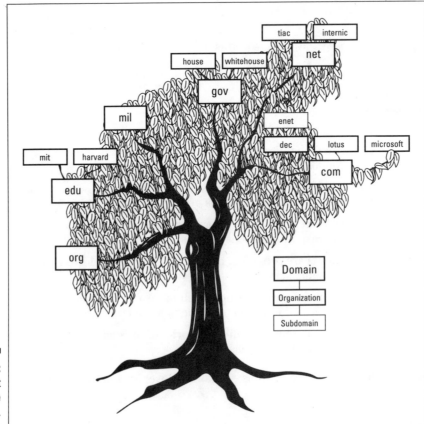

Figure 11-2:
Internet domains are hierarchical.

In the United States, the top-level domains have the generic organization types listed in Table 11-1. (You may recognize the three-character designators in the first column as the last part of many Internet addresses.)

Table 11-1	Top-Level Domain Names in the United States
Organization Type	*Definition*
com	Commercial enterprise
edu	Educational institution
gov	United States government
org	Organization
mil	Military service
net	Network services provider

In the United States, if you want your organization to be on the Internet, you must register it at a registry, such as the InterNIC. Most Internet Service Providers (ISPs such as AT&T's worldnet.att.net and RCN's erols.com) are empowered to do this for you. When you register, either directly with the InterNIC or via the ISP, your organization is assigned to live in one of the top-level domains listed in Table 11-1.

For information on other registries and registration activities around the world, browse Yahoo's index at www.yahoo.com/ Computers_and_Internet/Internet/Domain_Registration/.

Prove your good intentions with $$$

As the popularity of the Internet soared over the last few years, some entrepreneurs got a nasty idea: Register for some well-known domain names before the companies who really need them, and then sell them to the companies for a profit. For example, we could have registered for mcdonalds.com, and when the fast food company tried to get on the Internet, its name would be taken. The company would have a couple of options:

✔ Use another name, perhaps mcdonaldshamburgers.com

✔ Pay us our asking price to give up the domain name

To avoid the potential for this kind of blackmail, you now have to pay a fee to register a domain, plus an annual maintenance fee. This slows down the bad guys who were registering dozens of commercial domain names to sell to the rightful users. Additionally, the Internet Society has created an arbitration system to settle disputes over domain names when a trademarked name has been "stolen." The arbitration procedure reduces the incidence of lawsuits such as the one in which Hasbro Inc. had to go to court to prevent an adult nudie site from using candyland.com.

The InterNIC (www.rs.internic.net) charges $70.00 (U.S.) to register a domain name in some of the top level domains shown in Figure 11-2 (.com, .org, .net, .edu). The Internic's annual maintenance fee is $35.00 (U.S.). You can call the InterNIC 7 days a week, 24 hours a day, at Network Solutions, Inc., for information on registration services. The telephone number is 888-771-3000 for calls originating in the US, Canada, Puerto Rico, and the Virgin Islands, or 402-496-9798 elsewhere.

Go to www.registration.fed.gov to register a site in the .gov domain. To register a US military agency, go to the registry at www.nic.mil.

Subdomains

The top-level domains branch out into *subdomains,* which are usually named after your organization. A subdomain is any subdivision of a domain. So a subdomain of a top-level domain is a second-level domain. If your organization is large, it may further create its own subdomains for administrative purposes; these subdomains are third-level, fourth-level, and so forth. Refer to Figure 11-2 to see a few second-level domains (such as mit.edu and lotus.com), as well as a third-level domain (enet.dec.com).

The internationalization of the Internet

Outside the United States, the rightmost piece of the Internet address is the two-character country code specified by ISO standard 3166; a few of these top-level domains are listed in Table 11-2.

Table 11-2	International Domain Names
Country Code	*Country*
ca	Canada
in	India
uk	United Kingdom (Actually, the ISO code is gb, but it's hard to make a long story short about whether a country is in Great Britain or the UK.)
us	United States

When you communicate with someone outside the United States, be aware that the subdomains may (or may not) have different names. In Australia, they use the same style as in the U.S. (com.au, edu.au, and so on). But in the UK, administrative domains are named differently, as in co.uk (corporation) and ac.uk (academic community). So don't assume anything about subdomain names outside the U.S.; always look them up. As world geography changes rapidly in the 1990s, the Internet has been unable to keep pace. For example, the top-level domain yu still exists on the Internet, even though Yugoslavia no longer exists on the world map.

Fully qualified domain names

You have already seen some DNS domain names used in this book. (They can be part of e-mail addresses.) For example, when you send mail to mwilensky@abc.university.edu, the university.edu part of this address is the domain name. Each DNS domain has a unique name. This name is so important that it actually becomes part of each computer's name. The result is called a *fully qualified domain name,* or FQDN, pronounced by saying the letters F Q D N.

Here are some examples:

- ✔ The computer named hbs is part of the DNS domain named harvard.edu, yielding the FQDN hbs.harvard.edu.
- ✔ The mythical computer named viper is part of the mythical DNS domain named support.lotus.com, yielding the FQDN viper.support.lotus.com.

Figure 11-3 shows what these two FQDNs look like on the Internet tree.

You may wonder why FQDNs are so long. You may be able to use some shortcuts — depending on where you're sending e-mail from. If you send mail to mwilensky@abc.university.edu, the mail reaches him no matter where you are when you send it. However, that's a pretty long address to have to type. To make things easier, you don't always have to use an FQDN. If you don't, TCP/IP assumes the domain is the same as yours.

So if you, too, are on computer abc, you can simply send mail to the username mwilensky and save some typing. If you're on a different machine, say computer xyz, but your computer is also in the university.edu domain, you can leave out the domain name and just send to mwilensky@abc.

These shortcuts aren't limited to e-mail.

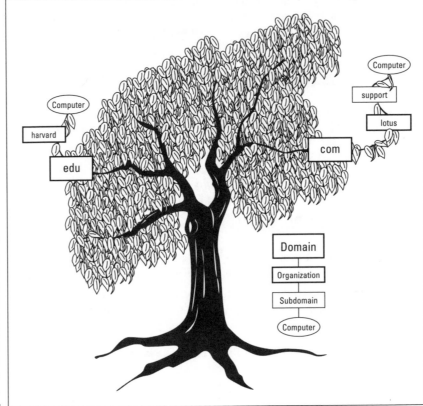

Figure 11-3:
An FQDN (fully qualified domain name) spans the DNS tree from leaf to root.

Servers, Authority, and Other Techie Stuff

You can have three types of servers in your DNS domain:

- The primary name server
- The secondary name server(s)
- The caching name server(s)

Before we examine their roles in the scheme of things, be sure you know your authority figures. Read on.

Who's in charge here?

In the DNS environment, a name server — any kind of name server — can be in one of three different states when queried by the client:

✔ It knows the answer authoritatively. That means it has the answer in its data files. This is the same as being responsible for the data.

✔ It knows the answer, but not authoritatively. That means it has stored (cached) the data in memory from some previous query.

✔ It doesn't know the answer and has to ask another server.

Primary name servers are the authority for their zone. A zone is often the same as a domain, but not always — a primary name server can delegate authority to a secondary name server, to lessen the primary's workload and to give it a backup. (Is this starting to sound like life at the office? To relieve stress, delegate!)

When the primary name server delegates authority, it ships the truth, in the form of the database, to the secondary name server. The more the primary can delegate, the more stress relief it gets. Each domain should have a primary and at least one secondary name server.

Caching name servers also help relieve stress, but they're not entirely trustworthy because they don't have the real truth in the form of database files on disk. Caching name servers have what they "believe" to be the truth, in the cache. (It's sort of like an office intern or apprentice — they're eager to help out, but do you trust them to do the tough stuff?)

All servers do caching, especially of the data for which they're not responsible. Caching servers do only caching because they have no data files and aren't responsible for any information.

The primary is master of the domain

The primary name server is the "big" one. It has authority for its whole domain. That means the master stores the databases for its zone. It can also delegate authority to secondary name servers. The primary server is the ultimate repository of truth — at least as far as the names and addresses in the domain are concerned.

Please don't confuse the DNS primary name server with an NIS master server. (NIS is covered in Chapter 10.)

The secondary name servers

In school, the little kids in primary school look up to the big kids in secondary school. But on the Internet, it's just the opposite: Secondary name servers download copies of name/address information from a primary or another secondary name server.

The more secondary name servers your organization has, the less chance there is of clogging up the primary name server, and the better protected you are from a failure of the primary. Secondary name servers are the backups for the primaries, and if the primary delegates authority, the secondary can answer address queries from any other name server in its zone.

The big difference between a primary name server and a secondary name server is where they get their information. The primary gets it from the database files; the secondary gets it from a primary or another secondary name server.

Caching servers

Caching servers have no authority in a DNS arrangement and don't store any databases on their disks. They depend on the kindness of other name servers for information. The caching servers query other servers for name address information and keep (that is, "cache") it in memory for users who are geographically close.

If Katherine sends mail to ken@beacon.com, her local caching server looks up beacon.com in the DNS and holds on to the information. When Katherine sends Ken another mail message, beacon.com's IP address is now quickly available from the caching server, and her request for the name-to-address translation is spared a long trip across the network.

If beacon.com is renumbered, Katherine's caching server may still hold the old address information. To avoid this problem, the cached data in a name server expires periodically.

To manage this expiration procedure, the administrator of the authoritative name servers (the ones responsible for knowing the truth) sets a *Time To Live,* or TTL, value for the name/address data. Think of the TTL as a timer that limits how long any name server can cache the data. When the timer runs out, the cached data must be discarded. Without the TTL, no updates would ever replace old information. Remember that the resolver issues a query for computer name-to-address translation every time you go out on the network, regardless of the application you're using.

Smaller TTL values mean that the data cached by nonauthoritative name servers (including the caching servers) is updated more often. The trade-off is that those name servers must query more frequently. Larger TTL values reduce network traffic but increase the likelihood that old, possibly incorrect, data are still alive.

Servers, lies, and videotapes

We lied. There are no videotapes. And there are more than three name server types.

Now that you're a name server expert, you should know about two more types: slave name servers and forwarding name servers. Although they're not as widely used as primary, secondary, and caching name servers, they have their uses.

A *slave name server* can function as a primary, secondary, or caching name server. The difference is that the slave has no direct contact with the Internet. If a slave name server doesn't have the information it needs to resolve an address query, it sends the query to a forwarding server. The slave server contains a list of the numeric addresses of the forwarding servers to use. It queries the forwarding servers in the list, in order, until it receives an answer or reaches the end of the list.

A *forwarding name server* is any server except a slave. The server (primary, secondary, or caching) that receives the slave's query is the forwarding server.

DNS versus NIS

Both DNS and NIS are naming services. Both provide lookup services for groups of computers called domains. DNS provides name/address lookups and translation. NIS works with smaller groups of computers, providing name/address lookups and UNIX system and account information.

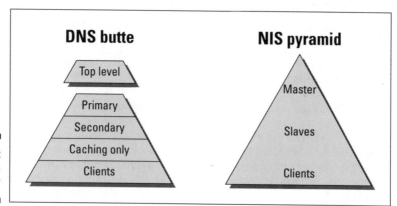

Figure 11-4:
Ain't it a butte?

In the beginning there were hosts files

Long ago, before the Internet was even a gleam in anyone's eye, keeping track of the names and addresses of a group of computers wasn't a big deal. A text file containing the addresses and names of the computers was the perfect solution. This was the *hosts file*, and each computer kept a local copy. *Host* normally means computer, but it can also refer to any other device connected to the TCP/IP network, including routers, hubs, and terminal servers (see Chapter 18). Local hosts files are still in use today. If your computer needs to communicate with only a small number of other computers, you can easily list them in your own local hosts file.

Every TCP/IP product on every operating system knows how to look in a local hosts file to resolve a computer's name into its numeric address. Every TCP/IP product on every operating system knows how to query DNS servers. Only UNIX systems and a few TCP/IP Windows products know how to query NIS servers for address resolution (see Chapter 10).

DNS has a strategic advantage over NIS. Although both use a tree structure, NIS is a mountain with a pointy top and DNS is a butte with a flat top, as shown in Figure 11-4. The top of the NIS mountain is the single master server in the domain and thus the single point of failure. DNS's "flattened" top is formed by a set of name servers, where no one server can be a single point of failure. That makes the DNS environment extremely robust — robust enough to serve the Internet.

Use DNS in the following circumstances

- ✔ If your own computers are connected to the Internet
- ✔ If you're a system manager or network administrator responsible for more than a few computers
- ✔ If many of your computers run an operating system other than UNIX, which means that NIS won't help you

When you have a large private internet, DNS is the best choice because it eases your maintenance burden. Manually updating and synchronizing local hosts files on all your computers is tedious, time-consuming, and risky. Moreover, those local hosts files can be enormous if your organization has thousands of computers, and each one needs its own copy. With DNS, if and when you do attach your organization to the Internet, your domain is ready to go.

Finding Information about Domains and Name Servers

Two tools can help you find information about DNS domains and name servers: whois and nslookup.

Where is whois?

Chapter 7 explains how to look up domains and servers in the Whois databases. The key to using whois is "If you don't succeed at first, try, try another whois database".

Figure 11-5 shows the results of asking for whois information about the domain lotus.com.

```
% whois -h rs.internic.net lotus.com
Lotus Development (LOTUS-DOM)
    55 Cambridge Parkway
    Cambridge, MA 02142

    Domain Name: LOTUS.COM

    Administrative Contact, Technical Contact, Zone Contact:
        Sanderson, William J.  (WJS2)  wsanders@ccmg.lotus.com
        617-693-1115

    Record last updated on 20-Oct-94.

    Domain servers in listed order:

    NIC.NEAR.NET                 192.52.71.4
    BU.EDU                       128.197.27.7
    NOC.CERF.NET                 192.153.156.22

The InterNIC Registration Services Host contains ONLY Internet Information
(Networks, ASN's, Domains, and POC's).
Please use the whois server at nic.ddn.mil for MILNET Information.
%
```

Figure 11-5:
The whois command tells you about domains and servers.

Your fishing pole: nslookup

To query a DNS server manually, you can use the nslookup utility (pronounced by saying N S lookup). Most TCP/IP products include this program. Because nslookup calls the same resolver routines as every other TCP/IP application, it's also a basic troubleshooting tool.

So why would you want to query a DNS server manually (that is, instead of from some application)? You say your applications take care of that for you? Okay — but inquiring minds want to know. And if you want to, you can use nslookup to

✔ Troubleshoot network connections

✔ See if the data in the name server's cache are current

✔ See how mail messages actually get where they're going

All the nslookup commands that you use for manually querying a name server are shown in Figure 11-6.

Be careful as you enter nslookup commands. Any typographical error is treated as a request for DNS information, so watch those typos. For example, if you want to set a timeout value, but you type **sit timeout=5** instead of **set timeout=5**, nslookup asks the name server for information about a computer named sit.

```
% nslookup ─────────────────────── Manually query a DNS server.
Default Server: dnsp.lotus.com
Address:  130.103.48.124          ──── The server we're querying announces itself.


> ? ─────────────────────────── Ask for online help. ───────
Commands:       (identifiers are shown in uppercase, [] means optional)

NAME             - print info about the host/domain NAME using default server
NAME1 NAME2      - as above, but use NAME2 as server
help or ?        - print help information
exit             - exit the program
set OPTION       - set an option
    all          - print options, current server and host
    [no]debug    - print debugging information
    [no]d2       - print exhaustive debugging information
    [no]defname  - append domain name to each query
    [no]recurse  - ask for recursive answer to query
    [no]vc       - always use a virtual circuit
    domain=NAME  - set default domain name to NAME
    root=NAME    - set root server to NAME
    retry=X      - set number of retries to X
    timeout=X    - set time-out interval to X
    querytype=X  - set query type to one of A,CNAME,HINFO,MB,MG,MINFO,MR,MX
    type=X       - set query type to one of A,CNAME,HINFO,MB,MG,MINFO,MR,MX
server NAME      - set default server to NAME, using current default server
lserver NAME     - set default server to NAME, using initial server
finger [NAME]    - finger the optional NAME
root             - set current default server to the root
ls NAME [> FILE]- list the domain NAME, with output optionally going to FILE
view FILE        - sort an 'ls' output file and view it with more
>
> exit ──────── All done!
%
```

Figure 11-6: These are the only nslookup commands. Anything else is a DNS query.

These are the commands. Anything else you type (that means typos!) is interpreted as a query an address to be resolved.

When you start nslookup, it connects to a default name server — the same one your computer normally uses for DNS queries. You can explicitly switch to another server any time you need to, using the `server` and `lserver` commands.

By default, nslookup only asks for address information. To find other kinds of information, use the `set type=` command, followed by a record type listed in Table 11-3. Figure 11-7 shows a real-life nslookup session.

Table 11-3   DNS Record Types to Use with Set Type= Command

DNS Record Type	Description
A	Address information (the default)
CNAME	Canonical name, also known as common name or alias
HINFO	Host information, such as computer model and operating system
MX	Mail eXchanger, a computer that receives mail on behalf of a computer and/or forwards it further on
any	I don't care; give me any and all information

```
% nslookup ───────────────────── Manually query DNS server.
Default Server:  dnsp.lotus.com
Address:  130.103.48.124 ──────┐
                               └─ Server we're querying announces itself.
>
> set type=any ───────────────── Report any kind of data you know about.
>
> mail.lotus.com.
Server:  dnsp.lotus.com               First query (mail.lotus.com)
Address:  130.103.48.124              has authoritative response,
                                      even though it's not
mail.lotus.com  internet address = 130.103.46.2   announced that way.
>
>
> hp.com
Server:  dnsp.lotus.com
Address:  130.103.48.124
```

Figure 11-7:
A sample nslookup session.

(continued)

(continued)

```
Non-authoritative answer:
hp.com   inet address = 15.255.152.4
hp.com   origin = relay.hp.com
         mail addr = hostmaster.hp.com
         serial=1002204, refresh=10800, retry=3600, expire=604800, min=86400
Authoritative answers can be found from:
NS.INTERNIC.NET inet address = 198.41.0.4
AOS.ARL.ARMY.MIL        inet address = 128.63.4.82
AOS.ARL.ARMY.MIL        inet address = 192.5.25.82
AOS.ARL.ARMY.MIL        inet address = 26.3.0.29
NS1.ISI.EDU     inet address = 128.9.0.107
C.PSI.NET       inet address = 192.33.4.12
TERP.UMD.EDU    inet address = 128.8.10.90

NS.NASA.GOV     inet address = 128.102.16.10
NS.NASA.GOV     inet address = 192.52.195.10
>
>
> hpl.hp.com ──────────────── Query to resolve this address.
Server:  dnsp.lotus.com
Address:  130.103.48.124          ── This server . . .

Non-authoritative answer:
hpl.hp.com      nameserver = hplns3.hpl.hp.com
hpl.hp.com      nameserver = hplabs.hpl.hp.com
hpl.hp.com      nameserver = hplns26.hpl.hp.com
hpl.hp.com      nameserver = pub.hpl.hp.com
hpl.hp.com      nameserver = hplb.hpl.hp.com
hpl.hp.com      nameserver = hplms26.hpl.hp.com
hpl.hp.com      preference = 20, mail exchanger = hplms2.hpl.hp.com
hpl.hp.com      preference = 23, mail exchanger = mlhub26.hpl.hp.com
hpl.hp.com      preference = 25, mail exchanger = hplms26.hpl.hp.com
hpl.hp.com      preference = 30, mail exchanger = hplabs.hpl.hp.com
hpl.hp.com      preference = 35, mail exchanger = hplb.hpl.hp.com
hpl.hp.com      origin = hplns3.hpl.hp.com
         mail addr = ns-admin.hplabs.hpl.hp.com
         serial=854, refresh=10800, retry=3600, expire=604800, min=86400
Authoritative answers can be found from:
hplns3.hpl.hp.com       inet address = 15.0.48.4
hplabs.hpl.hp.com       inet address = 15.255.176.47
hplns26.hpl.hp.com      inet address = 15.9.144.4
pub.hpl.hp.com inet address = 15.255.176.10
hplb.hpl.hp.com inet address = 15.255.59.2
hplms26.hpl.hp.com      inet address = 15.255.168.31
hplms2.hpl.hp.com       inet address = 15.0.152.33
>
> hpl.hpl.hp.com ──────────────── Another query.
Server:  dnsp.lotus.com
Address:  130.103.48.124
```

. . . delivers this infor- mation.

```
@ dnsp.lotus.com can't find hp1.hp1.hp.com: Non-existent domain ──┐
>                                                                  │
> hplms2.hp1.hp.com                                                │
Server:  dnsp.lotus.com                        There is no information
Address:  130.103.48.124                       for this address.

Non-authoritative answer:
hplms2.hp1.hp.com        inet address = 15.0.152.33
Authoritative answers can be found from:
hplns3.hp1.hp.com        inet address = 15.0.48.4
hplabs.hp1.hp.com        inet address = 15.255.176.47
hplns26.hp1.hp.com       inet address = 15.9.144.4

pub.hp1.hp.com  inet address = 15.255.176.10
hplb.hp1.hp.com inet address = 15.255.59.2
hplms26.hp1.hp.com       inet address = 15.255.168.31
>
> set type=mx ───────────────── Report only Mail Exchange data.
>
> hp1.hp.com
Server:  dnsp.lotus.com
Address:  130.103.48.124

Non-authoritative answer:
hp1.hp.com       preference = 20, mail exchanger = hplms2.hp1.hp.com
hp1.hp.com       preference = 23, mail exchanger = mlhub26.hp1.hp.com
hp1.hp.com       preference = 25, mail exchanger = hplms26.hp1.hp.com
hp1.hp.com       preference = 30, mail exchanger = hplabs.hp1.hp.com
hp1.hp.com       preference = 35, mail exchanger = hplb.hp1.hp.com
Authoritative answers can be found from:          NOTE: This
hplms2.hp1.hp.com        inet address = 15.0.152.33    is a subset
mlhub26.hp1.hp.com       inet address = 15.9.144.132   ─ of the data
hplms26.hp1.hp.com       inet address = 15.255.168.31  returned in
hplabs.hp1.hp.com        inet address = 15.255.176.47  earlier
hplb.hp1.hp.com inet address = 15.255.59.2             response.
hplns3.hp1.hp.com        inet address = 15.0.48.4
hplns26.hp1.hp.com       inet address = 15.9.144.4
pub.hp1.hp.com  inet address = 15.255.176.10
>
> exit
%
```

WINS (Windows Internet Name Service): Name Resolution According to Microsoft

Microsoft provides WINS as an alternative to DNS for resolving names to IP addresses. WINS replaces the need for local hosts files, DNS databases, and DNS servers. WINS is designed to be easier to set up and manage than DNS databases.

Although two RFCs (RFC 1001 and 1002) describe WINS and how WINS cooperates with TCP/IP, WINS isn't actually part of the TCP/IP protocol suite. It's a proprietary protocol from Microsoft.

WINS client and server services work only on computers that run Microsoft operating system software. You can run a WINS server only on the Microsoft Windows NT operating system. Why does anyone want to use WINS if it's so restrictive? Well, one use of WINS is to convert Microsoft's old (very ancient) proprietary NetBEUI protocol names to DNS names.

Windows NT 5.0 doesn't use Microsoft's proprietary protocol NetBEUI. It uses a native DNS to correlate all those ugly IP addresses with the names we like to use, so you can forget about WINS. In Windows NT 5, Microsoft uses a new service, Active Directory, to manage Windows NT resources, users, and groups. Active Directory uses Internet standards (DNS and LDAP), rather than proprietary technology (WINS) to manage resources.

WINS is fine for Microsoft-based networks that aren't connected to the Internet. WINS can work together with DNS, but if you're going to DNS anyway, for example, to run a name server that's connected to the Internet, why use both? You would need to maintain databases for both and monitor both for performance. We recommend that you make your life easier, and just use DNS for name resolution within your intranet and to the outside Internet.

Chapter 12

Feasting on Information

. . . .

In This Chapter

▶ Exploring hypertext and hypermedia

▶ Discovering the latest browser technologies

▶ Browsing the World Wide Web — quickly

▶ Finding meals on the Internet: Gopher Goulash, Web Wingdings, and malts with Archie and Betty

▶ Searching out search engines to find what you want on the Web

. . . .

*T*here is an absolute glut of information and files available on the Internet — so much that you may feel overwhelmed. Even when you know what you want, it can be really hard to find. The information services described in this chapter help you navigate the Net, including the World Wide Web.

Get ready to take your raw Internet data and bake them into succulent tidbits of information, using all of the latest tools in your information management repertoire — outlining, cross-referencing, indexing, summarizing, and condensing — all without having to copy the files to your own host. Here's even more good news: You don't need a Web browser to do these wonderful things. Even if you do have a graphical browser, it may pay off for you to read about some of the non-graphical tools in this chapter. When you get frustrated with how slowly your graphical Web access is going, you can speed up with Archie, Gopher, and WAIS.

TCP/IP applications give you more than one way of doing things. The applications described in this chapter give you options. There is no "best" way — only the way that you prefer. We don't recommend one way of finding information over another. It all depends on what suits your personal preference.

Surfers' paradise

Cruising around the Internet to see what's out there is often called *surfing the Net*. Vinton

Cerf is known as the Father of the Internet. So shouldn't it be Cerfing the Net?

Everybody, sing!
"Duke, duke, duke, duke of URL, duke, duke..."

If you've been paying attention to the Web pages throughout this book, you may have noticed the address box that starts with `http`. This string of characters is called a *Uniform Resource Locator,* or URL. (The acronym is usually pronounced by saying the letters U R L, but we love that song, and some people do pronounce it "earl.")

Here's an example URL:

```
http://www.lotus.com
```

The `http` is the protocol, HyperText Transfer Protocol, that you use to access the resource. Everything following the colon is the location of the Web resource. The location starts with

`//`, followed by the site name. If anything follows the final /, it is a filename on that host. (Throughout this book, we drop the "http://" part of the URL, because many browsers no longer make you type in that part.)

URLs don't only locate Web resources. Here are examples of URLs that point to an Anonymous FTP site and an LDAP server:

```
ftp://ftp.microsoft.com
ldap://ldap.bigfoot.com
```

While you're busy browsing, the Web can actually take you to a non-HTTP resource such as those just mentioned.

How Do Information Services Help Me?

In the last few years, a number of new information services have been developed and deployed on the Internet. When you go to that big TCP/IP banquet at Internet Hall, the tools introduced in this chapter represent the frills of the dinnerware set: the lobster picks, fruit knives, and demitasse cups that you don't even know you need until you sit down to eat.

Like most of the applications and services we talk about in this book, the Internet information services are client/server environments. You use a client application — either as software on your own computer or by connecting to a host that's running the client application — to communicate with a server.

Some of these information exploration tools have a *GUI* (graphical user interface), so to take full advantage of their features you need to run them from a Windows, Macintosh, or Motif-equipped computer. Other tools have only a plain-character interface that you can run from a DOS PC or even a dumb terminal connected to a minicomputer or mainframe. But whatever the user interface, there's usually a TCP/IP protocol in there somewhere. And the information you can access is much more than just plain text.

What Are Hypertext and Hypermedia?

You may have heard the terms *hypertext* and *hypermedia* used in conjunction with the latest and greatest Internet tools. However, both hypertext and hypermedia have been around for a long time and are used not only for Internet tools such as Gopher and browsers, but also for applications not related to TCP/IP and the Internet, such as Hypercard on the Macintosh.

✔ *Hypertext* is text that contains in-line pointers to other text in the same file or another file. A common example of hypertext is the Microsoft Windows help system, in which you click a highlighted word or icon or button and you receive more information about what you clicked on. The linked, multipage information you click around in is hypertext.

✔ *Hypermedia* extends the hypertext concept beyond just text and into multimedia. In hypermedia applications, a pointer can take you to a sound byte, or a graphic image, or even a video clip. These days, there's much more to life on the Internet than just text!

You may already be familiar with the most common use of hypermedia on the Internet — the World Wide Web. Later in this chapter you can read about Archie, Gopher, and WAIS, all of which help you handle the enormous amounts of information available on the Net.

The World Wide Web (WWW)

The World Wide Web (also called "the Web," "WWW," "W3," or "W cubed") is the worldwide hypermedia information service on the Internet, and it's amazingly hot these days. A common misconception among newcomers to the Information Superhighway is that the Web and the Internet are two different things. Actually, the Web is a subset of the computers and information on the Internet.

Netscape Navigator, Lotus Notes, and Microsoft Internet Explorer are popular Web clients. Lynx is another Web client, but it's completely text based. Web clients, which are also called *browsers,* communicate with the servers via HTTP, or HyperText Transfer Protocol.

A Web browser is an HTTP client that sends requests to web server software. When you type a URL (Uniform Resource Locator) or click on a hypertext link, your browser creates an HTTP request and sends it to the IP address that's represented by the *URL* (or Web address).

Thanks, but I'm just looking

To use the Web, you need a browser (client) and a TCP/IP connection to a web server. The browser is a TCP/IP application that comes with either graphical or text-based interfaces.

Many operating systems, such as Microsoft Windows 95, 98, and NT, come with browsers. Additionally, certain communication products have built-in browsers. Some examples include Lotus Notes and Netscape Navigator, which you can purchase separately or bundled with Netscape Communicator.

Help! I'm the only person in the universe who doesn't have a browser!

Don't worry if you don't have a browser. You can connect via telnet to a public host that has a non-graphical browser. Chapter 8 shows how to use telnet.

If you don't have a browser, and you prefer not to telnet to someone else's browser, you can use Anonymous FTP (see Chapter 9) to get a free browser. To find a non-graphical browser, use Archie (described in the "Using Archie to search FTP archives" section, later in this chapter) and type this command:

```
find lynx
```

Archie points you to FTP sites from which you can download the Lynx text-based browser and other browsers as well.

If you use a non-graphical browser, you need to know the commands listed in the following to help you navigate.

Browser Command	Function
home	Go to the home page
recall	Review documents you've already viewed
top	Go to the first page of the document
bottom	Go to the last page of the document
next	Follow the next link in the chain of information
previous	Retrace the prior link

A browser that speaks

IBM's talking browser, Home Page Reader for Windows, was developed for blind and visually-impaired Web surfers. Home Page Reader browser reads aloud the information on a Web site. Home Page Reader is available in Japanese and English. It uses Netscape Navigator to move around the Web and IBM's ViaVoice speech technology to speak the Web pages.

If you want a really efficient graphical browser, try Opera, from the Norwegian company, Opera Software. The program code is small enough to fit on 1 floppy. Program size is often an indicator of efficiency. Figure 12-1 shows Opera's interface. Opera is shareware, and you can get it from the Web at www.operasoftware.com. Because Opera is shareware, you get to use it for 30 days. If you want to keep Opera, you should pay them $35 U.S. Opera runs on Windows and OS/2, and a Macintosh version in the works.

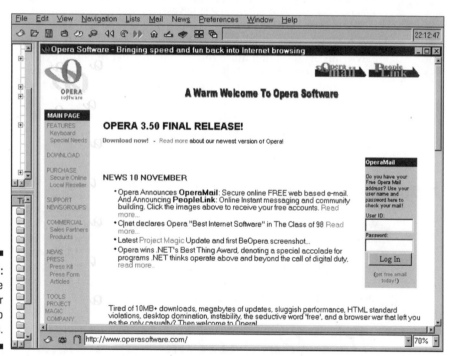

Figure 12-1: Rush to the Opera for speedy Web access.

If you're concerned about security on the Web, S-HTTP (Secure HTTP) is undergoing the Internet's Request For Comments process and should become an international standard. S-HTTP is basically HTTP with extensions for secure client/server communications. Chapter 19 has more information on S-HTTP.

Mousing across the Web

Graphical browsers bring the Web to life. To get started, just double-click on the icon for your browser and you get a *home page* — the Web term for a "welcome" screen. Typically, the home page explains what the Web site is all about and points you in the right direction for the information that you're looking for.

We talk a lot about the Internet in this book because TCP/IP and the Internet are really a package deal. You can't have the Internet without TCP/IP; nor would the world have had TCP/IP without the Internet. But in the greater scheme of things, this book is only skimming the general characteristics of the Internet in order to show you the relationship between the Net and its protocols and services. So if you think you're turning into an Internet junkie (or already are and always will be), the best place to find out more about the Internet is on the Internet itself.

The Netscape home page (www.netscape.com) is a great place to start. Just follow the links by clicking on topics that interest you. You don't have to use a Netscape browser to access this Web page. Any browser can get you here.

The Internet is emerging as an unlimited commercial site. In the future, you may wind up spending more time at an Internet mall than you do walking through the traditional kind — the ones with hard floors, recycled air, and salespeople who spray you with perfume. The Internet mall even has a food court! It has all kinds of restaurants to which you can e-mail an order, and they deliver. We have purchased airline tickets on the Internet and sent flowers to our niece, Sarah.

How Does Information Get on the Web?

Web authors use Web authoring technologies to write the text, place the pictures, and interact with you on the Web. Because a Web language isn't a protocol, service, or application, it's not part of TCP/IP. However, the Web wouldn't be the Web without all the creative, exciting pages created by the following languages and tools. The following sections discuss these Web authoring technologies and tools.

HTML (Hypertext Markup Language) and dynamic HTML

HTML tells a Web browser how to display a Web page's text and graphics.

You can use *dynamic HTML* (sometimes called *HTML 4.0*) to create snazzier Web pages than with HTML — with more animations and more response to user interaction than with HTML. For example, when you move your mouse over a graphic, the graphic speaks and changes color.

XML (eXtensible Markup Language)

The latest language to hit the Web is XML, and more and more companies are creating new Web languages and products based on XML. XML is more powerful than HTML, because it *describes* the Web data as well as how the data should look. This description makes Web searching more efficient. Because XML is more descriptive than HTML, Web searches are able to filter out the irrelevant topics that you often see in today's HTML-based world. If you use Internet Explorer 4.0 (IE4) from Microsoft, you have already used XML without even realizing it — it's the first browser to support XML. The Channel Definition Format (CDF) that IE4 uses to define channels is based on XML. Netscape plans for Navigator 5.0 to use XML technology.

Java and JavaScript

Java is a programming language specially created by Sun Microsystems for use on the Internet. A Java *applet* is a small program that's part of a Web page. A Java application can run on any operating system platform without having to be built specifically for it.

JavaScript is the Netscape scripting language. A scripting language is a mini-programming language. If you're creating Web pages, you can include JavaScript in HTML pages. The Web browser knows how to interpret the JavaScript code, which makes the browser act more like a Web application client. You can also run JavaScript on the server side with the Microsoft Active Server Pages (ASPs).

ASP (Active Server Page)

ASPs are HTML pages that include *scripts* (small programs) written by Web developers. The scripts are processed on a Microsoft Web server, which sends the HTML Web page to any browser. These pages are called *active* because you can use scripts to customize the pages for different users.

ActiveX

ActiveX, a set of object-oriented technologies, is the Microsoft answer to Java. An ActiveX *control* is a program that runs in the ActiveX environment, and is conceptually similar to a Java applet. ActiveX controls run on Windows 95, 98, and NT, and on Macintosh products. Microsoft also plans to support ActiveX controls for UNIX.

Lotus Domino

Domino is Lotus Development Corporation's Web application server program. In addition to all of its other messaging and groupware features, you can use Domino as a Web server with or without Lotus Notes as the Web client, on your intranet or over the Internet.

The Web Is a High-Calorie Feast

Yes, it is. And sometimes, it has a lot of empty calories. If you know what you want to see on the Web but not where it is, you need a search engine. A *search engine* is a site with specialized software that maintains a database of Internet sites. You tell the search engine what you want to look for, and it hunts through its database to give you links to the sites that match the word or words that you asked for. We had a lot of fun searching for our names. There were only a few matches, so it wasn't bad. When we searched for the name "Gates," we got 100,000 matches. Our favorite search engines are Alta Vista (www.altavista.com) and Hotbot (www.hotbot.com).

A search engine includes a program that compares your search request to the entries in the index, and then returns results to you. A search engine also includes a component called *spider, crawler,* or *bot* that searches every searchable page on the Web and reads it to see if it contains the information that you requested.

Check out the Easy Searcher site (www.easysearcher.com/index.html) to find the locations of hundreds of specialized search engines, including an index of other search engines.

Structured directories of topics are often miscategorized as search engines. Yahoo! (www.yahoo.com) is an example of a popular directory on the Web. Several Web portals, including Yahoo, combine both the search engine and directory approach to finding information. A *portal* is a Web site that's meant to be a starting site for users. A portal often contains content similar to an online service, such as America Online (AOL).

Reducing the Web's Wait

Some people think that WWW really means World Wide Wait. Web speed ranges from tortoise speed to warp speed. All of those fancy graphics that you see on Web pages are high fat and take a long time to get to you.

If you would like things to go faster, here are a few tips.

- ✔ **Use faster hardware.** A 56 Kbps modem or a cable modem should help — see Chapter 18 for the details.

- ✔ **Try a *Web accelerator.*** This is a program that pre-fetches Web pages and caches them on your local computer. So, while you're looking at that first recipe for cheesecake, the Web accelerator program brings the page with the next recipe to your local computer. You see the next recipe more quickly when you click to see it because it has already been moved from the Web site to your computer. We've seen Web accelerator programs at our local discount warehouse store for $40 to $50 U.S.

- ✔ **Automatically download files.** You don't have to sit in front of your computer to download Web pages and files. You can exercise and work off the junk food that this book makes you crave by using *download scheduling software.* You can use the software to download Web pages and files automatically on schedule. These scheduler programs disconnect from the Internet when your download successfully finishes. NetAttaché (`www.tympani.com`) is one example of this kind of software.

- ✔ **Use Lynx.** Little known Lynx saves lots of time. When surfing for text, use the Lynx browser for speed. Lynx outperforms Netscape Navigator and Microsoft Internet Explorer when reading pages of text and FAQ files. You can get a free copy of Lynx for Windows 95 or Windows NT at `www.fdisk.com/doslynx/lynxport.htm`.

- ✔ **Multitask.** Let your Internet connection do two things at the same time. Contrary to popular belief, you can surf while you download, or perform a couple of downloads at the same time and get good performance.

- ✔ **Avoid Web rush hour congestion.** Check MAE West's traffic report before you start browsing (`www.mfst.com/MAE/west.ds3.overlay.html`). MAE helps you pick the best times to surf and download files.

- ✔ **Upgrade to Windows 98.** Windows 98 automatically optimizes TCP/IP transmissions if you set the IP Packet Size to Automatic, by doing the following:

    1. **From the Start Bar, choose Settings⇨Control Panel.**

    2. **In the Control Panel dialog box, click the Network icon, click on Dial-Up Adapter, and then click on the Properties button.**

    3. **Click on the Advanced tab.**

4. Look at the list of Properties. The IP Packet Size entry should say "Automatic."

If not, click to list the IP Packet Sizes, and click on Automatic. Setting the IP Packet Size to Automatic allows the MTU size to match the connection speeds. By the way, Windows NT also has an automatic MTU adjustment feature.

MTU (Maximum Transmission Unit) defines how many bytes are in each packet that flows across a network. The ideal packet size depends on the kind of network and network hardware that's handling your packet. If a packet is too large for your kind of hardware, TCP/IP automatically breaks up the packet into smaller quantities. This slows down your network performance. The automatic setting in Windows 98 adjusts the packet size before it goes out from your PC onto the network.

Who's in Charge of the Web?

Well, the Web is part of the Internet. A fairly new group, the W3C (World Wide Web Consortium), develops protocols for the Web. The W3C consists of industry members from all over the world.

The W3C provides several practical services, including

✔ Sample applications that demonstrate technology that's coming to the Web.

✔ A library of information about the Web and its specifications. The library is useful for both application developers and users.

The W3C isn't part of the IETF — the Internet Engineering Task Force that researches Internet issues for the Internet Society (check out Chapter 2) — rather, it has a more commercial orientation. However, many members of the W3C also belong to the IETF working groups. W3C research and proposals can be put on the IETF track to become standards. The W3C and the IETF work together on the HTTP protocol. W3C specifications undergo a review and finalization process similar to RFCs. W3C members approve specifications in a process that goes through stages: working draft, proposed recommendation, and recommendation.

A Few Blasts From the Past Are Still Useful

The Web isn't all that's available to you. The following sections describe a few older, but still useful, tools.

Using Archie to search FTP archives

Archie is a client/server environment that helps you find out which Anonymous FTP archives hold the things you're looking for on the Internet. Archie is like a card catalog to the world's FTP libraries.

Archie is just a finder. After you find the location of what you're looking for, you have to go get it. So, you have to use Anonymous FTP to transfer the files you want to your own computer. Figure 12-2 shows a UNIX client accessing an Archie server on the Internet.

You can also telnet to an Archie server and log in as user `archie`, as our friend Betty has done in the session illustrated in Figure 12-3. Betty isn't asked for a password. That's because Archie servers are public.

Figure 12-2:
An Archie client asks the server to search for information on the IPv6 protocol.

```
$ archie -h archie.internic.net IPv6 ──── Show user Betty articles and files about IPv6.
─ Host ftp.library.uwa.edu.au

        Location: /pub
                    FILE -r--r--r--        22  Aug 19 1996  IPv6
─ Host sunsite.cnlab-switch.ch
                                        ╲ Ignore these. They're the UNIX file protections.
        Location: /MIRROR/RIPE          ╱
            DIRECTORY drwxr-xr-x ────╱       512  Mar  4 06:33  IPv6
        Location: /MIRROR/linux/Networking
                    FILE -rw-rw-r--        37884  Feb  7 18:06  IPv6
        Location: /MIRROR/linux/Networking/sunacm
                    FILE -rw-rw-r--          930  Jan  4 14:15  IPv6
─ Host thumper.bellcore.com

        Location: /pub/gja
            DIRECTORY drwxr-xr-x            1536  Mar  8 1996  IPv6
─ Host ftp.fh-rosenheim.de

        Location: /pub/systems/linux/Kernel
                    FILE -r--r--r--         8796  Jun 18 1996  IPv6
─ Here are four locations. You can use ftp to retrieve files from them.
```

Gophers go-fer Internet gold

Gopher is a menu-based client/server rodent for burrowing through the Internet. Gopher menus allow you to work your way around, up, down, across, and through the Internet feast. Gopher works harder than Archie. When you want to bring the information that you've found into your own computer, Gopher displays the information and then automatically starts telnet or FTP or whatever TCP/IP application that you need to deliver the information (see Figure 12-4).

```
% telnet archie.rutgers.edu ───────────────── Betty telnets to an Archie server.
Trying 128.6.21.13...
Connected to archie.rutgers.edu.
Escape character is '^]'.
Solaris 2 (dogbert.rutgers.edu) (pts/3)

login: archie ─────────────────────────────── She logs in as archie.
Last login: Thu Jun 19 21:03:06 from 206.25.35.10
Sun Microsystems Inc.    SunOS 5.5.1     Generic May 1996
------------------------Network Services ----------------

                      Welcome to Archie!
                         Vers 3.5

# Bunyip Information Systems, Inc., 1993, 1994, 1995

# Terminal type set to `vt100 24 80'.
# `erase' character is `^?'.
# `search' (type string) has the value `exact'.
archie> servers ──────────────────────────── She used the servers command.
-------------------< List of active archie servers >---------
                              Last Update: Jun 21 1996

    archie.au              139.130.23.2     Australia
    archie.univie.ac.at    131.130.1.23     Austria
    archie.belnet.be       193.190.248.18   Belgium
    archie.cs.mcgill.ca    132.206.51.250   Canada
    archie.funet.fi        128.214.6.102    Finland
    archie.cru.fr          129.20.254.2     France
    archie.th-darmstadt.de 130.83.22.1      Germany
    archie.ac.il           132.65.208.15    Israel
    archie.unipi.it        131.114.21.10    Italy
    archie.wide.ad.jp      133.4.3.6        Japan
    archie.hana.nm.kr      128.134.1.1      Korea
    archie.nz              140.200.128.13   New Zealand
    archie.uninett.no      128.39.2.20      Norway
    archie.icm.edu.pl      148.81.209.5     Poland
    archie.rediris.es      130.206.1.5      Spain
    archie.luth.se         130.240.12.23    Sweden
    archie.switch.ch       130.59.1.40      Switzerland
    archie.ncu.edu.tw      192.83.166.12    Taiwan
    archie.doc.ic.ac.uk    146.169.16.11    UK
    archie.sura.net        192.239.16.130   USA (MD)
    archie.internic.net    192.20.239.132   USA (NJ)

archie> whatis security
RFC 1037                    Greenberg, B.; Keene, S. NFILE - a file access
protocol. 1987 December; 86 p.RFC 1038
St. Johns, M.
Draft revised IP security option. 1988 January; 7 p.
cops              System Security analysis tool
forktest          Find security holes in shell-escapes
kerberos          Host security package
safe-mkdir        mkdir() and security hole *****FIX****
```

We edited out many Archie servers. Try Archie for yourself to see the rest.

Figure 12-3: Betty telnets to an Archie server and logs in as user *archie.*

```
% gopher
                                    Internet Gopher Information Client v2.1.3

                                    Other Gopher and Information Servers
    > 1. All the Gopher Servers in the World/
          2. Search All the Gopher Servers in the World <?>
          3. Search titles in Gopherspace using veronica/
          4. Africa/
          5. Asia/
          6. Europe/
          7. International Organizations/
          8. Middle East/
          9. North America/
         10. Pacific/
         11. Russia/
         12. South America/
         13. Terminal Based Information/
         14. WAIS Based Information/
         15. Gopher Server Registration <??>

Press ? for Help, q to Quit, u to go up a menu          Page: 1/1

                                    Internet Gopher Information Client v2.1.3

                                    Fun & Games

          1. Games/
          2. Humor/
          3. Movies/
    > 4. Music/
          5. Recipes/
```

Figure 12-4:
Gopher
burrows
around the
Internet to
find and get
what you're
looking for.

Get into Gopher by using Gopher client software on your computer (the most efficient choice, after you have the software) or by telnetting to a Gopher server and logging in as user gopher.

Gopher menus differ from server to server, but you navigate through the menus the same way. The up arrow and down arrow keys are the most convenient way to move through Gopher's menus. When something you want is highlighted, you press Enter, or you can type the number of your choice and then press Enter.

Figure 12-5 shows the top Gopher menu at the University of Minnesota.

You can use Gopher to ferret out everything from poetry to the *CIA World Fact Book* to song lyrics to — well, you get the idea.

Gopher a WAIS down the Internet

The Wide Area Information Service (WAIS), pronounced like the word "ways," is yet another client/server environment. WAIS searches the wide range of databases available across the Internet for the topics of your choice, from computers and networking to aeronautics to *soupe de poisson*.

```
$ gopher gopher2.tc.umn.edu
Press ? for Help, q to Quit       Retrieving Directory..\
Internet Gopher Information Client v2.1.3
 Home Gopher server: gopher2.tc.umn.edu

 1.  Information About Gopher/
 2.  Computer Information/
 3.  Discussion Groups/
 4.  Fun & Games/
 5.  Internet file server (ftp) sites/
 6.  Libraries/
 7.  News/
--> 8.  Other Gopher and Information Servers/
 9.  Phone Books/
 10. Search Gopher Titles at the University of Minnesota <?>
 11. Search lots of places at the University of Minnesota  <?>
 12. University of Minnesota Campus Information/

 Internet Gopher Information Client v2.1.3
  Other Gopher and Information Servers

 1.  All the Gopher Servers in the World/
 2.  Search All the Gopher Servers in the World <?>
 3.  Search titles in Gopherspace using veronica/
 4.  Africa/
 5.  Asia/
 6.  Europe/
 7.  International Organizations/
 8.  Middle East/
 9.  North America/
 10. Pacific/
 11. Russia/
 12. South America/
 13. Terminal Based Information/
--> 14. WAIS Based Information/
        15. Gopher Server Registration <??>
```

Figure 12-5:
The
University
of
Minnesota's
Gopher
menu.

Part III

TCP/IP Stew — A Little of This, a Pinch of That

The 5th Wave By Rich Tennant

"I can't seem to connect to the Mars Rover—I keep getting the Dummies Press Web site instead."

In this part . . .

TCP/IP is more than two protocols — it's a whole banquet of courses, soup to nuts, with all the necessary utensils, from the sardine can opener to the Ginsu knife to the pots and pans. Part III is a stew cooked up in a big pot starting with TCP/IP staples: names and addresses. Then, we spice up the stew with some of the more esoteric TCP/IP implements and ingredients.

Chapter 13 is a behind-the-scenes look at why mere mortals can use computer names, even though TCP/IP eats numbers at every meal.

Have you heard that the Internet is running out of addresses? Are you worried that, when you need to add a computer to the Internet, the Internet will be full? Chapter 15 introduces the next generation of IP, called IPv6, to calm your fears. Chapter 16 helps you find people, computers, and e-mail addresses on the Internet. Chapter 14 helps new network administrators figure out all those files that appear on computers that run TCP/IP.

Chapter 17 provides some of the dialup ingredients for our TCP/IP stew, including Virtual Private Networks (VPNs) and Mobile-IP. In Chapter 18, you get acquainted with some of the pots and pans that are used to cook the stew, from simple switches to complex gateways to some of the fastest connection methods. Chapter 19 includes some very important seasonings in Part III's *ragoût:* security considerations and techniques.

Chapter 13

Nice Names and Agonizing Addresses

- -

In This Chapter

▶ Using a new name for computers: hosts

▶ Understanding why you need both names and addresses

▶ Using TCP/IP network addresses — classy things or classless?

▶ Recognizing the parts and fields of IP addresses

▶ Figuring out how to get an IP address and an address on the Internet

▶ Comprehending subnets and supernets and why they wear masks

▶ Tasting IPv6

▶ Drinking CIDR to relieve Internet address space disorder (for now)

- -

*I*f your computer is already on a network, *and* you always call computers by name, *and* you don't give a fig what TCP/IP is doing to your computer's name behind the scenes, you can breathe easy in this chapter. The only thing you really need to know here is another term for a computer — a *host* — and what it means. In other words, you can go look up the term host in this book's Glossary and move on to Chapter 14 or some other chapter. This whole chapter is techno-geekism for you.

However, if you need to get your computer on the network or the Internet, or you want to know the meaning of all those strings of numbers and dots (not to mention IPv6's letters and colons and CIDR's slashes) that you see when you use an application such as FTP or telnet, stay right here. Most of the information in this chapter is aimed at you — especially if you're a beginning network administrator.

IPv6 is designed to expand greatly the numbering system used for the Internet, without changing the names we use for the computers. Some information about IPv6's impacts are sprinkled in the appropriate places, but most of it is together in Chapter 15. But don't head to Chapter 15 yet, unless you already understand IPv4 addresses because:

> ✔ IPv6 addressing builds on the IPv4 foundation.
>
> ✔ IPv4 and IPv6 will exist together for a long time to come.
>
> ✔ IPv6 isn't yet widely used.
>
> ✔ If you're not ready for Ipv6, you can use a workaround to the IP address shortage.

What Did You Say Your Computer's Name Was Again?

You have a name. When you were born, your parents gave it to you. They did this for several reasons: to fill in the big space on your birth certificate, to give them something interesting to yell when they call you for dinner, and because "Hey you!" is sorta rude (not to mention unspecific). Ultimately, though, your name uniquely identifies you. Sometimes it takes your entire name to identify you: Alfred E. Newman, Smokey the Bear, Thurston Howell III. Sometimes it only takes part of your name: Einstein, Gandhi, Gilligan.

You also have a number. You probably have more than one:

✔ A driver's license number

✔ Credit card number(s)

✔ A social security (or other government identification) number

You can change your name if you want. You may acquire a nickname, slapped on by one of your friends or maybe even chosen by you yourself. Maybe you write books under a pen name. If you're working as a spy, you probably assume a number of "covers." When you get married, you may elect to take your spouse's last name. You can even go to court and change your name legally.

Changing your numbers is a little harder. In most cases, you have to get some corporation or official agency to approve and make the change for you.

If your computer uses TCP/IP, your computer must have a name, too. If you're lucky, you may get to choose it yourself. Most likely, though, your organization has a naming policy that helps you select a name or limits your choices. In some cases, a system manager or network administrator gets to have all the fun and assign a name to your computer for you.

Getting to know you . . .

Your computer has a number, as well. That number is called the computer's *IP address,* and we spend the greater part of this chapter studying it. (Throughout much of this book, we call it a *numeric address* — now you know the correct technical term.) Your computer may have more than one IP address, depending on how many networks it's connected to.

Your computer's name and IP address can change, too. It may never write a book under a pseudonym or take a married name, but it can take on nicknames, change names, and have multiple identities. (If you use it for espionage, maybe your computer has a "cover," too — would you believe Agent 80586?)

A computer needs a name for several reasons.

- ✔ You need to be able to connect to a particular computer and the services it offers. Knowing that computer's name makes it easier to link up.

- ✔ You want your e-mail delivered to a specific place. Without computer names and addresses, e-mail would be impossible.

- ✔ Humans like naming things (dogs, cats, goldfish) and can remember names. Computers like dealing with numbers.

What happens if the computer name isn't unique on the network? In Chapter 11, we compare two Lotus companies — one makes cars; the other makes software. If you try to connect via FTP to a computer named just lotus, would you find files about cars or software?

Uniquely yours . . .

TCP/IP and the Internet require that each and every computer on the network, in the organization, in the world, in the solar system, be uniquely identified by both name and address. To identify computer lotus, then, we need more names — kind of like first, middle, last, and maybe more.

A computer's full name is called a *fully qualified domain name,* FQDN. (Go ahead, just try to say it three times fast.) So, for computer lotus, its FQDN may be

```
lotus.lotus.com
```

Computer name = lotus; organization name = lotus; and Internet top-level domain = com (short for *commercial organization*). Here's another example:

```
hbs.harvard.edu
```

The computer name = hbs; organization name = harvard; and Internet top-level domain = edu (short for *educational institution*).

What's the Local Hosts File?

You may usually call a computer on the network a "computer," or sometimes a "system," but now we get more technical and start calling it a *host*. Substitute the term *host* for *computer,* and you can then say that every host on a TCP/IP network has a name and a number.

In Chapter 11, we introduce you to the concept of a local hosts file. This file, residing on your own computer, lists by both name and number the hosts (computers) you want to communicate with.

- ✔ On UNIX, the hosts file is /etc/hosts.
- ✔ On the version of TCP/IP that we use with Microsoft Windows NT, the hosts file is c:\winnt\system32\drivers\etc\hosts.
- ✔ On non-UNIX systems, the hosts file's location varies with the TCP/IP product you're using.

Figure 13-1 shows the names and addresses in a small local hosts file.

```
# Copyright (c) 1993-1995 Microsoft Corp.
# This is a sample HOSTS file used by Microsoft TCP/IP for Windows NT.
#
# This file contains the mappings of IP addresses to host names. Each
# entry should be kept on an individual line. The IP address should
# be placed in the first column followed by the corresponding host name.
# The IP address and the host name should be separated by at least one
# space.
#
# Additionally, comments (such as these) may be inserted on individual
# lines or following the machine name denoted by a '#' symbol.
#
# For example:
#
#      102.54.94.97     rhino.acme.com          # source server
#      38.25.63.10      x.acme.com              # x client host

127.0.0.1        localhost
# Cardinal Consulting, Inc. LAN
130.103.40.55    redbird            #candace's computer
130.103.40.56    bluebird           #marshall's computer
130.103.40.61    oldbird            #VMS server
130.103.40.63    toughbird          #big UNIX server
130.103.40.64    mazarin            #Windows NT server
130.103.40.65    macbird            #the Mac
130.103.40.66    topbird            #admin mainframe
130.103.40.52    woodpkr            #library computer
130.103.40.53    oriole             #ancient 386 laptop
```

Figure 13-1: A local hosts file identifies each host by name and number.

If you're part of a large network, you probably want to use a naming service to replace or supplement your local hosts file. See Chapter 11 for information on the Domain Name System (DNS) to *resolve* (translate) host names into addresses.

The Many Faces of IP Addresses

Hosts on a network are identified by their numeric IP address. Yes, you usually type in the host's name, but somewhere along the way, TCP/IP resolves that name into an IP address. That's why you have a local hosts file, along with NIS and DNS. In the case of big networks (and can you get any bigger than the Internet?), DNS does the name/address resolution.

Why bother with a number if the computer has a name?

People like names. Computers like numbers.

What's in an IP address?

The address where you live is made up of several parts. It may include any of many elements that identify you — your street name, post office box, city, region (province, state, canton, county), country, postal code, and so forth. The same is true of your computer (host). The difference is that you know your address, and it is mostly text with a few numbers; but you may or may not know your computer's address, which is all numbers and dots.

The IP address (to be specific, the IPv4 address) is a set of numbers separated by dots. (IPv6 addresses are described later in this chapter.) It identifies *one network interface on a host*. Every device on the TCP/IP network — that is, every network interface on the network, because some devices may have more than one — needs a unique IP address. If your host is on a TCP/IP network, that host has an IP address, even if you've always called your computer by name.

You may have noticed this numeric address showing up in messages and wondered what it was. For example, telnet reports the IP address as it tries to connect to the remote host. Here's a code fragment that shows it. You connect to frodo by name, and telnet responds with frodo's IP address.

```
% telnet frodo
Trying 130.103.40.225 ...
Connected to frodo.
```

An IPv4 address is a 32-bit number. It is divided into two sections: the network number and the host number. (You can't see the division. Wait for the section on subnet masks later in this chapter.) Addresses are written as 4 fields, 8 bits each, separated by dots. Each field can be a number ranging from 0 to 255. This style of writing an address is called *dotted decimal notation*.

All hosts on the same network must use the same network number. Each host/network interface on the same network must have a unique host number.

Figure 13-2 shows some legal combinations of network and host numbers.

Figure 13-2:
Here are some legal combinations of network and host numbers.

A | Network. . . Host . . . .
B | Network. . . . . Host . . . .
C | Network. . . . . Host . . . .

Class A address 1.1.1.1
Class B address 130.103.40.210
Class C address 192.9.200.15

How Do I Get an IP Address?

Can you just pick any IP address that's unique on your network? Most of the time, the answer is no, unless you're the network administrator. If your organization uses DHCP, the DHCP server software can automatically assign an IP address to you.

Most organizations have network administrators (known affectionately as the network police) who tell you what to use for an address so that yours doesn't conflict with anyone else's. After all, you can't just pick any ol' house on the block and move in — someone else probably already lives there, right? So, your network police officer is there to make sure nobody squats at a network address that's already in use. If the police don't do their jobs and you set up your computer to use an existing address, don't come complaining to us that you never receive your e-mail or that you're receiving someone else's junk mail. Some implementations of TCP/IP check on the network to make sure the address your computer is about to start using is available.

Only if your network isn't connected to any other network is it okay for you or your network police to pick a host address out of the blue. If your network is connected, your address must be unique across the combination of linked networks.

On the Internet, where many thousands of networks are interconnected, no one person actually polices to make sure each and every address is unique. The assignment of the network number portion of the IP address keeps the organizations clearly identified and separate.

To connect your network to the Internet, you need an official block of addresses. The official bestower of IP addresses is the InterNIC. Regional Internet Service Providers also can give you your official addresses.

How do you find out who these Internet Service Providers are? The best way is by looking at lists on the Internet, but that's kind of a catch-22. One of the next best ways is to ask neighboring organizations that are already on the Internet whom they use. You can also look at the ads in almost any computer-related magazine. Many Internet starter kits in bookstores are preconfigured to link you to an Internet Service Provider.

If you think you want to connect your network to the Internet some day, you can save yourself a lot of work down the line by applying for IP addresses ahead of time. You can start using them locally as soon as you get them, and when you finally connect to the Internet, you won't have to renumber your network and all your hosts.

The Four Sections of the IPv4 Address

An IPv4 address looks like this:

```
field1.field2.field3.field4
```

The meaning of these fields depends on your network class. There are four classes of networks in TCP/IP. While only three classes are widely used today, the fourth is up and coming for a special purpose. Whether your organization connects to the Internet or is a private intranet, the first three classes work the same way.

As an example, we use the biggest internet we can think of — the Internet — to examine how network classes work.

Class A is for a few enormous networks

Theoretically, there can only be 127 class A networks on the Internet, but each one of those 127 can have a huge number of hosts: about 17 million each (16,777,216 to be exact). Only a few very large organizations need class A networks. (By the way, there is no class A network that starts with the number 0, and the entire class A network numbered 127 is reserved. This leaves only 126 class A networks.)

Class B is for lots of big networks

Although they're nowhere near as enormous as class A networks, class B networks are hefty, as well. Each class B network can have about 65,000 hosts — the size needed by some universities and larger companies. The Internet can support up to 16,384 class B networks.

Class C is for the thousands of small networks

Class C networks are much smaller, and the Internet has over 2 million (2,097,152) of these. Most of the networks connected to the Internet are class C. Each one can have only 256 hosts. (Actually, each class C network can have only 254 hosts; the numbers 0 and 255 are reserved.)

Class D is for multicasting

Class D networks are completely different from the other classes — they're used for multicasting, which is a special way of transmitting information from a server to a set of clients all at the same time. Multicasting is the technology that supports such cool applications as audio- and video-conferencing and radio and television stations that exist only on the Internet.

Days or weeks prior to the "broadcast," the sponsoring organization announces (via e-mail or Usenet news) the class D network address that the server is going to use for the transmission. (Radio and television stations are assigned permanent addresses so they can transmit constantly if they choose to.) There are plenty of available channels, because class D addresses go from 224.0.0.0 to 239.255.255.255. At the assigned date and time for the broadcast, you tune — that is, configure — your client software to the proper class D address. The broadcast works just like ordinary radio and television, but it's on the Internet.

Real-time applications require special purpose, multicast-aware *routers* (see Chapter 18 for more on those) so that the packets always arrive in the proper order and none are missing. These routers on the Internet form the MBone, or IP Multicast Backbone.

Take a look at Chapter 15 for more on multicasting, especially about its new uses in IPv6.

For Math Nerds Only: Biting Down on Bits and Bytes

Who decided how many hosts are in class A, B, and C networks? And why can there only be 127 class A networks when there can be a zillion (well, almost) of class C?

It all has to do with the arrangement of the bits inside the addresses. For example, class A addresses use the first field as the network section, and the next three fields as the host section. The more fields in a section, the bigger number you get. Because class A only has one field in the network section, it can only have a small number of networks. But the three fields in the hosts part allow each of those 127 networks to have a ton of computers.

Table 13-1 shows how the four fields of the IP address are assigned to the network section and host section.

Table 13-1	The Two Sections of the IP Address	
Network Class	**Network Section of IP Address**	**Host Section of IP Address**
A	field1	field2.field3.field4
B	field1.field2	field3.field4
C	field1.field2.field3	field4

Danger! There's math ahead. If you already understand binary numbers and how to convert from decimal to binary, skip ahead to the next section. If you don't understand binary, this section takes you back to high school. Get ready to look at place values in a whole new way.

Figure 13-3 takes the number 127 apart to show how it's constructed in binary. A computer looks at the number 127 as an arrangement of 0s and 1s. Computers ultimately do everything in *binary*, or base 2. So if you look at the place value columns in Figure 13-3, you don't see the familiar 1s, 10s, 100s, and so on, from the decimal system. Rather, you see the 1s, 2s, 4s, 8s, 16s, 32s, 64s, 128s, and so on. (Remember, in binary, the only possible values in a column are 0 or 1. Also remember that a byte contains 8 bits.) In the decimal system, it takes three columns — the 1s column, the 10s column, and the 100s column — to represent the number 127. To get to 127, then, a binary number has 7 columns: the 1s, 2s, 4s, 8s, 16s, 32s, and 64s.

Figure 13-3:
Binary
numbers
are as easy
as 1, 2, 3.
Oops, make
that 0 and 1.

Class A Network

128	64	32	16	8	4	2	1	Place value columns
0	1	1	1	1	1	1	1	Bit values (either 1 or 0)

High
order ◄─────────────────────────── order
bit   bit

Low

$127 = 1 + 2 + 4 + 8 + 16 + 32 + 64$

Classy bits

In a computer, each place-value column in a binary number is represented by a bit. In the early days of computers, you could look inside the cabinet and actually see circular magnets called cores; each magnet was a bit. A core magnetized in one direction (say, clockwise) meant the bit was set to 1. The other direction (counterclockwise) meant the bit was set to 0. Today's transistors and semiconductors have replaced the magnets, so it's harder to see what's going on inside — but the computer still uses bits of 1 and 0. All numbers inside the computer, from 0 to 1,000,000,000,000 and on up, are made from bits. The computer keeps adding the 1s and 0s until it reaches the total, such as 127.

If each and every bit of the class A network piece were set to 0 or 1, that would result in a higher number than the 127 allowed by the

Internet. Figure it out: 128+64+32+16+8+4+2+1. But TCP/IP requires that the high-order bit for a class A network always be 0. According to this rule, when you add up the bits you get 0+64+32+16+8+4+2+1 for the number of class A networks that a 32-bit address allows. To determine how many networks and hosts were allowable for each Internet class, the maximum value was calculated for the field combinations of each section. The rules for class B state that the first two high-order bits must be 1 and 0. For class C, the first two high-order bits must be 1 and 1.

The high-order bits are the bits at the end of the number. Which end depends on whether your computer reads from right to left or left to right. If a computer reads from right to left, as does a PC, the high-order bits are the ones on the far left end.

Administering Subnets and Subnet Masks

Subnets divide one network into multiple smaller networks. The separate networks are normally interconnected by network devices called *routers*. (Routers, hubs, and more are explained in Chapter 18.)

Not every environment requires subnets. For example, if your organization's class C network has 254 or fewer hosts and the network lives entirely in one building, there's no reason to subnet it. But if your organization's network does expand into multiple locations, the network administrator has a couple of options.

One option is to ask for another entire network number for each new facility, but this is sorta greedy if your existing network still has enough unassigned host numbers for future growth. The other option is to take your existing network and split it into pieces, one piece for each location.

When subnets are necessary, and the network administrator (this may mean you!) uses good common sense to subdivide the network, subnets do yield some advantages over one large network:

- Smaller networks are easier to manage and troubleshoot, even though there are more pieces.
- Network traffic overall is reduced, and performance may improve because most traffic is local to its subnet.
- Network security can be applied more easily at the interconnections between the subnets. For some mind-numbing details about network security, read Chapter 19.

Figure 13-4 shows a main network with two subnets. Each network and each host has an address. Look carefully at field3 in each address; can you find some subtle differences?

The address for a subnet uses the address for the main network and borrows some bits from the host part to extend the network section. The borrowed bits enable each subnet to have its own unique network address. Because the subnet addresses are derived from the main network's address, you don't have to ask the InterNIC for them. These addresses already belong to your organization; you've just decided to deploy them differently.

Mask-erading subnets

When the network administrator borrows bits from the main network address's host section, TCP/IP must be told which bits of the host section are borrowed to be used as the network address. The administrator uses a

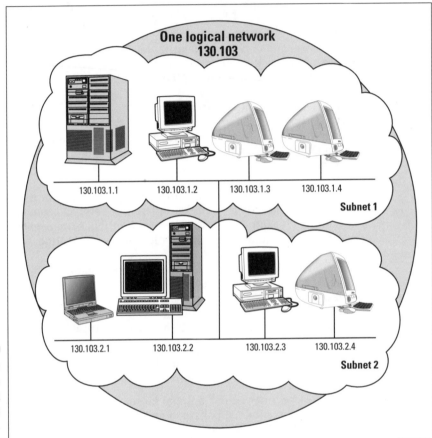

Figure 13-4:
Each
subnetwork
has its own
address.

subnet mask to borrow those host bits. A subnet mask is 32 bits, just like
the IP address. The bits for the network address are all set to 1, and the bits
for the host address are all set to 0.

Before defining a subnet mask, the network administrator needs to figure
out how many subnets to create and how many hosts will be in each subnet.
This determines how many bits should be set to 1.

The more bits used for the subnet mask, the fewer hosts can be on the
subnet.

Why do I have a mask if it's not Halloween?

Your network has a subnet mask even if it doesn't have subnets. Most TCP/IP implementations supply a default subnet mask, which says, "Hi. I'm a network that's not subnetted." Figure 13-5 shows the default subnet mask for each class of network. Some TCP/IP vendors (Microsoft, for example) automatically configure the default subnet mask for you.

Figure 13-5:
Each class has a default subnet mask.

A   255.0.0.0

| 11111111 | 00000000 | 00000000 | 00000000 |

B   255.255.0.0

| 11111111 | 11111111 | 00000000 | 00000000 |

C   255.255.255.0

| 11111111 | 11111111 | 11111111 | 00000000 |

The subnet mask must be the same for each computer on the network; otherwise, the computers don't understand that they're on the same network.

The subnet mask is applied to the IP address in every message in order to separate the network number and the host number. For example, when your computer examines the class C address 192.9.200.15 and applies the default subnet mask of 255.255.255.0, it sees the network number 192.9.200 and the host number 15.

How do you know that this works? Hold on to your techie hats. It's done by converting nice decimal numbers like 255 to not-so-nice binary numbers like 11111111. And then, after all the numbers are converted to binary, they get ANDed. AND is a binary mathematical operation. If you aren't fed up AND bored by now, read the upcoming sidebar "Boolean arithmetic: AND." Just remember, although this stuff may seem incomprehensible to you, your computer lives, breathes, and eats binary and thinks this is Really Fun!

p.s. The authors can't be held responsible for any medical or mental complications that result from reading beyond this point!

Boolean arithmetic: AND

In the AND operation, regardless of the value in the data bit, a mask bit of 0 yields a result of 0. And a mask bit of 1 preserves the value in the data bit, also regardless of the value in the data bit. Another way to say this is that the result bit is a 1 if, and only if, both the data bit and the mask bit contain 1. Otherwise, the result bit is 0. Here's a table that demonstrates this:

	0	1	0	1	Data
AND	0	0	1	1	Mask
	0	0	0	1	Result

Suppose you examine how a subnet mask is used to obtain the network number part of an IP address. In your computer, the fields of the dotted decimal IP address 192.9.200.15 are already in binary as

11000000 00001001 11001000 00001111

The fields of the dotted decimal subnet mask 255.255.255.0 are already

11111111 11111111 11111111 00000000

The AND operation yields the network number 192.9.200, as shown here:

11000000 00001001 11001000 00001111
IP address: 192.9.200.15

11111111 11111111 11111111 00000000
Subnet mask: 255.255.255.0

11000000 00001001 11001000 00000000
Result: 192.9.200.0

To get the host number, your computer inverts the bits of the subnet mask — each 1 becomes a 0, and each 0 becomes a 1 — and does another AND. Easy as pi, right?

11000000 00001001 11001000 00001111
IP address: 192.9.200.15

00000000 00000000 00000000 11111111
Subnet mask: 0.0.0.255

00000000 00000000 00000000 00001111
Result: 0.0.0.15

Subnetting 101

We're going to split one class C network with 256 hosts into two equal subnets of 128 hosts each. We must change the class C default subnet mask of 255.255.255.0.

Let's use network number 192.9.202, which means the 256 hosts are numbered 192.9.202.0 through 192.9.202.255. To split the network into two parts, with one part getting addresses 0 to 127 and the other getting addresses 128 to 255, you need the custom subnet mask 255.255.255.128. The 0 becomes 128 because you borrow the high-order bit from field4. (In binary, 128 is 10000000. Refer to the "Classy bits" sidebar if you need help with the math.)

In the 192.9.202 network, there are 128 addresses that happen to have the high-order bit of field4 set to 0, and another 128 addresses that happen to have the high-order bit set to 1. If you thought the custom subnet mask would be 255.255.255.1, you were close, but that mask borrows the low-order bit of field4. It puts all the even-numbered hosts (0, 2, 4, 6, and so on up to 254) in one subnet and all the odd-numbered hosts (1, 3, 5, 7, and so on up to 255) in the other.

Before subnetting this example network, it was easy to say that all of the hosts were in the 192.9.202 network. They still are.

Probably the most common use of subnetting is when an organization splits its class B network into 256 class C networks. To accomplish this, every host sets its subnet mask to 255.255.255.0.

If you hate this math, read about IPv6 in Chapter 15. The expanded address size removes the need for subnetting.

Expanding with Supernets and Supernet Masks

If your organization has grown, you may need to link two or more class C networks together. The result is one larger network, although it won't be as large as a class B network. In this supernet, the network number part of the address lends bits to the host number part — just the opposite of what happens in a subnet.

The networks being linked into a supernet should be "numerically adjacent." The meaning of "numerically adjacent" depends on whether you're using decimal or binary numbers. Adjacent binary numbers may well have nonadjacent decimal equivalents. For example, decimal 3 is adjacent to decimal 4, but their binary equivalents, 011 and 100, aren't adjacent. In this first supernet example, the two network numbers are "adjacent" in both their binary and decimal values. In the later examples, they're not.

Supernet Example 1: Suppose you link 192.9.200 and 192.9.201. You can skip over the 192 and 9 because they're the same in both addresses and concentrate on the 200 and 201. Your computer already stores the decimal number 200 as the binary number 11001000 and the decimal number 201 as the binary number 11001001. Notice that the only difference is the last bit. That means you only need to borrow the low-order bit of field3. To link these two networks together, you simply change from the default subnet mask of 255.255.255.0 to the custom supernet mask of 255.255.254.0.

Supernet Example 2: This next one is harder and points out the nasty side of the "adjacent" requirement. Here, you link 192.9.199 and 192.9.200. Once again, you can skip over the 192 and 9 and concentrate on the 199 and 200. Your computer already stores the decimal number 199 as the binary number

11000111, and decimal 200 as binary 11001000. Uh-oh, these binary numbers differ in all of the last four bits! The supernet mask that links them is 255.255.240.0 (240 in decimal is 11110000 in binary) — but that supernet mask actually links together the 16 networks 192.9.192 through 192.9.207. (Do the math yourself or just trust us. We know our binary.) So, if the other 14 networks don't belong to your organization, you've just created a mess, and this isn't the right answer for you. If all of the networks were yours, this may be okay, depending on what you really need to do.

Supernet Example 3: Okay, one last example and we're done. This one shows how two networks can be adjacent in their binary numbers even though they don't look adjacent in their decimal numbers. This time, you link 192.9.200 and 192.9.216. As usual, you can skip over the 192 and 9 and concentrate on the 200 and 216. Your computer already stores decimal 200 as binary 11001000, and decimal 216 as binary 11011000. Wow, the only difference is one bit, although it's in the middle — which means you only need to borrow that bit in `field3`. To link these two networks together, you use the supernet mask 255.255.239.0. It looks strange, but has been properly calculated.

A bit makes more than a bit of difference

It's more important that two supernet network numbers vary by one bit than it is for them to be plus or minus one decimal value. That's why 200 and 216 are "adjacent," but 199 and 200 aren't. Table 13-2 shows how many bits of supernet mask it takes to link networks together.

Table 13-2	Bits and Network Linkages
To Link This Many Networks	*The Network Numbers Must Differ In*
2 networks	Only 1 bit position
4 networks	2 bit positions
8 networks	3 bit positions
16 networks	4 bit positions
32 networks	5 bit positions
64 networks	6 bit positions
128 networks	7 bit positions
256 networks	8 bit positions

If you're a network administrator and need to configure subnets, a calculator that converts between binary and decimal is one of your most valuable tools. (Or if you're a seasoned IBM mainframer, you can look up binary-to-decimal conversions on your tattered old IBM 370 green card.)

Supernets — the bottom line

The supernet mask really links together separate networks into one network. By using the supernet mask value of 255, you can link together the 256 networks numbered from 0 to 255.

DHCP Gives Network Administrators Time to Rest

DHCP is the TCP/IP protocol that automatically assigns and keeps track of IP addresses while the network administrator takes a stroll on the beach.

One administrator's nightmare is another's fantasy

Imagine you're the person in charge of the White Pages of the telephone book. What a hard job it must be! You have to be sure that everyone's name and number are in the book correctly and in alphabetical order. When people move into your area, you have to assign them a number and list it in the directory. If people discontinue service, you have to remove their names and numbers. If you live where people move frequently, you spend all your time keeping that directory up-to-date.

Now imagine that the telephone company gets a new system. Whenever someone needs to be assigned a telephone number, you don't do anything. The telephone system magically assigns a number automatically. If someone no longer needs a number, the telephone system automatically removes it and later recycles the number to someone else. And forget about keeping the telephone book up-to-date. The telephone system magically does that, too. In fact, there's no permanent telephone book. If someone wants to call Emily, she picks up the telephone and says, "Please connect me to Emily's telephone, wherever that is." This system would make your life as a telephone administrator so easy that you could work at the beach with a novel in one hand and a cold drink in the other.

Fantasy? Yes, for telephone administrators, but not necessarily for network administrators. People communicate on an internet or intranet via computer names and IP addresses. The network administrator keeps these up-to-date in a hosts file or a DNS database. Maintaining this information is tedious and time consuming in a volatile environment, such as the international OOPS Corporation in Chapter 10. The salespeople constantly need to change IP addresses on their portable computers as they travel around the world selling those octopus pies and sushi.

Here's how it works — it's client/server again

When you turn on your computer (a DHCP client), it contacts your network's DHCP server and asks to *lease* an address. The client and server *negotiate* the lease and — voilà! You have an IP address to use for the duration of the lease.

Here's how it works:

1. **You turn on your computer.**

   TCP/IP starts, but remember, you're a traveler. You have no permanent IP address.

2. **Your DHCP client software asks to lease an IP address.**

   This request is called a *DHCP discover message.* The DHCP discover message contains the name of your computer and its hardware address. Your hardware address comes on your NIC (network interface card).

   You can read about your hardware address in the ARP section of Chapter 15.

3. **Your computer keeps broadcasting its lease request until a DHCP server responds.**

   If there's no DHCP server — maybe an earthquake destroyed it — your computer keeps trying, but never gets its address. That means you can't use any TCP/IP applications or services.

4. **All the available DHCP servers answer your message by offering your proposed IP address, the servers' IP address, a subnet mask, and the duration of the lease in hours.**

   Your computer grabs an IP address so that no one else can take it while you're negotiating.

5. **Your DHCP client takes the first offer and broadcasts its acceptance.**

   The other servers cancel their offers.

6. **Your selected DHCP server makes your IP address permanent and sends you an "acknowledged" message (DHCP*ACK*).**

7. **You have an IP address.**

   You can use TCP/IP applications and services as long as you want — or until your lease expires.

Oh no! My lease expired. Am I evicted?

Usually a DHCP server renews your lease with no problem. In fact, you don't have to do anything. The entire process is automatic and doesn't interfere with what you're doing.

If the DHCP server dies during your lease, you won't be able to renew. When your lease expires, so does your ability to use TCP/IP services and applications.

Because any DHCP server on the network can renew your lease, your network administrator should configure more than one server.

Is the Internet Getting Low on Addresses?

Yes.

Will the Internet Ever Run Out of Addresses?

No. Read all about IPv6, the next generation of IP, in Chapters 2 and 15. If you're not ready for Ipv6, read on about CIDR.

CIDR (Classless Inter-Domain Routing) Juices up the Internet

Have you heard about CIDR (Classless Inter-Domain Routing)? You pronounce it the same as cider, the drink made from apples. The key word if you're a class expert is "classless!" With the enormous growth of the Internet, everyone needs to accept that IP addresses are an endangered resource that must be managed for the good of the many. CIDR's goal is to create a strategy for allocating IP addresses in the Internet in a way that lets the Internet grow without getting obese.

What's CIDR?

CIDR is an addressing and routing scheme that enables routing decisions to be made more efficiently — CIDR reduces the size of routing tables. Reducing the size of anything in the Internet is a good thing. (Too bad TCP/IP doesn't have a protocol for reducing the size of our waists — excuse the digression.) If you're an Internet user who doesn't need to configure TCP/IP on your computer, you now know all you need to know about CIDR. Stop here if you don't want to read too many stressful techie details. If you're a network administrator, try to read on.

In late 1990, there were 2,190 routes to be managed by routing tables. In early 1999, that number exceeds 40,000 routes. It takes almost 64MB of computer memory and a powerful CPU to store 60,000 routes. If you use CIDR, you can save lots of computer memory and CPU power too.

How can CIDR offer a solution to the growing demand for IP addresses without making the Internet address space too hefty to manage? CIDR replaces a Class B address with a group of contiguous Class C addresses. This technique is called *address space aggregation*. It keeps the routing table size nice and slim. CIDR specifies that every IP address include a network prefix that identifies either one gateway or an aggregation of network gateways. The length of the prefix is also part of the IP address.

Taking CIDR apart

C is for *classless*. Classless means, "Let's revolt against the 4-class structure of IP addresses, especially class B networks (65,533 hosts), which often waste lots of IP addresses."

D is for *domain*. RFC 1518, *An Architecture for IP Address Allocation with CIDR*, defines a domain as the group of "resources under control of a single administration." Internet Service Providers (ISPs) are domains of domains. That is, ISPs let other domains hook into their network. Subscribers are the domains that connect to IPSs. A domain can be both an ISP and a subscriber simultaneously.

I is for *inter*. Inter-domain means that CIDR is used between domains. The gateways on the Internet's backbone network described in Chapter 2 use CIDR as the system for routing between each other. The Internet's regulating authorities now expect every Internet service provider (ISP) to use CIDR.

R is for *routing*. A router is a computer that runs software that connects two or more networks. Routers determine the path a packet should follow on the network as it moves toward its final destination. A router stores a table of the available routes for packet travel and figures out the most efficient route that a packet should follow.

A CIDR network address looks like this:

```
130.103.40.03/18
```

"130.103.40.03" represents the network address."/18" declares that the first 18 bits are the network part of the address. The last 14 bits represents host addresses.

CIDR works with the OSPF and BGP routing protocols. You can read about these routing protocols in Chapter 18.

The Internet is a network of networks. Corporate and campus networks attach to transit networks (such as regional networks). Most of these corporate and campus networks consist of subnetworks. These subnetworks are interconnected by routers to form the corporate or campus network.

You say subnet, NEToRAMA says supernet

Consider the example of a fictional Internet Service Provider (ISP) named NEToRAMA. NEToRAMA is allowed to give out addresses 192.9.*.* (where * represents 0 to 255). When you sign up with NEToRAMA, you get a piece of

the their address space, which is a subnet of its address space (numeric IP address range). From the NEToRAMA's perspective, it's supernetting your address space into 192.9.*.*. For example, company a.com gets 192.9.200.* and your company gets 192.9.201.*.

NEToRAMA has 100 customers. Before using CIDR, NEToRAMA's routing table had 100 entries — one for each customer's address. But what if NEToRAMA could somehow use only one entry to be shared among all 100 clients? That would be a much smaller and therefore more efficient routing table. This is what CIDR does. Now, apply this theoretical routing efficiency across the entire Internet address space. The efficiency savings are impressive! We wanted to say staggering, but maybe we're getting carried away — or maybe we drank too much hard CIDR.

Back to the Comfort Zone

Congratulations. You stuck with it and made it to the end of this arduous odyssey of agonizing addresses. If you're a network administrator, you need to work with numbers occasionally to set up IP addresses and possibly subnets, so you may be used to this stuff anyway. If you're an end user of TCP/IP and the Internet, you've just acquired a store of valuable mathematical trivia. We doubt that you need to use it, however, unless you become a contestant on Jeopardy, the Network Edition. (Don't laugh. Digital Equipment Corporation's Users Society has actually sponsored "Network Jeopardy" at its conventions.)

In any event, no matter what your role in network fun and games, for the rest of the book, you can relax. Well, you can relax if you don't need to know any technical stuff about IPv6. That's in Chapter 15. Sorry about that. But if you gotta know, you gotta know.

Chapter 14

Configuring TCP/IP —
Will Someone Please Set
the Network Table?

In This Chapter

▶ Previewing network security

▶ Looking at TCP/IP network administration

▶ Understanding what network files can do

▶ Peaking inside network files

*W*e begin Part II by comparing the TCP/IP protocol suite to a dinnerware set, with enough pieces to serve a banquet from soup to nuts to dessert. If you're going to use all those serving pieces, you need someone who understands etiquette to set your table. (Does the seafood fork go on the left?) With TCP/IP, the network administrator or system manager usually sets the TCP/IP "table" by configuring files to work with the protocols.

This chapter describes the contents of the basic files needed to support TCP/IP.

Are the Files Already on the Table?

Some of the basic files are supplied with TCP/IP. Others must be created by the network administrator (who is probably you). How you do this is up to you: A text editor works just fine. Or if you have a graphical interface to TCP/IP, you point your mouse, click, and type some text.

If you're really lucky, you have a tool that steps you through network setup in much the same way a tutorial would. Some operating systems provide tools that prompt you for all the required network configuration information. The tool then creates and maintains the files for you.

If you're using an operating system or TCP/IP product that's different from the ones we have on our networks, your files may vary slightly from the figures in this book. Don't worry. The files may be in a slightly different location, but the general content and the purpose of those files are the same, regardless of what directory they're stored in. If your local hosts file (covered in the upcoming section called "The Local Hosts File") isn't in one of the locations that we show, search your disks for something with the word "host" in it, and then go off and look at the file. "RTFM" also applies — "Read the Fabulous Manual" that came with your TCP/IP product.

Configuring TCP/IP

We use the Microsoft Windows client and Windows NT Server as examples. Microsoft gives you a Network applet in the Control Panel on Windows 95, Windows 98, and Windows NT. The *applets* (mini programs) are slightly different, but perform essentially the same function: helping you configure TCP/IP on the computer. Okay, okay, it also helps you configure any other network stuff you may need or want. As Figure 14-1 shows, the Control Panel applets are listed in alphabetical order.

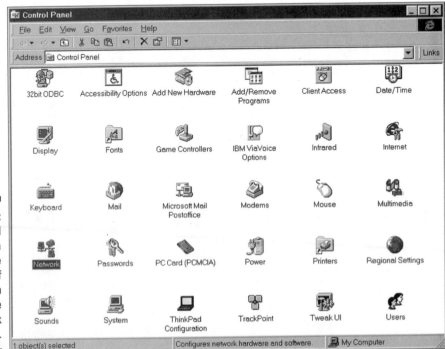

Figure 14-1: The Control Panel is a treasure chest full of loot, such as the Network applet.

Configuring TCP/IP on a Windows 95 or Windows 98 Client

Start by opening the Control Panel and double-click the Network applet to display the Network dialog box and the Configuration tab. (We don't discuss the other tabs in that dialog box — the Identification and Access Control tabs — in this book.) The first thing that you see is the list of network components installed on the computer, similar to the one shown in Figure 14-2. The exact number and type of entries that you see depend on your unique situation, but include

- **Clients:** Software that lets you use file and print servers.
- **Adapters:** Hardware, such as your NIC (Network Interface Card) or modem.
- **Protocols:** TCP/IP and other software for communicating on the network.
- **Services:** Software that lets your computer be a file or print server.

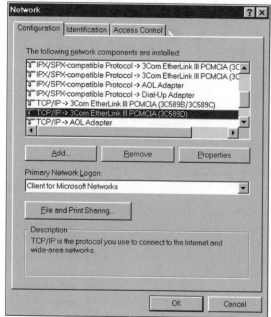

Figure 14-2:
Components
ahoy!
There's the
one we
want.

Right now, we're only concerned with configuring TCP/IP, so scroll down the list until you find a line with an icon of a network cable and TCP/IP, followed by the name of the adapter. Select it and click the Properties button (or just double-click on it) to open the TCP/IP Properties Configuration dialog box to the IP Address tab.

The default selection of Obtain an IP address automatically means that you want the computer to request a numeric IP address from a DHCP (Dynamic Host Configuration Protocol) server. See Chapter 13 for the scoop on DHCP. If you're lucky enough to work in a DHCP environment, you may be done with the Network applet. Click OK twice to exit. (You usually have to restart the operating system after making changes in the Network applet.)

Figure 14-3 shows you how to specify an IP address and subnet mask manually. Of course, you can't just use the numbers from the figure. You have to get your own numbers from your network administrator.

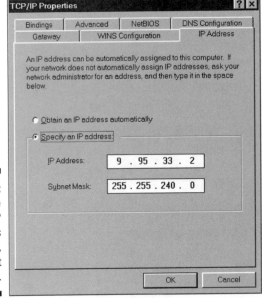

Figure 14-3: Enter the numeric IP address hook, line, and subnet mask.

While you can't simply copy the sample information from Figures 14-4 and 14-5, they show examples of supplying information on the DNS Configuration tab and Gateway tab. The Internet uses DNS (Domain Name System — see Chapter 11) to find domains, such as lotus.com, and translate their names into numerical IP addresses.

Make sure that your network administrator gives you of all the configuration data you need, such as:

✔ DNS Domain name and the numeric IP addresses of any DNS servers (for the DNS Configuration tab).

✔ Numeric IP addresses of the routers (for the Gateway tab).

✔ Numeric IP addresses of any optional WINS servers (for the WINS Configuration tab). WINS (Windows Internet Naming Service) is part of the Microsoft Windows NT Server — see Chapter 11. WINS is an alternative to DNS for associating workstation names with IP addresses in a strictly Microsoft environment.

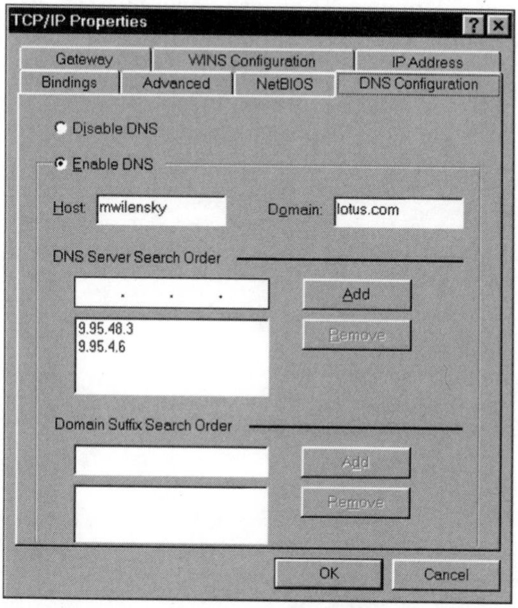

Figure 14-4: We christen thee the Jolly.Roger .com. Send the DNS lookouts to the crow's nest!

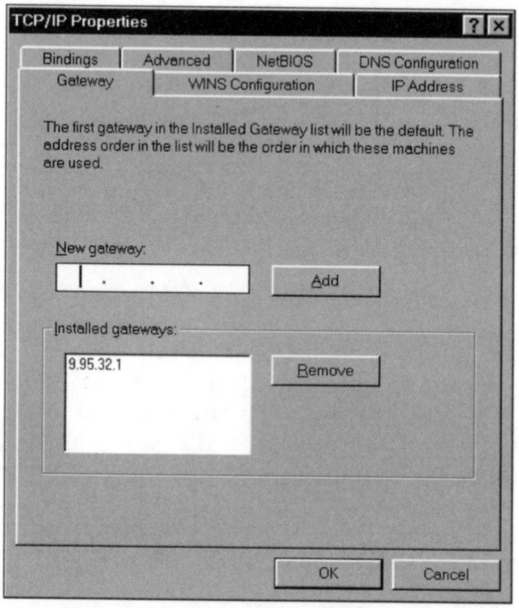

Figure 14-5: Avast maties! There be routers in these waters.

Those are the essential steps for configuring TCP/IP for Windows 95 and Windows 98.

Configuring TCP/IP on a Windows NT Server

To configure TCP/IP on a Windows NT Server, begin by logging in as Administrator. When you open the Control Panel and double-click the Network applet, the first thing you see is information in the Identification tab, similar to what's shown in Figure 14-6. Don't change anything there!

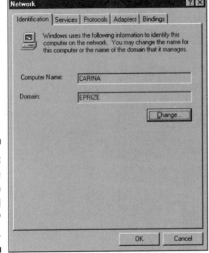

Figure 14-6:
Follow the map to the buried TCP/IP treasure.

You can find separate tabs for configuring services, protocols, adapters, and bindings. Wow, it sure looks different from Windows 95 and 98! That's partly because they're clients, while Windows NT is a server that can provide network services. Because you're interested in configuring TCP/IP, click on the Protocols tab. You should see a list of installed protocols, similar to what you see in Figure 14-7.

Choose TCP/IP Protocol from the list, and click the Properties button (or just double-click on TCP/IP Protocol) to get to the IP Address tab, as shown in Figure 14-8. If this computer is going to offer services to other computers, you won't be able to choose to Obtain an IP address from a DHCP server. Instead, you have to assign it a numeric IP address, subnet mask, and gateway address (see Figure 14-8). Remember that you can't use the values from our examples for your computer.

Figures 14-9 shows how you set the host name, DNS domain name, and the numeric IP addresses of the DNS servers.

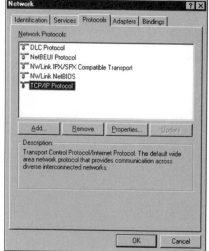

Figure 14-7:
Go two
paces East,
five paces
South, and
start
digging.

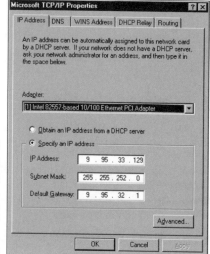

Figure 14-8:
Look
maties,
three
pieces of
eight.

The Local Hosts File

We start with the most fundamental file that you need for communicating with other computers on your network — the local hosts file.

In Chapter 11, we add the word *host* to your vocabulary — that's host as in a computer on the network. If you think it's host as in "Be our guest," take a look ahead at Chapter 19, about security.

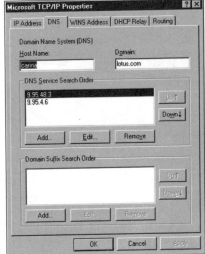

Figure 14-9:
We christen
thee the
Solemn.
Roger.
com. Send
the DNS
lookouts
aloft!

When you access another host by name on the Internet or any other internet, your computer needs to know the remote host's IP address. You can get remote host addresses from DNS (see Chapter 11) or from your computer's local hosts file. This file lists the names and addresses of other computers (hosts) known by your computer.

When you need to know about thousands of hosts on the Internet, maintaining the local hosts file is really too cumbersome a mechanism. Imagine having to spend all that time updating it as computers come and go or relocate on the Internet! In that case, you need DNS to locate remote hosts.

The location and name of the local hosts file depend on the operating system and version of TCP/IP you use. Table 14-1 lists the local hosts file locations for a few implementations of TCP/IP.

Performance: Let DNS and a local hosts file share the job

Many versions of TCP/IP allow you to use a combination of DNS and a local hosts file to find remote hosts by putting the most frequently accessed hosts into your local file. That way, you won't have the performance overhead of accessing a DNS name server on the network to get an address for the hosts that you connect to on a regular basis. Let DNS help you find addresses for hosts that you access only occasionally. This is really the best of both worlds: performance and accessibility.

Table 14-1	Popular Locations for Local Hosts Files	
Location	*Operating System*	*Vendor*
/etc/hosts	UNIX	Various
c:\windows\ ftptcp96\hosts	Microsoft Windows 95	FTP Software, Inc.
c:\winnt\system32\ drivers\etc\hosts	Microsoft Windows NT	Microsoft
c:\tcpip\etc\hosts	OS/2	IBM

How to maintain a local hosts file

Your operating system or TCP/IP product provides a local hosts file to get you started. You, the network administrator, the system manager, or whoever is in charge of network configuration maintains the local hosts file. As you add host names and addresses, you need to update the file. If your vendor did not include a network configuration tool, you get to use a plain old text editor to type in two columns of information — column 1 for the host's IP addresses and column 2 for its names.

What's in the local hosts file?

Figures 14-10 and 14-11 show the contents of two different local hosts files, one taken from a computer running UNIX and one from a PC running FTP Software's TCP/IP stack on Microsoft Windows 95. The files have exactly the same type of information, despite their origins. One was created with a simple text editor. The other was created with a GUI that allowed the network administrator to click to open windows and then fill in the blanks.

Looking at Figure 14-10, you may think there are several host names on a line. But the first name is the host name, and the following name(s) are nifty host name aliases. Look carefully at the entry for the host spiderman. Do you see a host name alias, peterparker? You can send mail to Peter on either spiderman or peterparker. Anything preceded by a # character is a free-form comment about things like the computer's owner, location, operating system, and whatever else you think is meaningful.

In Figure 14-11, can you tell whether the file was created with a text editor or with a GUI? Look carefully at the local hosts file. The software we used is called Secure Client, from FTP Software Inc., one of the few commercially available TCP/IP stacks that understand both IPv4 and IPv6.

```
#
# Sun Host Database
#
#
127.0.0.1        localhost
#
129.103.40.1     spiderman peterparker    # M Wilensky
129.103.40.3     reddwarf                 # Marshall Wilensky
129.103.40.6     giacomo                  # Netware server
129.103.40.7     grapeleaf                # OS/2 Notes server
129.103.40.17    kerwien                  # Erica Kerwien
129.103.40.24    vogon                    # Notes NLM Server
129.103.40.53    zugspitz                 # SparcStation
```

Figure 14-10: This local hosts file, created with a text editor, contains the IP address and the host name.

```
#
#   Copyright (C) 1993-1996 by FTP Software, Inc.  All rights reserved.
#
# This file contains a local host table used to resolve host names
#
# Format:
#<host address> <hostname(s)> <aliases>
#
# Sample:
#
# This is an IPv4 Sample Address
#
# 10.216.146.1chocolate.abc.com choc
#
# This is an IPv6 Sample Link Layer Address based on
# this Hardware Address: 0x12 34 56 78 90 12
#
# fe80::1234:5678:9012chocolate.abc.com choc
#
  5F00:2100:1024:9000:2580:800:2C37:7802   emmy.cardinalci.net casper
```

Figure 14-11: A local hosts file created with a GUI-based TCP/IP that understands IPv6.

Improving TCP/IP's digestion of the local hosts file

Without an up-to-date local hosts file, you may not be able to find other computers on the network, so it's important to update the file whenever a computer changes its name or address or joins or leaves the network. It's a good idea to list the computers in most frequently-used order. TCP/IP searches the local hosts file sequentially from top to bottom until it finds the computer it's looking for, so on a big network with a large local hosts file, ordering the computers appropriately gives you a performance advantage.

The Trusted Hosts File

On UNIX, the file `/etc/hosts.equiv` lists the other hosts on the network that your computer trusts; this is your *trusted hosts file*. This file is easy to create. It has only one column, which contains the host name of each computer you trust (see Figure 14-12).

Figure 14-12:
The `hosts`
`.equiv` file
lists trusted
hosts.

```
vogon
grapeleaf
spiderman
reddwarf
```

Be very careful with this file. Any remote computer listed here is a trusted host, and all of its users can log in to your computer without knowing a password.

Some operating systems implement trust using other methods besides a trusted hosts file. Microsoft Windows NT Server, for example, doesn't use the `hosts.equiv` file. Instead, you set up trust relationships when you set up security policies for your computer. Trust relationships are between NT domains (groups of computers) as opposed to individual hosts. See Figure 14-13.

The Trusted Hosts Print File

On UNIX you can use the `/etc/hosts.lpd` file to list the remote hosts that can print on the printer attached to your computer. The simplest `hosts.lpd` file possible contains just one asterisk (*) character, which means that any host on the network can share your printer. If you don't have a `hosts.lpd` file, it's the same as having the file with an asterisk in it. So, if you aren't prepared to be supergenerous with your printer, you'd better create one of these `hosts.lpd` files.

Speaking of generosity, how generous can you afford to be with your printer? If you share your printer with all of the hosts on your network, will the volume of remote print jobs mean that you always have to wait before you can print your own stuff? Will this same print job traffic clog up the network connection media (the cables)? You should ask yourself these questions before editing your `hosts.lpd` file.

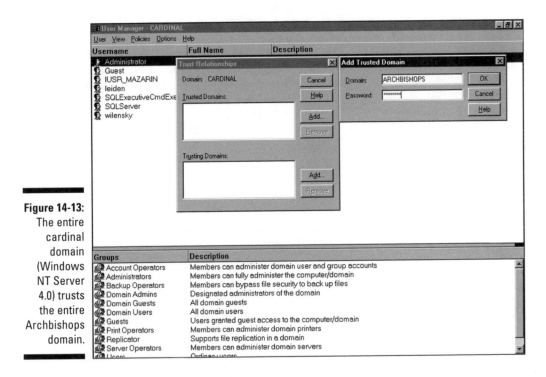

Figure 14-13:
The entire cardinal domain (Windows NT Server 4.0) trusts the entire Archbishops domain.

Freddie's Nightmare: Your Personal Trust File

You should be aware of a special (and dangerous) file that exists on a "per user" basis. This means that you and all the other users on a computer can create a personal trust file in your home directory. In UNIX environments, this file is named .rhosts, pronounced "dot are hosts." And yes, the dot is part of the filename.

The .rhosts file holds two pieces of information: the host name and the account name. Here are the contents of our niece Sarah's .rhosts file in her home directory on computer elmst. The file allows her sister, Emily (from computer mainst), to have the run of computer elmst without a password. If you live on Elm Street or elsewhere in cyberspace, don't let personal trust become a nightmare. Please be careful about letting evil players like Freddie into your .rhosts file.

```
#Local host    user       comment
mainst         emily      # Let in Emily from mainst
```

Most network administrators, like Freddie, consider .rhosts files to be potential security problems. These files list *trusted remote users* — those who are permitted to log in to your local account without entering a password. Logging in without a password allows users to copy any files from your directories with rcp and to remotely execute any command on your computer with rsh.

This is scary. Why would I ever want .rhosts?

If you do a lot of work on various hosts, it's quite convenient to rlogin as yourself on all the computers on which you have accounts. Your account may be Marshall on one computer, Wilensky on another, and Mwil on a third — with three different passwords. If all of these computers have a .rhosts file that lets you in from anywhere, you can skip remembering all those passwords.

Surprise! The curse of the network administrator lives

If Emily has been wandering all over computer elmst because Sarah lets her, Emily may get a big surprise one day when she tries to log in remotely and permission is denied. Network administrators frequently hunt down and kill these .rhosts files. After Sarah's .rhosts file is gone, Emily needs to know a valid password in order to log in.

The Networks File

Not only do you need a local hosts file (or DNS) to list the individual hosts with which you plan to communicate, along with their IP addresses, you also need a *networks file* to hold the network numbers and names with which you plan to communicate. Listing the network names lets you refer to all of the hosts on the same network (or subnet) as one group. The networks file supplied with the operating system or TCP/IP product rarely needs editing.

Figure 14-14 shows a networks file. On UNIX, the network file is /etc/ networks. The file can be at different locations, depending on the operating system. For example, Microsoft Windows NT Server stores the file in \winnt\system32\drivers\etc\networks, rather than in the traditional UNIX location.

Figure 14-14:
The networks file lists the network name and its address.

```
#
# Sun customer networks
# This file is never consulted when the NIS are running
#
loopback        127
sun-ether       192.9.200    sunether ethernet localnet
sun-oldether    125          sunoldether
#
# Internet networks
#
arpanet         10           arpa
ucb-ether       46           ucbether
```

When you create your networks file, be sure to list only the network section and not the host piece of the numeric IP address. If you're not sure about this, read about IP addresses in Chapter 13. In the file illustrated in Figure 14-14, some of the network addresses only have one piece, such as arpanet 10. The ending 0s are assumed. You can leave them out for convenience or you can list them explicitly, as in 10.0.0.

The Internet Daemon Configuration File

What a mouthful! The file named /etc/inetd.conf on UNIX systems lists all of the things you want the internet daemon, inetd (see the "Daemons — are we in hell again?" sidebar), to do. The name of this file is pronounced "eye net dee dot conf." Now try it three times fast.

The inetd.conf file shown in Figure 14-15 is nearly identical to the original copy supplied with the UNIX operating system. The TFTP lines were modified slightly and the bootp line was added to allow down-line loading of X Window terminals.

You don't have this file on Windows 95, Windows 98, or Windows NT. The configuration registry maintains this information for you.

Daemons — are we in hell again?

Daemons, in general, are programs that provide some sort of services — TCP/IP daemons are the servers for many of the TCP/IP client/server functions. The internet daemon program, inetd, is the heart and soul of TCP/IP services. (By the way, most daemons' names end in d.) Inetd supervises the other TCP/IP daemons. The internet daemon configuration file, inetd.conf, tells inetd what other servers it is responsible for.

```
# @(#)inetd.conf 1.24 92/04/14 SMI ──── This file comes with TCP/IP. Usually you don't
#                                          touch it except for good reasons.
# Configuration file for inetd(8).  See inetd.conf(5).
#
# To re-configure the running inetd process, edit this file, then
# send the inetd process a SIGHUP.
#
#
# Internet services syntax:
#  <service_name> <socket_type> <proto> <flags> <user> <server_pathname> <args>
#
# Ftp and telnet are standard Internet services.
#
ftp    stream   tcp   nowait   root   /usr/etc/in.ftpd    in.ftpd
telnet  stream   tcp   nowait   root   /usr/etc/in.telnetd   in.telnetd
#
# Tnamed serves the obolete IEN-116 name server protocol.
#
name  dgram   udp   wait   root   /usr/etc/in.tnamed   in.tnamed
#
# Shell, login, exec, comsat and talk are BSD protocols.
#
shell   stream   tcp   nowait   root   /usr/etc/in.rshd    in.rshd
login   stream   tcp   nowait   root   /usr/etc/in.rlogind   in.rlogind
exec    stream   tcp   nowait   root   /usr/etc/in.rexecd   in.rexecd
comsat  dgram   udp   wait   root   /usr/etc/in.comsat   in.comsat
talk   dgram   udp   wait   root   /usr/etc/in.talkd   in.talkd
#
# Run as user "uucp" if you don't want uucpd's wtmp entries.
#
uucp   stream   tcp   nowait   root   /usr/etc/in.uucpd   in.uucpd
#
# Tftp service is provided primarily for booting.  Most sites run this
# only on machines acting as "boot servers."
#
#####
#####   Enabled specifically for NCD X-terminals.
#####     Marshall Wilensky   Fri Feb  4 17:50:55 EST 1994
#tftp   dgram   udp   wait   root   /usr/etc/in.tftpd   in.tftpd -s /tftpboot
tftp   dgram   udp wait root /usr/etc/in.tftpd   in.tftpd -s /usr1/ncd-install/tftpboot
bootps  dgram   udp   wait   root   /etc/bootpd    bootpd
#
# Finger, systat and netstat give out user information which may be
# valuable to potential "system crackers." Many sites choose to disable
# some or all of these services to improve security.
#
finger   stream   tcp   nowait   nobody   /usr/etc/in.fingerd   in.fingerd
#systat   stream   tcp   nowait   root   /usr/bin/ps   ps -auwwx
```

> This file comes with TCP/IP. Usually you don't touch it except for good reasons.

> Network administrator updated this entry. Top of the directory tree for downloading files.

> Security note: This is the original entry.

> Security note: Here's where you can disable finger. Remove this entry or use # to make it a comment.

> A daemon for performance monitoring

Figure 14-15: The inetd configuration file lists TCP/IP services directed by the internet daemon.

(continued)

(continued)

```
#netstat    stream   tcp   nowait   root   /usr/ucb/netstat   netstat -f inet
#
# Time service is used for clock syncronization.
#
time    stream   tcp   nowait   root   internal
time    dgram   udp   wait   root   internal
#
# Echo, discard, daytime, and chargen are used primarily for testing.
#
echo    stream   tcp   nowait   root   internal
echo    dgram   udp   wait   root   internal
discard   stream   tcp   nowait   root   internal
discard   dgram   udp   wait   root   internal
daytime   stream   tcp   nowait   root   internal
daytime   dgram   udp   wait   root   internal
chargen   stream   tcp   nowait   root   internal
chargen   dgram   udp   wait   root   internal
#
#
# RPC services syntax: ———— Programmer's note: Don't forget to read Chapter 19.
# <rpc_prog>/<vers> <socket_type> rpc/<proto> <flags> <user> <pathname> <args>
#
# The mount server is usually started in /etc/rc.local only on machines that
# are NFS servers.  It can be run by inetd as well.
#
#mountd/1   dgram   rpc/udp   wait root /usr/etc/rpc.mountd   rpc.mountd
#
# The rexd server provides only minimal authentication and is often not run
# by sites concerned about security.
#
#rexd/1     stream   rpc/tcp   wait root /usr/etc/rpc.rexd   rpc.rexd
#
# Ypupdated is run by sites that support NIS updating.
#
#ypupdated/1   stream   rpc/tcp   wait root /usr/etc/rpc.ypupdated rpc.ypupdated
#
# Rquotad serves UFS disk quotas to NFS clients.
#
rquotad/1   dgram   rpc/udp   wait root /usr/etc/rpc.rquotad   rpc.rquotad
#
# Rstatd is used by programs such as perfmeter.
#
rstatd/2-4   dgram   rpc/udp   wait root /usr/etc/rpc.rstatd   rpc.rstatd
#
# The rusers service gives out user information.  Sites concerned
# with security may choose to disable it.
#
rusersd/1-2   dgram   rpc/udp   wait root /usr/etc/rpc.rusersd   rpc.rusersd
```

```
#
# The spray server is used primarily for testing.
#
sprayd/1   dgram   rpc/udp   wait root /usr/etc/rpc.sprayd   rpc.sprayd
#
# The rwall server lets anyone on the network bother everyone on your machine.
#
walld/1      dgram   rpc/udp   wait root /usr/etc/rpc.rwalld   rpc.rwalld
#
#
# TLI services syntax [not yet implemented]:
# <service_name> tli <proto> <flags> <user> <server_pathname> <args>
#
#
# TCPMUX services syntax [not yet implemented]:
# tcpmux/<service_name> stream tcp <flags> <user> <server_pathname> <args>
#
#
# rpc.cmsd is a data base daemon which manages calendar data backed
# by files in /usr/spool/calendar
100068/2-3   dgram   rpc/udp wait root /usr/etc/rpc.cmsd   rpc.cmsd
# Sun ToolTalk Database Server
100083/1    stream  rpc/tcp wait root /usr/etc/rpc.ttdbserverd rpc.ttdbserverd
```

For each service, the `inetd.conf` file contains a line with the following fields:

- **Service name:** The service must also have a corresponding entry in the `/etc/services` file.

- **Socket type:** An interprocess communication mechanism that's a bit too techie for this chapter. This field usually specifies `stream` if the service uses TCP, and `dgm` or `dgram` for datagram if the service uses the UDP protocol. You may also see `raw` in this column.

- **Protocol:** The protocol used by the service.

- **Flags:** Another technoid. Flags are set to either `wait` or `nowait` to specify whether inetd can accept another connection without waiting for the current server to finish.

- **User:** This field holds the account name that's the owner of the service. On UNIX systems, it's usually the username of the privileged user, `root`.

- **Server path:** This is the directory and filename for the daemon program.

- **Arguments (args):** The name of the daemon or the command that runs a tool and any other command arguments.

The Protocols File

The protocols file lists the TCP/IP protocols. You may need to update this file if you add protocols to your TCP/IP configuration.

Figure 14-16 shows an example of a UNIX protocols file, /etc/protocols. Look at Figure 14-17 for a similar example from a Microsoft Windows NT Server protocol file. On Microsoft Windows NT, the file is named protocol, with no *s* at the end.

Figure 14-16:
On UNIX, the /etc/ protocols file lists TCP/ IP protocols used on the network.

```
# @(#)protocols 1.9 90/01/03 SMI
#
# Internet (IP) protocols
# This file is never consulted when the NIS are running
#
IP        0      IP    # internet protocol, pseudo protocol number
icmp      1      ICMP  # internet control message protocol
igmp      2      IGMP  # internet group multicast protocol
ggp       3      GGP   # gateway-gateway protocol
tcp       6      TCP   # transmission control protocol
pup       12     PUP   # PARC universal packet protocol
udp       17     UDP   # user datagram protocol
```

Figure 14-17:
On Microsoft Windows NT Server, the protocol file is located in /winnt/ system32/ drivers/ etc/ protocols.

```
# Copyright (c) 1993-1994 Microsoft Corp.
#
# This file contains the Internet protocols as defined by RFC 1060
# (Assigned Numbers).
#
# Format:
#
# <protocol name>  <assigned number>  [aliases...]  [#<comment>]

ip        0      IP       # Internet protocol
icmp      1      ICMP     # Internet control message protocol
ggp       3      GGP      # Gateway-gateway protocol
tcp       6      TCP      # Transmission control protocol
egp       8      EGP      # Exterior gateway protocol
pup       12     PUP      # PARC universal packet protocol
udp       17     UDP      # User datagram protocol
hmp       20     HMP      # Host monitoring protocol
xns-idp   22     XNS-IDP  # Xerox NS IDP
rdp       27     RDP      # "reliable datagram" protocol
rvd       66     RVD      # MIT remote virtual disk
```

Any port in a network

With so many services, how does an application know which one it should use? Well, certainly not by name — that would be too easy, even though many applications, services, and protocols are named the same. Take FTP, for example, which is the name of an application, a service, and a protocol.

Applications communicate with services via an object called a *port id number.* ID numbers 1 through 255 are reserved for the most commonly used services, such as telnet and FTP.

Port numbers can also be created, as needed. If you write your own TCP/IP application and service, you simply use a port number greater than 255.

When an application says to TCP/IP, "Here I am, ready to work," TCP/IP doesn't really care about the application's name. Instead, TCP/IP sees only the numbers: the Internet address of the host that provides the service and the port number through which the application intends to communicate.

The Services File

The /etc/services file lists the network services being used on your computer. You don't usually have to maintain this file yourself. TCP/IP does it automatically when you enable or disable new services.

Each line in the file has the following columns:

- ✔ Service name
- ✔ Port number
- ✔ Protocol (separated from the port number by a /)
- ✔ Aliases (other, optional names for the service)

Figure 14-18 is a services file from a UNIX system, and Figure 14-19 is a services file from a Microsoft Windows NT Server system. Pop quiz: Can you see the difference? Answer: It's a trick question. Although the computers in the examples run specific services to support their users (Ingres on the UNIX system, for example), and although the file is located in different directories on the two operating systems, the basic file format is the same.

```
# @(#)services 1.16 90/01/03 SMI
#
# Network services, Internet style
# This file is never consulted when the NIS are running
#
tcpmux       1/tcp                         # rfc-1078
echo         7/tcp
echo         7/udp
discard      9/tcp          sink null
discard      9/udp          sink null
systat       11/tcp         users
daytime      13/tcp
daytime      13/udp
netstat      15/tcp
chargen      19/tcp         ttytst source
chargen      19/udp         ttytst source
ftp-data     20/tcp
ftp          21/tcp
telnet       23/tcp
smtp         25/tcp         mail
time         37/tcp         timserver
time         37/udp         timserver
name         42/udp         nameserver
whois        43/tcp         nicname       # usually to sri-nic
domain       53/udp
domain       53/tcp
hostnames    101/tcp        hostname      # usually to sri-nic
sunrpc       111/udp
sunrpc       111/tcp
#
# Host specific functions
#
tftp         69/udp
rje          77/tcp
finger       79/tcp
link         87/tcp         ttylink
supdup       95/tcp
iso-tsap     102/tcp
x400         103/tcp                       # ISO Mail
x400-snd     104/tcp
csnet-ns     105/tcp
pop-2        109/tcp                       # Post Office
uucp-path    117/tcp
nntp         119/tcp        usenet        # Network News Transfer
ntp          123/tcp                       # Network Time Protocol
NeWS         144/tcp        news          # Window System
#
# UNIX specific services
#
# these are NOT officially assigned
```

Figure 14-18:
A UNIX
services file,
/etc/
services.

```
#
exec          512/tcp
login         513/tcp
shell         514/tcp      cmd              # no passwords used
printer       515/tcp      spooler          # line printer spooler
courier       530/tcp      rpc              # experimental
uucp          540/tcp      uucpd            # uucp daemon
biff          512/udp      comsat
who           513/udp      whod
syslog        514/udp
talk          517/udp
route         520/udp      router routed
new-rwho      550/udp      new-who          # experimental
rmonitor      560/udp      rmonitord        # experimental
monitor       561/udp                       # experimental
pcserver      600/tcp                       # ECD Integrated PC board srvr
ingreslock    1524/tcp
```

You may notice some interesting security services, including Kerberos, in Figure 14-19. Check out Chapter 18 to see what that dog of a service is all about. Speaking of dogs, look for a UNIX service named biff. According to UNIX mythology, this service is named after a dog who barked at the letter carrier. Biff is, of course, the mail notification service (chuckle).

Figure 14-19:
A Microsoft
Windows NT
Server
services file,
\winnt\
system32\
drivers\
etc\services.

```
#
# This file contains port numbers for well-known services as defined by
# RFC 1060 (Assigned Numbers).
#
# Format:
#
# <service name>  <port number>/<protocol>  [aliases...]   [#<comment>]
#

echo          7/tcp
echo          7/udp
discard       9/tcp        sink null
discard       9/udp        sink null
systat        11/tcp
systat        11/tcp       users
daytime       13/tcp
daytime       13/udp
netstat       15/tcp
qotd          17/tcp       quote
```

(continued)

(continued)

```
qotd            17/udp      quote
chargen         19/tcp      ttytst source
chargen         19/udp      ttytst source
ftp-data        20/tcp
ftp             21/tcp
telnet          23/tcp
smtp            25/tcp      mail
time            37/tcp      timserver
time            37/udp      timserver
rlp             39/udp      resource        # resource location
name            42/tcp      nameserver
name            42/udp      nameserver
whois           43/tcp      nicname         # usually to sri-nic
domain          53/tcp      nameserver      # name-domain server
domain          53/udp      nameserver
nameserver      53/tcp      domain          # name-domain server
nameserver      53/udp      domain
mtp             57/tcp                      # deprecated
bootp           67/udp                      # boot program server
tftp            69/udp
rje             77/tcp      netrjs
finger          79/tcp
link            87/tcp      ttylink
supdup          95/tcp
hostnames       101/tcp     hostname        # usually from sri-nic
iso-tsap        102/tcp
dictionary      103/tcp     webster
x400            103/tcp                     # ISO Mail
x400-snd        104/tcp
csnet-ns        105/tcp
pop             109/tcp     postoffice
pop2            109/tcp                     # Post Office
pop3            110/tcp     postoffice
portmap         111/tcp
portmap         111/udp
sunrpc          111/tcp
sunrpc          111/udp
auth            113/tcp     authentication
sftp            115/tcp
path            117/tcp
uucp-path       117/tcp
nntp            119/tcp     usenet          # Network News Transfer
ntp             123/udp     ntpd ntp        # network time protocol (exp)
nbname          137/udp
nbdatagram      138/udp
nbsession       139/tcp
NeWS            144/tcp     news
sgmp            153/udp     sgmp
```

```
tcprepo          158/tcp    repository     # PCMAIL
snmp             161/udp    snmp
snmp-trap        162/udp    snmp
print-srv        170/tcp                   # network PostScript
vmnet            175/tcp
load             315/udp
vmnet0           400/tcp
sytek            500/udp
biff             512/udp    comsat
exec             512/tcp
login            513/tcp
who              513/udp    whod
shell            514/tcp    cmd            # no passwords used
syslog           514/udp
printer          515/tcp    spooler        # line printer spooler
talk             517/udp
ntalk            518/udp
efs              520/tcp                   # for LucasFilm
route            520/udp    router routed
timed            525/udp    timeserver
tempo            526/tcp    newdate
courier          530/tcp    rpc
conference       531/tcp    chat
rvd-control      531/udp    MIT disk
netnews          532/tcp    readnews
netwall          533/udp                   # -for emergency broadcasts
uucp             540/tcp    uucpd          # uucp daemon
klogin           543/tcp                   # Kerberos authenticated rlogin
kshell           544/tcp    cmd            # and remote shell
new-rwho         550/udp    new-who        # experimental
remotefs         556/tcp    rfs_server rfs# Brunhoff remote filesystem
rmonitor         560/udp    rmonitord      # experimental
monitor          561/udp                   # experimental
garcon           600/tcp
maitrd           601/tcp
busboy           602/tcp
acctmaster       700/udp
acctslave        701/udp
acct             702/udp
acctlogin        703/udp
acctprinter      704/udp
elcsd            704/udp                   # errlog
acctinfo         705/udp
acctslave2       706/udp
acctdisk         707/udp
kerberos         750/tcp    kdc            # Kerberos authentication-tcp
kerberos         750/udp    kdc            # Kerberos authentication-udp
kerberos_master  751/tcp                   # Kerberos authentication
```

(continued)

(continued)

```
kerberos_master    751/udp                # Kerberos authentication
passwd_server      752/udp                # Kerberos passwd server
userreg_server     753/udp                # Kerberos userreg server
krb_prop           754/tcp                # Kerberos slave propagation
erlogin            888/tcp                # Login and environment passing
kpop               1109/tcp               # Pop with Kerberos
phone              1167/udp
ingreslock         1524/tcp
maze               1666/udp
nfs                2049/udp               # sun nfs
knetd              2053/tcp               # Kerberos de-multiplexor
eklogin            2105/tcp               # Kerberos encrypted rlogin
rmt                5555/tcp    rmtd
mtb                5556/tcp    mtbd       # mtb backup
man                9535/tcp               # remote man server
w                  9536/tcp
mantst             9537/tcp               # remote man server, testing
bnews              10000/tcp
rscs0              10000/udp
queue              10001/tcp
rscs1              10001/udp
poker              10002/tcp
rscs2              10002/udp
gateway            10003/tcp
rscs3              10003/udp
remp               10004/tcp
rscs4              10004/udp
rscs5              10005/udp
rscs6              10006/udp
rscs7              10007/udp
rscs8              10008/udp
rscs9              10009/udp
rscsa              10010/udp
rscsb              10011/udp
qmaster            10012/tcp
qmaster            10012/udp
```

Test yourself by trying to recognize some familiar services in these examples. Can you find telnet and SMTP?

On Microsoft Windows NT, you can open the Control Panel and use the Services applet to get information about services, such as whether they're running and whether they start automatically. Figure 14-20 shows the Control Panel running the Services applet. Do you recognize any TCP/IP services?

Dealing with the Devil

Earlier in this chapter, we tell you that inetd is the father of all daemons. The following sections give you descriptions of a few other TCP/IP daemons that you should know about.

routed (here we go again)

The routed daemon manages routing tables (explained in Chapter 18). No, don't say "row-ted" or even "roo-ted." It's either "rowt dee" or "root dee." The routed daemon uses RIP, the Routing Information Protocol (also explained in Chapter 18).

named

The named daemon is pronounced "name dee" (are you getting the hang of it yet?). This handy daemon is the one that runs on your name server to manage DNS and to do the host name/IP address resolution covered in Chapter 11.

More handy-dandy daemons

There are lots more daemons. All have names that ends with d and are pronounced by saying the name of the service followed by "dee." Some of the more famous daemons are listed in Table 14-2 along with the services that they provide. Figure 14-21 shows some popular daemons running on a UNIX system.

Table 14-2	Popular Services and Their Daemons
Service	*Daemon*
finger	fingerd
ftp	ftpd
telnet	telnetd
Service	*Daemon*
rlogin	rlogind
rsh	rshd
rexec	rexecd
talk	talkd
NFS client	nfsiod
NFS server	nfsd

Figure 14-21:
This
computer
has some of
our favorite
daemons
running.

```
$ ps auwx
USER        PID %CPU %MEM  VSZ  RSS TT  STAT STARTED  TIME COMMAND

root         65  0.0  0.0 1160  992 ??  Ss   Thu12PM    1:31.58 named
root         68  0.0  0.0   52  108 ??  Ss   Thu12PM    0:08.83 rwhod
root         70  0.0  0.0   60  108 ??  Is   Thu12PM 5:13.29 nfsiod 4
root         77  0.0  0.0   56   16 ??  I    Thu12PM    1:47.96 nfsiod 4
root         78  0.0  0.0   56   16 ??  I    Thu12PM    0:48.53 nfsiod 4
root         79  0.0  0.0   56   16 ??  I    Thu12PM    0:20.84 nfsiod 4
root         80  0.0  0.0  444  132 ??  Ss   Thu12PM 0:17.39 inetd
root      22947  0.0  0.0   96   72 ??  I    10:28PM    0:00.48 rlogind
root      15491  0.0  0.0  120  172 ??  I    1:00PM     0:00.35 telnetd
root      20008  0.0  0.0  224  556 ??  S    3:03PM     0:00.40 ftpd
root      20033  0.0  0.0   28  232 ??  S    3:03PM     0:00.07 ntalkd
```

If you have a problem using one of the services in Table 14-2, a quick troubleshooting technique is to check and see whether the daemon is started. On Windows NT, use the Services applet to see if it's running. On UNIX you can do this with ps, one of the tools covered in Chapter 16. In the ps output, check the last column of each entry and look for the name of the daemon (ending in d). If you don't see the daemon required for the service, that's the problem. To use the service, you need to get the daemon started in whatever way your operating system allows. You may simply have to click on an icon, or you may have to type in a command.

Any port in a storm?

In the figure below, Microsoft lists the port for Kerberos, a security function (read more about it in Chapter 19), as 750. Here is a services file from FTP Software's Secure Client TCP/IP version 6 stack. Read the comments about the use of port 750.

```
#  Copyright (C) 1993-1996 by FTP Software, Inc.  All rights reserved.
#
#  This file contains port numbers for well-known services
#
#  Format:
#
#  <service name>   <port number>/<protocol>  [aliases...]   [#<comment>]
ftp              21/tcp        # File Transfer [Control]
telnet           23/tcp        # Telnet
smtp             25/udp        mail            # Simple Mail Transfer
domain           53/tcp        # Domain Name Server
tftp             69/udp        # Trivial File Transfer
gopher           70/tcp        # Gopher
finger           79/tcp        whois                    # Finger
www              80/tcp        # World Wide Web HTTP
#
#  Note, the official port for kerberos is 88, however, a large portion
#    of the installed base of Kerberos V4 is using port 750.  The PC/TCP
#    V4 KINIT.EXE will use port 750 by default.  To override this default,
#    uncomment the following lines for kerberos:
#
#  kerberos         88/tcp        # Kerberos
#  kerberos         88/udp        # Kerberos
pop3             110/tcp       # Post Office Protocol - Version 3
pop3             110/udp       # Post Office Protocol - Version 3
nntp             119/tcp       # Network News Transfer Protocol
snmp             161/tcp       # SNMP
biff             512/udp       # notify user of mail delivery
router           520/udp       route routed   # local routing process
```

Instructions for Kerberos

Chapter 15

IPv6 — IP on Steroids

*I*f you're interested in the new IPv6 protocols and addresses, this chapter is for you. Take a deep breath, count to ten, and know that IPv6 can make your life a lot easier. But first, here are the reasons why Internet sites can benefit from implementing IPv6:

 ✔ The Internet is in danger of running out of network numbers within the next decade.

 ✔ Large, cumbersome routing tables of addresses slow down the Internet.

 ✔ The Internet may possibly run out of addresses because it connects over 200 million computers and other devices. (The exact number isn't nearly as important as the fact that the number of computers and devices is growing by leaps and bounds.)

IPv4's 32-bit numbering already provides for 4 billion addresses. How many networks? The Internet probably won't run out before 2010. (That's a wild guess. If we could predict the future, do you think we would be authors?)

If you're a network manager, don't wait until December 31, 2009. Start planning your migration path to IPv6 now! In the meantime, IPv4 and IPv6 can coexist.

Some analysts believe that everyone in the world should be connected to the Internet. Predictions estimate the world population to exceed 10 billion by 2020. Does that mean 10 billion computers on the Internet? Not really, because people have more than one computer. Think about it. Do you think you have only one computer? How about:

✔ Your car

✔ Your sewing machine

✔ Your home's alarm system

✔ Your pacemaker

✔ Your video game

Now how many computers do you have? But, you say, these computers aren't on the Internet. Not yet, anyway. Think of the possibilities. You're driving along when your car's computer detects a failing fuel pump. It transmits a message via TCP/IP to your service station to have a replacement ready, uses the Global Positioning System to determine the location of the nearest towing service, and calls for a tow truck. This isn't a fantasy — a concept car like this already exists.

Chapter 13 urges you to call your computer a "host," but in this chapter, we change the name of computers again. We're not trying to drive you crazy, we promise! In the IPv6 world, a computer is now called a *node*. Actually, we're not talking just about computers. Any device, such as a router, on an IPv6 network is called a node.

If It Ain't Broke, Don't Fix It — Well, Improve It Just a Little

IPv6 retains most of IPv4's characteristics — especially for the stuff that works. For example, fully qualified domain names (FQDN) stay the same. Thank goodness!

Some things do change, though. Every piece of TCP/IP is affected by a new, longer address format. While the name resolution services (local hosts file, NIS, WINS, and DNS) still exist, there should be less need for them in the future thanks to autodiscovery, autoconfiguration, and autoregistration (more about these in this chapter).

Some other things can go away (such as supernet masks and ARP), while still other things could simply stand some improvements (such as switching to a different network number). In this chapter, we highlight the key topics.

If you need a refresher course on IPv4 addressing, see Chapter 13.

Wow! 8 Sections in an IPv6 Address?

A 32-bit IPv4 address provides 4 billion addresses. Every IPv6 address is 128 bits long, or four times longer than an IPv4 address. That doesn't mean that there are only four times as many address; it means there are an ENORMOUSLY HUGE number of IPv6 addresses because we're talking about exponential growth! The number is so big we broke three calculators trying to figure it out.

An IPv6 128-bit address is taken as 8 groups of 16 bit numbers, separated by colons. Each number is written as 4 hexadecimal (hex) digits. This means that IPv6 addresses range from

```
0000:0000:0000:0000:0000:0000:0000:0000
```

to

```
FFFF:FFFF:FFFF:FFFF:FFFF:FFFF:FFFF:FFFF
```

Here's a sample IPv6 address EFDC:BA62:7654:3201:EFDC:BA72:7654:3210. (Hey, these are even more agonizing than v4 addresses.) Aren't you glad that fully qualified domain names are still valid?

Why use hexadecimal?

Hexadecimal is very compact inside a computer, saving memory and disk space. It's also easier to write large numbers in hex than it is in decimal.

The Microsoft Windows 95 calculator can convert decimal to hex and vice versa. The calculator is in the Accessories folder in the Start menu.

There's good news and there's bad news

The good news is that if you're what the computer industry calls an end user, you don't really need to worry about this. You still send e-mail to Candace by typing her address, `leiden@tiac.net`.

The bad news is that if you're a system manager or network administrator, you may have to type these awkward addresses into files to set up the network for the lucky end users.

Reading hexadecimal, or since when is F a number?

Everyone knows that digits are 0 through 9. That's true for decimal (or base 10) numbers, but other numbering bases also use letters. In hexadecimal (also called hex and base 16), the allowable digits are 0 through 9 plus A through F. Zero through nine are the same as good old decimal, but then there's

- A = decimal 10
- B = decimal 11
- C = decimal 12
- And so on

So the decimal value 15 can also be written as hex F.

Fact of life: People love decimal. Computers love hex.

Here's where we get advanced: hex 10 = decimal 16. Yikes! We're talking place value here. Take a look at a decimal example. Remember the 1s, 10s, and 100s columns.

```
100s 10s 1s
  1   3  0    = one 100s plus three 10s plus zero 1s = 130
```

In hex, the columns are 1s, 16s, 256s, 4096s, and so on. Try the hex number 101. What number is it in decimal?

```
256s 16s 1s
  1   0  1    = one 256s plus zero 16s plus one 1s
             = 256 plus 1
             = 257
```

Here's another hex number to test yourself, AC4.

```
256s 16s 1s
  A   C  4    = A 256s plus C 16s plus four 1s
             = ten 256s plus twelve 16s plus four 1s
             = 2,560 plus 192 plus 4
             = 2,756
```

For fun, try FFF. That's

```
256s 16s 1s
  F   F  F    = F 256s plus F 16s plus F 1s
             = fifteen 256s + fifteen 16s + fifteen 1s = ??
```

Now is a good time to get our your calculator and figure it out. Don't call us if it breaks, though.

Shorthand For Non-Stenographers

We know it seems like a lot of work to read and write these addresses. Thank goodness IPv6 has some shortcuts to make these addresses easier to handle.

The leading zero (0000) shortcut

When you write an IPv6 address you can omit any leading zeros — and there may be lots of them — in each group of 4 hex digits. For example, you can write

```
1060:0000:0000:0000:0006:0600:200C:326B
```

as

```
1060:0:0:0:6:600:200C:326B
```

The double colon () shortcut

Then there's the double-colon (::) shortcut. In an address, you can replace one sequence of single zeros and colons with a double colon. You can only use the double-colon shortcut once in an address, though. For example, you can write

```
1060:0:0:0:6:600:200C:326B
```

as

```
1060::6:600:200C:326B
```

To re-expand a double-colon address, you have to figure out how many colons are missing and which ones. You may want to draw an address template with *s instead of any hex digits and with all seven colons in place, like this:

```
****:****:****:****:****:****:****:****
```

Then look at the address you need to expand and find the :: — everything to the left of it must start at the beginning of the address. Line up any colons you can. Everything to the right of the :: must end at the end of the address. Again, line up any colons you can. Insert spaces or leading zeros to help yourself. Now you can tell which colons are missing, and how many!

For example, to re-expand `1060::6:600:200C:326B`, the `1060` (before the `::`) must start at the beginning of the address, and the `6:600:200C:326B` (after the `::`) must come at the end, like this:

```
****:  ****:  ****:  ****:  ****:  ****:  ****:  ****
1060:     :      :      :     6:   600:  200C:  326B
```

This means that `0:0:0` is what's missing. Don't worry about the leading zeros before the `6` and `600`. They're optional.

Be careful. Sometimes — as in `::8267:2805` or `FEC0:1:A0::` — the double-colon appears at the start or end of the address.

The IPv4 coexistence shortcut

IPv4 addresses are a subset of the IPv6 address space. You can convert an IPv4 address into an IPv6 address by inserting zeros at the beginning. All of IPv4 fits in

```
0000:0000:0000:0000:0000:0000:****:****
```

which can also be written as

```
::****:****
```

For example, the IPv4 address `130.103.40.5` is also the IPv6 address

```
0000:0000:0000:0000:0000:0000:8267:2805
```

or

```
::8267:2805
```

There's also a hybrid notation called *IPv4 mapped addresses* in which you can still use dotted decimal notation. It looks like this:

```
0000:0000:0000:0000:0000:0000:0000:130.103.40.5
```

or this:

```
::130.103.40.5
```

Thanks to mapped addresses, you can reduce the risk of typos caused by broken calculators.

What about Subnet and Supernet Masks?

IPv6 addresses maintain the notion of a network part and a host part, but it's much harder to say where the division is. Subnet masks, discussed thoroughly in Chapter 13, aren't completely eliminated in IPv6, but they're much less visible. The systems know what to do and that's what matters. Don't worry about it. Supernet masks are completely obsolete. We're absolutely positive that it will be years before anyone will need to link together multiple chunks of IPv6 address space. (At least we hope so.)

In fact, subnets, masks, and supernets have been designed to work around the fact that Class A, B, and C networks are different sizes. This means that these networks are typically either too large or too small.

Several proposals are being debated regarding how to allocate chunks of IPv6 addresses. Right now, the winner is *provider-based distribution,* in which Internet service providers get whole chunks to assign to their customers. The distribution is designed to facilitate the routing of packets. Provider-based distribution of addresses consumes only one-eighth of the total IPv6 address space, so plenty of room is left for experiments with other allocations.

Special IPv6 Addresses

IPv6 reserves certain addresses for special purposes. These special addresses include the unspecified address, the loopback address, site-local addresses, link-local addresses, and multicast and unicast addresses.

The unspecified address

The *unspecified address* is 0:0:0:0:0:0:0:0 (or just ::). It can be used by a system that needs to send a packet for broadcasting or DHCP client requests but hasn't yet received an address. It can't be used as a destination address.

The loopback address

The *loopback address* is 0:0:0:0:0:0:0:1 (or just ::1). It lets a system send a message to itself for testing.

Site-local addresses

Site-local addresses begin with `FEC0:` — they're designed for use within an organization's intranet and can't be routed on the Internet.

Link-local addresses

Link-local addresses begin with `FE80:` — they're designed for use on a single network segment and aren't forwarded by any router. Link-local addresses permit communication with only those neighboring systems directly connected to the same part of the network (link). They allow a system to learn about its neighbors and their services without having a router get involved. (Feeling brave? Read all about routers in Chapter 18.) This kind of address saves time and has a side security benefit. A system can automatically generate a IPv6 address for itself from the link-local address prefix (FE80), the double-colon shortcut (`::`), and the 48-bit hardware address from its Network Interface Card (NIC). The NIC is the network controller hardware for your computer. The NIC may be inside your computer or you may have an external NIC. For example, your link-local address may be `FE80::0800:2BBE:1124`. You can find out more about hardware addresses in Chapter 16.

Multicast addresses

Multicast addresses begin with `FF**:` — while a unicast address identifies one NIC, a multicast address identifies a group of NICs for a group of computers. If a packet is sent to a multicast address, all the members in the group receive that packet.

Anycast addresses

Anycast addresses also identify a group of NICs. The difference between anycast and multicast is that a packet sent to an anycast address goes only to the nearest member of the group. Anycast addressing is new in IPv6 and is designed to help you find the servers closest to you. For example, you can use anycasting to find the closest DHCP server.

IPv6 — And the Using Is Easy

Suppose you receive a new computer that you need to connect to your organization's IP network or you take your laptop computer to the branch office and want to connect to the intranet. How does your computer get an

IP address? In the IPv4 environment, you have to contact your network administrator. He or she configures your laptop with an IP address and updates the appropriate network management files (see Chapter 14). In two or three days (assuming the network administrator isn't on holiday and not swamped with requests), your IP address is ready, and you can get on to the network and work. If your site uses DHCP, you may be able to plug your laptop into your intranet and request an address from the DHCP server.

How does your computer get an IPv6 address? The answer is autodiscovery, autoconfiguration, and autoregistration. Together they provide easier management of a dynamic network with no manual intervention. The next sections are pretty technical and more than a little boring, but we spent a lot of time on them, so humor us. Give them a try.

IP is your dinner plate and IPv6 is the platter. You can fill up with lots more tasty network dishes if you have the platter.

Checking out the network buffet with autodiscovery

Autodiscovery, also called Neighbor Discovery, uses the link-local addresses and the new *Neighbor Discovery Protocol* (NDP) to find out about the network and the nearby systems. NDP uses ICMPv6 informational messages. The routers on the network segments use Router Advertisement (RA) multicast packets to

- Advertise the routers' existence
- Announce the *on-link prefix* (the "network part" of an IPv6 address)
- Signal whether systems should perform stateless or stateful configuration

Hosts hear these advertisements and can generate their own addresses (stateless) or request an address from a DHCPv6 server (stateful), as directed. (See the discussion of autoconfiguration in the next section.)

So how does your computer exchange address information with the other computers on the network? We're so glad you asked — although you may regret it. The following process isn't just for computers, but also for routers and every other network-attached device.

Whenever your computer creates an IPv6 address for itself, it transmits a Neighbor Solicitation (NS) query to that address and waits for a response. If your computer doesn't receive a response, the address is available. If another system responds with a Neighbor Advertisement (NA), the address is already in use. Try again. Your system caches the address for that neighbor in case it needs to use it later.

Your computer listens to all of the NA confirmations and all the data communication traffic on the network to learn that the neighbors are still alive and what addresses they're using. Your computer caches this information so it's available whenever it's needed.

In the absence of NA confirmations and data traffic, your computer periodically transmits an NS query. An NA response is a "Yes, I'm here" confirmation that includes the hardware address. If there's no response, the neighbor is unreachable. Address information can be deleted when it expires this way. We could call this "autoforgetfulness," and it's an important piece because it supports the renumbering of systems.

NS, NA, and this Duplicate Address Detection (DAD) process totally replace the Address Resolution Protocol (ARP). Take a look at Chapter 16 to find out about ARP.

Let someone else fill your platter — use autoconfiguration

Autoconfiguration is a kind of IP address "plug-and-play" process. It automatically assigns an IPv6 address to a NIC. As we describe in the preceding section, the Router Advertisement (RA) packets contain the on-link prefix and indicate whether systems should perform stateless or stateful configuration.

Autoregistration says "Let us serve you"

If your computer is just acting as a client of the services on your organization's network, it should be completely satisfied by autodiscovery and autoconfiguration. But what about the servers — the computers responsible for the services on the network? How do they make sure that the clients can find them? Autoregistration!

Autoregistration refers to the automatic, dynamic adding or updating of a computer's hostname and address information in DNS. You need autoregistration so that the new IPv6 address that a server receives via autoconfiguration is available to the clients as soon as they need it. So maybe there won't be that many typos and broken calculators after all. Even now, we can hear the contented sighs of network managers everywhere. Too bad they have to wait for more IPv6 deployment.

The computer without a country — stateful or stateless

In stateless configuration, your computer builds an IPv6 address by taking the on-link prefix and appending its hardware address. Of course, it must now use Duplicate Address Detection (DAD) to check that the address is okay to use.

In stateful configuration, your computer requests an IPv6 address from a neighboring DHCPv6 server.

In both stateless and stateful configuration, the address has a specified lifetime in order to support automatic renumbering. That means that your assigned IPv6 address isn't permanent.

Other Delicious IPv6 Morsels

IPv6 delivers other features, too. Some are continuations of stuff that works under IPv4 while others are new concepts. While we won't go into detail here, we thought you should hear a little about them.

Security for all

Security services such as packet authentication, integrity, and confidentiality are part of the design of IPv6. These capabilities can guarantee that packets are actually from the indicated sender, haven't been altered in transit, and can't be seen by hackers. Because the security services are built into IPv6, they're available to all of the TCP/IP protocols, not just specific ones such as SSL, PPTP, and S-HTTP. This means your organization's network can be easily made more secure, but don't assume that you can relax completely. Governmental restrictions against exporting or importing security technology may limit the availability of some capabilities, and hackers can be amazingly crafty.

The new IPSec protocol, a component of IPv6, adds an additional level of security for IPv6 and creates a secure, TCP/IP-level, point-to-point connection. In fact, IPv6 offers security to applications that currently lack built-in security and adds security to applications that already have minimal security features.

Faster, better multimedia

IPv6 provides new capabilities for high-quality, streaming, multimedia communications, such as real time audio and video. Huge opportunities for research and experimentation exist in this area of communication, especially as the Internet continues to grow and evolve.

Sharing the Planet — IPv6 and IPv4 Can Coexist

Now that it's here, do you have to use IPv6? No, not for decades. First of all, only a few vendors sell the IPv6 protocol stack yet. Also, IPv6 is built to manage both v4 and v6 addresses. If your server has the latest and greatest IPv6, your client computer with IPv4 doesn't have to change. IPv6 server software is backward compatible. That means it understands both IPv4 and IPv6 dialects. Your server knows what to do.

Don't bother upgrading your client computer to v6 until your network administrator upgrades your servers and routers. Your client won't have anyone who understands its dialect if other network devices are still at v4. IPv4 software isn't forward compatible.

A key reason to upgrade your routers is to enable the autos — autodiscovery, autoconfiguration, and autoregistration, thereby enabling network administrators to have a well-deserved week at the beach.

Whew . . . You Made It!

Wow, are we ever impressed! You made it all the way here. Or do you just jump to the end of each chapter to read our clever summaries and segues? In any case, if you're interested in more details regarding IPv6 and its advanced features and capabilities, you can find many RFCs, articles, and books. Or you can get on the Internet and see what's happening on the 6-Bone, the real world deployment of IPv6.

Although there are more than 15 RFCs about IPv6, we recommend that you start with these two:

- ✔ RFC1924, by R. Elz, "A Compact Representation of IPv6 Addresses"
- ✔ RFC1883, by S. Deering and R. Hinden, "Internet Protocol, Version 6 (IPv6) Specification"

Chapter 16

Is Anyone There?

● ●

In This Chapter

▶ Finding out who and what are on your network

▶ Recognizing who and what are on the Internet

▶ Figuring out if someone is "borrowing" your computer from across your network or the Internet

▶ Deciphering if the other users on your computer are accessing the network

▶ Uncovering what TCP/IP services and applications are running on a computer

● ●

*H*ow do you find someone to "talk" to? How can you look up someone's e-mail address? How many people are on your network and what hosts are available? If you want to use telnet or browse the Web (see Chapters 8 and 12), how can you determine if the server is up and running? The answers to these and other questions about checking out what's happening on the network are in this chapter.

Information, Please

Perhaps you just need to verify an e-mail address. Maybe you're a network administrator who needs to see how many people and machines are slowing down your network and why. Whatever your reason for looking around an internet or the Internet, you can find TCP/IP tools to help you.

We didn't have to work very hard on the humor in this chapter. For that, we have the names of the tools themselves. Many of them originated in UNIX (which is a pretty funny name itself, especially the first time you hear it pronounced without seeing the spelling). Take a look at Figure 16-1. It shows a Microsoft Windows for Workgroups program group with the icons for TCP/IP services and tools, and some of them are real giggles.

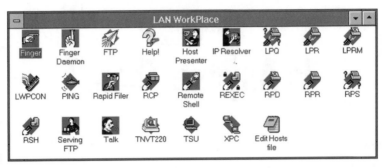

Figure 16-1:
A set of
graphical
TCP/IP
services
and tools.

If you don't have a graphical user interface (GUI), such as Windows or Mac, you can use most of the same tools represented in Figure 16-1, but you have to do more typing because you have to start them with commands. Some of the examples in this chapter are from UNIX systems without a GUI, and some are from GUI-equipped computers, so you can see for yourself the difference in the interfaces.

When you use TCP/IP at work, keep in mind that it's not the interface that's giving you network information, it's TCP/IP. All the tools and services described in this chapter are TCP/IP — regardless of the plain or fancy wrapping.

Fingering Your Friends and Enemies

Take it easy — this isn't what you may be thinking. Nevertheless, prepare yourself for some strange-looking terms: fingering, for example. Finger is a client/server environment for getting information about the users on a computer. It's the first application we tackle in this chapter because of the wealth of information it provides.

You use a finger client application to ask for information about one or more users on a computer — the computer you're on or a remote host. If you're fingering a remote computer and the finger server is running there, it answers your query. If the finger server isn't running on the remote computer, you get an error message such as

```
connection refused
```

When you use finger, it looks in the file that holds user account information for the operating system. Finger searches this file for a match on any keywords you supply. If you don't offer any keywords, finger looks in the user account file and returns information about every user currently using the computer.

Too much fingering may be harmful to your network's health

Finger is a tool to help you find out who is on your network and (possibly) what they're doing. It's also a great toy. You can discover all kinds of really cool information on the Internet by fingering computer hosts to see what they may tell you. Just remember, fingering can be addictive, and excessive use of finger can also slow down network performance. Remember to go outside and get some fresh air once in a while. After you check the cola machine.

This section gives you several examples showing the kind of information you can get with various uses of the finger command. Most of these examples were done on a UNIX system, but, to show the difference, we include a few from a graphical version of finger running on Microsoft Windows. TCP/IP doesn't care about your interface. Whether you point and click or type commands, it looks at your request and returns the information you've requested.

Some system managers disable the finger server because they feel the information it provides may be used to break into the computer in question. In this situation, you can still run the finger client application, but there's no server to answer your request. (You get a `connection refused` message.) You find more about finger and security in Chapter 18.

Fingering a user

Example 1: In this example, the unadorned `finger` command (that is, the command without any keywords) asks finger to look for everyone on the computer.

```
% finger
Login      Name                    TTY Idle  When           Where
wilensky   Marshall Wilensky No    co        Fri 17:40
leiden     Candace Leiden          p0        Fri 17:22
jtf        cia ss.psy.emigre.in    s4     3  Aug 22 14:35
```

Example 2: Here, we ask finger to look for a particular user, so we get more (and more specific) information:

```
% finger wilensky
Login name: wilensky                        In real life:
            Marshall Wilensky
Directory: /usr1/wilensky                   Shell: /bin/csh
On since Aug 20 17:40:09 on console
Mail last read Fri Aug 22 17:14:24 1998
No Plan.
```

Example 3: In this example, we ask finger to look for Marshall by entering `Marshall` as the keyword. Although `wilensky` is actually the correct account name for Marshall's user account, finger encounters `Marshall` in a documentation field and therefore returns the information from that record. If Candace's account record had `Marshall` somewhere in it, finger would find her, as well.

```
% finger marshall
Login name: wilensky                        In real life:
            Marshall Wilensky
Directory: /usr1/wilensky                   Shell: /bin/csh
On since Aug 22 17:40:09 on console
Mail last read Fri Aug 22 17:14:24 1998
No Plan.
```

Fingering a user who has projects and plans

Normally, finger lists just the basic user information, such as login name, home directory, real name, and when mail was last read. However, if a user has created project and plan files, finger tells you more.

If you want to provide more information about yourself to someone who fingers you, you can create a project file and/or a plan file. In these files you can describe the projects you're working on (if they're not Top Secret), your plans for the future, or anything else you want other people to see.

Consult the finger utility's documentation for your version of TCP/IP to find out where to put project and plan information.

Example 4: In this example, we ask finger to look for one of your authors, who happens to have created both a project file and a plan file. Notice the additional information finger displays in this case.

```
$ finger leiden
Login: leiden                              Name: Candace
         Leiden
Directory: /home/leiden                    Shell: /bin/bash
On since Fri Aug 22 14:53 (EST) on ttyq7 from bed-lp3
New mail received Fri Aug 22 12:25 1998 (EST)
      Unread since Thu Aug 21 19:10 1998 (EST)
Project:
Get a life.
Plan:
Get away from the snow. Visit Morocco.
```

Fingering the users on a host

You can also ask finger to look for the information for all users on a particular host.

Example 5: Here we ask finger to find out about everyone currently on the computer frodo:

```
% finger @frodo
[frodo]
Login       Name              TTY Idle   When     Where
wilensky Marshall Wilensky No  co         Fri 17:40
leiden   Candace Leiden         p0         Fri 17:22
```

Example 6: In Figure 16-2 we use a GUI-based finger to look for everyone on a host, but instead of specifying the host name, we give the IP address.

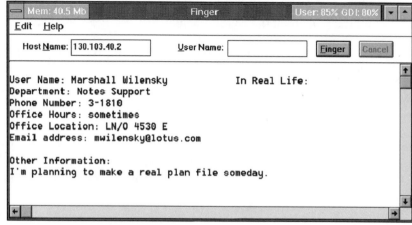

Figure 16-2: If you don't know the host name, you can use the IP address.

Using a Finger Gateway

If you're browsing the Web, you don't have to exit to a command window to look at a finger site — there are many finger gateways on the Web. Finger gateways are Web sites that connect to a finger server for you. The following section shows finger fun sites via a gateway, and some of the results of searching the Web for locations of finger gateways. Try one or two and have fun.

TCP — The Cola Protocol?

Once upon a time there were some students at Carnegie Mellon University who really liked cola. And they liked it cold. If they made a trip to the soda machine and it was out of cola, or if the cola had recently been refilled and wasn't cold enough yet, the students were beside themselves with disappointment. To spare themselves the anguish of arriving at a below-par soda machine, they connected the machine to their network!

The students set up finger so that they could check up on the availability and temperature of the soda. And then, because they were enterprising students, they put the machine on the Internet so that, today, everyone in the world can check on the status of this particular soda machine. You never know, after all, when you're going to be in Pittsburgh and thirsty. So, if you want to know how many colas are in that machine (or you just want to find out if we're pulling your leg), you can finger the machine. And if you're hungry, you can find out about these students' favorite kind of candy, as well.

Figure 16-3 contains our fingering of that soda machine — believe it or not. You'd better grab a diet soda before they're all gone. Too bad there's no information about the candy machine.

Oh, by the way, this isn't the only soda machine on the Internet. There are dozens (see Chapter 22 for more information)!

Fun with finger

It turns out that you can find out a lot about a lot of things with finger. You can discover more about earthquakes, space, the Space Shuttle — just by fingering computers on the Internet. The next few examples illustrate some of the more interesting uses of finger.

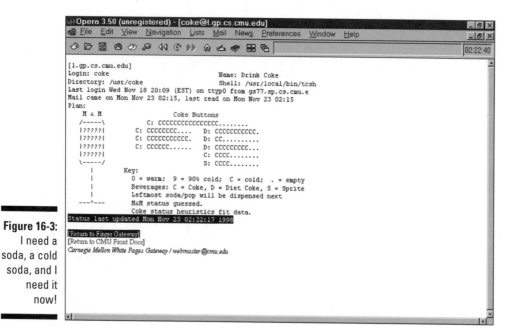

Figure 16-3:
I need a soda, a cold soda, and I need it now!

TCP Tremor Control Protocol?

Take a look at Figure 16-4. There you find the result of fingering an earthquake information system. If you live in quake country, you may be especially interested in this one.

Figure 16-4:
Use finger to find out more about earthquakes in the United States.

```
<HEAD>
 <TITLE>Finger Gateway -- quake@scec.gps.caltech.edu</TITLE>
 </HEAD>
 <BODY>
 This page generated by the <A HREF="http://www.cs.indiana.edu/finger">IU finger
 gateway</A><HR>
 <H1>
 quake@scec.gps.caltech.edu
 <IMG ALT=""
 SRC="http://www.cs.indiana.edu/faces/domains/edu/caltech/gps/unknown/face.gif">
 <IMG ALT="" SRC="http://www.cs.indiana.edu/faces/domains/edu/caltech/unknown/face.gif">
 </H1>
 <PRE>
 Login name: quake       In real life: SCSN Data Access
 Directory: /export/scec/user1/quake  Shell: /usr/local/bin/tcsh
 Last login Wed Nov  4 07:32 on ttyp8 from redhot.wr.usgs.g
 No unread mail
 Plan:
  WELCOME TO THE SOUTHERN CALIFORNIA EARTHQUAKE CENTER DATA CENTER (SCEC_DC)
 AUTOMATED LOCATIONS OF THE CALTECH/USGS SOUTHERN CALIFORNIA SEISMIC NETWORK

  This is a list of automated locations for earthquakes of magnitude 2.0 or
  greater, an RMS less then 0.5 and at least 8 phases in the solution,
  recorded by the CALTECH/USGS Southern California Seismic Network (SCSN)
  in the past 7 days. All times are Greenwich Mean Time.
  Subtract 8 hours for Pacific Standard time, and 7 hours for Pacific
  Daylight time.  Depths are in km.
```

(continued)

(continued)

```
 * Entries marked with a "*" are PRELIMINARY and have NOT BEEN HUMAN REVIEWED *
   Entries may contain ERRORS and may be UPDATED or DELETED at any time.
   Entries with origin times within 30 seconds may represent a single event.

   MAGNITUDE TYPES:
     MGN = empirically calibrated ML based on readings from high-gain components
     MLG = ML based on synthetic Wood-Anderson response from low-gain components
     ML  = ML based on synthetic Wood-Anderson response from TerraScope stations

   (Q) - EVENT LOCATION QUALITY
     The quality of the location is specified by the "Q" designation, with
     "A" representing the best quality, and "D" representing the worst.
 ========================================================================
   DATE     UTC TIME   LAT.    LON.   DEPTH  MAG. Q      COMMENT
   yy-mm-dd hh:mm:ss  (deg.)  (deg.)  (km)   typ
   -------- --------  ------  ------  -----  ---- -  -------------------------
   98/11/16 07:34:33  32.94N 116.23W   6.0  2.1ML  C  16 mi. SSW of Ocotillo Wells, CA
   98/11/16 08:12:38  34.15N 116.42W   2.8  2.1ML  A   3 mi. NNE of Yucca Valley, CA
   98/11/16 11:19:35  32.41N 115.33W   6.0  2.6ML  C  20 mi. SSE of Calexico, CA
   98/11/16 12:23:14  32.39N 115.33W   6.0  2.0MC  C  21 mi. SSE of Calexico, CA
   98/11/16 15:27:13  33.70N 116.82W  17.8  2.1ML  A   7 mi. WSW of Idyllwild, CA
   98/11/16 18:41:29  34.15N 116.43W   7.6  2.3ML  B   2 mi. N   of Yucca Valley, CA
   98/11/16 19:10:43  35.17N 119.18W  26.3  2.0MC  B  15 mi. E   of Taft, CA
   98/11/17 00:41:26  32.42N 115.33W   6.0  2.2MC  C  20 mi. SSE of Calexico, CA
   98/11/17 16:13:57  34.64N 116.53W   4.2  2.2ML  A  27 mi. ENE of Lucerne Valley, CA
   98/11/17 18:14:17  34.15N 116.43W   9.2  2.0ML  A   2 mi. N   of Yucca Valley, CA
   98/11/17 20:44:17  36.07N 118.01W   3.0  2.0MC  A   5 mi. WNW of Coso Junction, CA
   98/11/17 21:44:07  32.01N 116.30W   6.0  3.0MC  C  53 mi. SSW of Ocotillo, CA
   98/11/17 22:58:54  31.98N 116.32W   6.0  2.8MC  C  56 mi. SSW of Ocotillo, CA
   98/11/17 23:44:53  33.36N 115.71W   1.6  2.0MC  A   2 mi. ENE of Bombay Beach, CA
   98/11/18 00:29:57  33.66N 117.06W   0.0  2.0MC  A   8 mi. SW  of Hemet, CA
   98/11/18 02:29:30  34.32N 119.27W  10.5  2.4ML  A   3 mi. NNE of Ventura, CA
   98/11/18 06:27:15  36.04N 117.72W   1.3  2.1MC  A  12 mi. E   of Coso Junction, CA
   98/11/18 06:46:34  33.47N 116.50W   6.0  2.0ML  C  11 mi. ESE of Anza, CA
   98/11/18 07:14:51  32.66N 117.35W   6.0  2.0MC  A  10 mi. SW  of Mission Beach, CA
   98/11/18 15:49:02  34.33N 116.84W   5.8  2.9ML  A   4 mi. N   of Big Bear City, CA
   98/11/18 16:50:09  34.29N 118.76W  15.9  2.0ML  A   3 mi. W   of Simi Valley, CA
   98/11/18 18:19:17  31.80N 115.99W   6.0  2.4MC  D  65 mi. S   of Ocotillo, CA
   98/11/18 18:38:25  34.32N 116.84W   5.8  2.3ML  A   4 mi. N   of Big Bear City, CA
   98/11/18 20:13:12  34.32N 118.47W   4.3  2.8ML  A   3 mi. NW  of San Fernando, CA
   98/11/18 20:30:21  34.33N 116.85W   6.1  2.2ML  A   4 mi. N   of Big Bear City, CA
   98/11/18 22:37:28  33.92N 118.74W  15.3  2.1MC  C   6 mi. SSE of Pt. Dume, CA
   98/11/18 22:41:38  31.90N 115.77W   6.0  2.5MC  D  56 mi. SSW of Calexico, CA
   98/11/18 23:39:35  35.98N 117.83W   6.3  2.0MC  A   7 mi. SE  of Coso Junction, CA
   98/11/19 00:15:40  33.68N 117.02W   0.0  2.4ML  A   6 mi. SSW of Hemet, CA
   98/11/19 01:03:13  32.11N 115.42W   6.0  2.5MC  D  39 mi. S   of Calexico, CA
   98/11/19 02:20:58  33.68N 116.80W  16.9  2.0ML  A   7 mi. SW  of Idyllwild, CA
   98/11/19 04:29:01  33.79N 118.60W   6.0  2.0MC  C  10 mi. W   of Palos Verdes Point, CA
   98/11/19 06:24:58  32.01N 115.42W   6.0  2.9MC  D  45 mi. S   of Calexico, CA
   98/11/19 06:33:20  32.08N 115.44W   6.0  2.6ML  D  41 mi. S   of Calexico, CA
   98/11/19 07:08:33  35.98N 117.83W   6.6  2.1MC  A   7 mi. SE  of Coso Junction, CA
   98/11/19 10:21:14  34.33N 116.84W   6.1  2.1ML  A   4 mi. N   of Big Bear City, CA
   98/11/19 11:39:21  31.93N 115.77W   6.0  2.1MH  D  54 mi. SSW of Calexico, CA

   98/11/20 10:33:45  34.28N 118.52W   3.7  2.0ML  A   1 mi. WNW of Granada Hills, CA
   98/11/20 11:13:48  34.17N 116.43W   5.3  2.2MC  A   3 mi. N   of Yucca Valley, CA
   98/11/20 18:28:18  34.34N 118.26W   6.0  2.0MC  C   6 mi. NNE of Sunland, CA
   98/11/20 23:58:09  34.22N 117.44W   8.0  3.3ML  A   3 mi. W   of Devore, CA
   98/11/21 09:39:17  32.05N 115.43W   6.0  3.0ML  D  43 mi. S   of Calexico, CA
   98/11/21 15:39:40  32.61N 117.27W   6.0  2.1MGN C* 10 mi. SW  of San Diego, CA
   98/11/22 12:33:34  33.24N 116.79W   5.5  2.1MGN C*  2 mi. W   of Lake Henshaw, CA
   98/11/23 03:30:40  35.97N 117.90W   4.4  2.3MGN A*  6 mi. SSE of Coso Junction, CA
   98/11/23 04:42:57  34.10N 116.93W   6.6  2.1MGN C*  6 mi. W   of Mt. San Gorgonio, CA
 ---------------------------------------------------------------------------
   &lt;&gt; Last update was on 23-NOV-1998 04:44 gmt
      (List is updated when catalog is modified, not at regular intervals)

   The SCEC_DC, Caltech, and USGS are members of the Council of the National
 Seismic System.
 </PRE>
 </BODY>
```

Spaced out

You can find out what's going on in space (outer space, not cyberspace) by fingering a host at the Massachusetts Institute of Technology (see Figure 16-5).

```
This page generated by the IU finger gateway
--------------------------------------------------------------------
nasanews@space.mit.edu
nasanews: [space] Mon Nov 23 02:12:13 1998
               MIT Center for Space Research
--------------------------------------------------------------------
This NasaNews service is brought to you by the Microwave Subnode of
NASA's Planetary Data System. It is also available via World Wide Web
at "http://space.mit.edu/nasanews.html". AOL users can receive this
bulletin as: keyword "Gopher" > Aerospace and Astronomy > Nasa News.

We also maintain an email listserver for planetary microwave inform-
ation at "pds-listserver@space.mit.edu", an anonymous ftp server at
"delcano.mit.edu", and a WWW home page at "http://delcano.mit.edu/".
If you have any suggestions for how we might improve our services,
please mail them to "pds-requests@space.mit.edu".

Similarly, Kennedy Space Center status reports and press releases are
available by sending a message to "domo@news.ksc.nasa.gov". In the
body of the message, type "subscribe shuttle-status" or "subscribe
ksc-press-release" (no quotes). To remove yourself from the list, send
a message to the same address with a line "unsubscribe shuttle-status"
or "unsubscribe ksc-press-release".

NASA bulletins are also frequently posted to the "sci.space.news"
Usenet newsgroup, and are also available via anonymous ftp from the
"NASA.News" directory of "spacelink.msfc.nasa.gov", or via World Wide
Web from "http://spacelink.msfc.nasa.gov/".
--------------------------------------------------------------------
                        C O N T E N T S
  1   Thu Nov 19 14:39   GSFC   Landsat-7 Launch Scheduled
  2   Fri Nov 20 07:07   STScI  Hubble Status Report
  3   Fri Nov 20 14:04   DFRC   NASA Aircraft Sets New Record
--------------------------------------------------------------------
Date: Nov 19 14:39 UTC
Subject: Landsat-7 Launch Scheduled

LANDSAT-7 LAUNCH SCHEDULED FOR APRIL 15

NASA has selected a new launch date of April 15, 1999, for the
Landsat-7 Earth science satellite. The launch, originally scheduled for
December 1998, will take place from Vandenberg Air Force Base, CA, on a
Delta II launch vehicle.
--------------------------------------------------------------------
Date: Nov 20 07:07 UTC
Subject: Hubble Status Report

HUBBLE SPACE TELESCOPE DAILY REPORT #2255

PERIOD COVERED:  0000Z (UTC) 11/19/98 - 0000Z (UTC) 11/20/98

The WF/PC-2 was used to make observations of a high-Z supernova in
order to determine the cosmological parameters Omega and Lamda. The
observations were executed as scheduled, and no anomalies were noted.
--------------------------------------------------------------------
Date: Nov 20 14:04 UTC
Subject: NASA Aircraft Sets New Record

NASA AIRCRAFT SETS NEW WORLD ALTITUDE RECORD

A NASA ER-2 aircraft set a new world altitude record for medium weight
aircraft on Nov. 19, 1998, reaching 68,700 feet, almost twice the
cruising altitude of most airliners.
```

Knock, Knock — Who's There?

The *who* utility is a UNIX program that shows all interactive users on a host. If the fourth column (after the date and time) is filled in, the user has logged in to the computer from a remote host — in other words, IT'S HARLEY TIME! (For cycle stealing, that is.) You can use who to find out if someone is stealing cycles from your computer.

Although it's not a part of the TCP/IP stack, the who program returns information about who (literally) is using TCP/IP, and from what remote host. In the following example, look for the FQDN or the numeric IP addresses (the ones with four fields separated by dots). On this host, lp stands for local port, so the users who are designated by the letters lp in the right-hand column are local users.

```
$ who
sylvie    ttyp9    Aug 24 08:26    (wor-lp10)
emily     ttypb    Aug 24 14:18    (lwl-lp5)
kidman    ttyq5    Aug 24 14:29    (134.174.120.50)
kld       ttyq6    Aug 24 15:04    (132.245.33.7)
leiden    ttyq7    Aug 24 14:53    (bed-lp3)
cruise    ttyqc    Aug 24 13:51    (143.251.97.106)
kath      ttyrc    Aug 24 13:00    (bgray.avid.com)
```

w-ant to Know More?

The *w* utility is similar to who. (And please don't send us grammar lessons on who versus whom. This is *TCP/IP For Dummies,* not *English For Dummies.*) Not only does w tell you who (literally) on your host is using TCP/IP services, it also tells you what they're doing — for example, running Gopher or telnet. In Figure 16-6, w reveals that most users on the host computer are running network applications and exactly which network applications they're using.

```
$ w
  3:07PM  up 1 day,  2:19, 36 users, load averages: 0.32, 0.76, 1.00 ──────── More UNIX
 USER    TTY FROM             LOGIN@  IDLE WHAT    ┌─ Network location      to ignore
 suixcco  p0 bed-1p3          3:02PM     0 telnet main.com 4444
 Brianc   p2 1w1-1p5          1:23PM     0 irc (irc-2.6)
 frownig  p4 1w1-1p5          2:18PM     0 irc (irc-2.6)
 blnk     p5 bed-1p9          3:03PM     0 rlogin -1 jolea  199.232.40.10
 nifte    p7 bed-1p3          2:34PM     0 ftp
 chrispx  pb 1w1-1p5          2:18PM     0 telnet lerret.cs.ohiou.edu 4000
 mlspeake pf bed-1p11         3:03PM     0 gopher marvel.loc.gov
 electra  q0 bed-1p3          1:26PM     0 telnet realms.dorsai.org 1501
 mcmah    q4 bed-1p3          2:10PM     0 telnet btech.netaxs.com 3056
 leiden   q7 bed-1p3          2:53PM     0 script tools.txt
 dirienzo q8 bed-1p11         2:35PM     0 telnet infosoc.com
 shephrdr qc 143.251.97.106   1:51PM     3 tin
 aerie    qe bed-1p8          2:12PM    10 telnet 134.2.62.161 4252
 JIMH     qf bed-1p6          2:51PM     0 telnet infosoc
 rrestyn  r5 bed-1p6          8:58AM     0 telnet
 dogerb   rd redpanties.gradi 2:29PM     0 gopher
 teeny    s7 bed-1p12         2:40PM     0 telnet alumni.caltech.edu
 kaf      s8 bed-1p12         2:41PM     0 mail baker-j@pix.netway.com
```

Figure 16-6: On this computer, people really use telnet a lot, but some people like to chat.

rwho There, You Devil?

You've seen who and w show the users on one host. Now take a look at *rwho*, another Berkeley r utility, which shows all the users on the network — that is, all users on computers whose system administrators allow the rwho daemon to run.

The rwho daemon creates a packet that lists users on the computer on which the daemon runs and broadcasts this across the network every few minutes. The program is called a *daemon* because the UNIX programmers who created it were devils — at least, that's the opinion of some system and network administrators, because of the way rwho's broadcast packets can clog up a network.

The broadcasts aren't a problem when just a few computers are on the network, but as that number rises, so does the number of packets. Soon the network is so clogged with rwho broadcast packets that there's no room for yours. Together, the rwho daemons on all the network's computers keep all that data from all those broadcasts, ready to display for anyone who enters the rwho command!

Some system managers and network administrators may refuse to run the rwho daemon at all, so don't be surprised if you get no information back from your rwho command.

Here is a sample of output from rwho. The second column tells you where the user is signed on.

```
$ rwho
Betteb     max:ttyp2        Aug 24 13:23
JMJK       max:ttyqf        Aug 24 14:51
eve        min:ttype        Aug 24 14:24
blakbird   nec:ttys0        Aug 24 14:40
blink      max:ttyrb        Aug 24 14:28
bmunts     nec:ttyra        Aug 24 14:27
breedst    max:ttyr5        Aug 24 08:58
bryanc     millenium:ttyp6  Aug 24 13:06
leaf       dalek:ttyp4      Aug 24 12:41 :04
```

ruptime, Cousin of rwho

The *ruptime* utility (that's right, it's another Berkeley r utility) displays a list of the computers that are up and running on the network and some bonus data about them.

Like rwho, ruptime uses the rwho daemon's broadcast packets, so ruptime, too, can rupture your network in terms of performance. As in the case of rwho, system managers and network administrators may choose not to configure the rwho daemon, so you may not see every host on your network (or any information at all).

Here's a sample of output from ruptime. In the left-hand column is the computer name; the next column is the computer's status; next is how long it's been up and how many users are logged on. You can ignore the UNIXy techno-data on the right; it's about the load average on each computer.

```
$ ruptime
dalek     up 13+17:08,    2 users,  load 1.28, 1.28, 1.28
max       up  1+02:06,   37 users,  load 1.46, 1.19, 1.13
millenia  up    14:49,    7 users,  load 1.34, 1.19, 1.10
```

The World According to ARP

The *arp* utility displays the TCP/IP Address Resolution Protocol (ARP) tables. The tables are cached in memory and are maintained automatically, for the most part. Only rarely does a system manager or network adminis-trator have to modify a table entry manually.

The arp utility learns the physical (hardware) address of a computer's network interface card by means of an arp request. Your computer issues the arp request when it discovers that the ARP table doesn't have the physical address of the computer with which yours wants to communicate. The arp request is a broadcast message asking the computer with a specific IP address to respond with its physical address, and the response is loaded into the table for future use. Each computer on the network maintains its own ARP table, cached in memory, and benefits from the responses to all arp requests, even the ones it didn't issue.Without the ARP tables, this process would have to be done each time you access a host. For example, if you send frequent mail messages every day to wilensky@frodo.lotus.com, you don't want to have to go out across the network for every message to find out the physical address of frodo's network interface card. By keeping frodo's physical address in the ARP tables, the computer can speed up performance and reduce network traffic.

To find out what IP addresses are listed in the ARP tables for your computer, use the arp utility. Figure 16-7 shows sample arp output, listing the frequently accessed IP addresses and their corresponding hardware addresses.

On the Internet, routers and gateways use routing protocols such as RIP (Routing Information Protocol) and OSPF (Open Shortest Path First) to supplement ARP. (See Chapter 18.)

IP address   Hardware address

```
% arp -a
cisco.tiac.net (199.0.65.1) at 0:0:c:0:a2:94
zork.tiac.net (199.0.65.2) at 0:80:29:e3:95:92
kickoff.tiac.net (199.0.65.3) at 0:40:33:21:d6:9a
lit-lp16.tiac.net (199.0.65.7) at 0:c0:5:1:13:7d
mvy.tiac.net (199.0.65.8) at 8:0:20:f:20:fa
sundog.tiac.net (199.0.65.9) at 8:0:20:b:bb:94
bed-lp13.tiac.net (199.0.65.10) at 0:c0:5:1:10:88
bed-lp1.tiac.net (199.0.65.12) at 0:c0:5:1:2:5e
bed-lp2.tiac.net (199.0.65.13) at 0:c0:5:1:4:9a
bed-lp3.tiac.net (199.0.65.14) at 0:c0:5:1:7:e5
bed-lp4.tiac.net (199.0.65.15) at 0:c0:5:1:9:e9
lwl-lp5.tiac.net (199.0.65.16) at 0:80:ad:4:d8:d3
bed-lp6.tiac.net (199.0.65.17) at 0:c0:5:1:d:ea
mvy-lp7.tiac.net (199.0.65.18) at 0:c0:5:1:1a:a9
bed-lp8.tiac.net (199.0.65.19) at 0:c0:5:1:b:d8
bed-lp9.tiac.net (199.0.65.20) at 0:c0:5:1:c:b7
boris.tiac.net (199.0.65.21) at 0:40:33:28:bc:df
millenium.tiac.net (199.0.65.24) at 0:40:33:25:c7:48
toybox.tiac.net (199.0.65.25) at 0:40:33:28:b6:51
bed-lp12.tiac.net (199.0.65.26) at 0:c0:5:1:10:6a
zima.com (199.0.65.27) at 0:40:33:21:9a:7d
bed-lp11.tiac.net (199.0.65.29) at 0:c0:5:1:10:81
bobafet.tiac.net (199.0.65.32) at 0:40:33:29:43:eb
wor-lp10.tiac.net (199.0.65.55) at 0:c0:5:1:e:db
laraby.tiac.net (199.0.65.80) at 0:40:33:2b:35:77
mar-lp15.tiac.net (199.0.65.102) at 0:c0:5:1:12:f4
t1-1.Bedford.MA.tiac.net (199.0.65.111) at 0:c0:5:0:f:c6
lwl-lp19.tiac.net (199.0.65.114) at 0:c0:5:1:17:c7
bed-lp17.tiac.net (199.0.65.121) at 0:c0:5:1:15:d5
kin-lp18.tiac.net (199.0.65.171) at 0:c0:5:1:13:96
t1-2.Bedford.MA.tiac.net (199.0.65.225) at 0:c0:5:0:13:b0
davros.tiac.net (199.0.65.235) at 0:40:33:2d:40:cc
? (199.0.65.255) at (incomplete)
%
```

Figure 16-7:
The ARP tables show a computer's "other" address — the physical address.

What's a physical address? Isn't the IP address enough?

When you buy a network interface card, it comes with a unique hardware address, also called the *physical address.* This hardware address is the ultimate address (final resting place) of your computer on a network. Just as TCP/IP associates your computer's name with its IP address, the IP address is associated with a hardware address. After all, when you send e-mail, you're sending it from one piece of hardware to another. The ARP piece of TCP/IP is what provides this IP address/hardware address resolution.

The nslookup Utility

Look in Chapter 11 for examples of using *nslookup* to look up IP addresses from a name server, as well as a list of nslookup commands.

The showmount Utility

To see which NFS clients have mounted shared disk space from an NFS server, run the *showmount* utility on the NFS server. Showmount is also an important tool for system managers and network administrators who are responsible for network security. You find more about this utility in Chapter 19.

Reach Out and Touch Something, with ping

The *ping* utility, which we introduce you to in Chapter 9, lets you find out if a remote computer is available. It uses the network "sonar" — the Internet Control Message Protocol (ICMP). Ping bounces a message off a computer; if there is a reply, the computer is alive and well.

Ping is one of the first troubleshooting commands a system manager or network administrator uses when investigating system and network problems. After all, if there's a problem, you need to know if the wounded computer is dead or alive.

Here is an example of ping checking a computer named "millenium" to see if it's alive. At the end are some summary statistics about packets sent, packets lost, and how long the ping round trip took. Also, Figure 16-8 shows a use of a GUI version of ping on a PC and ping's output. Notice that the PC version doesn't show the packet traffic data.

```
$ ping millenium
PING millenium.tiac.net (199.0.65.24): 56 data bytes
64 bytes from 199.0.65.24: icmp_seq=0 ttl=255 time=1.518 ms
64 bytes from 199.0.65.24: icmp_seq=1 ttl=255 time=1.624 ms
--- millenium.tiac.net ping statistics ---
2 packets transmitted, 8 packets received, 0% packet loss
round-trip min/avg/max = 1.581/1.624/2.571 ms
```

Figure 16-9 shows an example of ping from a computer that's running IPv6. This time we use the IPv6 address instead of the host name.

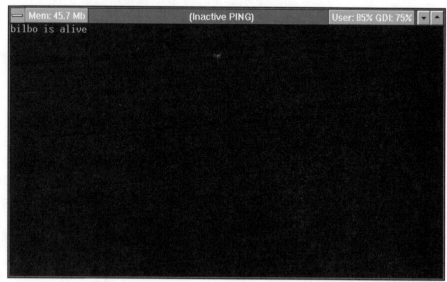

Figure 16-8: A GUI version of ping is fun, too.

Figure 16-9:
Notice how
long the IP
addresses
are.

```
% ping 5F00:2100:1024:9000:2490:800:2B37:7802
PING (5F00:2100:1024:9000:2490:800:2B37:7802): 56 data bytes
64 bytes from 5F00:2100:1024:9000:2490:800:2B37:7802: icmp6_seq=0 hlim=64 time=0 ms
64 bytes from 5F00:2100:1024:9000:2490:800:2B37:7802: icmp6_seq=1 hlim=64 time=0 ms
64 bytes from 5F00:2100:1024:9000:2490:800:2B37:7802: icmp6_seq=2 hlim=64 time=0 ms
5F00:2100:1024:9000:2490:800:2B37:7802 PING Statistics----
3 packets transmitted, 3 packets received, 0% packet loss
round-trip (ms)  min/avg/max = 0/0/0 ms
```

Did you notice that the IPv4 version of ping has TTL information, while the IPv6 version uses hlim instead? *TTL* means "time to live" — how long this packet should be allowed to survive before being discarded. It sounds like it is measured in units of time, such as milliseconds, but TTL is actually measured in hops from computer to computer across the network. Hlim means hop limit. It means about the same thing as TTL, but is a more accurate term.

ps, We Love You

No, we're not hitting on you. The *ps* utility is often thought of as a UNIX performance monitoring tool, but it also lets you see what kinds of network processes, including daemons, are running on your computer. For example, if a network administrator decides to disable the rwho daemon, ps can be used to make sure it is no longer running. Figure 16-10 shows ps output from a host with lots of network processes.

In this chapter, we describe the most commonly used tools for finding out many network-related facts about your computer and about what's going on across your network. Depending on what TCP/IP product you have, you may be able to use additional tools for these information-gathering tasks. Microsoft Windows NT, for example, includes arp, finger, and ping, in addition to supplying its own graphical Performance Monitor that tracks users and processes such as daemons and supplies dozens of network utilization statistics. Other vendors, as well, support most of the basic lookup-style tools along with their own additions and extensions.

Afraid to Ask for Directions? Traceroute Tells You Where You're Going

Traceroute is a TCP/IP utility for deciphering the route that packets follow on their way to a destination. You can use traceroute to test and measure transmissions on the network.

```
$ ps auwx
USER       PID %CPU %MEM   VSZ  RSS TT   STAT STARTED   TIME COMMAND
leiden   20113  3.0  0.0   348  172 p3   R+    3:06PM   0:00.04 ps auwx
root        65  0.0  0.0  1160  992 ??   Ss   Thu12PM   1:31.58 named
root        68  0.0  0.0    52  108 ??   Ss   Thu12PM   0:08.83 rwhod
root        70  0.0  0.0    60  108 ??   Is   Thu12PM   0:00.09 portmap
root        76  0.0  0.0    56   16 ??   S    Thu12PM   5:13.29 nfsiod 4
root        77  0.0  0.0    56   16 ??   I    Thu12PM   1:47.96 nfsiod 4
root        78  0.0  0.0    56   16 ??   I    Thu12PM   0:48.53 nfsiod 4
root        79  0.0  0.0    56   16 ??   I    Thu12PM   0:20.84 nfsiod 4
root        80  0.0  0.0   444  132 ??   Ss   Thu12PM   0:39.04 sendmail:
accepting connections (sendmail)
root        83  0.0  0.0    76  100 ??   Ss   Thu12PM   0:17.39 inetd
root     22947  0.0  0.0    96   72 ??   I    10:28PM   0:00.48 rlogind
patt     22948  0.0  0.0   468   76 p1   Is+  10:28PM   0:00.53 -bash (bash)
WiseGuy  27152  0.0  0.0   312   72 r6   I+   12:36AM   0:01.55 ncftp
root      5542  0.0  0.0    96   88 ??   I     8:26AM   0:23.60 rlogind
sylvan    6137  0.0  0.0   148  112 r0   I+    8:36AM   0:30.77 telnet
netcom.com
anmary    6792  0.0  0.0   568  476 p6   S+    8:52AM   0:35.11 irc (irc-2.6)
root      7004  0.0  0.0    84   88 ??   S     8:58AM   0:38.18 rlogind
root     15491  0.0  0.0   120  172 ??   I     1:00PM   0:00.35 telnetd
Bryant   16380  0.0  0.0   452  480 p2   S+    1:23PM   0:21.04 irc (irc-2.6)
root     16444  0.0  0.0    84  196 ??   S     1:26PM   0:15.52 rlogind
ellend   16534  0.0  0.0   156  260 q0   S+    1:29PM   0:07.03 telnet
realms.dorsai.org 1501
root     16936  0.0  0.0   120  200 ??   I     1:41PM   0:03.15 telnetd
shepherd 17449  0.0  0.0  2940  372 qc   I+    1:53PM   0:18.34 tin
ellend   17573  0.0  0.0   156  260 q0   T     1:56PM   0:00.47 telnet main.com
4444
root     17891  0.0  0.0    28  196 ??   S     2:05PM   0:00.46 comsat
deepwatr 18126  0.0  0.0  5408  592 s3   I+    2:11PM   1:08.44 trn
root     18127  0.0  0.0    96  216 ??   I     2:12PM   0:04.62 rlogind
shift    18943  0.0  0.0   276  372 p7   S+    2:34PM   0:02.70 ftp
rdf      19827  0.0  0.0   152  260 s8   I+    2:58PM   0:00.13 mail
batsoid@xx.netcom.com
root     19833  0.0  0.0   484  168 ??   I     2:58PM   0:00.06 sendmail:
server relay3.UU.NET cmd read (sendmail)
whitehed 20008  0.0  0.0   224  556 ??   S     3:03PM   0:00.40 ftpd:
dip27n8.drc.com: whitehd: RETR pgp262.zip\r\n (ftpd)
root     20033  0.0  0.0    28  232 ??   S     3:03PM   0:00.07 ntalkd
mlspeake 20060  0.0  0.0   440  356 pf   I+    3:04PM   0:00.42 gopher
```

Neat! The rwho daemon is running.

Users might come in via rlogin.

Looks like a version of ftp.

They're both using IRC to chat, but probably not to each other.

Someone's using telnet.

Someone's getting a file via FTP.

Figure 16-10: With ps, you find that this computer has lots of TCP/IP networking going on.

Traceroute sends three UDP packets called *probes* out onto the network. Traceroute works by counting the hops that your probes make as they move from host to host across the network. In fact, it counts each packet three times — that's why the report lists three times in the last three columns. Traceroute uses two retry hops, and shows the round trip times for all three hops.

The following lines of code show a successful traceroute command to "mazarin". Notice that traceroute shows both the name and the IP address of the router. On the Internet, the router is a fully qualified domain name.

The following code is from a UNIX system. When using a Microsoft Windows operating system, you spell the command "tracert".

```
%  traceroute mazarin
traceroute to mazarin (130.3.3.6), 30 hops max, 40 byte
         packets
1 redbrd (130.3.3.1) 2 ms 3 ms 2 ms
2 blubrd (130.3.3.2) 4 ms 4 ms 4 ms
3 tweeti (130.3.3.3) 6 ms 7 ms 5 ms
4 mazarin (130.3.3.6) 12 ms 8 ms 8 ms
```

Chapter 17

Mobile-IP, Dialup Networking, and IP Telephony

*Y*ou may have full network access from your office, but what about from your home or when you travel? Dialup networking and mobile computing give you access to remote computers, network services, and the entire Internet. You can even use your computer to make long distance phone calls at local rates. This chapter describes three recent developments for TCP/IP internetworking:

✔ **Mobile-IP:** Roam freely across the Internet without worrying about changing your IP address.

✔ **Dialup connections:** Dial the Internet or your corporate network from any telephone line.

✔ **IP telephony:** Telephone and fax without incurring any telephone company charges.

Mobile-IP for Hassle-Free Travel

Mobile-IP, a special version of IP, is the heart of mobile computing. Mobil IP makes it possible to use hardware that ranges from those as common as a laptop computers and personal digital assistants (PDAs) to handheld computers and strange devices, such as the wearable computer shown in Figure 17-1.

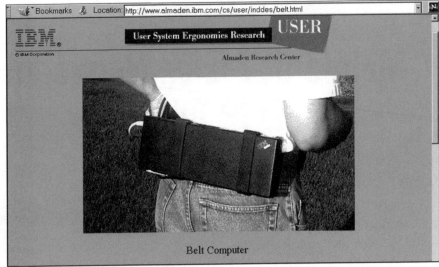

Figure 17-1:
Is it a
computer or
a belt
buckle?

Mobile-IP is an enhancement to IP that allows a computer to roam an intranet or the Internet without changing its IP address. This is a neat trick because every IP address includes a network number. Imagine that your office network number is 226, and this is where you work on your notebook computer four days a week. Every Friday, you take your laptop to a customer's site, where the network number is 103. It would seem that if you want to connect your laptop to your customer's network, you need to change your IP address so it says that you're on network 103. The DHCP (Dynamic Host Control Protocol, described in Chapters 6 and 13) could help you by giving you a new address just for Friday. In fact, every Friday, if you use DHCP, you receive a different IP address.

Mobile-IP differs from DHCP because even when you carry your laptop from your home office to a customers's office, your laptop can keep its original IP address. You don't have to reconfigure your TCP/IP settings on the laptop or use DHCP. Your IP address is your IP address wherever you go, and your laptop computer (or any other portable computing device) becomes a *mobile host* (MH).

RFC 2002 defines IP Mobility Support. RFC 2005 is the Applicability Statement for IP Mobility Support.

Mobile-IP — too good to be true?

The Mobile-IP architecture, developed by the IETF, defines two components:

- ✔ Home agent (HA)
- ✔ Foreign agent (FA)

The HA and the FA cooperate to allow your mobile host (MH) to move anywhere on your internet or the Internet without changing its IP address. A network that has mobility support needs a computer to act as a mobility agent — that's a computer that serves as either the HA, the FA, or both.

Think of mobility support as the U.S. Postal Service. When you move to a new home, you notify the post office of your new address. The post office captures mail that comes to your old address and pastes a new address label over your old address. Then, the post office forwards the mail to your new home.

In the same way, Mobile-IP allows your MH to move around by pasting new address labels on your packets. Your MH is affiliated with one home network that's part of your MH's permanent IP address. IP always delivers packets for the MH to this network. When a MH is traveling, the network's home agent (HA), intercepts and forwards your packets to whatever exotic Internet spot you're visiting.

Whenever you move your MH from your home network to a foreign network, your MH tells a foreign agent (FA) on the new network to notify your HA where you've gone. If you're jet-setting with your MH, packets always arrive for you on your home network. Then, the HA and sends the packets to the FA on the network you're visiting.

The post office occasionally has problems when you move. A letter may get lost in the process of forwarding it to your new home. Unfortunately, the post office doesn't have a TCP working for it.

With Mobile-IP, if you move your MH, it's possible that some packets get lost as the HA and FA adjust to your travels. Remember, however, that IP doesn't live alone. Connections maintained by TCP are able to survive packet losses and resend them.

Mobilizing security

Security is always an issue in computing, and even more so when you're moving your computer all over the Internet. With Mobile-IP computing, your home network depends on advanced firewall technologies to protect you wherever you may go. Firewalls protect mobile access by using secure logon procedures and Digital Certificates for authentication (see Chapter 19) so that no one else can try to put a portable on your corporate network and say it's you.

Connecting with Dialup Protocols

Your dialup choice depends on what you want to do from your "other" locations and what capabilities are available at the site you're dialing in to. Will you be connecting to a UNIX system, a Windows NT system, or something else? Can you manage with limited services — just e-mail and Usenet news, for example? Or do you need all of the network services that you have at work (telnet, FTP, NFS, DNS, Web browsing)?

Depending on what you're looking for, the answer may be UUCP, SLIP, CSLIP, or PPP. If you need to connect to your organization's private network via the Internet, you need PPTP. What do all these mean? The next sections tell you.

SLIP your way onto the network

SLIP, Serial Line Internet Protocol, is TCP/IP over direct connections and modems. It's also known as *dialup TCP/IP*. You pronounce the acronym SLIP just as you do the word "slip."

In Chapter 3, we introduce Ethernet and token ring, two types of networks on which TCP/IP runs. After all the years of experience making it work over all those networks, TCP/IP developers found it pretty easy to get TCP/IP to work over low-speed serial links. SLIP was the result. The bulk of the changes made were at the physical and data link layers (see Chapter 5). A serial port and a modem take the place of a network interface card (NIC).

With SLIP, one computer can connect to another computer or to a whole network, or two networks can connect to each other with the help of a network device such as a router or terminal server or one of the other devices described in Chapter 18.

PPP (no, not "the bathroom protocol," silly!)

Just a year or two ago, SLIP was the most commonly used dialup protocol, although there was a brand new protocol just starting to be used. PPP, the Point-to-Point Protocol (pronounced by saying the letters P P P), is that "new" dialup network solution. Today, PPP has overtaken SLIP in popularity with good reason. PPP isn't limited to carrying TCP/IP traffic. It can be used to carry other network protocols, such as SPX and AppleTalk, and can transport them all simultaneously.

Serial for breakfast

Have you ever looked at the back of your computer? That's where you find the ports into which devices are plugged so they can run with your computer. Modems are plugged into a *serial port,* also called a COM port (or, to those of you with old geezer computers, an RS-232 port). The following figure illustrates two different types of serial ports, one with 25 holes and one with nine holes, to hold the pins of your device connector (in this case, a modem). Sometimes the modem is inside your computer, so the connection is less obvious. You can read more about modems in Chapter 18.

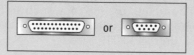

The point-to-point part of PPP's name is a little misleading because this connection method can be used to link one computer to another computer, one computer to a network, and/or one network to another network.

Using PPTP to create VPNs (Virtual Private Networks)

A *VPN* (Virtual Private Network) is a restricted communications environment carried on the (very public) Internet. A VPN is secure because it runs through a private tunnel on the Internet. That tunnel uses a new TCP/IP protocol, PPTP (Point to Point Tunneling Protocol).

PPTP lets you work remotely — at home or in a hotel room — and connect to your organization's intranet via the Internet. You dial and connect to your local Internet Service Provider (ISP). PPTP is the protocol that lets you connect (via a secure "tunnel") from there to a private intranet. Why wouldn't you simply dial directly into your organization? Two main reasons involve cost. The third reason is security.

- ✔ **Telephone charges:** If it's a long distance call, you save your company a lot of money if you can dial a local number. If your organization consists of lots of telecommuters, local calls can be a big savings.

- ✔ **Easier (and cheaper) management:** In a VPN, the major investment is in modems for the telecommuters. Plain old analog modems are cheap. Also, the network administrator at your site doesn't have to spend time configuring large dialup environments. The telecommuting employees use the Internet Service Provider's resources.

Why is SLIP's popularity slipping away?

PPP is more rigidly and formally defined than SLIP, which means that vendors must spend more time implementing, debugging, and offering PPP as part of their products. PPP is more reliable and is multiprotocol. Microsoft Windows NT Server uses PPP to implement its Remote Access Service (RAS) Server.

✔ **Security:** PPTP allows the network administrator to set up filtering. Filtering allows the administrator to say what kinds of network messages are allowed into the intranet, such as TCP only, IP only, UDP only, or some combination. The administrator can also deny all communications except through PPTP.

In UUCP, the U lies and the C misleads

UUCP is a dialup communication protocol that's not actually part of TCP/IP but is still worth your attention in this chapter. If you need only a few basic remote functions, such as e-mail, Usenet News, and file copy, UUCP can be a very inexpensive networking solution. UUCP stands for UNIX to UNIX CoPy (pronounced by saying the letters U U C P). But check it out: The U lies and the C deceives!

Don't let the UNIX word scare you off — implementations of UUCP exist for other operating systems, too. That's what we mean when we say that the U lies. For example, one version of UUCP for personal computers is called UUPC. (Yes, we know, UUPC is only a typo away from UUCP, but we didn't pick the name, so don't blame us. Dyslexics, untie!)

And how does the C mislead? By underrating UUCP's role. UUCP allows you to do more than copy files.

Think back — w-a-a-a-y back — to your first phone. Perhaps it was two tin cans strung together with a long string, used by you and the neighbor kids for many a private conversation through a hedge or across a creek. UUCP is the network equivalent of that homemade "telephone." Two computers use UUCP to establish a temporary point-to-point network between them. Either computer can initiate the two-way communication by calling the other.

How does UUCP work?

In a modern system using UUCP, the system manager (who is also the UUCP administrator in this case) configures the UUCP software to establish dialup connections with many other computers. The connections are scheduled for regular, periodic intervals, but the UUCP administrator can also force a connection at any time. Two computers often share the connection initiation responsibilities in order to share any telephone charges. The connection lasts only as long as needed to perform the work. Then, the computers disconnect and hang up the phones.

So, what's UUCP good for?

The ability to copy files from one computer to another is certainly useful, but most network users need additional services, so UUCP also has the following capabilities:

- ✔ E-mail
- ✔ Remote printing
- ✔ Usenet News

For the file transfers and remote command executions to work properly in the services described here, UUCP must be installed and running on both computers.

The good, the bad, and the UUCP

First the good news: UUCP is inexpensive and secure.

The UUCP software is included free on UNIX systems, and public domain (free) versions exist for other operating systems, too. The only communications charges involved are for the phone calls. However, if you can find a UUCP site close by, you only make local phone calls.

Even if the site you do find is a toll call away, there are ways to cut costs. Get the computer you're communicating with to make some of the calls; then you can split the charges. You can also schedule the connections to take advantage of lower telephone rates. It's truly wonderful how many UUCP sites are willing to help you out with connection charges as much as possible.

Now the bad news: UUCP is hard to manage and hard to find.

Getting UUCP set up and keeping it running smoothly can be difficult for the system manager. As more and more sites use real TCP/IP and real connections to the Internet, UUCP is fading away. Over time, the number of sites with which to link is shrinking. If you need to connect to an outside network but aren't ready to deploy TCP/IP, UUCP can be an interim solution. It has been popular and quite useful, and it may be around for a long time to come — but it's no TCP/IP.

Which dialup solution is for you?

Use the dialup connection that best balances the features and functionality you need, the availability of the protocol for your operating system, and the cost you're willing to pay. Use the best solution that's available, but sure you balance your capabilities against the remote site's. PPP is more flexible than SLIP and, because it piggybacks other protocols, can share the dialup line with protocols such as AppleTalk. PPP also includes error correction for packet transmission. Although PPP is perhaps the better overall protocol, if you need to communicate with a computer that only has SLIP, you need SLIP.

If you're able to choose from several alternatives, try to make your selection based on the following order of priority:

- ✔ Mobile IP, so you can use a real network connection at full bandwidth (the rate at which information can be transferred over a network).

- ✔ PPP, used over the fastest modems you can afford.

- ✔ SLIP, used over the fastest modems you can afford.

If you need to connect to an organization's intranet, let the Internet be part of your VPN by using PPTP.

Dialup security

Protect your dialup communications in the same way you protect your network. Some of the dialup security features that you may run into include the following:

- ✔ **Username and password challenges:** When you dial in to your network, you should be challenged for a valid username and password before you're allowed to connect. Usernames and passwords are security controls that you may already be familiar with because you need them to log in to many computers.

- ✔ **Dial-back modems:** A modem is the device that connects your telephone and your computer (see Chapter 18). When you call your network, you go through the username/password challenge. If you're using a dial-back modem, the network disconnects you, and its modem calls you back at an authorized phone number that the network administrator set up. Even if an intruder has stolen your username and password, he or she can't get into your network (unless he or she can get into your home or remote office).

- ✔ **Encryption:** Is anyone listening in on your phone line? Ecryption is standard with PPTP and optionally available for SLIP and PPP. Encryption puts your data into a secret code before it goes over the wires. Eavesdroppers can't understand the code. Check out Chapter 19 for more information on encryption.

Understanding IP Telephony

Telephony refers to carrying voice, fax, and other information over connections provided by the public switched telephone network (PSTN) — what people usually call "the phone company." *IP telephony* is telephony without the telephone. Calls travel as packets of data on the Internet instead of over the telephone lines. What a way to avoid telephone charges! The challenge for IP telephony is to deliver the voice, fax, video, and other packets reliably and with high quality.

Who provides IP telephony services?

Internet Service Providers most commonly offer IP telephony services, but watch for local and long distance telephone companies and cable TV companies to participate much more in the future.

Who's in charge of IP telephony?

Whereas traditional telephone service is regulated by the government in most countries, IP telephony is not. In the United States, the Federal Communications Commission (FCC) regulates telephone connections. The FCC doesn't plan to regulate connections between a telephone user and an IP telephony service provider. Might that change in the future? Your guess is as good as ours, but it will be interesting to see what agencies get involved as more and more people take advantage of the Internet for phone and fax.

VoIP — Voice information in packets

VoIP, pronounced Vee Oh Eye P, is a major part of IP telephony. To deliver voice using IP means sending voice information in packets rather than using telephone technology. Like other forms of IP telephony (IP Fax, for example) VoIP avoids the charges of ordinary telephone service.

A practical use for IP telephony

GTE Internet uses computer-to-phone IP telephony so that customers can talk with an Internetworking service representative. When customers at the Web site click on the icon, they're automatically connected to the customer service representative's phone line.

With new technology comes new standards

Yes indeed. The VoIP Forum is a group that works to standardize sending voice and video over IP both on the Internet and in private intranets. More than 140 organizations around the world, including Cisco, IBM, Microsoft, France Telecom, Lucent Technologies, Hitachi, Telstra Corporation Australia, and 3Com, participate in the VoIP Forum.

How can I use VoIP?

Using IP to send voice communications over the Internet gives you a lot of calling flexibility. Here are some of the services you can take advantage of:

- ✔ **Computer-to-computer calling:** If both you and the person you're calling have compatible software, you can speak to each other through the microphone connected to your computer.

- ✔ **Computer-to-phone calling:** You can start the call on the computer and make the phone ring at the other end. If the person you're calling is home, you have a conversation. If your "callee" isn't home, you may be able to leave voice mail.

- ✔ **Computer-to-fax-calling:** You can send long distance fax transmissions through a fax gateway on the Internet for the cost of a local call to your Internet Service Provider (ISP).

You need a microphone to send your voice and speakers to hear people talking. These may be built in to your computer, or you may need to buy them. Luckily, they're not too expensive. You can also add telephone features to your computer by adding a telephony card that combines the functions of a modem, a sound board, a speakerphone, and a voicemail system.

Chapter 18

The Dreaded Hardware Chapter

In This Chapter

▶ Arranging all your pots and pans for the network banquet

▶ Understanding the marriage between hardware and software

▶ Speeding up your network connections

▶ Taking a look at modems and things that are called modems (but are something else)

*T*oday's world is divided into two kinds of people: hardware people and software people. Although very few mutants exist — people who have combined hardware and software traits — successful marriages have been known to occur between hardware and software people. Their differences, thank goodness, are complementary.

If you're reading this book, you're probably a software person (after all, network protocols are software). Or, you may be a hardware person who wants to see how the other half lives. If you're a hardware person, you probably already know what's in this chapter and can go on to some other one if you want. And if you're wondering why a software book includes a hardware chapter at all, remember that software runs on hardware. Software can't work without hardware, and there's no point in having hardware if there's no software for it.

Network administrators usually have to configure both the hardware and the software for a network. This chapter covers the most commonly used network hardware devices — how they work to extend your network and enable it to communicate with other networks — and offers a little advice on making choices.

Why doesn't this work anymore?

Our personal favorite excuse when anything goes wrong is, "It's a hardware problem." Try it. Say it over and over while you click your heels three times, and if you're wearing Dorothy's red shoes maybe you can get by with it!

Catering a Network Banquet

Ever been to a big wedding reception? With separate tables for adults and children? With cocktails, the salad bar, sit-down tables, and the dessert buffet all in different, but connected, rooms? With lots of round and rectangular tables, big and small, holding all kinds of foods from soup to nuts?

Are you in charge or did you just come to eat?

Whoever organizes the banquet has a lot of planning to do. How many tables in how many rooms? What's the traffic pattern going to be? Will the hallways connecting the rooms be long and crowded? Or will guests be able to move smoothly from one room into another so everyone can chow down before the food gets cold? And what about the kitchen? A banquet this size needs more than just regular dinnerware. You have to have hardware — ranging from small sauté pans to huge kettles, soup tureens, deep fryers, roasting pans, and so forth. It's a lot of stuff that you and your guests don't want to have to think about, let alone wash up when it's over.

Like wedding receptions, networks vary in size. Maybe you're just having a party with two tables of four, and serving an appetizer, main course, salad, and dessert — nothing fancy. And you can use your everyday dishes. In network parlance, what you have there is a small *local area network* (LAN) with a few hosts and some cable but no fancy network devices or specialized hardware. But consider the Internet and all its miscellaneous interconnected pieces and network hardware all over the world — now, there's a shindig!

If you're not a system manager or network administrator, you're probably just interested in eating from the salad bar (e-mail, storing and copying files, and so on), so you can skip this chapter. But you system managers and network administrators out there are the caterers, so stay with us. Whether big or small, a network banquet has to be organized so that everyone gets enough to eat. That's your job. And if you're supervising the system managers and network administrators, you should definitely stay with us. Getting to know a little about network hardware will help you understand why your employees are always asking for faster, more powerful stuff.

What's hardware got to do with it?

Even though TCP/IP is software, it has to run over hardware. Like love and marriage, TCP/IP and hardware go together like a horse and carriage. And if you're responsible for a network, you can't be just "a software person" — no matter now hard you try. You need to pick up a little hardware knowledge and jargon to do your job right. Part of having a good marriage is understanding and appreciating each other's differences.

So, the answer to the question "What has hardware to do with doing a good job in network management?" is this: Network cables (and other media), along with TCP/IP software, link computers together so that they can provide communication for and among your users. Computers are just hardware devices that happen to run some software — often, too slowly. If you're the caterer and the hot buffet is cold, your guests are unhappy. If you're the network manager and the software runs too slowly, your users complain. And the problem may not be with the software. Just as the caterer needs enough pots, pans, kettles, and chafing dishes, you need network hardware to satisfy guests at the TCP/IP banquet. Your network needs some other hardware devices to create the infrastructure, too — unless it runs across the dining room table the way ours does.

Keep Layers in Mind

Chapter 5 lists a major benefit of TCP/IP software — that it is independent of the underlying hardware. TCP/IP protocols do, however, work with hardware.

Some of the hardware discussed in this chapter communicates only with the physical (bottom) layer of the TCP/IP network layer cake, and protocols aren't an issue. Nevertheless, we have included information on these hardware devices. When designing or paying for a network, you may need to choose between a simple hardware device that has nothing to do with the middle (transport/internet) and upper (session/presentation/application) layers of the cake where TCP/IP is located, and, a more complicated solution consisting of both hardware and TCP/IP software. We include descriptions of some physical layer devices so that you can compare their features to the devices that work with TCP/IP protocols.

All of this information helps you organize your network wedding banquet with confidence, and that means you can build your network with the most appropriate components.

Packets Chew through Network Layers

Your network message is put into packets (see Chapter 3) along with some control information and sent out onto the network. We use the life of a packet to explain the layers in the network model.

A packet's life begins when an application creates it. Each packet travels down through the layers of the sending host, out across the network cables, up through the layers of the destination host, and into the appropriate application.

As the packets travel down through the layers of the sending host, control and formatting information and directions are added. When the packets reach the destination host, that information is read and stripped out as the packets move upward through each layer. For example, if you FTP a file from computer A to computer B, the data in the file is "packetized" at the application layer and sent through all the layers on computer A. By the time the packets are sent out across the wire, they have gained some weight — it's all that added network information. After the roly-poly packets reach the destination host, they start to slim down, and when they arrive at the top layer and deposit your file, they're positively svelte again.

Figure 18-1 shows an FTP put operation; a packet travels from the application layer on computer A out on to the network wire and up to the application layer on computer B. You can see how the packet gains weight at each of computer A's layers and then goes on a diet as it moves up through computer B's layers. Yo-yo dieting may be unhealthy for humans, but it works great for packets on the network.

The rest of this chapter helps you understand some of the devices that you can use to extend your network, how they're different, and how to decide whether you need one on your network or internet.

Figure 18-1:
Packets
can eat
TCP/IP
wedding
cake all
day.

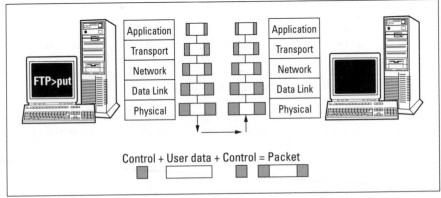

| Application | Transport | Network | Data Link | Physical |

Control + User data + Control = Packet

Modem Munchies

A computer likes digital data. Your regular telephone line likes analog data. This is a Latin/Pig Latin communication problem. You need a translator. A *modem* translates a computer's digital data into analog signals that telephone lines understand. This process is called *modulation/demodulation — modem* for short. In the olden days (the early 1990s), the simplest way to connect to the Internet or any network was to connect a modem into your computer and dial the network's or the ISP's (Internet service provider's) telephone number. Your big decision was how fast you wanted the modem to transmit data versus how much you wanted to pay.

These days, you may be faced with a huge number of choices in modems that can communicate at many thousands of bits per second (Kbps), but consider yourself fortunate to be living in such speedy times. Both of your doddering authors have actually done work dialed in at a rate of 300 bps. Notice there's no K! (Windows hadn't even been invented yet, although UNIX had. And DOS was an IBM mainframe operating system.)

A "plain old" modem is still the simplest way to connect to a network, short of being permanently wired to it. The latest international standard for modems is known as V.90 (pronounced vee-dot-ninety) and it specifies data rates up to 56 Kbps. Your telephone wires may keep you from ever zooming along at top speed, though.

If V.90 still isn't fast enough for you, check with your ISP to find out if you can use two modems and two phone lines simultaneously to increase your speed limit to 112 Kbps. (Ask them if they support "multilink PPP.") Some companies now make cards with two modems and two telephone jacks. That may be a good choice if you're going to upgrade your internal modem, but not as appealing if you already have a high-speed modem card inside your computer.

Satisfy Your Need for Speed with Other Things That People Call Modems

Some new connection devices, also commonly called modems, give you even more speed, although they may add layers of complexity as well. These newfangled "modems" include cable, ISDN, and satellite dishes.

Why do we say these devices aren't really modems? The term *modem* comes from the modulating and demodulating of a digital signal into an analog one, and vice versa. While cable modems and ISDN terminal adapters connect you to a network, they don't do the same modulation/demodulation as conventional modems. (Motorola makes a device that combines an ordinary modem and an ISDN terminal adapter.) So, although they may seem to function like modems, electronically, they do something else. It may seem like a fine point to you, but think how superior you can feel to all those folks who haven't got a clue.

Cable me up

A cable "modem" connects your computer to your coaxial TV cable, which, in addition to letting you watch the sci-fi channel 'til all hours, becomes your Internet connection medium. Accessing the Internet over cable TV cables is *fassssssst*, up to 27 Mbps (million bits per second). The actual speed you get may be closer to 1.5 Mbps, depending on the capacity of the link between your ISP and the Internet and the number of other cable modem users in your neighborhood. That's still a lot faster than normal analog modem connections and it's available 24 hours per day.

A cable modem replaces a traditional modem, but before you buy a cable modem, make sure your cable TV provider offers Internet access. Cable modem access is a fairly new service, and not all cable companies offer it. With a cable modem, your cable TV provider becomes your Internet service provider as well. The monthly fee varies, depending on your cable TV provider. Our cable company, Media One, charges $39.95 U.S., per month as of this writing. Check with your cable company for promotional prices and savings. And if you're thinking of setting up a server for other people to use, ask if you can have a permanently assigned TCP/IP address instead of a periodically changing DHCP address. (See Chapter 6 for the basics of DHCP and Chapter 12 for details of numeric addresses.)

ISDN: Immediate Surfing Down the Net?

ISDN (Integrated Services Digital Network) connects you to the Internet over a telephone line. Did we hear you ask, "So what's the big deal? My modem does that now." We forgot to mention that the telephone line isn't a regular voice line. An ISDN line is a special super-speedy phone line.

ISDN, pronounced by saying the letters I S D N, allows you to stay home and connect to the Internet or your organization's intranet as efficiently as if you signed on to a powerful mainframe computer. Instead of transmitting data at modem speeds, you can use ISDN to zoom along at up to 128 Kbps. That's more than twice as fast as 56 Kbps. If you do a lot of downloading, think of the time you can save. Instead of surfing the slow, gentle wavelets of the Web, you get to accelerate as if you were cresting the Wedge at top speed on the slickest fiberglass surfboard.

Surf the Web from your couch

The WebTV device is a TV set-top box that allows you to access the Internet using your television set instead of using a computer. That's right — you can browse the Web from the comfort and safety of your living room or even your bedroom. (Don't pull the covers over your head.) With WebTV Plus, you can even watch and surf at the same time! The WebTV Classic Terminal or the WebTV Plus Receiver connects to your TV and to a telephone line. Basically, the WebTV box is a special-purpose computer that uses your television set as the screen.

WebTV doesn't use a cable modem. You connect to the Internet via the telephone, not the cable TV service. You need call waiting if you want to receive calls while you're surfing, and you'll have to stop browsing to make calls. Check out www.webtv.com if you're intrigued.

Although ISDN has been around for a decade, it is just starting to heat up as a popular network connection medium. ISDN has languished for almost ten years for several reasons:

- ✔ Most telephone companies did not provide the service, or if they did, the price was outrageous.

- ✔ Communications standards organizations couldn't get together on developing a common standard.

- ✔ The equipment was incompatible from one installation to the next (see the preceding bullet).

Thankfully, these problems have lessened over time. ISDN has finally become more practical for a few reasons:

- ✔ The exploding use of the Internet by home users, telecommuters, and small businesses is driving demand for ISDN.

- ✔ Standards groups have agreed on interfaces that make it practical for phone companies to link ISDN services to the other services on their networks.

- ✔ Most major ISDN hardware vendors have solved equipment compatibility problems.

You get ISDN from your telephone company. You usually have to pay an installation charge plus a monthly charge. Bell Atlantic, our telephone company, also has a data usage charge.

Try to get your telephone company to install ISDN service at a special promotional rate. If your phone company isn't currently running the rate, ask if it plans to have a "sale" any time soon. These promotional rates are almost as common as cable TV's promotions.

We live in New England, which is Bell Atlantic country. As of this writing, their Web site (www.bellatlantic.com) estimated a $67.07 installation fee, a monthly fee of $24.90, and up to $0.08 per connection minute. Your phone company's rates may be better — or worse. There's a wide variation in rates across the United States.

Besides the telephone charges, you need an ISDN terminal adapter (ISDN TA). Many people incorrectly call it an ISDN modem. However, when we say "ISDN modem," everyone seems to understand what we're talking about. The sales representative offered to sell us an ISDN TA for $199.00. Not awful, but a lot more expensive than our new 56 Kbps modem.

Before you get too excited about ISDN, remember that not every telephone company office has the equipment to provide ISDN service.

In some of its service areas, Bell Atlantic offers another high speed network service based on a technology called ADSL (Asymmetrical Digital Subscriber Line). With ADSL, you can have voice and data activity at the same time over your ordinary telephone wires. After you pay for the specialized modem and the network connection/installation, you pay a monthly fee based on the speed you crave: 640 Kbps costs $59.95 per month, 1.5 Mbps costs $99.95 per month, and 7.3 Mbps costs $189.98 per month. You receive data at that speed but transmit at something slower, hence the "asymmetrical" nature of the communication.

Beam me down, Scotty!

Another high speed connectivity option is a satellite dish. Now, don't start cutting down trees to make room for a concrete base underneath a huge earth station dish. We're talking about devices such as the Hughes Network Systems DirecPC dish. It's less than 36 inches across. You receive data from the satellite at 400 Kbps, but you transmit data over an ordinary modem connection. The incoming data gets a free trip into outer space and back — the satellite is in orbit 22,300 miles above the Earth — but the second half of the trip is downhill all the way.

With DirecDuo dish from Hughes, you can also receive TV programming at the same time as your Internet data. This isn't the same as WebTV, though. (See the sidebar "Surf the Web from your couch" for more on WebTV.) The television signals are delivered to your TV and the network traffic is delivered to your PC.

For more information, check out www.DirecPC.com or www.DirecDuo.com. (Because the TV portion is available only within the continental United States, DirecDuo is limited.)

Serve Your Guests with Terminal Servers

The terminal servers discussed in this section have absolutely, positively nothing to do with the Microsoft Windows NT Terminal Server that we tell you about in Chapter 8.

Even in this age of networked PCs, Macintoshes, and workstations, the majority of guests at most network weddings are terminals needing to attach to hosts. The most common terminal type is a "dumb" VT100-compatible terminal. A dumb terminal doesn't have any processing power. All of the brain power comes from the computer that it connects to. Not all terminals are as dumb as a VT100, however. Certain terminals have small computer "brains" inside them. The more powerful the computer brain inside it, the smarter a terminal is. IBM terminals are smarter, and X Window system terminals are really quite bright.

Regardless of how smart your terminals are, the users of those terminals need to connect to the network in order to communicate with their host computers. A *terminal server* is a special device that helps terminals connect to any computer on the network.

Figure 18-2 illustrates three different uses for terminal servers:

- ✔ Without a terminal server, each terminal must be attached directly to a single computer. In Figure 18-2, the terminals attached to Terminal Server 1 can connect to host A, host B, and host C.

- ✔ Terminal servers can also be used to create modem pools for dial-up arrangements between remote terminals and a host. The modems and telephone lines attached to Terminal Server 2 help remote terminals dial in to host A, host B, and host C. Terminal Server 2 also lets the hosts dial out to remote computers.

- ✔ When a terminal server is used "backwards" — that is, with its ports facing a host computer — the terminal server can be used to provide a network interface for a computer. Terminal Server 3 provides host C's network interface. Notice that the terminal server's serial ports face the host and not the users. The number of users that can connect to host C is determined by the number of serial ports linking the host and the terminal server.

Do you need terminal servers? If you already have a large number of terminals attached to your computer, you probably already have terminal servers. If you're designing a network and people work at terminals, terminal servers are a valuable asset. And when you need a modem pool or a creative solution for a network interface, terminal servers really shine. If your organization is using personal computers, you don't need these terminal servers, but you may want to investigate the Microsoft Windows NT Terminal Server.

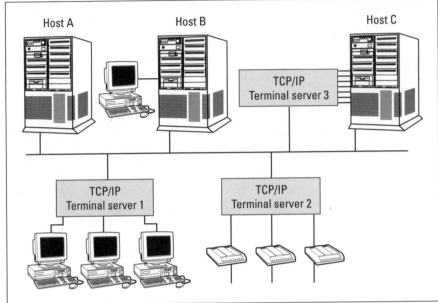

Figure 18-2: Some terminal servers are born great, some achieve greatness, and others have greatness thrust upon them.

Stretching the Network Dinner Party into a Banquet

Networks come in all sizes, shapes, and media. No matter what media your network runs on, each type has its own distance limitations. Take a look at Table 18-1 and examine Ethernet's cable limits.

Table 18-1	Ethernet Cable Maximums for Best Signal Transmission	
Cable Type	*Description*	*Maximum Limit, in Feet /Meters*
10Base5	Thick coaxial cable	1640/500 (Ethernet originally ran on this)
10Base2	Thinwire cable	606/185
10BaseT	Twisted-pair wire	328/100
10BaseF	Fiber optic cable	6560/2000
100BaseT	Twisted-pair wire	1351/412
1000BaseT	Twisted-pair wire	328/100

You may be able to exceed these maximums (for example, by using thinwire cable that's 620 feet long) and get by; the limits usually have a small amount of play built in. But remember that your data is transmitted as an electronic signal across a cable. The longer that signal has to travel, the weaker it gets. The maximums in Table 18-1 indicate the point when the signal starts to weaken.

Think about the banquet. If the kitchen is up two flights from the bar and you plan to serve the appetizers in the bar, you'd better not count on hot appetizers unless you have a dumbwaiter. Likewise, if you need to "exceed" the recommended limits for your cable type, you must use a hardware solution — the network equivalent of a dumbwaiter — to deliver your signal on time and while it's still hot.

The hardware options for extending your network beyond the cabling limits in Table 18-1 include the following (all covered in the following sections):

- ✔ Hubs
- ✔ Switches
- ✔ Routers
- ✔ Gateways

Hubba, Hubba

Suppose Table 18-1 shows that your twisted-pair wires, though cheap, aren't long enough to extend across your building as planned. Think twice before you throw away the wire and buy some expensive optical cable, which could extend your network not just across the building but across the county. Optical cable may extend your network, but it will also seriously shrink your budget.

 Don't panic. There are other answers, including a device called a *hub* that ties multiple segments of wire or cable together. The hub also retransmits the signal so that it can travel longer distances, despite the limitations of the wires and cables. When you extend a cable with a hub, you can put more physical devices, such as computers, on the cable. Most people think hubs are the things under their desks for easily connecting multiple computers to the network — and they're right — but a hub also helps extend your network cable.

You can use hubs to extend a LAN by linking multiple network segments. These segments must be of the same type. In other words, all Ethernet is fine, but mixed Ethernet and token ring is not fine (see Chapter 3). The hub takes the electronic signals from one network segment and retransmits them on the other segments. It never thinks about packet formats or network protocols.

Although the hub can be a potential point of failure within the network configuration, a hub is a simple device and doesn't usually fail on its own. If you're thinking of using hubs to extend the distance your network wires span, be sure to consider the history of power outages in your area. Hubs don't have built-in power-failure features, such as battery backup. They're simple and inexpensive, and they do the job — but they don't have a lot of advanced options.

Keep large animals away from your network wiring! Although hubs are durable and reliable network devices, if your pet elephant steps on one, it breaks. If you have a hub under your desk, try not to kick it too often.

There's Ethernet and there's Fast Ethernet

If Ethernet isn't fast enough at 10 Mbps, you can get Fast Ethernet at 100 Mbps. Fast Ethernet is called 100BaseT, and is part of the original IEEE 802.3 standard. If Fast Ethernet isn't fast enough, you can try Gigabit Ethernet at 1 Gbps (that's 1,000 Mbps). Wow! Things just keep getting faster by factors of 10.

Fast Ethernet uses twisted-pair wire, like that in your house, or it can use fiber-optic cable. You also need a NIC (Network Interface Card) and other hardware, such as hubs and routers, that understand the speed of Fast Ethernet. The nice thing for network administrators is that your knowledge of Ethernet (is it slow Ethernet now or regular Ethernet?) is transferable. You don't need extra training or new books.

Gigabit Ethernet is an extension to the IEEE Ethernet standard. After two and a half years of work, the IEEE 802.3z standard (Gigabit Ethernet over fiber optic cable, also known as 1000BaseSX and 1000BaseLX) was formally approved in June of 1998. The Gigabit Ethernet Alliance is now working for the approval of IEEE 802.3ab (also known as 1000BaseT) for Gigabit Ethernet over twisted-pair wire. You can keep track of their efforts by monitoring www.gigabit-ethernet.org and standards.ieee.org/catalog/ IEEE802.3.html. If standards groups moved as fast as these new Ethernets, the standards would be done in a matter of hours.

Gigabit Ethernet is still pretty new. Not every vendor can supply what you need.

Fast hardware is one way to speed Web access. But just because you have fast hardware doesn't mean that you will see a miraculous increase in speed. You need faster hardware not just on your desk, but at your ISP and throughout the Internet. These lessons apply to your intranet, too.

Who really needs to go that fast?

You may be surprised. Fast Ethernet is becoming popular for connecting servers and powerful desktops, such as the high-end graphics stations that create the animated movie *Antz*. If desktops and servers run at such high speeds, there must be a need for the backbone network or superserver to run even faster. And there's probably someone out there on a Mac who's saying "I need to go even faster," right now.

A Switch in Time Saves Nine Intranet Hassles

A *switch* is a network device that extends a LAN by linking multiple network segments. Gee, that sounds like a hub, doesn't it? Well there are similarities, but there are many differences:

- ✔ Switches normally live in wiring closets and computer rooms, rather than under desks.

- ✔ A switch increases the available network bandwidth by connecting network segments together only when a packet needs to pass between them.

- ✔ A switch makes connection decisions based on address information inside the packet. The address information is either a NIC's hardware address (from layer 2, the data link layer) or a numeric IP address (from layer 3, the network layer). (Flip to Chapter 5 for a discussion of TCP/IP's layers.)

- ✔ A packet may pass through several switches on its journey from the sending computer to the receiving. Each switch must make its own connection decision, because switches don't talk among themselves.

A switch is designed to be very fast, but not super-intelligent. While it's great for your intranet, it doesn't support WANs, so you can't use one on the Internet. For that you need routers.

Rowter or Rooter? Doesn't Matter

In the original work on TCP/TP, the designers wanted to be able to move data across the network even if parts of the network became disrupted. For example, if a network link were taken out by enemy attack, the traffic on that link would automatically be rerouted to a different link. This reliable scheme is call *dynamic rerouting*, but your system doesn't have to be a victim of an enemy attack for dynamic rerouting to be valuable. If a forklift cuts a cable in a warehouse, for example, dynamic rerouting means that inventory data can still be sent across a network via a different route.

According to Webster's, a *router* ("rowter") is a woodworking tool. A *router* ("rooter") is a sports fan with a bet on the Big Game; it's also a horse that's trained for distance races. In network parlance, however, you can pronounce it any way you want, so pick a side and join the battle. People pronounce it both ways and some are willing to fight for their choice. We prefer to remain nootral.

If your network suffers an identity crisis when its segments are linked together, a router may be the therapy it needs. A *router* extends a LAN by linking two or more network segments that may or may not use the same media type. The router permits each connected network to maintain its independent identity and address.

What makes routers special is that they're intelligent enough to understand IP addresses. In fact, the decisions the router makes about directing the packets of your data are based on the network portion of the IP address. A router contains a network interface card for each segment of the network that it connects. Each network interface card has a different IP address because the router itself is a member of each network.

How does routing work, anyway?

Routers work at the internet, data link, and physical layers of the TCP/IP structure.

A router resembles an octopus whose tentacles represent all of your cabling types. Routers are aware of multiple paths your data packets can take across the network to their final destination. The router knows about other routers on the network and can choose the most efficient path for the data to follow. This efficient path may change as network devices change and traffic comes and goes.

For example, on Monday, the most efficient path may be from network A to network C to network B. On Tuesday, however, the most efficient path may be from network A to network D to network B, because network C is broken. Because it knows about any problems on the network path, the router can detour your data when necessary.

Routers use a routing protocol to learn about the entire network and to determine the optimal path for sending a packet on to its destination. What's optimal? Is it the shortest path (fewest hops from one host to another)? Or the fastest path (more hops on speedier links)? Or the least-congested path?

Suppose you want to go from Boston to New York City to visit the World Trade Center. Your top three choices are probably these:

✔ Drive to NYC on Interstate 95 and use a city map to find the World Trade Center.

✔ Drive to Boston's Logan Airport. Fly to JFK Airport in NYC. Take a taxi to the World Trade Center.

✔ Drive to Boston's South Station. Take a train to Penn Station in NYC. Take the subway to the World Trade Center.

Which way do you think would get you there fastest? If you've never driven to Logan Airport during rush hour, most of you would guess that flying from Logan to JFK is the fastest route. However, depending on city traffic, flying may actually be the slowest way. Trust us on this — we've had the experience to prove it over and over again.

The shortest way isn't always the fastest way. Nor is the most direct route always the fastest way. And if you never go to New York City even once in your life, these facts are rules to live by on the network, as well.

Routing protocols

When you buy a router, your purchase includes proprietary software that functions as a mini-operating system, which the network manager — probably you — must install and configure. The router also includes an installation guide. If you have to configure router software yourself, be sure to follow the instructions. Many routers load their "operating system" software from a server on the network via the BOOTP or TFTP protocols described in Chapter 6.

When you configure the router, you also need to select the appropriate routing protocol(s); these protocols, too, come with the router. There are several, but the three most prevalent routing protocols are discussed in the following sections.

RIP (Routing Information Protocol)

RIP was developed by Xerox, which was way ahead of its time as a computer company — so ahead of its time, in fact, that it didn't catch on as a computer company. But the legacy of Xerox lives on in networking, especially in Ethernet. RIP has been part of UNIX TCP/IP since the beginning and is also a part of almost every TCP/IP product on the market today. Because RIP was developed before the corresponding RFC (RFC 1058), you find differences in the various implementations.

Are you getting the point by now that RIP is old? Some people think it's old as in Old Reliable. Some people think it's old as in Rest In Peace. Though RIP is intelligent and routes your packets to their destinations just fine, it's a slow learner when it comes to network changes, such as the appearance of new routers and faster paths. RIP is one of the Interior Gateway Protocols, which means that, if it's in use at all, RIP is used within an organization and not on the wider Internet.

OSPF (Open Shortest Path First)

The Open in OSPF isn't a verb; in this case, it's open as in open systems (see Chapter 1). OSPF is a descendant of and supersedes older protocols such as IS-IS (Intermediate System to Intermediate System). OSPF is built on the concept of *designated routers* — that is, all routers are created equal, but some get elected to positions of importance. OSPF is the most common Interior Gateway Protocol.

BGP (Border Gateway Protocol)

BGP is the protocol the Internet's routers use to exchange routing table information. Because it is used between organizations, BGP is an Exterior Gateway Protocol — in fact, it replaced a protocol with that name.

CIDR (Classless Inter-Domain Routing)

CIDR is the key technology that has kept the world from running out of IP addresses and it helps routers do their job as efficiently as possible. (Check out Chapter 13 for the essential information.) These days, every ISP is required to use CIDR . Because it isn't exactly a protocol itself, CIDR works with OSPF (for intranets) and with BGP (for the Internet).

For all the gory details of CIDR and the conservation of IP addresses, check out RFC 2050, Internet Registry IP Allocation Guidelines.

Configuring a router on Windows NT Server

While most routers are dedicated hardware devices running specialized software, you can use a general purpose computer to perform the same function. The computer must have two or more NICs and must be connected to two or more network segments. The TCP/IP implementation must include routing capabilities. Figures 18-3 and 18-4 show a Windows NT system that's in the process of being configured as a router. Notice that one NIC has already been installed, and a second NIC is in the process of being installed.

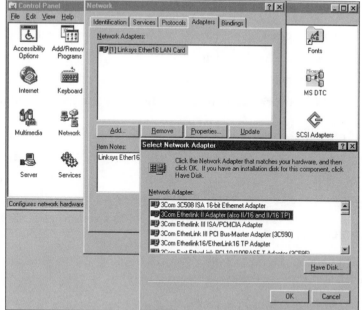

Figure 18-3:
Configure
your NICs
before
enabling
routing.

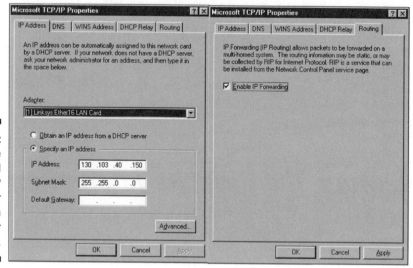

Figure 18-4:
Configure
TCP/IP and
enable IP
routing for
each NIC in
your
computer.

Here's what you do:

1. **From the Start menu, choose Settings⇨Control Panel.**

2. **Click on the Network icon.**

   This brings up the Network dialog box, shown in Figure 18-3.

3. **In the Network dialog box, click the Adapters tab to configure the NIC.**

4. **Click the Add button.**

   A list of Network Adapters appears in the Select Network Adapter dialog box.

5. **Click on your NIC from the list displayed.**

   If your NIC isn't on the list, you need a disk with the software driver for that NIC.

To configure a NIC for TCP/IP, follow these steps. You need to do this for each NIC installed in your router.

1. **After configuring your NIC, click the Protocols tab in the Network dialog box.**

2. **Click on TCP/IP to open the Microsoft TCP/IP Properties dialog box.**

3. **Click the IP Address tab.**

4. **In the Adapter drop-down menu, fill in the address numbers as shown in Figure 18-4.**

5. **Click the Routing tab and click on the Enable IP Forwarding checkbox.**

6. **You're done!**

Gateways: The Ultimate Interpreters

When the wine list is all French, most people need a knowledgeable *maître d'* or a *sommelier* to help out. Similarly, to do translations on the network, you need a gateway. Gateways work at all the TCP/IP layers, from the bottom physical layer right up to the top application layer, to move data across networks of any type. They translate and repackage information from one application to another — even from one protocol to another.

Chapter 7 talks all about the SMTP gateway, which sends and receives mail between non-SMTP sources and destinations. When a gateway does a translation, it looks at the addressing and routing information and the data being sent and converts it all into the format of the protocols and data on the receiving network.

A common gateway myth

Many people assume that a gateway extends the size of a network. Actually, a gateway extends the connectivity of the network by overcoming cultural and packet format differences between connected networks, including differences in protocols.

Because of all the translation involved, a gateway has more work to do than the other network devices in this chapter. You can go down to a computer store and buy a hub, and then go home or to work and clamp it on your cables and put it right to work. A gateway, on the other hand, is usually a computer with two or more network interface cards, one for each different network being connected. And like most computers, a gateway has to be configured with an operating system and network protocols before you can put it to work.

The Party's Over — It's Decision Time

Table 18-2 summarizes the capabilities and features of the network devices described in this chapter.

Table 18-2	Network Devices Compared			
	Hub	*Switch*	*Router*	*Gateway*
Intelligence	None	Moderate	High	Genius
Relative Cost	Very Low	Medium	High	Very High
Configuration Complexity	Simple	Average	High	High
Network Model Layer	Physical	Physical, data link, internet	Physical, data link, internet	All
Addresses Understood	N/A	Hardware, IP	Hardware, IP	Hardware, IP

Don't just blindly add devices to the network without doing any planning. Suppose you decide that all you need is a hub. Before you write the check, consider whether that hub will still meet your needs in a month, in six months, or in a year. If your network is growing, in just a few months you many need to divide it with a switch or router. In that case, even though all you need today is a hub, you probably should go ahead and purchase a more complex device that will still work for you later.

Chapter 19

Security — Will the Bad Guys Please Stand Up?

Security, especially network security, is a hot topic. Being connected to a network, especially the Internet, comes with some security risks. Is it worth it? For most people and organizations, the answer is yes, but a few important precautions are usually necessary.

Some of the topics in this chapter aren't strictly related to TCP/IP, but are general security topics that apply to all computers and every network protocol. Before you even think about securing your network, you must secure the computers on it. As classic wisdom says, "A chain is only as strong as its weakest link." And sometimes your network is the weak link.

The information in this chapter is intended for everyone, but the tips are targeted at system managers and network administrators, for the most part. And we pose some questions without answering them. We do this on purpose, to get you thinking about certain issues — especially the ones that don't have easy answers. Chapter 23 lists some more real life, practical tips for keeping party crashers from feasting on your internet, intranet, extranet, or Virtual Private Network.

In the Good-Ol' Days

ARPANET security depended on the physical isolation of the network and the fact that the hosts and users were trustworthy. IP didn't have much in the way of built-in security. Back then, the concepts of encryption, authentication, and secure transactions were totally alien. As the network grew into the Internet, minimal security features were bolted onto TCP/IP. The world isn't such a friendly place now, and most sites need more than those early minimal security features.

What's Involved in Network Security?

Network security involves everything:

- ✔ Hardware: the computers and other devices on the network
- ✔ Operating systems to provide security features such as user accounts and passwords
- ✔ Software: the applications themselves
- ✔ The file system, offering mechanisms for protecting directories and files
- ✔ Network design: the whole kit and caboodle
- ✔ Organizational policies and procedures
- ✔ Training and education for users
- ✔ Rules and regulations, including punishments for breaking the rules
- ✔ Physical security, such as locks on computer room doors

Everyone involved in setting up security must consider a variety of questions. What are you protecting and from whom? Are the regular users on your network a greater threat than outsiders trying to break in? How much are you willing to pay, and for how much protection? How much inconvenience will legitimate users tolerate?

RFC 1173, "Responsibilities of Host and Network Managers: A Summary of the 'Oral Tradition' of the Internet," describes the security responsibilities of system managers and network administrators.

RFC 2196, "Site Security Handbook" contains good information to help your organization establish security policies and about the security risks of connecting to the Internet.

RFC 1470, "FYI on a Network Management Tool Catalog: Tools for Monitoring and Debugging TCP/IP Internets and Interconnected Devices" (also known as FYI 2), is a catalog of tools available to network administrators and system managers.

Who's responsible for network security?

Everyone is responsible for network security:

- ✔ Users, who must not reveal their passwords
- ✔ System managers, who configure the services and monitor the computers
- ✔ Network administrators, who implement and manage the connections
- ✔ Organization management, which establishes policies and procedures regarding unacceptable behavior as well as punishments for breaking the rules (We could tell you what these are, but then we'd have to kill you!)
- ✔ Information management security staff, who enforce everything

Don't practice "security by obscurity;" that is, don't assume that users are stupid. Some users are smarter than your assumptions, and others make the most amazing mistakes.

Here's a simple example: Leo configures his organization's Anonymous FTP server so that it is publicly writable and assumes that no one will find out simply because he doesn't announce the change. Leo is attempting to practice security by obscurity.

What's the worst that can happen?

Four main categories of security problems put networks at risk:

- ✔ Software bugs that allow outsiders to damage network and Web servers.
- ✔ Outsiders finding out how to break into your server (this overlaps the first risk).
- ✔ Confidential data (such as your password or credit card number and expiration date) being intercepted and stolen.
- ✔ Confidential documents (such as your company's plan to market a unique new product) being stolen.

IPSec (IP Security Protocol)

The IETF working group for IPSec (see Chapter 2 to review what the Internet Engineering Task Force does) has so far produced 28 Internet drafts on the way to creating a security standard for VPNs (Virtual Private Networks).

There's good news ...

Using Internet resources to create corporate VPNs can save large organizations lots of money, especially in hardware costs. Saving money — that sounds great!

... and bad news

If your company's VPN can't infallibly authenticate the users and networks that connect to the VPN, all kinds of unauthorized spies and spooks will find their way into your corporate data and resources.

IPSec is a work in progress. The goal is to develop a standard for securing VPNs. As of this writing, work needs to be done to flesh out IPSec. For example, IPSec provides very strong encryption for data, but still needs a standard method for authenticating users.

The TCP/IP Banquet Is By Invitation Only

Every layer in the TCP/IP layer cake offers, and needs, different security components. (Take a look at Chapter 5 to find out about layers.) The following sections explores some layer-specific security steps.

Tales from the crypt

At the bottom of the TCP/IP structure, in the physical and data link layers, you can encrypt the data on the wire. This is one of the most common security techniques used in communications. Encryption, and some of the other terminology used for computer security, comes straight out of the world of secret agents. Here are definitions of some of these concepts.

Cryptography

This is the process of scrambling (*encrypting*) and deciphering (*decrypting*) messages in secret code. We have seen some authors use the term *cryptology*, but as far as we know, that's the study of crypts.

Encryption

Encryption is the process of scrambling a message into code to conceal its meaning. A common method of encryption is to use a pair of keys — a public key and a private key to encode data so that only the person who is intended to see it can read it. If Marshall sends a message to Helen, Candace's mother, he encodes the message with Helen's public key. She decodes the message with her private key. Only Helen's private key can decode the message. Candace can't peek at what Marshall and Helen are saying about her.

Encryption key

The *encryption key* is the essential piece of information — a word or number or combination — used in encrypting and decrypting the message, but it isn't the algorithm (process) used for encryption.

IPv6 allows applications to encrypt an entire packet (maximum security) or just the data portion using various mathematical methods (more on IPv6 in Chapter 15).

Import and export regulations

Much, but not all, of the research and development on computer security takes place in the United States. The U.S. government won't allow the best U.S.-designed encryption systems to be exported beyond North America. The U.S. has traditionally considered encryption products that use keys with more than 40 bits as weapons. Maybe it's national ego or paranoia left over from the cold war. There are signs that the U.S. government may be loosening up, though. In September 1998, the U.S. eased export restrictions so that 56-bit encryption software can be exported to most other countries.

IPSec requires at least 56 bits in encryption keys. Imagine the consequences if the U.S. hadn't loosened up a bit (actually, 16 bits). By the way, 56-bit encryption products are about 64,000 times harder to break than 40-bit products.

Other countries have their own initiatives and import or export controls. For example, France won't allow strong encryption systems to be imported. This causes some vendors to create two or even three versions of a product. The North American version of the Netscape Commerce Server, for example, uses keys that are 128 bits long. The more bits there are, the harder it is to break the code. The international version also has encryption, but it uses 40-bit keys.

If you need international encryption products, a good place to start looking is at CERN (www.cern.ch), the European Laboratory for Particle Physics and the birthplace of the World Wide Web. (CERN is an acronym for its original French name — Conseil Européen pour la Recherche Nucléaire.) CERN has a low-end security scheme called CERN Access Authorization Protocol.

You should also keep your eyes on TrustWorks, headquartered in the Netherlands (www.elvis-plus.com — the name has nothing to do with Elvis Presley, it's just that the company originated in Russia, where the Cyrillic letters of the company's name look like "ELVIS+"). TrustWorks' products for secure VPNs make export restrictions a non-issue. With TrustWorks' Open CryptoAPI, your organization can plug in any encryption scheme that's legal in your country. For example, you can use a 128-bit encryption scheme developed in Switzerland to communicate with a 128-bit version from the United States.

Public key/private key cryptography

In the public key/private key coding process, one encryption key is used to encrypt the message, and another key is used to decrypt the message. There's a relationship, usually mathematical, between the two keys. The public and private keys are very long prime numbers that are numerically related (factors of another, larger number). Possession of one isn't enough to translate the message, because anything encrypted with one can only be decrypted with the other.

Every user gets a unique pair of keys, one that's made public and the other kept secret. Public keys are stored in common areas, mailed among users, and may even be printed in newspapers. Private keys must be stored in a safe place and protected. Anyone can have your public key, but only you should have your private key.

It works something like this: "You talkin' to me? I won't listen unless you encrypt the message using my public key, so I know no one else is eavesdropping. Only my private key, which no one else has, can decrypt the message, so I know no one else can read the message. I don't care that lots of other people have my public key because it can't be used to decrypt the message."

PGP, which stands for Pretty Good Privacy, is an exportable, public-domain (free) software package for public key/private key cryptography. PGP is the technical underpinning for adding security to applications.

The X-Files — tales of authentication

In the middle of the layer cake, in the internet and transport layers, there's a security measure for authentication of computer names and addresses that an application may use. Authentication goes beyond identifying yourself. You have to prove that you are who you say you are.

Knock, knock.

"Who's there?"

"Special agent Fox Mulder, FBI."

Do you believe the breathy voice on the other side of the door and open up? Or do you authenticate him by looking at his ID? Can you really believe his ID? Do you even know what an FBI ID should look like? Do you call the Federal Bureau of Investigation headquarters and try to verify his identity? What if he's really a space alien in disguise?

In TCP/IP, the process of authentication must be built into the applications. For example, an Anonymous FTP server does only very basic authentication.

To interact with the FTP server, you need an FTP client program, a user account name (anonymous), and a password (just your e-mail address). Username/password authentication is the easiest kind to crack. Encrypting the username and password makes cracking them much more difficult. Certain applications, such as Lotus Notes and electronic commerce Web sites, use much more stringent authentication controls, such as *certificates* and *signatures*.

What's a certificate and how do you get one?

Just as your passport proves that you are who you say you are to an immigration official, network authentication proves that you are who you say you are to an application or server. Sometimes your passport is sufficient to allow you to enter a country, but not always. Some countries require a visa, an additional piece of identification, for security purposes. Network and computer security works the same way. Sometimes an application or server accepts your simple authentication by itself and you're allowed to access the application and server resources. Sometimes, however, the application or server requires additional electronic identification for security purposes. That "electronic visa" is called a certificate and it contains your encryption keys.

In real life, you have separate forms of identification for specific purposes: passport, driver's license, employee ID, and so on. For these identification papers to be trustworthy, they must come from a recognized authority, such as the government or your employer. On a network, you may need a separate certificate for each application or server that you need to use. For these certificates to be trustworthy, they must come from a *Certification Authority*.

To obtain a certificate, submit a certificate request to a Certificate Authority, an organization that issues certificates. If your certification authority is a vendor, you must pay a service fee, because the certifier verifies that all requesters are who they claim to be. This validation process protects you and your organization. For example, when you get a certificate for your server, your certificate protects you in the following ways:

- ✔ People who communicate with your server are assured that your server really belongs to your organization, not to an imposter's.

- ✔ You're legally set up to conduct transactions on the Internet.

- ✔ Your server is able to establish secure connections with other servers and clients such as Web browsers via SSL (TCP/IP's Secure Sockets Layer).

Your organization acts as the Certification Authority when it issues the certificate you need to access intranet resources. The Web has trusted third-party Certification Authorities that issue electronic IDs only after verifying the identities of the requesters. You can get a personal certificate from a company called Verisign to use with your Web browser by completing an application at www.verisign.com. Some applications and software are responsible for creating certificates. For example, when you're registered as a Lotus Notes user, Notes creates a user ID that contains your certificate and public key/private key pair.

Authentication on the World Wide Web isn't just about you proving who you are to a Web server. It's also about the reverse. Are you sure that the Web site you've reached is really the site it says it is? Could it be a fake site created by an evildoer who wants to steal your credit card information? Certificates to the rescue! A Web server that has a certificate proves that it is the site it says it is and can encrypt the data communications traffic between itself and your browser.

Are digital signatures as legal as "real" signatures and how do you get one?

Sometimes you must sign a document in the presence of a witness. When the witness is a notary public, he or she can emboss the document with a seal. The signed and sealed original document is then obviously different than a photocopy or facsimile, and is more difficult for a forger to counterfeit. As part of an network application, a digital signature is even more reliable than a notary's seal. (Just in case you were wondering, a digital signature isn't a graphical representation of your handwriting.)

Digitally signed documents are even harder to counterfeit than handwritten, signed papers because the digital signature and the document are bound together and the document is certified to be exactly the same as the original. However, no one has challenged the validity of digital signatures in the courts yet, so who really knows if they're legal.

A network application that supports digital signatures creates one for you each time you want or need one. For example, when you sign an e-mail message, the application uses a certificate to create a digital signature and then binds it to the message.

RFC 1422, "Privacy Enhancement for Internet Electronic Mail: Part II: Certificate-Based Key Management," explains more about certificates and e-mail privacy.

To catch a thief

At the top of the TCP/IP layer cake, in the application/presentation/session layer, the applications can have their own security features.

Some network applications (FTP, rexec) employ passwords, which are a good safeguard, but the use of passwords can open up other vulnerabilities. For example, someone may try to break into your system by telnet, and guess passwords. You can run some kind of accounting or system-auditing utility that can help alert you when your system is under attack, but most Bad Guys are wise to that scheme. To get around it, they may use FTP to test out their guesses instead of using telnet to log in directly. Because different implementations of FTP may or may not provide the same level of auditing that logging in does, make sure the ones you use link to the accounting/auditing system so you know you're under attack.

Tunneling through the Internet

IP tunneling ensures secure, private communication for your online activities. If you telecommute, IP tunneling lets you connect to your office via the Internet without worrying that hackers can read your organization's data. IP tunneling software encrypts your data before sending it over the Net. You need software on your computer that supports tunneling, and your organization needs matching software as well — usually as part of its firewall. You can read about firewalls in the "What's a Firewall?" section, later in this chapter. Chapter 17 introduces you to VPNs and the PPTP protocol.

If all you want to do is surf the Web, you absolutely don't need tunneling. If you want to surf your intranet's web, you may need tunneling.

Be Aware of Security Pitfalls in Your Applications

Now, we look at some of the additional security precautions that you can apply to specific applications, protocols, and services.

Put limits on TFTP

The Trivial File Transfer Protocol, TFTP, provides down-line loading and remote booting. Imagine the damage if people were using TFTP not just to download an operating system to a diskless computer but also to grab your password file. So make a careful decision about whether you really need TFTP. If you do, configure it properly and carefully so that you limit which files can be fetched and by whom.

Test TFTP yourself — but only on your own computers. Testing other people's systems is probably illegal. Try fetching your system's critical files. If you've secured things properly, the transfer fails.

If you don't need TFTP, don't run the daemon that enables it.

Be careful of what's anonymous

Because anyone from anywhere can use Anonymous FTP, configure it carefully so that you limit the files that can be fetched. As with TFTP, Anonymous FTP could be used by an evildoer to grab your password file.

When you configure Anonymous FTP, you specify the topmost directory holding the files that you're offering. But that makes any subdirectories under the specified directory automatically accessible (normal file and directory permissions should still apply). So, after you configure Anonymous FTP, test it to make sure you aren't making critical files available. You also need to make sure that users aren't able to change to a directory outside the tree you specify.

Consider dedicating a computer to Anonymous FTP, and don't put anything on it that you're not willing to share.

Don't believe everything you read, Part One: E-mail

You can never be sure that an e-mail message came from the person it says it's from. Anyone who wants to send fraudulent e-mail messages can change the name of his or her computer and even his or her username. When the message goes through, SMTP doesn't verify the username, computer name, or even the sender's e-mail address. It just passes the message through with the counterfeit information. Figure 19-1 shows the SMTP dialog between the sending and receiving computers.

On many computers, you can't change your username or the computer's name (unless you're the system manager), but on a personal computer you don't have such limitations. It's your machine and you can call it anything you want — even `whitehouse.gov`!

PEM, Privacy Enhanced Mail, is a more secure mail environment implemented by means of a new mail user agent (MUA) in conjunction with good old SMTP. (For more information on SMTP, MUAs, and MTAs, flip to Chapter 7.) PEM knows how to send and receive mail in a secure fashion, but both you and your correspondent must agree to use PEM's privacy functions. Specifically, you both must have public key/private key pairs as well as access to each other's public keys.

For example, a user named Ben can't send his sister Rachel an encrypted message unless both the following requirements are met:

Figure 19-1:
The
receiving
SMTP
computer
believes
what the
sending
computer
tells it.

```
% mail -iv mwilensky@lotus.com
Subject: File to put on floopy
~rtools.txt
"tools.txt" 623/34384
.
Cc: leiden
leiden... Sent
mwilensky@lotus.com... Connecting to crd.lotus.com. (smtp)...
mwilensky@lotus.com... Connecting to lotus.com. (smtp)...
220 lotus.com Sendmail 4.1/SMI-4.10801.1994 ready at Wed, 31 May 95 09:49:27 EDT

>>> HELO max.tiac.net───────── SMTP trust that you are who you say you are.
250 lotus.com Hello max.tiac.net, pleased to meet you
>>> MAIL From:<leiden@max.tiac.net>
250 <leiden@max.tiac.net>... Sender ok────── SMTP doesn't ask to see your ID.
>>> RCPT To:<mwilensky@lotus.com>
250 <mwilensky@lotus.com>... Recipient ok
>>> DATA
354 Enter mail, end with "." on a line by itself
>>> .
250 Mail accepted
mwilensky@lotus.com... Sent (Mail accepted)
Closing connection to lotus.com.
>>> QUIT
221 lotus.com delivering mail
You have mail in /usr/spool/mail/leiden
%
```

✔ Rachel has a public key that Ben can access. He may find it in a central repository, or she could e-mail it to him.

✔ Ben has software (especially an MUA) that can use a public key for encryption, and he knows how to use it.

Even if both these requirements are met, that's not good enough. Suppose Ben could create a public key/private key pair for Rachel and use the brand-new public key to encrypt the mail message he's sending her. After she receives the message, how does she decrypt it? Ben not only would have to give Rachel her public key but also would have to be sure that Rachel knows how to decrypt and encrypt mail. Did he keep a copy of her private key? Can Rachel trust Ben? As Johnny Carson used to say, "Who do you trust?"

Privacy Enhanced Mail may be useful, but you and your correspondents must be synchronized.

Don't believe everything you read, Part Two: Usenet news

When you're reading Usenet news articles, you have the same lack of assurance about their authors as you do about e-mail senders. It's not impossible for a clever villain to generate deceitful news articles. To help you here, NNTP, the Network News Transfer Protocol (see Chapter 7), provides some optional authentication features.

The NNTP server can be configured so that it only accepts news articles if it can authenticate the source computer and author. For this to work, both the NNTP server and the client must use the authentication features. Most clients today aren't using them, however.

Because NNTP authentication only works with the cooperation of the users (at properly configured NNTP clients), it only ensures that the good guys are who they say they are. The villains aren't going to use software that inhibits their misdeeds — at least, not voluntarily.

Usenet news articles can be trusted only if all the authentication pieces are properly coordinated.

We trust only Johnny Carson and Walter Cronkite

The trust-based services (rsh, rcp, rlogin) know which computers and which users to trust, but only because of the contents of an ASCII text file. Are these files and their directories protected so only authorized users can change the contents? (On UNIX systems these include /etc/hosts.equiv and the .rhosts files in users' home directories.)

The security of your trusted TCP/IP network services is, in reality, a function of operating system security. Any user of rsh, rcp, and rlogin, including the system manager, can open holes in security — accidentally or on purpose.

Whenever you state a computer's name when you're using rsh, rcp, and rlogin, always specify the FQDN. Otherwise, if you say you trust lotus, you're trusting every computer named lotus everywhere on the Internet, not just the one at the car company.

NFS = No File Stealing!

On UNIX systems, the file named /etc/exports lists the disk space that your NFS (Network File System) server is willing to share. It also allows you to limit access to only the NFS clients you name, as well as to restrict the actions of the privileged users on those NFS clients.

Here are some tips for keeping your NFS servers safe and secure:

- ✔ Be specific about the disk space you're sharing. Only list the directories that need to be shared.
- ✔ Be specific about the NFS clients you support. Put their FQDNs in the file.

✔ Don't allow privileged users on NFS clients to have privileged access to your disk space. State (in /etc/exports) that those clients aren't allowed privileged access.

Use the showmount command on the NFS server to see the disk space that the NFS clients are using. Here's an example:

```
% showmount -a
frodo:/var/spool/mail
frodo:/usr1/emacs
bilbo:/var/spool/mail
bilbo:/usr2/xmosaic
```

If you ever see a numeric IP address instead of the name of the NFS client, it could indicate a security problem. It means the NFS server was unable to look up the name of the client in the local hosts file, the NIS, or the DNS.

If you want to review NIS and NFS, look in Chapter 10; we explain DNS (Domain Name System) in Chapter 11.

Sweat the small stuff!

Don't get so involved in security complexities that you forget the basics. Without the following simple practices, all the fancy network security tips in the world are useless.

✔ Require users to change their passwords on a regular basis. Use a password-checking program to discover if users have selected passwords that are too easy for evildoers to guess.

✔ Deploy virus-scanning applications widely and use them regularly.

✔ Back up your systems regularly and store the backup media (tapes, disks, floppies, or whatever) offsite.

How Promiscuous Is Your Network Controller?

Normally your network controller is only interested in looking for packets addressed to it — it ignores all the rest. Some network monitoring and management software, however, is able to place the network interface card in "promiscuous mode," making it keep and display every packet. These kinds of tools are useful for debugging network problems, but they should be available to and used by authorized network administrators only.

Anyone using this software, or any network analyzer, can see the contents of any packet — perhaps even an unencrypted password or an e-mail message — as it travels by. This network monitoring and management software is easy to get for personal computers; perhaps too easy. It may be difficult to protect yourself and your network.

Credit Card Shopping on the World Wide Web

More and more, World Wide Web surfers want to do more than just browse published data. The Web's clients and servers need two-way communication in order to provide more sophisticated services. Corporations need this interchange in order to conduct business over the Internet. The goal is for a consumer to be able to browse a product offering, fill out an order form, and supply credit card information (or a checking account number for electronic funds transfer, or the like). Both parties need to be sure that the transaction is done in a secure manner.

How does the S-HTTP (Secure HTTP) protocol help?

Secure HTTP (HTTP with security enhancements) addresses the issue of moving data securely across a public environment such as the Web. HTTP is HyperText Transfer Protocol (check out Chapter 12), which is how browsers communicate with servers on the Web.

RFC 2069, "An Extension to HTTP: Digest Access Authentication" describing S-HTTP, is on the Internet standards track.

S-HTTP provides transaction security services and confidentiality as well as authentication. It builds encryption into the application level before you even get to the Web server. HTTP, on the other hand, makes the client try to access the Web server before issuing a username and password challenge, if needed. Secure HTTP doesn't require any changes to HTML, the language that makes the Web's pages look so good. (Although HTML is also getting new features, they're driven by other requirements.)

If you need S-HTTP, upgrade to new versions of World Wide Web browsers and servers as soon as they're available. By the way, S-HTTP also supports Kerberos security. You can browse www.commerce.net for S-HTTP information and demonstrations. Or, you can use Anonymous FTP to get the S-HTTP specification (/pub/standards/drafts/shttp.txt) from ftp.commerce.net.

How does the SSL (Secure Socket Layer) protocol help?

The SSL protocol ensures privacy between a client and server by using certificates to authenticate the server and optionally the client, and it ensures confidentiality by encrypting the data they exchange. No one can put a computer on the network and fool SSL into believing the spoofing server should receive the client's confidential credit card information. If you're shopping on the Web, you want the commerce server to prove that it is who it claims to be. Do you remember the alien impersonating Fox Mulder earlier in this chapter? SSL won't let that happen. SSL also has an option to authenticate the client so a server can be sure you're who you claim to be. SSL requires a reliable protocol for the transport — TCP, not UDP.

SSL isn't tied to a particular application. This is a great advantage. You can layer any application or protocol, such as HTTP or FTP, over SSL. SSL sits on top of TCP/IP, taking care of encryption, security keys, authenticating the server, and — possibly — authenticating the client before the application sends or receives any data.

To ensure complete Internet privacy, be sure that SSL is implemented on both your client and the server.

Security software that's based on SSL can't protect you from disreputable people. In TCP/IP, as in life, security makes it much harder for the bad guys to take advantage of you, but in networking (as in real life), you have to trust someone. Even special agent Mulder trusts his partner, Scully.

For example, when you buy something over the telephone, you trust the person who takes your order with your credit card information. When you buy something over the Internet, you trust the server administrator at the site with your credit card information. The server administrator maintains the security software, the physical security of the computers, and the security of passwords and private keys.

Do You Have Any ID? A Digital Certificate Will Do

A Digital Certificate verifies the connection between who a server claims to be and the server's public key. Your passport works like a Digital Certificate by connecting who you are (your photograph) with your identification (name, age, birthplace, citizenship).

Netscape Navigator and Netscape Commerce Server deliver server authentication using signed Digital Certificates issued by trusted third parties known as *Certificate Authorities* (CAs). Other client and server products can do the same thing.

A Digital Certificate is an encrypted, password-protected file that contains

- ✔ The name of the certificate holder
- ✔ The holder's e-mail address
- ✔ The public key for verifying the digital signature of a message sender by matching the sender's private key
- ✔ The name of the issuing certification authority (CA), for example, Verisign or RSA Certificate Services
- ✔ The certificate's validity period

The CA digitally "signs" and guarantees the file (certificate).

How Digital Certificates are used

Digital Certificates secure communications between Web browsers and servers (for example, via SSL or SET) or between two e-mail clients using S/MIME (Security-enhanced Multipurpose Internet Mail Extensions).

RFC 2312 describes how certificates and S/MIME work together. By the way, as of this writing, there are currently nine Internet drafts about S/MIME.

Organizations on the Internet use Digital Certificates to establish mutual trust so that the participants can trust other's identity during transactions such as

- ✔ Internet credit card purchases
- ✔ Internet banking and investing
- ✔ Enrolling and checking benefits with healthcare organizations
- ✔ Communication between employees on private corporate information

How to get a Digital Certificate

Here's how to get a signed Digital Certificate:

1. **Submit a request to a Certificate Authority (a company that checks that your server and organization are who they say they are).**

For example, Netscape Communications gets the certificates for the secure product, Netscape Commerce Server, from RSA Certificate Services, a division of RSA Data Security, Inc.

2. Pay the service fee to cover the necessary investigation.

E-Commerce — a Shopper's Dream?

E-commerce, electronic commerce, is high-volume and hopefully high-speed shopping over the Internet's Web. It can also be over an intranet's web.

Watch out, Big Four!

If e-mail, FTP, telnet, and browsing are the most widely used Internet/intranet applications, e-commerce is the fastest-growing application area. Many Fortune 500 companies, as well as thousands of medium-sized and small companies and individual entrepreneurs, are on the Web.

What kind of business can you do over the Internet?

There's no limit to the potential. As an end user you can

- ✔ Browse through a company's catalog.
- ✔ Look at price lists.
- ✔ Place secure credit card orders using SET, the Secure Electronic Transaction protocol. (See Chapter 6 for a description of SET.)
- ✔ Check your order status.

You can do all of these 24 hours a day, 7 days a week, 365 days a year (24 x 7 x 365 in computer lingo).

If you're a corporation, you provide electronic shopping and ordering services for end users. To offer a full range of e-commerce functions, corporations need servers with the following Internet capabilities:

- ✔ **Continuous availability:** You don't have to close your store because the front door of the mall is broken.
- ✔ **High reliability:** If Marshall buys a new Lamborghini over the Internet, he may be upset if he receives a Kia. By the way, is that for Candace's birthday?

> ✔ **Secure transactions that use appropriate encryption and authentication:** When Marshall purchases the car, the "store" has a responsibility to protect the credit card information. For more information on secure transactions, flip though the SET protocol section in Chapter 6.

CommerceNet is a non-profit organization comprising over 500 companies and organizations. Its goal is to promote the Internet as an international electronic marketplace. Give it a look at www.commerce.net. Other organizations have similar goals.

Commonly Held Myths about Network Security

It's amazing, the things that some people say and believe about network security! Here's a random and scary sample. We don't believe these and neither should you.

- ✔ No evil people are connected to computer networks.

- ✔ Only evil people connect to networks.

- ✔ There are no security concerns about putting your computer on a network.

- ✔ It is impossible to have a secure network.

- ✔ After your network is secure, you don't have to worry it about anymore.

- ✔ Accounting and auditing utilities have too much overhead to be worth the expense.

There's shopping and then there's SHOPPING!

The country of Singapore is an example of e-commerce on a grand scale. Singapore is setting up an Electronic Procurement System (EPS) for all government purchasing agencies. The Singapore government plans EPS to be an e-commerce system that manages all procurements from more than 10,000 suppliers and distributors. By coordinating their activities through EPS, all government departments combine their buying power to get the best possible service and prices. Singapore expects tremendous savings in manpower and time.

Protecting Your Network

When you think about securing your network, you need to look at it from the bottom up, in this order:

- ✔ Connection media
- ✔ Computers and network devices
- ✔ Users

Can you protect the cables?

Are you the person who decides what devices are and aren't attached to your network? Could someone illicitly attach to a network cable and "tap in" to your network?

The security of your network depends primarily on the network design and physical installation. The efforts you need to make to keep illegal devices off the network will vary with the media you employ. Here are some things to keep in mind:

- ✔ The cable on a traditional token ring network is shielded twisted-pair. The cable and connectors, plus the circular nature of the network, make it difficult to tap in illicitly.

- ✔ Traditional Ethernet coaxial cable (10Base5) can be tapped without cutting through it, but you need special tools and a transceiver to make the illicit connection.

- ✔ Thinwire Ethernet cable (10Base2) is extremely easy to tap, especially at the tee connectors and terminators. It's virtually impossible to prevent additional connections on active network segments.

- ✔ Twisted-pair Ethernet (10BaseT and 100BaseT) cable is regular wire that you can buy in any hardware store. So to make your wiring secure, be sure to run the wires into locked communications closets.

- ✔ In all wiring closets, unused ports on hubs should be deactivated, as should the jacks in unused offices.

- ✔ Fiber-optic cable is extremely difficult to tap. The network fails completely when the cable is cut, so illicit taps announce themselves pretty clearly.

- ✔ Wireless links — including infrared, radio frequency, lasers, microwaves, and satellite dishes — are all interceptible broadcasts. How do radio and TV stations know how many people are listening/watching, you ask? And how do you know if someone is eavesdropping on your radio waves? The answer is that you don't, so you need to encrypt the data so that eavesdroppers can't use it.

Can you detect an unauthorized host or device on your network?

To locate an unauthorized host or device on your network, you could try to ping every network address, but that's impractical on most networks — hard to automate and really boring to do manually. Plus, you're looking for things that shouldn't be there, and you may be distracted by things that should be there and aren't. What if one node is broken or down on purpose?

In one common security attack — called a *spoof* — an evildoer replaces a valid, known host with an impostor. The evildoer turns off or otherwise disables the valid system and brings up the impostor (Ms. Evildoer's own PC, possibly) with the valid system's name and IP address.

Wiring hubs may have some management controls, but you need a real network management solution based on TCP/IP's SNMP, the Simple Network Management Protocol (pronounced by saying the letters S N M P). Here are a few SNMP network management products:

- ✔ Hewlett-Packard's OpenView
- ✔ IBM's SystemView

You can also get free (public domain) SNMP based network management software. Here are two locations:

- ✔ Carnegie-Mellon University ftp from `ftp://ftp.net.cmu.edu/pub/snmp`
- ✔ Massachusetts Institute of Technology ftp from `ftp://thyme.lcs.mit.edu/pub.snmp`

Fort Knox is on the Internet — is our gold at risk?

If you take a look at the Fort Knox home page at `http://147.238.100.101`, you may notice that the site doesn't have any links to the U.S. gold reserves. If you search for "gold," Fort Knox returns 33 items concerning gold — gold medals and such — but no gold as currency. If you want access to any gold in Fort Knox, you have to do it the way they tried in the movie, Goldfinger — storm the gates and hope that James Bond isn't around. We don't have to remind you that this is illegal.

Automatic teller machines aren't on the Internet either — they're on private networks. That's why criminals yank them out of the walls to steal them and the money inside — although some evildoers have probably tried to connect to the network and tell the machines to spit out money.

Can you keep unauthorized users off your computers?

Unauthorized tapping into your physical network may be less of a problem for you than protecting your network and your computers from improper use by authorized and semiauthorized users. If your organization's network is linked to the Internet, that means anyone linked to the network — legally or illegally — can potentially reach one of your computers or any network device.

So how do you protect yourself? Don't give them access. See the sidebar "Fort Knox is on the Internet — is our gold at risk?" and the upcoming section on firewalls.

What's a Firewall?

Make sure you read Chapter 18 before diving into this section — don't say we didn't warn you!

Webster's Ninth New Collegiate Dictionary defines a firewall as "a wall constructed to prevent the spread of fire." Notice it doesn't say anything about putting out the fire. A real firewall actually only slows the fire's movement through a building.

A *network firewall* is more like a dam with a hydroelectric power plant. The dam has a specific number of very carefully built openings and spillways that allow some of the water through in a controlled way. And "damn!" is what you may say while you try to set up a network firewall, and what your users may say when they try to do work through one. We can also compare a network firewall to the passport control and customs at an international airport. Before you're allowed into or out of a country, you must pass a series of checkpoints. In a network firewall, every packet has to pass certain checks before it's allowed to continue on its way.

In terms of network traffic, normally you're more concerned with inbound traffic (from the Internet to your network) than with outbound. Letting your users out onto the Internet is more or less essential these days. Some people you simply have to trust to behave responsibly — and others you don't. You have some control over the people in your own organization, but you have much less control over the outsiders.

How can you identify the Medusa Evildoers? You can't, and there's no easy way to look in every packet and find out "what the heck is this for?" You have to use what's there — the source address, the destination address, and the port (the service that's being used) — to determine which services are allowed through the firewall and which aren't.

How a firewall works

The firewall examines every packet and decides whether it's allowed in or out. If the firewall refuses to let it pass, the packet is thrown away. The sending system gets the idea when there's no response. Most applications take the lack of response as bad news; they may try again or give up and go away. (What does a caller do if you don't answer your phone when it rings?)

Types of firewalls

You can take many approaches to establish a firewall. The following sections describe some solutions for minimal, good, and better protection against undesirable traffic, and offer suggestions for setting them up. We aren't particularly recommending any of these; we are simply introducing you to the basic concepts so you can decide for yourself.

If you're connected to the Internet via a commercial Internet Service Provider, ask your provider about its own security precautions and the services it can extend to you. You can also hire a network consultant to help you with customized solutions.

Minimal protection: "No default route"

The most common way to tell your computer how to send a message to a network number different than its own — including the Internet — is to establish a *default route value*. If you don't designate the default route, your computer can't send packets to a different network. This inability to send outbound traffic also offers some protection from inbound traffic because almost all TCP/IP services need two-way communication.

Here's an example: If Internet users try to obtain one of your files with FTP, they won't be able to — because their FTP requests need your computer to answer. But your computer can't send anything out, either. Of course, this also means you can't use FTP to get a file from another computer on the Internet because your computer can't send your request to the destination.

So, with "no default route" you get protection from undesired access, but at the cost of services. Sure, boarding up the doors and windows in your house makes it more difficult for someone to break in, but you'll soon be dead because you can't go out for groceries.

This basic approach, then, isn't really a true firewall, but it's cheap.

Good protection: Packet filtering by routers

You can establish a typical and more effective firewall using a router on your network. A *router* looks at the destination address in each packet to determine where the packet goes. You build your firewall by establishing filters. A *filter* is a rule that you establish on the router to train the router to drop certain packets on purpose. Nothing less intelligent than a router can do this be-cause of the software required.

The three fields that can trigger the filters are the source address, the destination address, and the port number:

- ✔ **The source address** answers the question, "Where did this packet come from?" Remember that Medusa Evildoer can set her computer's IP address to anything she wants. Depending on how her computer is attached to the network and how its packets reach your computer, you can't necessarily trust the validity of that source address. The DNS helps her by telling her what IP address to use for spoofing attacks. But your filter can say, "I don't trust this computer at all and will not talk to it."

- ✔ **The destination address** answers the question, "Where is this packet going?" When the destination is one of your computers, you can decide whether any packet is allowed to go there at all. Your filter can say, "Look, this computer doesn't receive packets directly from outside. Forget it. No way." Sometimes you may choose to redirect the packet to a special server. In this case your filter can say, "The packet is okay, but send it over there instead." E-mail is a good example of a service that you may want to redirect. You can disallow receipt of e-mail directly from outside, arranging for all e-mail to be routed instead through a single point of contact. The DNS mail exchange records, known as *MX records,* are designed specifically for this.

- ✔ **The port number** answers the question, "What service is this packet destined for?" If you're not running a particular server, why should you accept any packets of that protocol? For example, if you're not running a World Wide Web server, you can freely and safely ignore any HTTP packets. Your filter can say, "I refuse to talk about that subject."

Better protection: A gateway

Like a router, a *gateway* is a combination of hardware and software, but a gateway is even smarter than a router because it has a whole computer for a brain. Anything that a router can do, a gateway can do better. The problem is, someone has to build the gateway software, and each one is a custom solution.

Network management considerations when setting up a firewall

A simplistic firewall is a single router that links the internal and external networks, examines every packet, and decides whether or not to let each one pass. A single router offers some protection, but is it enough? In this most basic approach, there may also be a question of ownership and control: Who owns the router, you or your Internet Service Provider? Where is the router installed, on your premises or the service provider's?

Some organizations choose to add another router and another network segment. The Internet Service Provider owns one router and you own the other. Fortunately, routers are invisible to the network users. In this arrangement, you must decide carefully how the network's computers are arranged — the computers need to be placed on the correct network segment, based on their function within the network.

This intermediate approach has one major advantage: If you decide to disconnect from the Internet by turning off your own router, your organization still appears to be on the network, because some of your computers are still active, even though no traffic is coming in. E-mail can be queued for later delivery inside; external users can still get to the Anonymous FTP server; and the World Wide Web server can still be browsed. On the other hand, if the service provider must turn off its router, your organization is off the network!

Some computers, such as your Anonymous FTP server and your World Wide Web server, need to be accessible from outside your organization (that is, from the Internet side of the firewall). But do they have to be directly accessible from inside your organization (that is, from your side of the firewall) as well? You can always move files onto the servers by floppy or other external media, but how inconvenient would that be? Is the trouble worth the benefit of the extra level of security?

Some computers and services must be accessible from both inside and outside your organization in order to be useful. E-mail and telnet are prime examples.

Sometimes the firewall's protection interferes with services your own users need, such as Anonymous FTP and the World Wide Web. One easy solution is to add a compute server on the network segment with your

Is your intranet safe?

Suppose your organization is well protected from outside intruders. Is it protected from inside attack as well? Your firewall may well keep the bad guys out, but are you sure there aren't any bad guys inside the organization — perhaps a disgruntled employee or just an ignorant one? Intranets use Internet technology, such as Web browsers. Do you need to prevent the salespeople from browsing engineering data? Or vice versa? Do you need to protect human resource data, such as salary and medical information? If so, you need internal firewalls as well as external ones.

externally accessible servers. To surf the Net, your users must connect to
this system first. This arrangement is somewhat annoying, however, both for
the users and for the system manager, who has to create user accounts on
this doorway computer. Another solution is to establish a proxy server,
which redirects packets toward their real destination. Figure 19-2 demonstrates using Anonymous FTP with a nearby proxy server.

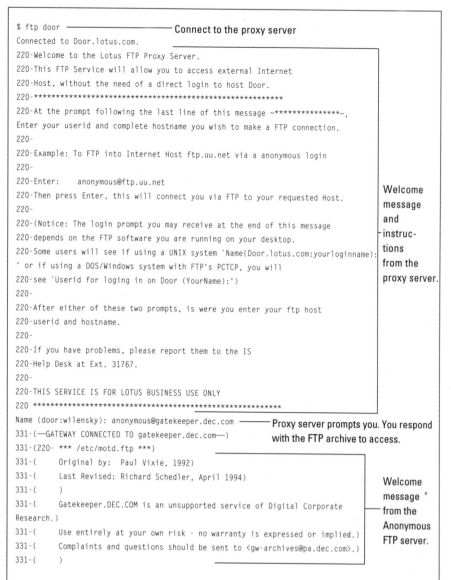

```
% ftp door ————————————————— Connect to the proxy server
Connected to Door.lotus.com.
220-Welcome to the Lotus FTP Proxy Server.
220-This FTP Service will allow you to access external Internet
220-Host, without the need of a direct login to host Door.
220-************************************************************
220-At the prompt following the last line of this message ~***************~.
Enter your userid and complete hostname you wish to make a FTP connection.
220-
220-Example: To FTP into Internet Host ftp.uu.net via a anonymous login
220-
220-Enter:    anonymous@ftp.uu.net
220-Then press Enter, this will connect you via FTP to your requested Host.
220-
220-(Notice: The login prompt you may receive at the end of this message
220-depends on the FTP software you are running on your desktop.
220-Some users will see if using a UNIX system `Name(Door.lotus.com:yourloginname):
' or if using a DOS/Windows system with FTP's PCTCP, you will
220-see `Userid for loging in on Door (YourName):')
220-
220-After either of these two prompts, is were you enter your ftp host
220-userid and hostname.
220-
220-If you have problems, please report them to the IS
220-Help Desk at Ext. 31767.
220-
220-THIS SERVICE IS FOR LOTUS BUSINESS USE ONLY
220 ************************************************************
Name (door:wilensky): anonymous@gatekeeper.dec.com ——— Proxy server prompts you. You respond
331-(—GATEWAY CONNECTED TO gatekeeper.dec.com—)            with the FTP archive to access.
331-(220- *** /etc/motd.ftp ***)
331-(    Original by: Paul Vixie, 1992)
331-(    Last Revised: Richard Schedler, April 1994)
331-(    )
331-(    Gatekeeper.DEC.COM is an unsupported service of Digital Corporate
Research.)
331-(    Use entirely at your own risk - no warranty is expressed or implied.)
331-(    Complaints and questions should be sent to <gw-archives@pa.dec.com>.)
331-(    )
```

Welcome
message
and
instruc-
tions
from the
proxy server.

Welcome
message
from the
Anonymous
FTP server.

Figure 19-2:
A proxy
server
helps with
Anonymous
FTP.

(continued)

(continued)

```
331-(    EXPORT CONTROL NOTE: Non-U.S. ftp users are required by law to follow U.S.)
331-(    export control restrictions, which means that if you see some DES or)
331-(    otherwise controlled software here, you should not grab it. Look at the)
331-(    file 00README-Legal-Rules-Regs (in every directory, more or less) to learn )
331-(    more. (If the treaty between your country and the United States did not )
331-(    require you to respect U.S. export control restrictions, then you would)
331-(    not have Internet connectivity to this host. Check with your U.S. embassy)
331-(    if you want to verify this.))
331-(    )
331-(    This FTP server is based on the 4.3BSD-Reno version. Our modified sources)
331-(    are in /pub/DEC/gwtools.)
331-(    )
331-(220 gatekeeper.dec.com FTP server (Version 5.97 Fri May 6 14:44:16 PDT 1994) ready.)
331 Guest login ok, send ident as password.
Password: ───────────────────────────────── You enter your e-mail address, but it doesn't display.
230 Guest login ok, access restrictions apply.
ftp> dir ──────────────────────────────────── Your normal FTP session starts here.
200 PORT command successful.
150 Opening ASCII mode data connection for /bin/ls.
total 27639
-r-r-r-  1 root    system        858 Dec 11  1992 00README-Legal-Rules-Regs
-r-r-r-  1 root    system      33298 Apr 28  1994 GATEWAY.DOC
-r-r-r-  1 root    system        211 Sep  6  1989 GATEWAY.DOC;1
-r-r-r-  1 root    system      51925 Apr 28  1994 GATEWAY.PS
-r-r-r-  1 root    system   10894531 Jan 20 05:04 Index-byname
-r-r-r-  1 root    system    1974469 Jan 20 05:03 Index-byname.Z
-r-r-r-  1 root    system   10894531 Jan 20 05:15 Index-bytime
-r-r-r-  1 root    system    2207675 Jan 20 05:21 Index-bytime.Z
-r-r-r-  1 root    system       4037 Jan 20  1994 README.ftp
-r-r-r-  1 root    system       4156 Nov 12 15:35 README.nfs
-r-r-r-  1 root    system       4152 Apr 13  1994 README.nfs~
-r-r-r-  1 root    system       6002 Jan 20  1994 README.www
-r-r-r-  1 root    system        647 Aug  5  1993 US-Legal-Regs-ITAR-NOTICE
lrwxr-xr-x 1 root    system         30 Jan 16 01:18 gatekeeper.home.html
-> hypertext/gatekeeper.home.html
dr-xrwxr-x 8 root    system        512 Jan 16 01:41 hypertext
dr-xr-xr-x 2 root    system       1024 Dec 28 12:58 pub
226 Transfer complete.
3483 bytes received in 18 seconds (0.19 Kbytes/s)
ftp> cd pub ─────────────────────────────── Move down the directory tree.
250 CWD command successful.
ftp> dir ─────────────────────── Look at files in the pub directory.
200 PORT command successful.
150 Opening ASCII mode data connection for /bin/ls.
total 38
lrwxr-xr-x 1 root    system      11 Dec 28 12:58 Alpha -> ../.b/Alpha
lrwxr-xr-x 1 root    system       9 Dec 28 12:58 BSD -> ../.0/BSD
lrwxr-xr-x 1 root    system       9 Dec 28 12:58 DEC -> ../.2/DEC
```

Files in the top-level directory.

Berkeley UNIX information here.

```
lrwxr-xr-x  1 root     system           3 Dec 28 12:58 Digital -> DEC
lrwxr-xr-x  1 root     system           9 Dec 28 12:58 GNU -> ../.8/GNU
lrwxr-xr-x  1 root     system          10 Dec 28 12:58 Mach -> ../.b/Mach
lrwxr-xr-x  1 root     system          10 Dec 28 12:58 NIST -> ../.b/NIST
lrwxr-xr-x  1 root     system          12 Dec 28 12:58 athena -> ../.b/athena
lrwxr-xr-x  1 root     system          10 Dec 28 12:58 case -> ../.b/case
lrwxr-xr-x  1 root     system          10 Dec 28 12:58 comm -> ../.b/comm
lrwxr-xr-x  1 root     system          17 Dec 28 12:58 conferences -> ../.8/conferences
lrwxr-xr-x  1 root     system          10 Dec 28 12:58 data -> ../.b/data
lrwxr-xr-x  1 root     system          14 Dec 28 12:58 database -> ../.8/database
lrwxr-xr-x  1 root     system           9 Dec 28 12:58 doc -> ../.b/doc
lrwxr-xr-x  1 root     system          13 Dec 28 12:58 editors -> ../.b/editors
lrwxr-xr-x  1 root     system          12 Dec 28 12:58 forums -> ../.b/forums
lrwxr-xr-x  1 root     system          11 Dec 28 12:58 games -> ../.b/games
lrwxr-xr-x  1 root     system          13 Dec 28 12:58 recipes -> ../.2/recipes
226 Transfer complete.
2916 bytes received in 2 seconds (1.4 Kbytes/s)
ftp> cd NIST
250 CWD command successful.
ftp> dir
200 PORT command successful.
150 Opening ASCII mode data connection for /bin/ls.
total 21
lrwxr-xr-x  1 root     system          31 Jan 19 06:37 00README-Legal-Rules-Regs
-> ../../00README-Legal-Rules-Regs
-r--r--r--  1 root     system       14352 Sep 26  1991 GOSIP.README
dr-xr-xr-x  2 root     system         512 Jan 19 06:37 eval_guide
dr-xr-xr-x  2 root     system         512 Jan 19 06:37 gnmp
dr-xr-xr-x  2 root     system         512 Jan 19 06:37 gosip
dr-xr-xr-x  2 root     system         512 Jan 19 06:37 gug
dr-xr-xr-x  5 root     system         512 Jan 19 06:37 oiw
226 Transfer complete.
499 bytes received in 0.34 seconds (1.4 Kbytes/s)
ftp> get GOSIP.README gosip.txt
200 PORT command successful.
150 Opening ASCII mode data connection for GOSIP.README (14352 bytes).
226 Transfer complete.
local: gosip.txt remote: GOSIP.README
14996 bytes received in 0.97 seconds (15 Kbytes/s)
ftp> cd gosip
250 CWD command successful.
ftp> dir
200 PORT command successful.
150 Opening ASCII mode data connection for /bin/ls.
total 2072
lrwxr-xr-x  1 root     system          34 Jan 19 06:37 00README-Legal-Rules-Regs
-> ../../../00README-Legal-Rules-Regs
-r--r--r--  1 root     system       47067 Sep 26  1991 gosip_cover.ps
```

Move down to the NIS (National Institute of Standards and Technology) directory.

List the files that relate to standards.

Copy information about OSI.

Go down to the GOSIP directory.

List the files.

(continued)

(continued)

```
-r—r—r—  1 root      system      20852 Sep 26  1991 gosip_cover.ps.Z
-r—r—r—  1 root      system       2649 Sep 26  1991 gosip_cover.txt
-r—r—r—  1 root      system       1613 Sep 26  1991 gosip_cover.txt.Z
-r—r—r—  1 root      system     958466 Sep 26  1991 gosip_v2.ps
-r—r—r—  1 root      system     215753 Sep 26  1991 gosip_v2.ps.Z
-r—r—r—  1 root      system     255271 Sep 26  1991 gosip_v2.txt
-r—r—r—  1 root      system      80603 Sep 26  1991 gosip_v2.txt.Z
-r—r—r—  1 root      system     232748 Sep 26  1991 gosip_v2.w50
-r—r—r—  1 root      system     232744 Sep 26  1991 gosip_v2.wp5
```

— Lots of OSI information here.

```
226 Transfer complete.
827 bytes received in 0.46 seconds (1.8 Kbytes/s)
ftp> cd /pub/doc
```
———————————————— Change to another directory.
```
250 CWD command successful.
ftp> dir
200 PORT command successful.
150 Opening ASCII mode data connection for /bin/ls.
total 643
lrwxr-xr-x  1 root      system              31 Jan 19 06:39 00README-Legal-Rules-Regs ->
../../00README-Legal-Rules-Regs
drwxr-xr-x  3 root      system             512 Jan 19 06:39 DECUS
-r—r—r—  1 root      system              75 Jun 24  1990 README
dr-xr-xr-x  3 root      system             512 Jan 19 06:39 security
-r—r—r—  1 root      system           67113 Nov 26  1989 telecom.glossary.txt
226 Transfer complete.
1221 bytes received in 0.58 seconds (2 Kbytes/s)
ftp> get telecom.glossary.txt telecom.txt
```
———————————— Get another file.
```
200 PORT command successful.
150 Opening ASCII mode data connection for telecom.glossary.txt (67113 bytes).
226 Transfer complete.
local: telecom.txt remote: telecom.glossary.txt
68700 bytes received in 2.6 seconds (26 Kbytes/s)
ftp> quit
```
———————————— Done at last!
```
221 Goodbye.
```

When you leave the Anonymous FTP server, you are automatically disconnected from the proxy server.

Firewall protection any more sophisticated than what we cover in this section is beyond the scope of this book. For additional solutions, consult your Internet Service Provider or a network security consultant. For more information, look at these resources:

- ✔ The document titled "Thinking About Firewalls" on the Web at `www.tis.com/docs/products/gauntlet/ThinkingFirewalls.html`.

- ✔ The "Internet Firewalls Frequently Asked Questions" list at `www.clark.net/pub/mjr/pubs/fwfaq/index.htm`.

- ✔ The Internet firewalls mailing list. To subscribe, send an e-mail message to `majordomo@greatcircle.com`. The subject doesn't matter, but the body must contain `subscribe firewalls`. You can get the back issues by Anonymous FTP from `ftp.greatcircle.com`.

✔ The newsgroup `comp.security.firewalls`.

Approaching Secure Environments

Vendors and researchers in network technology are aware of today's security issues and are trying to find ways to address them. There are two dominant approaches to secure communications between separate systems.

✔ Allow only specific activities between cooperating computers and ensure that they've agreed on all the details. Add security (such as encrypted data traffic), to which both sides must agree. For example, a Lotus Notes client communicates with a Lotus Domino server. Both ends have agreed on exactly how to communicate in a secure manner. For another example, think of a primitive network consisting of two cans connected by a string. For security purposes, the kids on that network decide to speak only in Pig Latin so that their parents can't understand the conversation.

✔ Allow two computers to do whatever the heck they want, "safe" in the knowledge that they're who they say they are. This approach is in conflict with publicly accessible computers. If you allow open access by any random computer to a publicly accessible service (such as Anonymous FTP), how can you be sure you can trust the random computer to be who it says it is?

For your consideration...

The following rhetorical questions are intended to get you thinking about the security issues in your environment. Do you have to know in advance who's allowed to talk to you and how? Or are you willing to talk to anyone, anytime? If the latter is true, how do you do that in a secure manner? Can you add security to what's currently happening on the network? Can you build new applications that are aware and secure? Can you identify who the sender really is? Is the sender trustworthy?

We don't have all the answers, but we want you to understand that there are lots of questions.

To find out more about specific security problems and solutions, we recommend visiting the Web site for the U.S. Department of Energy Computer Incident Advisory Capability (CIAC) at `ciac.llnl.gov`. You can read all about security problems. While at CIAC, you can also find out about Internet hoaxes — as if real computer viruses aren't enough to worry about. Now, some strange people think it's funny to circulate warnings about viruses that don't even exist.

Kerberos — Guardian or Fiend?

Project Athena at the Massachusetts Institute of Technology was dedicated to research into very large computing environments — "very large" meant thousands of computers. Kerberos was the security part of that research. Kerberos is also a protocol used by the component parts of a secured computing environment. It's a client/server environment (but isn't everything these days)? See Chapter 4 for more on client/server.

The Kerberos master server — there's only one in your secure network — provides an authentication service used for security in an internet environment. Encrypted user-account information is stored in a database on the Kerberos master server rather than in a local password file or an NIS map.

The secured computing environment needs coordinated time services so that all computers synchronize their ticket expirations properly. (Aha, that's a new piece of the pie: tickets. More about tickets shortly.)

RFC 1510 describes the Kerberos Network Authentication Service.

Playing at Casino Kerberos

Suppose we walk through what happens when you're running under Kerberos. Meet Barry, who likes to play roulette. One fine day, Barry knocks on the special door at the back of Casino Kerberos. (Barry types his username at a Kerberos-enabled computer.)

Barry asks the bouncer for permission to enter the secret inner casino. (Barry's computer asks the Kerberos master server for a ticket-granting ticket, which is permission to talk to the ticket-granting server.) The bouncer then asks Barry for the casino password. Barry gives the right response and is allowed in. (Barry's computer asks him for his password and uses it to verify the response from the Kerberos master server.)

Barry is happy. He goes to the cashier window and buys some gaming chips. He has a choice; the casino games all require different chips. The chips are only valid for a short time. When that time is up, his chips are worthless. (Barry's computer sends a request to the ticket-granting server requesting an application service ticket. These tickets have a limited lifetime.)

Barry is ready to play. He can now lose money at the casino game of his choice, as long as he uses the correct chips at the gaming table he chooses. If he wants to move to a different gaming table, he must have the correct chips or he must return to the cashier window to get them. (Barry's computer can now present the application service ticket to an application server, as permission to use the service.)

By the way, everyone in the casino speaks Pig Latin. (All communications — between Barry's computer and the Kerberos master server, between Barry's computer and the ticket-granting server, and between Barry's computer and the desired application — are encrypted.)

When all of this is in place and operating properly, Barry can be sure he's at the right table and that everyone else standing around the table is playing by the rules. (Barry knows he's talking to the computers and services that he wants to talk to, and the computers and services can be sure that Barry is who he says he is.) Everybody's happy, right?

Catch-22 at Casino Kerberos

Here's the bad news. There aren't very many wheelers and dealers (applications) that work in Casino Kerberos. If you want or need this level of security, you need Kerberos-ed applications. But these days you won't find any in the local software store.

Kerberos is all about a secure environment in which you can trust the computers and the users on them. The reason it hasn't taken off is because most environments aren't closed that way. Most are linked to other environments. Kerberos is complicated and saddled with the catch-22 typical of computer science: Kerberos isn't widely deployed because there aren't many Kerberos-ed applications, and there aren't many applications because Kerberos isn't widely deployed.

In Greek mythology, Kerberos was a three-headed dog with the tail of a snake and snakes wrapped around his neck; he guarded the entrance to Hades. If you got past Kerberos, you were in hell. For the time being, we have to wonder if this is what MIT intended.

Microsoft is using Kerberos in its security model for Windows NT v5.0.

Training the dog — one step per head

A system or network administrator has a lot of work to do before Kerberos is ready to protect a network. Here are the basic steps to configure (Kerberize) the computers and applications on your network:

1. **Start the Kerberos server.**

   Attention network administrators! Forget about sleep and regular meals until you finish this step. You have to install software, edit files, create a database, and insert records for people and computers.

2. **Register principals.**

   A Kerberos principal works like a regular computer account. The name of the principal looks like this:

```
You choose this part@YOUR.REALM
```

If you love chocolate, you probably love chocolate brownies frosted with more dark chocolate. If you love security, you will love the idea of a Kerberos principal. The encrypted principal is the frosting on the Kerberos security brownie. (Gotcha — we bet you thought there would be no food in this chapter!) A principal looks something like an e-mail address, but the resemblance ends there. Kerberos knows just how to use it in a secure environment. You get to choose the part before the "@". A typical choice is your regular account name. The part after the @ sign is the name of the realm. It may look like your computer name for convenience. Each principal is encrypted with a Kerberos master key so that not just anyone can examine it and is stored in the Kerberos database. The principal includes the name, password, and some techie stuff.

3. **Get programmers to Kerberize applications.**

   Kerberizing involves checking to see who is using the application, validating that user's identity, checking to make sure that the user has the right ticket, and getting the user the appropriate ticket.

We're CERTainly Interested in Security

CERT, the Computer Emergency Response Team, is an independent agency that helps organizations defend themselves from attacks. CERT's mission includes helping members of the Internet community deal with computer security incidents and researching ways to improve computer systems security. The people at CERT also maintain information on the security weaknesses of operating systems and applications and how to repair them. CERT doesn't publicize security vulnerabilities without telling you how to work around the problem or how to get a patch to fix it.

You have your choice of ways to sample CERT security advisories:

- ✔ Browse the CERT Web site, `www.cert.org`.
- ✔ Look through their Anonymous FTP archive at `ftp.cert.org`.
- ✔ Subscribe to CERT's mailing list by sending e-mail to `cert-advisory-request@cert.org` with the word SUBSCRIBE in the subject line.
- ✔ Read their Usenet news group, `comp.security.announce`, for security alerts.
- ✔ Telephone 412-268-7090, CERT's 24-hour emergency hotline in the U.S.

Are you a security glutton? If you need more security tidbits, flip to Chapter 23 for ten juicy security tips.

Part IV
The Part of Tens

The 5th Wave   By Rich Tennant

"WELLL, I'M REALLY LOOKING FORWARD TO SEEING THIS WIRELESS DATA TRANSMISSION
SYSTEM OF YOURS, MUDNICK."

In this part . . .

At the network buffet, these chapters are the TCP/IP nuggets, with your choice of dipping sauce. Gobble up our salty little morsels of trivia and silliness, with some valuable information thrown in for nutrition.

As you work through this part, you may notice that "ten" does not always equal 10 — that's computer math for you. Are we talking decimal numbers or binary? Hex, maybe? In octal, 10 means 8. In binary it means 2, and in hexadecimal it means 16. We reserve the right to count in whatever base we like!

Chapter 20

Ten Reasons to Use TCP/IP

In This Chapter

▶ Making money on the Web

▶ Preventing e-mail withdrawal

▶ Finding gaming buddies

▶ Traveling the world without leaving your house

*T*CP/IP provides the broadest level of network connectivity you can get. This is reason enough for many organizations to use TCP/IP. If you're looking for a concise list of convincing arguments, though, for deploying TCP/IP throughout your organization and connecting to the Internet, start with the list in this chapter.

You Want to Sell Your Wares on the Web

Are you a photographer? Do you provide consulting services? Do you have a part-time home business making soap? We know people who do. All of these people advertise and sell their products on the Web. They like the exposure they get on the Web and the low overhead of doing business. If you have a product or service, or a hobby that you would like to turn into a product, look into getting started on the Web. It reaches millions of potential customers.

You Need E-Mail

For many of us, a day without electronic mail is a day without sunshine. For others, a day without e-mail nowadays is a miracle, or a clue that something's wrong with the network. Of course, some people still believe that "no news is good news."

Why do you need e-mail? Professor Irwin Corey (a famous humorist) always said that these complex questions require multipart answers. Why? Because!

Do you need e-mail? Sure you do — so that you can do the following:

✔ Keep in touch with your friends who live far away — but for much less than the price of a telephone call.

✔ Tell your boss that you're taking vacation in the middle of a big project because you don't have the nerve to tell her face-to-face.

✔ Correspond with an electronic pen pal. Some e-mail acquaintances fall in love before they ever meet in person.

✔ Order a deli platter when you don't have time to go out for lunch.

✔ Contact the President of the United States.

✔ Send your Christmas wish list to Santa Claus.

All sorts of interesting people have e-mail addresses. Try fingering the stars to see whose e-mail addresses you can find. (See Chapter 16.)

You Live to Shop

The Internet mall. It's really here — 24 hours a day, 7 days a week, and worldwide. We'd tell you more, but we'd be tempted to pick up a few things after we log on.

You Want to Run Programs on Other People's Computers

Here's a significant TCP/IP bonus! If you have a pathetically powered computer without enough disk space to hold all the programs, games, and tools that you want, rlogin and telnet are an answer to your prayers. They let you steal computer power from all over the world (see Chapter 8).

You Want Someone to Play With

Life shouldn't be all work and no play. Although the Internet offers innumerable ways for people to work together, it also gives you lots of opportunities to play — by yourself and with others. For example, network-enabled versions of the latest computer games let you compete against other players rather than just against your computer. Multiplayer gaming services on the Internet such as www.mplayer.com help you locate worthy and not-so-worthy adversaries. Because the players can interact aggressively as well as cooperatively, the dynamics of the game change constantly as players arrive and depart.

Sneakernet Is Wearing You Out

Have you ever used Sneakernet? That's when you copy files from a computer onto a floppy disk or tape and run down the hall to another computer and load them up. Then you realize you brought the wrong floppy disk or copied the wrong file, so you run back to the other office, where you realize you left the . . . well . . . you get the picture.

If you don't have all the computers in your workplace or other environment linked together by TCP/IP, this runaround may be the aerobic portion of your day. Who needs Jazzercise? But after you have TCP/IP on all the computers, you can relax, get comfortable in your chair, and transfer files to your heart's content — and only get up to go to the junk food machine or to the Jazzercise class that you now need!

But you can also find soda and candy machines on the Internet. (See Chapter 22.) If you network your vending machines with TCP/IP, you can check whether they're loaded up with your favorite brand before you lift yourself out of the chair.

You Have Files to Procure

While you were in the bookstore to purchase *TCP/IP For Dummies,* 3rd Edition, you may have accidentally looked at some other computer books. (We forgive you.) Did you notice that some books come with diskettes or CD-ROMs? Much of that software is available for free on the Internet. You get it via Anonymous FTP (flip to Chapter 9).

You Dream of Untangling the Web

Face it — the World Wide Web is the place to be. The price of admission is

- ✔ A good connection to the Internet — a dialup network connection, at least.
- ✔ A Web browser. Netscape Communicator and Microsoft Internet Explorer are the front-runners, but you can find many more to choose from.
- ✔ Lots of spare time.

Your browser has some built-in starting points for getting caught up in the Web, and we suggest others in Chapter 12. Web pages come and go, so don't get angry when you find some changed or gone. That's part of the fun.

After you get started, you may have trouble stopping. But please don't forget to bathe and eat periodically.

You've Always Wanted to Hear a Free Concert

On November 18, 1994, the Rolling Stones became the first major rock band to broadcast part of a concert on the Internet. Both audio and video signals were transmitted to over 60,000 sites. These days, you can see and hear much more than concerts. We like to go to www.broadcast.com to see the schedule of live events, such as concerts, sports, horse racing, and radio and television broadcasts from the BBC and Voice of America. Figure 20-1 shows the announcement for a Tony Bennett concert broadcast on December 7, 1998. Who knows, maybe you'll find the date for the next Stones concert!

Figure 20-1: TCP/IP helps you tune in to hip concerts.

Live By Request is a Registered Trademark and is used by permission. Tony Bennett's image is used by permission.

Chapter 21

Ten Frequently Asked Questions about TCP/IP and the Internet

*T*his chapter contains straightforward answers to some common questions. In some cases, the discussion is a summary of chapters you may have already read — unless you're still standing in the bookstore and haven't bought this book yet! (If that's you and you like what you see here, just wait until you spend some time in the other chapters!)

What Software Do I Need to Get on the Internet?

TCP/IP — that's all you need to navigate and work on the Net. The TCP/IP protocol suite always includes FTP and telnet client applications. If you want some of the fancier tools, such as Archie or Gopher and a Web browser, check with your operating system and TCP/IP vendors — most operating systems with TCP/IP include browsers, but you may need to download free copies of Lynx, Archie, and Gopher to do text-based searching.

If you plan to use Archie and Gopher only occasionally (see Chapter 12), you can also telnet to a public site that provides Archie and Gopher services.

A protocol suite is a set of protocols, services, and applications that work together.

If you don't get the tools that you want from your vendor, Chapters 9 and 12 show you how to find them and use Anonymous FTP to transfer them from other Internet sites. Most of the newer computer systems come with an Internet browser, but if yours didn't, skip ahead to "How Can I Get a Browser?" or use Anonymous FTP to get one from Netscape (ftp. netscape.com) or Microsoft (ftp.microsoft.com).

Do I Need UNIX to Run TCP/IP?

Absolutely not. The reason TCP/IP supports the Internet is that TCP/IP runs on practically any operating system. Yes, it started out on UNIX back in the early days, but it has migrated everywhere. You can count on UNIX to include TCP/IP, and many other operating systems are starting to include it as well. Flip through the examples throughout this book — there are more examples from Windows operating systems than from UNIX.

Can I Have a Web Server and Still Have Security?

Yes, but be cautious. When you install a Web server that connects to the outside world, you turn your own intranet into a free buffet for Internet grazers. Most visitors just taste what you display, but some may try to consume things that aren't meant for the public. Others may attempt to force their way into the kitchen (your organization's information system structure). Be sure that all CGI scripts installed at your site are written by careful programmers and are bug free. Bugs in your Web programs and CGI scripts are potential security holes. See Chapter 19 for tips on protecting your Web site.

How Can I Get a Browser?

Here's a Catch-22. Use a browser to get a browser: Read the document at www.boutell.com/faq/index.htm. It tells you how to obtain and use a browser for almost every operating system — even strange or old ones such as Amiga, Acorn RISCOS, and NeXt. The document also tells you how to get batch-mode browsers and where to find browsers accessible by telnet. Don't forget that you can use Anonymous FTP or Gopher to get a browser.

Does the Web have a Card Catalog?

You can find plenty of catalogs or indexes of information on the Web. Were you hoping to hear a definitive answer here? Sorry, there is none. The Web has no built-in mechanism to create a single Web-wide catalog of subjects. Yahoo (www.yahoo.com) is a complete index of Web sites, listed by subject. It also has a search facility. The original catalog of the web is the WWW Virtual Library (www.w3.org/hypertext/DataSources/bySubject/Overview.html), created at CERN in Switzerland and now maintained by the W3 Consortium — it's a good place to find resources on a particular subject.

What's a Cookie?

To us, it's got chocolate chips and nuts in it, but on the Internet's table, a *cookie* is information that a Web server sends to your browser when you connect to a site for the first time. Thereafter, the browser returns a copy of the cookie to the server each time it connects. Because cookies aren't part of the standard HTTP specification, only some browsers (such as recent versions of Microsoft Internet Explorer and Netscape Navigator) support them.

Cookies can't invade your computer system. Cookie lovers claim that cookies allow Web servers to serve you better by knowing your preferences. For example, if you say that you like to travel in an airplane window seat, a server puts your preference into a cookie and sends it to your browser. The next time you contact the site, your browser returns the cookie, showing you the flights that have window seats available.

Your browser may ask if you want to accept a cookie. Your authors usually say, "No thanks," because you leave behind some information about yourself, such as the name and IP address of your computer, your brand of browser, your operating system, and the URL, each time you visit a Web page. It may be difficult for someone to follow your trail of bread crumbs, but dastardly spies may be able to find out way too much about you from cookies.

If you want to know more about cookies, read the file cookies.txt, found in the following places:

✔ Netscape users on Windows can find this file in the C:\Programs\Netscape\Navigator directory.

✔ Macintosh users should look in their System Folder under Preferences\Netscape.

✔ Microsoft Internet Explorer users can find the file in C:\Windows\Cookies.

What's a Robot?

A *robot* is a program that automatically navigates the Web, looking for things you tell it to. Robots can be quite useful, but they can also make a mess of things and clog up Internet traffic.

Read the document, "World Wide Web Robots, Wanderers, and Spiders" (web.nexor.co.uk/mak/doc/robots/robots.html) to read about robots and to keep up with emerging standards for keeping of robots out of areas where they're not wanted.

What's CGI?

While browsing the Web, have you ever noticed a URL that had "CGI" in it? CGI stands for *Common Gateway Interface*. CGI programs (also called *scripts*) automate things a Web page needs to do, such as opening a connection to a database. If you've spent much time on the Web, you've probably run a CGI script, probably without even knowing it.

Can I Catch a Virus by Looking at a Web Page?

Probably not. The Web page itself doesn't pass on a virus. The executable programs that you download from an untrustworthy Web site are what can infect your computer. This is the same risk you run when downloading programs from bulletin board systems or Anonymous FTP.

What's VRML?

VRML, the Virtual Reality Modeling Language, extends Web graphics into the world of 3-D. VRML "worlds" depict realistic or fantasy environments. For more information about VRML, including where to find VRML browsers, consult the VRML site (vrml.wired.com) for general information and the WebSpace site (www.sgi.com/Products/WebFORCE/WebSpace) for the first VRML viewer to become available.

What's Java?

Java is a language developed by Sun Microsystems that allows Web pages to contain code that runs on your browser. Java programs are portable and interoperable because they run on any system that has a version of Java. A steaming application is called HotJava — it's a Web browser written to showcase Java language. Check it out at the HotJava home page (java.sun.com/).

How Do I Get a Usenet News Feed?

Keep in mind that you may not need a Usenet feed if you read news from your Web browser. One of our favorite sites for doing this is www.dejanews.com. This site not only lets you read news, it also includes a search tool to search all newsgroups or to search a single category for keywords. This is how we decided on a kitty litter pan and toys for Sybil, Hank, and Hannah, the cutest and the baddest kitties we know. We went to dejanews with our browser and searched for "litter pan." We were able to see the various kinds of doodads that cats in the real world use, before we spent tons of real money. You can use dejanews to search for "TCP/IP" to see what hints and tips other people have discovered. In fact, if you search enough, you can see this book and many others mentioned in informal reviews.

If your system manager or network administrator has already set up a Usenet news feed, you just need a newsreader client, like the ones we mention in Chapter 7.

If you don't have access to a Usenet news feed, you have a little more work to do. First, get Usenet server software, which is available for many operating systems via Anonymous FTP. You also need to find an existing Usenet site that's willing to support a connection to your computer. Often, this "connection" is nothing more than some extra traffic over existing Internet access channels.

One well-known Anonymous FTP archive site that has the software you need, as well as more information about Usenet, is ftp.uu.net. Look for a news directory that contains subdirectories for the software.

News.announce.newusers is a good newsgroup to start with because it helps new users get oriented to the Internet.

Chapter 22

Ten Strange but Real TCP/IP Network Devices (No Kidding!)

In This Chapter

▶ Checking out the Internet pantry

▶ Recognizing that not everything on the Internet is a host

▶ Discovering some mighty strange things that are connected to the Internet

This chapter offers some fun stuff on the Internet — a few of which are just plain silly. You can access the devices in this chapter with any Web browser, so start yours and play around.

To get to the appropriate Web page, just type in the *URL (Uniform Resource Locator* — see Chapter 12). Don't forget that things change rapidly on the Internet, so some of these devices may have taken a powder or may be hanging out elsewhere.

Soda Machines

Engineering students are a thirsty bunch and don't like making unsuccessful forays for quenching, so they have a long-standing tradition of hooking vending machines to the network. That's right — in addition to the one at Carnegie Mellon University that we tell you about in Chapter 14 (www.cs.cmu.edu/~coke), you can find several soda machines on the Internet. You can see a list of Internet-accessible soda machines on the Web at www.cse.ucsd.edu/users/bsy/coke.html.

The machines can be examined by various clients, including finger, telnet, and especially Web browsers. Figure 22-1 shows the images of two at the Computer Science House at the Rochester Institute of Technology in Rochester, New York. To get a firsthand look, access this URL with your Web browser: www.csh.rit.edu/proj/drink.html.

File Edit View Go Bookmarks Options Directory Window Help

Location: http://www.csh.rit.edu/proj/drink.html

CSH Drink Machine(s)

Figure 22-1:
A pair of
Internet-
accessible
soda
machines
wait to
serve you.

Toasters

Network toasters are a favorite device of vendors for showing the capabilities of their *SNMP* management stations. (We discuss SNMP, the Simple Network Management Protocol, in Chapter 19.) With the right connections between the host and the toaster, it's easy to control the darkness of the toast and the amount of time your bread or muffin is inside.

We can't find any toasters that are permanently connected to the Internet, so look for them at trade shows and technical conferences, or look at the picture of one at www.internode.com.au.

Coffee Pots

What's toast without some coffee? The University of Cambridge Computer Lab (that's Cambridge in the United Kingdom, not Massachusetts) has a coffeemaker that's on the Internet. Well, actually, they cheat just a little — there's a video camera pointed at the coffeemaker, and the images collected by the camera are available on the Internet. With your Web browser, access this URL: www.cl.cam.ac.uk/coffee/coffee.html.

If this coffee pot isn't in a convenient location for you, consult this list to find other coffee machines: `dir.yahoo.com/Computers_and_Internet/ Internet/ Interesting_Devices_Connected_to_the_Net/ Coffee_Machines/`.

Other Video Goodies

So now you have coffee and toast. How about some protein? Everybody knows that fish and insects are good sources of protein.

The fish are at this address: `www.netscape.com/fishcam/fishcam.html`.

And you go to Steve's place to see his ant farm (see Figure 22-2): `www.atomicweb.com/AntFarm2.html`.

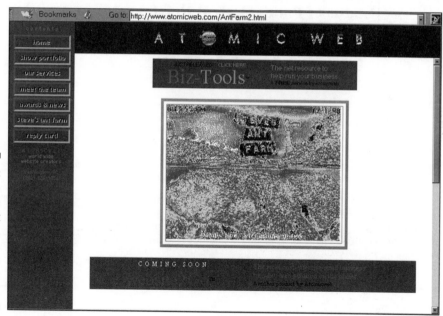

Figure 22-2: Keep them away from my toast and coffee, unless they're chocolate covered.

A Refrigerator

Paul Haas has connected sensors to parts of his spare refrigerator (`www.hamjudo.com/cgi-bin/refrigerator`). It's for sale, by the way. As you can see from Figure 22-3, a computer monitors the sensors and reports the

✔ Temperature in the refrigerator

✔ Temperature in the freezer

✔ Temperature of a can of Diet Coke (no, it's not in the freezer)

✔ Status of the light bulb

✔ Status of the door

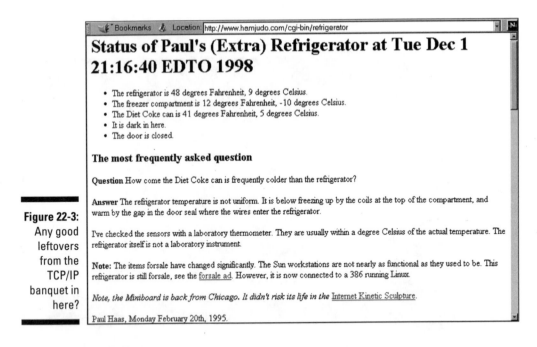

Figure 22-3: Any good leftovers from the TCP/IP banquet in here?

A Hot Tub

Paul Haas is at it again, this time with his hot tub. Figure 22-4 shows the conditions, but neglects to say whether it's in use. There's no video camera here — perhaps we should be grateful? — so you may want to send e-mail to Paul before dropping by. If you're browsing the Web, the hot tub and the hot tub FAQ are at `www.hamjudo.com/cgi-bin/hottub`.

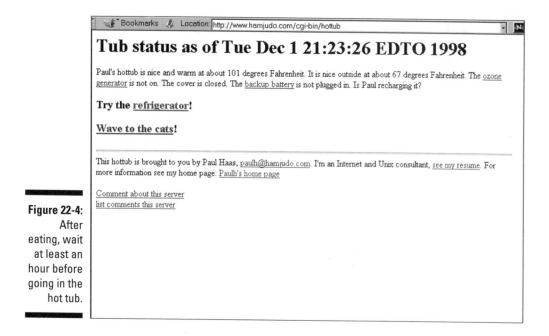

Figure 22-4:
After
eating, wait
at least an
hour before
going in the
hot tub.

The Streets of Seattle

The city of Seattle, Washington, has electronic sensors embedded in the roads and video cameras mounted on lampposts in order to monitor the flow of traffic in and around the area. The sensor information is linked to a map in order to display the traffic in a user-friendly format. Marshall has been to Seattle only once, so the map still doesn't mean that much to us, but you can look for yourself at www.wsdot.wa.gov/regions/northwest.NWFLOW/.

Weather Stations

Weather data are collected constantly by instrument packages around the world. We considered telling you about the one at the University of Washington so that you could decide whether or not to take that drive around downtown Seattle. But instead, why don't you investigate the ones in Norway: www.adm.uit.no/studie/foreign/index.htm.

Or Sweden: www.ausys.se/vadret/default.asp/Sprak=1.

Or see how the penguins are coping in Antarctica at www.antdiv.gov.au/stations/mawson/mawson_aws.html.

IBM PC

It's true! These days, an original IBM PC — with 64K of RAM, two 5.25-inch floppy drives, and no hard disk — is considered a "pretty strange" network device. And these old fogies are still out there, we guarantee it.

The International Space Station

Okay, the international space station isn't connected to the Internet — yet — but you can observe some of NASA's (U.S.'s National Aeronautics and Space Administration) operations at `www.ambitweb.com/nasacams/ nasacams.html` and at `www.nasa.gov`. We're certain that many more Web sites will pop up as the participating countries around the world launch the ongoing efforts to create and operate the space station.

Beepers

We can understand why you want to make it easy for people to beep you (that is, send you an alphanumeric page) and that connecting your beeper to the Internet provides that. But why would you publicly announce to the entire world how to access it? That's right, you can be beeped at any time of the day or night by complete strangers — people around the world who are Web surfing from the comfort and safety of their homes, in time zones different from yours. Somehow we doubt that you'll call them back, especially because they may not provide a valid phone number, if they include one at all. We suppose you could try reversing the charges to avoid the global long distance telephone costs.

If you still want to connect your beeper to the Internet, you may want to contact Bindo Wavell (`ugrad-www.cs.colorado.edu/~wavell/ page.chtml`) or Jonathan Rosenson (`www.rosenpages.com`). If they call back, perhaps they can tell you how to proceed.

Chapter 23

Watch Your Back — Ten Practical Security Tips

In This Chapter

▶ Protecting yourself and your browser

▶ Browsing incognito

▶ Finding and removing hidden evidence of your browsing

Advanced security features are contributing to the rapid growth and commercialization of the Internet. If you're doing business over the Internet, including your holiday shopping, be sure that the site you're dealing with protects you with encryption, authentication, and Digital Certificates — the major concepts in Chapter 19. But you can also do things to protect yourself. Remember the old saying, "The Internet protects those who protect themselves." Okay, you caught us. The "old saying" is only a couple of seconds old — we made it up. But as you chew your way across the Internet and Web, try saying it over and over. This chapter provides a smorgasbord of tasty delights that protect you from being eaten alive by security breaches.

Be Paranoid

Cover your tracks. If you don't want anyone watching you browse the Web, do it anonymously. Look for Web sites that offer to hide your identity. One site you can start your surfing from is www.iproxy.com. As of this writing, it's free for a 30-day trial and conceals your IP address from cookies and other tracking devices.

Be CERTain You Know the Dangers

Internet-savvy folks get themselves on the CERT (Computer Emergency Response Team) mailing list. CERT keeps you up-to-date on the latest security vulnerabilities and how to solve or work around them. To get on CERT's mailing list, send e-mail to `cert-advisory-request@cert.org`. Put the word "subscribe" in the subject line.

Take a look at Chapter 19 for a list of other CERT resources and how to access them.

Know What Your Browser's Doing

Be sure that your browser uses a security protocol such as SSL v2 or v3 that supports encryption. Also be sure that the protocol is activated so that you can use SSL connections when you're sending private information, such as a credit card number, over the Internet.

Be able to identify, view, and delete the personal public key certificates that you request from Certificate Authorities. Figure 23-1 shows the information that you receive by pressing the Ctrl+Shift+I key combination in Netscape Navigator 3.0 (Window⇨Security Info menu). Figure 23-2 shows similar functionality in the View⇨Internet Options menu in Microsoft Internet Explorer 4.0 (IE4).

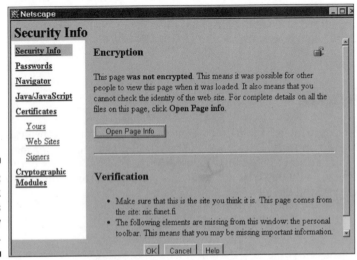

Figure 23-1: Check Navigator's security settings.

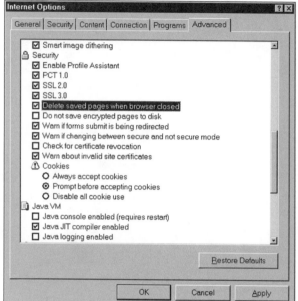

Figure 23-2:
Check
Internet
Explorer's
security
settings.

Keep your browser's security up-to-date

When software vendors find security holes in their browsers (and they do, unfortunately), they publish fixes, called *patches,* that you can download to fix the problem. Look for Internet Explorer security patches at the Microsoft site, www.microsoft.com/security/, and then follow the link to updates to Internet Explorer 4.0. Microsoft updates its site often, so be sure to check frequently. For Netscape security bugs and patches, browse the security solutions page at home.netscape.com/products/security.

Maintain your privacy

Your browser disk cache keeps a copy of every page you access. If you leave your computer unattended, some nosy person can check in your cache directory to see what you've been browsing. Clear the cache so that inquiring minds don't find out anything about your browsing habits. Different browsers provide different methods for managing the cache. Figure 23-3 shows how an Opera user chooses Preferences⇨Cache from the menu.

When a browser displays an encrypted page, it leaves an unencrypted copy of the page in your disk cache. See Chapter 19 for more information.

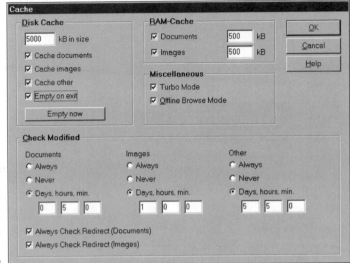

Figure 23-3:
Cleaning
out the
cache foils
snoopers.

To empty your Internet Explorer 4.0 cache, choose View⇨Options⇨General, and then click on the Delete Files button. To empty your Netscape Navigator disk cache, choose Edit⇨Preferences⇨Advanced⇨Cache, and then click on the Clear Disk Cache button.

You can set the security options to empty your disk cache when you exit a browser session. Refer to Figures 23-1 and 23-2.

Cover your browser's tracks in the Windows Registry

This tip is for totally paranoid people. Most prying people won't know to look in your Windows Registry, but it is another place on your hard disk where snoops can see where you've been browsing. When you type URLs into Internet Explorer, you can pull them down later from a menu, and that means that those URLs have to be stored somewhere to offer you the pull-down convenience. That place is the *Windows Registry.* You can use the Registry Editor to cover your tracks.

Here's how to wipe out those URLs:

1. **Close Internet Explorer.**

2. **Choose Run and type** regedit. **Click on the Enter button.**

3. **Keep expanding "Hkey_Current_User/" until you get to "Software/ Microsoft/Internet Explorer/TypedURLs" on the left side of the display.**

   Figure 23-4 shows these Registry values.

   For Netscape Navigator, expand "Hkey_Current_User/" until you get to "Software/Netscape Navigator/URL history." Figure 23-5 shows an example.

4. **Examine the list of the Web links starting with url1.**

5. **Delete the URLs.**

When you delete a URL, the others that follow numerically are no longer visible on the pull-down browser list in IE4. They still exist in the Registry, however.

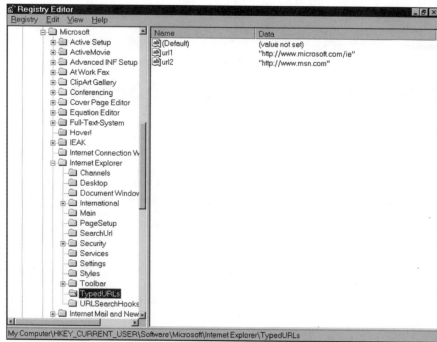

Figure 23-4:
Don't leave
a trail of
URLs from
IE4 in the
Registry.

Figure 23-5:
Delete your
trail of
URLs from
Navigator
in the
Registry.

Some Yummy Tips about SPAM

SPAM is unsolicited junk mail, sent in bulk. Junk mailers usually get you on their mailing lists by extracting your e-mail address from your Usenet News postings. But you don't need to give up News to avoid being overwhelmed by junk mail — simply add an expression such as NOSPAM to your outgoing e-mail address. Choose any phrase you want as long as the expression makes no sense as an e-mail address. And, of course, we know you wouldn't choose anything naughty! Do this when you set up your news reader. For example, Candace would change `cardinalci@aol.com` to `cardinal@NOSPAMARAMA.aol.com`.

Be nice to your fellow newsies. Write a reminder in your posting that says "If you want to reply, remove NOSPAM from my e-mail address." Legitimate newsies realize what you're doing, but automated e-mail gatherers for SPAM can't figure out your bogus address.

Chapter 24

Ten Ways to Get RFCs

*T*he most common and easiest way to get an RFC (Request For Comments) is to find it online on the World Wide Web. If you need or want your own copy, you can get it with Anonymous FTP. RFCs are available from many sites around the world, but especially from the IETF's RFC Editor (www.rfc-editor.org). Figure 24-1 shows the RFC Editor's home page.

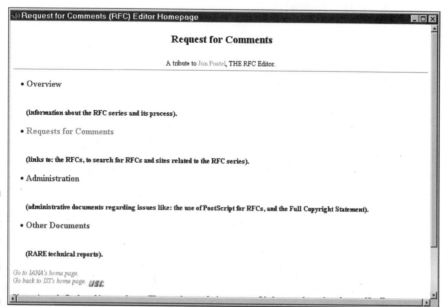

Figure 24-1: The IETF RFC Editor maintains all kinds of RFCs.

All RFCs have titles, but their numbers are the key to finding the documents, especially if you use Anonymous FTP. After you find the number of the RFC you want, you can just go after it. (Skip ahead to either the "Using the Web to

Get an RFC" or the "Using Anonymous FTP to Get an RFC" section if you know the number of the RFC you want.) Unless you've memorized all the RFCs by number — there are over 2,400 as of this writing! — your first task is finding an RFC Index.

Finding an RFC Index

An RFC Index is a list of all the RFCs, usually with both their numbers and their names. Several RFC Indexes are available on the Web and as text files that you can copy with Anonymous FTP.

See the section "Using Anonymous FTP to Get an RFC," later in this chapter to find out how to get your own copy of the RFC Index.

Understanding entries in an RFC Index

The contents of an entry in an RFC Index vary depending on who's maintaining the index. The entries in the IETF's RFC Index contain the following information:

- ✔ RFC number
- ✔ Author
- ✔ Title
- ✔ Date issued
- ✔ Number of pages
- ✔ Format — text (.txt) or PostScript (.ps)
- ✔ Type — whether the RFC is also an FYI or STD
- ✔ Relationship of this RFC to any others — whether this RFC is an update of an existing RFC, has made a previous RFC obsolete, or has been rendered obsolete by another RFC

For example, the entry for RFC 1129 contains the following information:

```
1129        D. Mills, "Internet time synchronization: The
            Network
               Time Protocol", 10/01/1989. (Pages=29)
          (Format=.ps)
```

This entry tells you RFC 1129 is authored by D. Mills and titled "Internet time synchronization: The Network Time Protocol." It was issued October 1, 1989, and contains 29 PostScript pages. It hasn't been updated or replaced by any other RFC. It isn't an FYI or a STD. (Remember, this is an example. Things may have changed by the time you're reading this.)

RFC name format

RFC filenames use these naming conventions, where the #### represents the RFC number without leading zeros:

```
rfc####.txt
rfc####.ps
```

The .txt extension indicates a text file; the .ps extension indicates a PostScript file. The PostScript version often contains figures and graphics that can't be represented in plain text, but you need a PostScript printer or PostScript previewer software to use the file.

So a PostScript version of RFC 1291 is located in the file named rfc1291.ps.

When you fetch a copy of an RFC with Anonymous FTP, make sure that you copy the file that's in the format you want.

Using the Web to Get an RFC

When you read an RFC on the Web, you don't have to worry about the file format because HTML takes care of everything. Reading RFCs on the World Wide Web is easy — just surf to www.rfc-editor.org/categories. The RFC Editor groups the RFCs into categories to make them easier to find. Figure 24-2 shows the RFC Editor's categories page, showing seven Web sites that hold RFCs.

RFCs are stored on many Web servers around the world. To find a server near you, use a Web search engine to find the sites that have the RFC Index or the specific RFC that you want.

Other people and organizations have Web sites that hold RFCs. Figure 24-3 show a favorite of ours, www.garlic.com/~lynn/rfcietf.html. Besides the RFCs, Lynn Wheeler's site includes links to a useful set of references about TCP/IP and the Internet. Philippe Dax also has a Web site that includes RFCs and user guides (in French) for TCP/IP protocols, including IPv6 (see www.infres.enst.fr/~dax/services/rfc/). Figure 24-4 shows the RFC page from his Web site. When you're done reading RFCs, browse up a level to M. Dax's home page to see an abundance of information in French.

LEO-Link Everything onLine is another well organized site to find RFCs (www.leo.org/pub/comp.doc/standards/rfc).

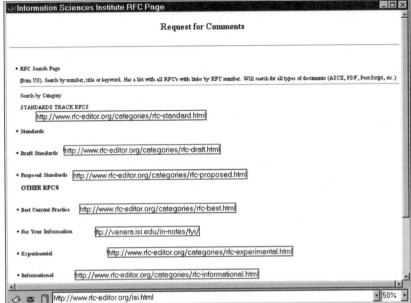

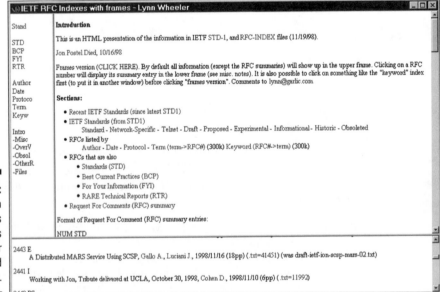

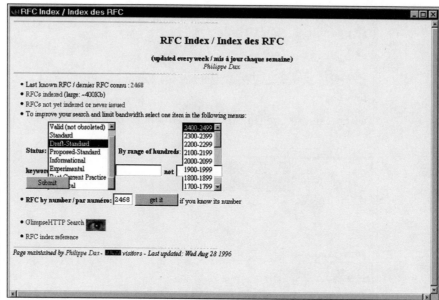

Figure 24-4:
After
reading
RFCs, try
browsing
around this
site.

Using Anonymous FTP to Get an RFC

If you want your own copy of an RFC Index, or if you have the number of the RFC you want to copy, you're ready to fire up your Anonymous FTP client. If necessary, read Chapter 9 to brush up on your knowledge of Anonymous FTP.

1. **Connect to an Anonymous FTP site that maintains a list of RFCs.**

   Figure 24-5 shows a useful Web site, `www.tile.net/ftp/rfcs.html`, that lists Anonymous FTP sites that store RFCs. It sounds a little strange — going to the Web to find FTP archives, but believe us, it's worth it to get such a comprehensive list.

2. **Move into the directory where the RFCs are stored by using the ftp command** `cd /rfc`.

3. **Use the ftp** `get` **command to transfer the files you want to your computer.**

   For example, you should use `get rfc-index.txt`.

In Figure 24-6, we retrieve RFC 1077 in plain text format.

RFCs are stored on many Anonymous FTP sites around the world. Here's a list of some of them:

  ✔ `nis.garr.it`
  ✔ `src.doc.ic.ac.uk`

- ✔ `ftp.isi.edu`
- ✔ `wuarchive.wustl.edu`
- ✔ `nisc.jvnc.net`
- ✔ `sunsite.unc.edu` (in the `/pub/docs/rfc` directory)
- ✔ `ftp.ta.jcu.cz`
- ✔ `ftp.sunet.se` (in the `/pub/internet_documents/rfc` directory)

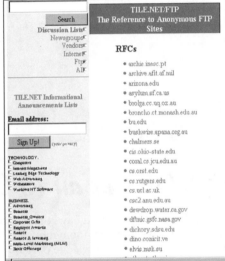

Figure 24-5:
Go to
the Web
before you
Anonymous
FTP.

```
C:\WINDOWS>ftp cs.ucl.ac.uk
Connected to cs.ucl.ac.uk.
220 cs.ucl.ac.uk FTP server (SunOS 4.0) ready.
User (cs.ucl.ac.uk:(none)): anonymous
331 Guest login ok, send ident as password.
Password:
230 Guest login ok, access restrictions apply.
ftp> dir
dr-xr-xr-x  2 0      0        512 Mar  1 1996 mmanela
dr-xr-xr-x  4 0      0        512 Apr 19 1996 osisec
dr-xr-xr-x  9 0      0        512 Nov 23 14:54 papagena
dr-xr-xr-x  7 0      0       1536 Jun  5 1997 pyggy
dr-xr-xr-x  3 0      0        512 Nov 24 09:47 rbordini
dr-xr-xr-x  2 0      0        512 May 29 1996 relate
dr-xr-xr-x  3 0      0        512 Oct 13 1994 research
dr-xr-xr-x  2 0      0      31232 Dec  8 17:42 rfc
dr-xr-xr-x  6 0      0        512 Nov 11 13:55 toast
dr-xr-xr-x  9 0      0        512 Mar  5 1998 vr
226 ASCII Transfer complete.
4393 bytes received in 1.64 seconds (2.68 Kbytes/sec)
ftp> cd rfc
250 CWD command successful.
ftp> dir rfc1077*
200 PORT command successful.
150 ASCII data connection for /bin/ls (32.100.56.23,2170).
-r--r--r--  1 0      0     113877 Jun 23 1989 rfc1077.txt
226 ASCII Transfer complete.
67 bytes received in 0.05 seconds (1.34 Kbytes/sec)
ftp> get rfc1077.txt
200 PORT command successful.
150 ASCII data connection for rfc1077.txt (32.100.56.23,2171) (113877 bytes).
226 ASCII Transfer complete.
116449 bytes received in 13.51 seconds (8.62 Kbytes/sec)
ftp> quit
221 Goodbye.

C:\WINDOWS>
```

Figure 24-6:
It's easy to get a copy of an RFC.

Chapter 25

Ten RFCs Worth Tasting

*T*he RFC process that we describe in Chapter 2 is the cornerstone of TCP/IP and of Internet development and growth. You can find over 2,400 RFCs (Requests For Comments), and many of them function as excellent sleep aids — but the ones we list in this chapter are of at least marginal interest.

Because the Internet and TCP/IP are so closely intertwined, many RFCs refer not only to the protocols, but also to the Net and its Web.

Chapter 24 tells you how to get the current list of all the RFCs that are available. For some strange and funny ones, get the RFC index and look for the RFCs dated April 1.

A View from Mars

RFC 1607: A View from the 21st Century. This RFC is really entertaining. It's written by Vinton Cerf (Big Daddy of the Internet) as a series of letters from someone working on Mars, circa 2023. It's a humorous treatment of the history of Internet growth as it may appear to people in the not-so-distant future. Some of Cerf's comments about the Internet running out of addresses are very funny, especially in light of the work being done on IPv6 (see Chapter 15) and the new IP address space.

You Need the Right Tool to Do the Job

RFC2151: A Primer on Internet and TCP/IP Tools and Utilities. This RFC is a guide to TCP/IP applications, utilities, and tools, including nslookup, ping, finger, telnet, ftp, whois, Archie, Veronica, WAIS, Gopher, and many others. It also lists newsgroups and mailing lists and includes a guide to perusing the Internet.

The Hitchhiker's Guide

RFC 1118: The Hitchhiker's Guide to the Internet. This RFC was written to help new Internaunts understand how the Internet came to be and where it's going. You also find guidance on how to find online information about using the Internet and being a good Interneighbor. It's an excellent introduction for newcomers to TCP/IP, as well, because the development of the Internet and TCP/IP are joined at the hip.

How Do I...?

RFC 1594: FYI On Questions and Answers — Answers to Commonly Asked "New Internet User" Questions. If you're new to the Internet and you have a question, read this RFC. Odds are good that your question has already been asked and answered.

RFC 1594 is a special type of RFC called an *FYI* (For Your Information). Instead of proposing a standard or commenting on a proposal, the purpose of an FYI is to inform and educate. RFC 1594 is also known as FYI 4.

The Whole RFC Catalog

RFC 1000: The Request for Comments Reference Guide. This RFC is historical — it tells a tale of the birth of the protocols and how the RFC process came to be. It also lists the various categories in which an RFC may be classified, because not all RFCs define standards — some are informational (FYIs), while others are humorous.

It's Official

RFC 2400: Internet Official Protocol Standards. This RFC describes the IAB's (Internet Advisory Board) process for standardizing protocols. This RFC is itself an Internet Standard. RFC 2400 also lists the protocols by the following categories:

- ✔ Standards
- ✔ Draft standards
- ✔ Proposed standards
- ✔ Experimental protocols
- ✔ Informational protocols
- ✔ Historic protocols
- ✔ Obsolete protocols

Are You Feeling Insecure?

RFC 2084: Considerations for Web Transaction Security. This RFC lists requirements for Web transaction security that should be provided either by extensions to HTTP or as a separate security protocol. The services include confidentiality, transaction integrity, user and server authentication, and proxy servers.

Trust No One?

RFC 1244: Site Security Handbook. This RFC has some guidelines in managing security for computers on the Internet. It's a good beginning for network administrators and security officers to help create the policies and procedures of an organization.

This RFC is oriented toward security practices in the United States. If you're managing a network elsewhere, the ideas and concepts in this RFC are useful, but many of the resources listed are only available in the U.S.

Here are some of the topics discussed in RFC 1244:

- ✔ Understanding the need for security policies
- ✔ Instituting security policies and procedures
- ✔ Deciding what resources need to be protected

✔ Securing your system when policies are violated

✔ Monitoring unauthorized activity and break-ins

✔ Responding to unauthorized activity and break-ins

The Truth Is Out There

RFC 1462: What Is the Internet? This is another FYI-type RFC, also known as FYI 20. It's written by the User Services Working Group of the Internet Engineering Task Force (IETF) — this group comprises more of the good-hearted people that we mention in Chapter 2. This RFC includes information from the book *The Whole Internet User's Guide and Catalog,* by Ed Krol.

This RFC also discusses commercial opportunities on the Internet. Commercialization of the Net is one of the hottest Internet topics today, and this RFC has some information about the origins and directions of commercial use.

The Cookbook

RFC 1180: A TCP/IP Tutorial. This is a technical tutorial explaining the step-by-step path followed by an IP datagram as it moves from the source host to the destination via a router. If you're writing a TCP/IP application or implementation, this RFC is invaluable.

Separate Tables — Advice for Subnetters

RFC 1219: On the Assignment of Subnet Numbers. Unless you're *subnetting* (breaking a network into smaller, interconnected pieces), don't bother with this RFC. However, if you're managing subnetted networks, you may find RFC 1219 useful — it suggests procedures for assigning subnet numbers within your organization's main network.

RFC 1219 is a commentary on RFC 950, the standard for subnet masks. A *subnet mask* helps a computer know how the network is split up. See Chapter 13 for the scoop on subnets and subnet masks.

Chapter 26

Ten Web Sites for TCP/IP Information

In This Chapter

▶ Finding some great sites on the Web

▶ Exploring the ins and outs of TCP/IP

*T*he Web is one of the best places to find more of TCP/IP to chew on — from the basic ingredients (protocols) to the utensils (applications) to the recipes (standards and procedures for the Internet). This chapter lists some other favorite TCP/IP and networking sites. We list commercial sites that are fun, as well as informative. We deliberately don't include any of the Internet Society sites, such as IANA and IETF, because you can find them yourself if you read enough of this book.

While we can't vouch for the technical accuracy of each item on each link that you may follow from these Web sites, we have recently visited each site and were impressed by the materials that we sampled.

Nibbling on NetGuide's Net Newbie

The Net Newbie site, www.netguide.com/Internet/Netnewbie/, is a fun place to sample Internet and TCP/IP morsels without a lot of fat. Some of the tidbits we tasted at this site include Web performance information, how to fight SPAM, tips for communicating online, and ways to chat online. We like their links to other sites too, especially "The History of the Internet" and "The Internet Privacy Coalition."

Gobbling Up Everything at ZDNet

We love this Ziff Davis site, www.zdnet.com. It includes a lot more than TCP/IP, but the sections on the Internet, TCP/IP, and networking are excellent. It's a good place to follow breaking news not just about the Internet, but about the computer world in general. You can also read articles from ZD magazines, such as *PC Week, PC Computing,* and *PC Magazine,* and you can even get a free e-mail account at ZDNet. The only problem with this site is that if you try to digest all the information, your brain may explode.

Noshing at Netscape

Because the Netscape Netcenter at www.netscape.com is a portal, you can find everything there from soup to nuts. We like the "Computing and Internet" category for researching Internet issues, such as security. You can also download browsers and tools, subscribe to Internet news (as in all the news that's fit to print, not Usenet). You can even find out how to create Web pages by building a Web site there and linking to live demos.

Chewing on CNET

CNET, www.cnet.com, is one of those giant sites with something for everyone. We recommend that you sample their "Beginner's Guide to Computing." Please don't get insulted, if you aren't a beginner. We recommend this guide because it includes

- The beginner's guide to downloading
- E-mail tips for (almost) everyone
- CNET's ultimate ISP guide
- 20 questions: how the Net works

Sampling InterNIC

Visit the InterNIC Web site (www.internic.net) to find out almost everything about TCP/IP and networks. The InterNIC provides:

- **Internet documentation:** All the technical documentation for TCP/IP protocols.
- **What's New listings:** Keeps you up-to-date on the latest Internet technologies.

✔ **The 15-Minute series:** Online training on Internet topics.

✔ **WebFinder:** The InterNIC's special Internet search engine that searches for Web servers.

✔ **Internet Service Provider (ISP) search engines and directories:** Helps you find a local Internet Service Provider.

✔ **White and Yellow Pages directories:** Helps you find people and businesses on the Internet.

✔ **World Wide Web subject directories:** Allows you to browse and search directories of Internet information by subject.

✔ **Mailing lists directories:** Helps you find e-mail discussion groups or Usenet newsgroups.

✔ **Online libraries:** Allows you to search library catalogs and resources all over the world.

✔ **Usenet Search Engines:** Searches Usenet news archives.

Trying the AlterNIC

Although AlterNIC is a young site (in business since 1995), it's been in the news recently for promoting new top level domain names. When you visit this company's site, you find a lot more there than just domain registration information. The AlterNIC home page, www.alternic.net, points you to RFCs, information about SPAM and privacy issues, security, and encryption services.

What's Whatis?

Whatis, www.whatis.com, is a super glossary for computing terms, including TCP/IP and internetworking terms. Besides providing definitions, whatis includes links to other sources that supplement the excellent definitions. Anyone can suggest a term and a definition to be included. Why not connect to whatis and see if they've missed any terms that you need to know? If so, follow their instructions and suggest that they include the term.

Toasting Web ProForums

Presented by the International Engineering Consortium, this site (www.webproforum.com/wpf_internet.html) includes links to tutorials presented by various organizations. We downloaded the "Internet Security Tutorial" from Sun Microsystems. It only took a couple of minutes to download on our 56 Kbps modem. The tutorial even comes with a little self-test so you can check your level of understanding. You can also find pointers to other tutorials.

Tasting the Dot Com Series

Online training at this site (`networksolutions.com/DOTCOM/`) helps you get your business set up on the Internet, including explaining about domains and electronic commerce basics.

Savoring Spectral

If you comb through this book and decide to get even more technical, the TCP/IP training here (`spectral.mscs.mu.edu`) is a good place to start. This university site also includes Java and HTML training.

Trying NetworkDNA

This site (at `networkdna.com`) includes a collection of tutorials and FAQs about TCP/IP in general and on Windows NT and Linux (the hottest free version of UNIX today). Be sure to visit the link to the Linux Resource Kit — don't let the "Linux" in the title frighten you, because this site contains a lot of general TCP/IP training materials and tutorials.

Sipping Secret Agent's Networking Page

This techie site (`www.secretagent.com/networking/ip.html`) includes a set of how-to's on various parts of TCP/IP, including routing, subnets, and SNMP network management.

Flipping through Cisco Systems' Internetworking Technology Overview

This site (at `www.cisco.com/univercd/cc/td/doc/cisintwk/ito_doc/index.htm`) contains a complete online book. You may not want to read the entire book, but if you need to go into depth on TCP/IP, start with the "Introduction to Internetworking" chapter. Then, try the "Internet Protocols" chapter.

Glossary

● ●

10Base2: The coaxial cable used for thinwire Ethernet. Over 10Base2 Ethernet, the maximum network transmission rate is 10 megabits of data per second.

10Base5: The thick coaxial cable used for the original thickwire Ethernet. Over 10Base5 Ethernet, the maximum network transmission rate is 10 megabits of data per second.

10BaseT: Twisted-pair Ethernet cable. Over 10BaseT Ethernet, the maximum network transmission rate is 10 megabits of data per second.

100BaseT: Twisted-pair wire for Fast Ethernet. The maximum network transmission rate is 100 megabits of data per second.

ACK (acknowledgment): The response from the recipient back to the sender that data was successfully received. TCP uses ACKs as part of its reliable transmission scheme. If an ACK is not received, data is retransmitted. See also *NAK* and *retransmission.*

Active Server Page: See *ASP.*

Active X: A set of object-oriented technologies from Microsoft. An ActiveX control is conceptually similar to a Java applet. See also *applet* and *Java.*

address mask: The set of bits used to mask an Internet address to create a subnetwork. See also *subnet mask.*

address resolution: The translation of an Internet address into the physical (hardware) address of your network interface card. The Address Resolution Protocol (ARP) does the address resolution.

Address Resolution Protocol: See *ARP.*

Anonymous FTP: See *FTP.*

ANSI (American National Standards Institute): The organization that defines standards for the United States, including network standards.

API (Application Programming Interface): The routines that an application program uses to interface with lower operating system services.

applet: A small program. Some examples of applets include Java enhancements to Web pages and the items found in the Control Panel of Windows 95, Windows 98, and Windows NT.

Archie: A program and a group of network servers that help you locate files on the Internet. Archie is strictly a file finder; after locating the file you want, you can use FTP to copy the file to your own computer.

ARP (Address Resolution Protocol): The TCP/IP protocol that translates an Internet address into the hardware address of a network interface card.

ARPA (Advanced Research Projects Agency): The United States government agency that funded the ARPANET, predecessor to the Internet. ARPA is now called DARPA, Defense Advanced Research Projects Agency.

ARPANET (Advanced Research Projects Agency Network): The U.S. government-funded network that evolved into the Internet.

article: A message posted in a Usenet news newsgroup.

ASP (Active Server Page): HTML pages that include scripts that are processed by the Microsoft web server. The pages are called "active" because the scripts customize the pages for different users.

authority zone: The part of a DNS domain for which a name server has responsibility. Authority is sometimes called "knowing the truth" about network name/address translation.

backbone: The physical cable in a building from which network segments radiate. 10Base5 (thickwire Ethernet) and fiber optic cable are two popular backbone media.

bandwidth: The range from highest to lowest frequencies transmitted on a network. Bandwidth measures network capacity.

batch browser: A kind of Web browser.

baud rate: The speed rating of network transmissions. Theoretically, baud rate is equal to the number of bits transmitted per second; however, transmission overhead reduces the actual data transfer rate, and data compression increases it.

Berkeley UNIX: The UNIX operating system developed by the University of California at Berkeley. It was the first version of UNIX that included TCP/IP.

binary: A number system based on 2. The place columns of the number are based on powers of 2: 1, 2, 4, 8, 16, 32, 64, 128, 256, and so on. A network administrator who creates subnet masks must understand binary-to-decimal conversion (or have a calculator that understands it).

bit: Each unit of binary data. A bit's value is either 1 or 0.

BOOTP (Bootstrap Protocol): The TCP/IP protocol for remote booting of diskless computers and other network devices.

bps: Bits per second. A unit for measuring data transmission speed. You don't want to work at bps speed. See also *Kbps* and *Mbps.*

bridge: A network device that connects two networks that use the same protocols. The bridge forwards packets between the connected networks, if necessary.

broadcast: The transmission of packets to all hosts attached to a network.

brouter: A network device that combines bridge and router functions.

browser: A client program for navigating the hypermedia information on the World Wide Web. The latest browsers are graphical (such as Netscape and Internet Explorer), but text-only browsers (such as Lynx) are also useful, especially on low-speed dialup links.

browser cache: A directory (or directories) that stores files of recently browsed Web pages. Look in these directories if your hard disk suddenly fills up and you have no idea why. See also *cache.*

CA (Certificate Authority): A trusted third party that issues Digital Certificates.

cable modem: A device for connecting your computer to the Internet via coaxial cable lines provided by your cable TV company.

cache: An area of memory where disk data is stored for faster access. Also a directory (or directories) that stores files of recently browsed Web pages. See also *browser cache.*

caching server: A DNS name server that stores in memory the information it receives from other servers. See also *DNS* and *DNS domain.*

Cello: A World Wide Web browser. See also *browser.*

Certificate Authority (CA): See *CA.*

chat: See *IRC.*

CGI (Common Gateway Interface): A CGI script or program automates things that a web server needs to do in order to customize a Web page. CGI also stands for *computer graphics imaging,* the visual special effects for movies and television.

client: A program that requests services from a server. The DNS resolver is an example of a client program. It requests name/address resolution services from a DNS name server. See also *client/server* and *server.*

client/server: A style of computing that allows work to be distributed across hosts (computers). For example, a PC client can request file access from a file server. TCP/IP uses a client/server architecture and enables development of client/server applications. See also *client* and *server.*

coaxial cable: A kind of wiring used in networks and also to transmit cable TV signals.

collision: Occurs on an Ethernet network when two hosts transmit packets at the same time. See also *CSMA/CD.*

Common Gateway Interface: See *CGI.*

Communicator: A suite of applications from Netscape that includes their Web browser, called Navigator. See also *Navigator.*

connection: A link between network processes running on different computers.

connectionless service: An IP delivery service that sends each packet (including the source and destination addresses) across the network without expecting an ACK (acknowledgement) to signify that the packet was received. Connectionless delivery services may lose packets and do not guarantee that packets will be delivered in order. See also *ACK.*

cookie: Information stored in a file that a web server may want to send to your computer, so that a Web site has information about you and your preferences.

CSLIP (Compressed Serial Line Internet Protocol): An optimization of SLIP. CSLIP reduces the need to transmit redundant address information. See also *SLIP* and *PPP.*

CSMA/CD (Carrier Sense Multiple Access/ Collision Detection): A network transmission scheme by which multiple network devices can transmit across the cable simultaneously, possibly causing collisions. If a collision occurs, both devices retransmit after waiting a random amount of time. Ethernet is the most well-known network type using CSMA/CD technology.

cyberspace: A virtual world of computers, applications, and services. Another term for the Internet.

daemon: A program that runs continually to provide a service for a protocol or application. TCP/IP daemons include the rwho daemon and the inet configuration daemon. Similar to a TSR program in DOS. Daemons are very common in UNIX.

DARPA (Defense Advanced Research Projects Agency): See *ARPA.*

data link layer: Layer 2 in the ISO OSI Reference Model and the TCP/IP network model. This layer handles logical connections between networked computers. See also *ISO OSI Reference Model.*

DCA (Defense Communication Agency): The organization responsible for the DDN (Defense Data Network) and the Department of Defense InterNIC. See also *DDN.*

DDN (Defense Data Network): A broader term for MILNET and the United States military components of The Internet. See also *MILNET.*

default gateway: The address IP uses when the destination address is not on the local subnet. It's usually the router's IP address.

DHCP (Dynamic Host Configuration Protocol): The TCP/IP protocol for allocating IP addresses dynamically when they are needed.

Digital Certificate: An electronic identification card that's issued by a Certificate Authority (CA) and used with client software, such as a Web browser. A Digital Certificate contains your name, encryption keys, and other information that uniquely identifies you to a server. See also *CA.*

digital signature: An electronic version of sealing wax that identifies the author of a document or the sender of an e-mail message. It also ensures that a message hasn't been edited or damaged since it was signed. A digital signature is *not* a graphic of your handwriting. See also *Digital Certificate* and *CA.*

distributed computing: Programs and/or data that function together and are spread across networked computers. Client/server computing can be a form of distributed computing if the client and server are on different computers.

DNS (Domain Name System): The name/address resolution service that uses a distributed database containing FQDNs and addresses. DNS makes it easy for people to refer to computers by name rather than by numeric address. DNS is the name/address resolution service used by the Internet. See also *FQDN* and *name/address resolution.*

DNS domain: A group of computers using the same DNS name servers and managed within the same administrative unit.

dog's breakfast: A little of this, a lot of that.

domain: See *DNS domain* and *NIS domain.*

domain name server: A program that converts FQDNs into their numeric IP addresses, and vice versa. The computer that runs the program. See also *FQDN.*

Domain Name System: See *DNS.*

dotted decimal notation: Used to represent IP addresses. Each part of the address is a decimal number separated from the other parts by a dot (.). For example, 130.103.40.4 is an IP address in dotted decimal notation.

dumb terminal: A terminal that has no processing capabilities and no graphics support, such as a VT100 terminal.

Dynamic Host Configuration Protocol: See *DHCP.*

Dynamic HTML (Dynamic HyperText Markup Language): Extensions to the language used to write pages for the World Wide Web (HTML) that allow the pages to be customized on-the-fly for each individual user. See also *HTML.*

dynamic routing: A way of moving data across an internet; when one path is unavailable, dynamic routing can use an alternate one. Originally designed to ensure that the Internet would be available if a military attack disabled any of the network paths.

e-mail: Electronic mail; also called email and mail.

epoch: The current era, starting January 1, 1900, as far as the Internet is concerned. Many network applications measure time as the number of seconds since the start of the epoch.

Ethernet: A LAN technology that uses CSMA/CD delivery. Ethernet runs over many different media, ranging from thick cable (10Base5) to twisted-pair wire (10BaseT). Most Ethernet networks operate at 10 megabits per second. Fast Ethernet runs at 100 megabits per second. Gigabit Ethernet runs at 1000 megabits per second. See also *LAN* and *CSMA/CD.*

Ethernet address: The hardware address that identifies the Ethernet network interface card inside a computer. Also called the physical address. No two Ethernet addresses are identical. See also *hardware address.*

eXtensible Markup Language: See *XML.*

FA (Foreign Agent): Part of Mobile-IP. When you connect your computer at a remote site, the site tells an FA on the new network to tell your Home Agent (HA) where you are. See also *HA, Mobile-IP,* and *MH.*

FAQ (frequently asked questions list): A FAQ is usually provided as part of each Usenet newsgroup to introduce new users to the newsgroup and its etiquette.

FDDI (Fiber Distribution Data Interface): A token ring network technology based on fiber optic cables made of bundles of glass or plastic. Used for high-speed and/or long-distance networks. The typical network transmission rate is 100 megabits per second. See also *optical fiber.*

Fiber Distribution Data Interface: See *FDDI.*

Fiber optics: A data transmission medium that uses light sent through glass or plastic fibers.

file server: A computer that provides file-sharing services to client computers on the network.

file services: Applications and services that allow network users to share disk space on networked computers. NFS is an example of a file service.

finger: A client/server application that displays information about users on the network. System administrators may disable the finger server for security reasons. See also *whois.*

firewall: A network security measure that works by allowing and preventing receipt of certain kinds of network messages.

Foreign Agent: See *FA.*

FQDN (Fully Qualified Domain Name): The "full" name of a computer, including all subdomain and domain names, separated by dots. For example, `frodo.support.lotus.com` is an FQDN.

frequently asked questions list: See *FAQ.*

FTP (File Transfer Protocol): A TCP/IP application, service, and protocol for copying files from one computer to another. Before the server will transfer the files, it requires the client to provide a valid username and password. Anonymous FTP is used at public network sites. It allows file transfer using a standard username, "anonymous," plus the user's e-mail address as the password.

ftpmail: The process of accessing an FTP archive via e-mail, rather than via an FTP client.

FYI: The television newsmagazine on the old television show *Murphy Brown.* Okay, not really. An FYI is an RFC that documents something just For Your Information. See *RFC.*

gated (gateway daemon): A program that must run on a computer using TCP/IP's RIP protocol. See *RIP.*

gateway: A computer that connects multiple networks, and routes packets among them. Also, any computer that translates information from one format to another. See also *SMTP gateway.*

Gbps: Gigabits (billion bits) per second.

good-deed doers: Volunteers. To name a few: RFC authors and reviewers, the inventors of MIME, the organizations that provide Anonymous FTP sites, and the creators of ftpmail and GopherMail.

Gopher: A client/server system for publishing information on the Internet in a menu-oriented fashion. To access Gopherspace, you use your own Gopher client or use telnet to get to a publicly accessible system and use its Gopher. See also *Veronica,* a program to help users navigate Gopherspace.

GopherMail: The process of navigating Gopherspace via e-mail rather than via a Gopher client.

Gopherspace: The worldwide collection of Gopher servers and the information they publish on the Internet.

GOSIP (Government Open Systems Interconnect Profile): A government's procurement standard that requires the OSI network model for networked computers.

graphical user interface: See *GUI.*

GUI (graphical user interface): An application or operating system appearance that usually involves windows, icons, and a mouse.

HA (Home Agent): Part of Mobile-IP. An organization's HA intercepts and forwards packets to your computer when it's connected at a remote site. See also *FA, Mobile-IP,* and *MH.*

hardware address: The physical address for the NIC (network interface card). Used by the low-level hardware layers of a network. TCP/IP's ARP protocol translates IP addresses into hardware addresses. The NIC vendor gets the address from the IEEE and assigns it permanently to the NIC. Also called the MAC (Media Access Control) address. See also *physical address.*

Home Agent: See *HA.*

host: A computer on a TCP/IP network. Sometimes means any device on the network.

hosts file: A text file that lists host names and their IP addresses on a network. For small networks, the hosts file is an alternative to DNS. Also called a host table by some TCP/IP vendors.

HotJava: A graphical World Wide Web browser from Sun Microsystems that demonstrates the benefits of Java. See also *Java.*

HTML (HyperText Markup Language): The language used to write pages for the World Wide Web. See also *Dynamic HTML.*

HTTP (HyperText Transfer Protocol): The TCP/IP protocol for transferring World Wide Web pages across the Internet or an intranet.

hub: A network device that ties multiple segments of wire or cable together. The hub also retransmits the signal so that it can travel longer distances, despite the limitations of the wires and cables.

hypermedia: A system for linking related multimedia objects, such as a text file and sound and video clips, that reside on different network sites.

hypertext: A text system for linking related documents, such as a main document, an attachment, and footnotes, that reside on different network sites.

IAB (Internet Architecture Board): The group of people responsible for research into the direction of the Internet and the development of TCP/IP. The IAB creates task forces to research Internet issues.

ICMP (Internet Control Message Protocol): The TCP/IP protocol used to report network errors and to determine whether a computer is available on the network. The ping utility uses ICMP.

IEEE (Institute of Electrical and Electronics Engineers): A group of scientists and engineers that advises on standards for the American National Standards Institute (ANSI). The standards committee for LAN technologies, such as Ethernet.

IESG (Internet Engineering Steering Group): Group that manages the IETF.

IETF (Internet Engineering Task Force): Part of the IAB; responsible for research into Internet issues. RFCs document the IETF specifications.

IGP (Interior Gateway Protocol): A protocol used by routers and gateways to transfer routing information. RIP is a well-known IGP.

IMAP4 (Internet Message Access Protocol v4): A client/server protocol that specifies how e-mail is held for you by your Internet server.

Interior Gateway Protocol: See *IGP.*

internet, an: A group of interconnected networks using the TCP/IP protocol suite.

Internet, the: The international collection of internets that use TCP/IP to work together as one immense logical network. You really didn't have to look this up after reading the book, did you? We'll assume you just chanced on this entry.

Internet Activities Board: See *IAB.*

Internet address (IP address) v4: A 32-bit unique numeric address used by a computer on a TCP/IP network. The IP address consists of two parts: a network number and a host number.

Internet address (IP address) v6: A 128-bit unique numeric address used by a node (computer or other device) on a TCP/IP network.

Internet Control Message Protocol: See *ICMP.*

Internet Engineering Steering Group: See *IESG.*

Internet Engineering Task Force: See *IETF.*

Internet Explorer: A graphical World Wide Web browser from Microsoft.

internet layer: Layer 3 of the TCP/IP network model.

Internet Message Access Protocol v4: See *IMAP4.*

Internet Research Task Force: See *IRTF.*

InterNIC (Internet Network Information Center): The Internet administration center that registers networks as part of the Internet. RFCs are available from the InterNIC. The InterNIC is sometimes called the NIC for short, but an organization may run its own NIC for its internet. A computer's network interface card is also called a NIC. You have to tell from the context which NIC is which.

interoperability: The capability of diverse hardware and software from different vendors to cooperate and communicate. For example, a Macintosh can share a file that's on a UNIX computer.

IP (Internet Protocol): One of the two main parts of the TCP/IP protocol suite. IP delivers TCP and UDP packets across a network. IP works at the network layer. Currently, IP is either v4 or v6 (also called IPng). IPv6 also understands IPv4 addresses. IPv4 can not understand IPv6 adresses.

IP address: See *Internet address v4 and Internet address v6.*

IPX: A Novell Netware protocol. TCP/IP allows IPX packets to be transmitted over IP.

IRC (Internet Relay Chat): A way for many people on the Internet to "chat" electronically, unlike the talk program, which allows only two people to converse. IRC conversations are live, as compared to Usenet news, which is not.

IRTF (Internet Research Task Force): The part of the IAB that is responsible for research and development of TCP/IP.

ISDN (Integrated Services Digital Network): A high-speed digital telephone line for high-speed network communications.

ISDN TA: An ISDN terminal adapter, often called an ISDN modem by those not in the know.

ISO (International Standards Organization): A group that defines international standards, including network standards. ISO defined the seven-layer network model for network protocols, called the ISO OSI Reference Model.

ISO OSI Reference Model: The ISO-defined seven-layer network model for network protocols. From the bottom up, the layers are: physical, data link, network, transport, session, presentation, and application.

Java: A programming language developed by Sun Microsystems for writing portable programs.

JavaScript: A programming language developed by Netscape for executing programs inside a Web browser.

Kbps: Kilobits (thousands of bits) per second.

Kerberos: A TCP/IP security scheme developed at MIT for authenticating log-ins and passwords and for accessing Kerberosed network services in a secure fashion.

LAN (local area network): A network that spans small distances, for instance, between buildings in an office park. Ethernet is a well-known example of LAN technology.

link: A general term referring to a network connection between two processes or computers.

local area network: See *LAN.*

Lotus Domino: A Web application server, messaging server, and groupware server from Lotus Development Corporation (an IBM company).

mail: In this book, mail means electronic mail, or e-mail.

mail transfer agent: See *MTA.*

mail user agent: See *MUA.*

Mbps: Megabits (million bits) per second.

MAN (metropolitan area network): A large LAN or set of connected LANs, operating over metropolitan-size areas at high speeds.

MH (Mobile Host): A computer that's configured for Mobile-IP. See also *Mobile-IP, HA,* and *FA.*

MILNET (Military Network): A spin-off from the ARPANET.

MIME (Multipurpose Internet Mail Extensions): Extensions to the standard SMTP e-mail message body to support attachments and other nontext data. See also *SMTP, MTA,* and *MUA.*

MIT: Massachusetts Institute of Technology.

Mobile Host: See *MH.*

Mobile-IP: An enhancement to IP that allows a computer to roam an intranet or the Internet without changing its IP address. See also *HA, FA,* and *MH.*

modem (modulator/demodulator): A device for connecting to networks and other computers across telephone lines. Modems may be internal or external to the computer.

modem pool: A set of modems established for shared use.

Mosaic: A graphical World Wide Web browser.

MTA (mail transfer agent): The TCP/IP application that uses SMTP to move an e-mail message to another MTA until the message reaches the addressee's computer, where the message is delivered. See also *MUA.*

MUA (mail user agent): The mail program used by the end-user to create and read e-mail messages. The MUA passes the message to the local MTA.

NAK: The response from the recipient back to the sender that data was not successfully received. A NAK says that the data almost arrived, but there was some kind of error. See also *ACK* and *retransmission.*

name server: See *domain name server.*

name/address resolution: Translation of a computer name or FQDN (for instance, `bilbo.support.lotus.com`) into a numeric address (for instance, `130.103.140.12`). Local hosts files or domain name servers do the name resolution.

Navigator: A graphical World Wide Web browser from Netscape. See also *Communicator.*

Network File System: See *NFS.*

network information center: See *InterNIC.*

Network Information Service: See *NIS.*

network interface card: See *NIC.*

Network News Transfer Protocol: See *NNTP.*

network number: The section of the IP address that is the same for a group of computers on the same network.

network operations center: See *NOC.*

network throughput: The amount of data that can be transferred across the network medium in a fixed time period.

news server: See *NNTP server.*

newsgroup: A "category" for a set of articles written by users of the Internet's Usenet news. Each Usenet newsgroup is about one general topic, and the articles are on related subtopics. Internet users can use newsgroups to share information, opinions, and feelings without actually meeting.

newsreader: A program for reading and responding to Usenet news articles. Examples are tin and rn. Newsreaders communicate with a news server via NNTP.

NFS (Network File System): A protocol and service that allows networked computers remote, transparent access to directories and files. The remote files appear to a user to be local.

NIC (Network Interface Card): A computer's network controller board (network adapter), required for transmitting and receiving signals on a network. A computer, especially a laptop, may have

an external network adapter rather than an internal one. The electrical connection to the network is done at the NIC level. NIC is also a nickname for the InterNIC. See also *InterNIC.*

NIS (Network Information Service): A service for networked computers, providing a single, shareable copy of common system and configuration files. Developed by Sun Microsystems and licensed to all UNIX vendors. Formerly called Yellow Pages. See also *YP.*

NIS domain: A group of UNIX computers that share a single copy of system administration files such as the passwd file.

NNTP (Network News Transfer Protocol): The TCP/IP protocol used to transfer Usenet news articles between two NNTP servers and between a newsreader and an NNTP server.

NNTP server: The computer and/or program that sends and receives Usenet news articles to and from other NNTP servers and newsreaders.

NOC (network operations center): The "nerve center" for monitoring and managing a network. For many organizations, the network administrators and SNMP management stations are located in the NOC. See also *SNMP.*

NSFnet (National Science Foundation Network): The backbone for a collection of networks started with funds from the United States National Science Foundation.

open systems: Open systems provide a standards-based computing environment, possibly including but not limited to UNIX, TCP/IP, APIs, and GUIs.

Open Systems Interconnect: See *OSI.*

Opera: A graphical World Wide Web browser from Opera Software.

optical fiber: Plastic or glass network medium. Theoretical maximum transmission speed is the speed of light.

OSI (Open Systems Interconnect): A set of protocols specified by ISO for interconnecting networks.

OSI Reference Model: See *ISO OSI Reference Model.*

packet: A network message that includes data, a header, error control data, and addressing information. When data is sent, each network layer adds information to the packet before passing the packet to the next layer down. When data is received on a computer, each layer strips off the data added by the sending layer before passing the packet up one layer.

physical address: The hardware address for the NIC (network interface card). See also *hardware address.*

ping (Packet Internet Groper): A program that sends an ICMP echo request to a remote computer and waits for the computer to reply that it is reachable across the network. Tests the network availability of a remote host.

Point-to-Point Protocol: See *PPP.*

Point-to-Point Tunneling Protocol: See *PPTP.*

POP3 (Post Office Protocol version 3): The protocol that you use to download your e-mail from a POP3 mail server to your computer, which must be a POP3 client. See also *client, server,* and *client/server.*

port: A number used by TCP and UDP to indicate which application is sending or receiving data. See also *socket.*

portal: A Web site that's meant to be a starting site for users. A portal contains content similar to an online service, such as America Online (AOL). Some popular portal sites include Netscape, Yahoo!, Excite, Lycos, and AltaVista.

PPP (Point-to-Point Protocol): A protocol that provides serial line connectivity (that is, dialup with a modem) between two computers, between a computer and a network, or between two networks. PPP can handle several protocols simultaneously. (Compare to SLIP, which handles only TCP/IP.) See also *SLIP* and *CSLIP.*

PPTP (Point-to-Point Tunneling Protocol): A protocol that allows private communications to be carried on the Internet. See also *VPN.*

print server: The software that allows a printer on one computer to be shared by computers across a network; and/or the computer to which the shared printers are attached and on which the software is running. Printers that are attached directly to the network allow sharing, too, although technically they are not called print servers.

protocol: Rules and message formats for communication between computers in a network.

protocol layers: The divisions of a hierarchical network model. Each layer performs a service on behalf of the layer directly above it. Each layer receives services from the layer directly below it.

protocol stack: A group of protocols that work together across network layers.

proxy server: A server that sits between a user's client and the Internet. Working with a firewall and a gateway server (which separates an organization's intranet from the Internet), the proxy server helps ensure security and provides caching of Web pages for quicker access. See also *firewall, gateway,* and *cache.*

ps: The UNIX program for seeing what programs and daemons are running on the computer.

r utilities: Berkeley UNIX and TCP/IP programs including rcp, rlogin, and rsh.

rcp: One of the Berkeley UNIX r utilities. The rcp utility allows users to copy files between computers on their internet and the Internet. It's functionally similar to FTP.

reference model: See *ISO OSI Reference Model.*

remote: Describes other computers, disks, directories, and files that are across a network from your computer.

Remote Procedure Call: See *RPC.*

repeater: A network device, operating at the physical layer, that amplifies and repeats electrical signals from one network segment to another, thereby allowing the network segment to be lengthened.

Request for Comments: See *RFC.*

resolver: The client that queries DNS name servers for computer name/IP address resolution on a TCP/IP network on behalf of an application such as telnet or ftp.

resources: System and network components, such as memory, disk space, and CPU.

retransmission: Resending a packet that was not received at the destination computer. The sending computer knows to retransmit because it receives a NAK or it does not receive an ACK from the remote computer. See also *ACK* and *NAK.*

RFC (Request for Comments): The documentation for the Internet, TCP/IP, and other networking standards. RFCs are maintained by the IETF and are publicly available from the InterNIC and numerous Anonymous FTP sites. Among other things, RFCs describe network and TCP/IP protocol standards, answer questions about TCP/IP and the Internet, and propose changes to TCP/IP. Some RFCs are also FYIs or STDs. See also *FYI* and *STD.*

RIP (Routing Information Protocol): Nope, it's not Rest In Peace. RIP is one of the TCP/IP protocols for dynamically routing information along a LAN. RIP requires routed (the route daemon) to be running.

rlogin: One of the Berkeley UNIX r utilities. The rlogin utility allows users to log in to remote computers on an internet or the Internet. Functionally similar to telnet.

route: The path that network data follows from the source computer to the destination computer. Each packet in a message may or may not follow the same route before arriving at the destination.

routed (route daemon): The program that is a prerequisite for RIP to route network data.

router: A network device that interconnects multiple network segments and forwards packets from one network to another. The router must determine how to forward a packet based on addresses, network traffic, and cost.

Routing Information Protocol: See *RIP.*

routing table: A table that lists all the possible paths data can take to get from source to destination. The routing table is stored in memory on routers, gateways, and computers.

RPC (Remote Procedure Call): A programming mechanism for clients to call routines over the network. RPC was originated by Sun Microsystems and is defined by RFC 1057. RPCs are often used to create distributed applications.

rsh: One of the Berkeley UNIX r utilities. The rsh utility allows users to run programs on remote computers on an internet or the Internet.

RTFM: Read the Fabulous Manual.

S-HTTP: Secure HTTP, the TCP/IP protocol for transferring World Wide Web pages across the Internet, with extensions for secure electronic transactions.

Serial Line IP: See *SLIP.*

server: A computer program that provides services to clients, and/or the computer that runs the server program. The FTP client, for example, requests file transfer services from the FTP server. In a networked environment, the server may be on a different computer from the client.

shielded twisted-pair: See *STP.*

Simple Mail Transfer Protocol: See *SMTP.*

Simple Network Management Protocol: See *SNMP.*

SLIP (Serial Line IP): The TCP/IP protocol that enables dialup networking from a computer equipped with a modem. RFC 1055 describes SLIP. See also *CSLIP* and *PPP.*

SMTP (Simple Mail Transfer Protocol): The TCP/IP protocol for sending and receiving e-mail across a network. SMTP specifies that all messages must be text. SMTP is specified in RFC 821. See also *MIME, MTA,* and *MUA.*

SMTP gateway: A computer program that translates e-mail messages from one format to another to interconnect two different e-mail systems when one system uses SMTP and the other does not. May also refer to the computer that runs the SMTP gateway program.

SNA (System Network Architecture): IBM's proprietary network architecture and protocols. You need an SNA gateway to move data between the Internet and an SNA network.

SNMP (Simple Network Management Protocol): The protocol used by management stations (computers that monitor network activity and performance) to communicate with one another and the computers (agents) they are monitoring. RFCs 1065 through 1067 describe SNMP.

socket: A data structure that allows programs on an internet to communicate. A socket is an API (Application Programming Interface) used by programmers who are writing network applications. It works as a pipeline between the communicating programs. The socket consists of an address and a port number.

STD: An RFC that documents a standard component of TCP/IP. See also *RFC* and *FYI.*

STP (shielded twisted-pair): Shielded twisted-pair cable. Most token ring networks use STP.

subnet: A piece of an internet. The act of splitting an IP network range into pieces by means of a subnet mask. For example, an organization may subnet its class B network into 256 class C networks. See also *subnet mask, supernet,* and *supernet mask.*

subnet mask: A 32-bit number used to separate the network and host sections of an IP address. A custom subnet mask subdivides an IP network into smaller pieces. See also *subnet, supernet,* and *supernet mask.*

supernet: An internet formed by combining two subnets into one network. See also *supernet mask, subnet,* and *subnet mask.*

supernet mask: A custom subnet mask used to link together two or more IP networks into a supernet. See also *supernet, subnet,* and *subnet mask.*

System Network Architecture: See *SNA.*

talk: A program that lets two users "converse" on an internet. See also *IRC.*

TCP (Transmission Control Protocol): One of the two principal components of the TCP/IP protocol suite. TCP puts data into packets and provides reliable packet delivery across a network (packets arrive in order and are not lost). TCP is at the transport layer in the network model, just above the internet layer and the IP protocol. RFC 793 is the specification for TCP.

TCP/IP (Transmission Control Protocol/ Internet Protocol): A set of network protocols that connect the Internet. This whole book is about TCP/IP. You didn't really expect to get a complete answer here in the Glossary, did you?

telnet: The TCP/IP protocol, service, and application for logging in to remote computers. Telnet provides VT100 terminal emulation for PCs and workstations. RFC 854 is the specification for telnet. See also *tn3270.*

terminal server: A network device that connects dumb terminals to a host. Can also provide a modem pool for dial-in or dial-out use. Can act as a network interface card when used "backward."

TFTP (Trivial File Transfer Protocol): The TCP/IP protocol used for downloading software and remote booting for diskless computers. TFTP is a subset of the FTP protocol, but it does not require a valid username and password. TFTP depends on another TCP/IP protocol, UDP (User Datagram Protocol). RFC 783 is the specification for TFTP.

thickwire: See *10Base5.*

thinwire: See *10Base2.*

throughput: See *network throughput.*

time to live: See *TTL.*

timeout: Occurs when a timer expires, usually because data was sent, but not acknowledged. When a timeout occurs, the protocol usually retransmits the data.

tn3270: A version of telnet that provides IBM 3270 terminal emulation. See also *telnet.*

token: A set of bits that permits a computer on a token ring network to transmit messages. Computers on a token ring wait to receive a token before transmitting on the network. The token controls the transmission of all traffic on the network.

token ring: A LAN technology that runs over various network media, most often shielded twisted-pair cable. Most token ring networks operate at 16 megabits per second, but some older ones run at only 4 megabits per second.

traffic: The data on the network.

Transmission Control Protocol: See *TCP.*

transport layer: Layer 4 in the ISO OSI Reference Model and TCP/IP network model. The TCP and UDP protocols reside at the transport layer.

Trivial File Transfer Protocol: See *TFTP.*

TTL (time to live): The amount of time a network object remains valid. For example, the amount of time a DNS server can store information in the cache.

UCB (University of California at Berkeley): The site where BSD UNIX and some of the early components of TCP/IP were developed.

UDP (User Datagram Protocol): A TCP/IP protocol found at the network (internet) layer, along with the TCP protocol. UDP sends data down to the internet layer and to the IP protocol. Unlike TCP, UDP does not guarantee reliable, sequenced packet delivery. If data does not reach its destination, UDP does not retransmit as TCP does. RFC 768 is the specification for UDP.

Uniform Resource Locator: See *URL.*

unshielded twisted-pair: See *UTP.*

URL (Uniform Resource Locator): The standard notation for referencing information on the Internet and especially the World Wide Web; for example, `http://www.lotus.com`. The first part of a URL, before the colon, specifies the protocol for accessing the information. The rest of the URL, after the colon, specifies the location of the information.

Usenet news: A TCP/IP service consisting of a worldwide collection of online newsgroups. Each newsgroup is an electronic conversation group about a particular topic.

User Datagram Protocol: See *UDP.*

UTP (unshielded twisted-pair): Unshielded twisted-pair cable. Telephone wire and 10BaseT are examples of UTP.

UUCP (UNIX-to-UNIX Copy Program): Older, non-TCP/IP dialup networking. SLIP and PPP, both TCP/IP protocols, are better choices.

Veronica: A program that helps users navigate Gopherspace; stands for Very Easy Rodent Oriented Network-wide Index to Computerized Archives. It lets you know which of Gopher's many menus have information on topics you request. Veronica does for Gopher what Archie does for FTP.

Virtual Private Network: See *VPN.*

VPN (Virtual Private Network): A private communications environment carried on the Internet using PPTP. See *PPTP.*

VRML (Virtual Reality Modeling Language): A language that extends Web graphics into the world of 3-D.

VT100: The industry-standard dumb terminal (except for IBM's 3270 terminal), created by Digital Equipment Corporation. Many Internet hosts and programs (such as telnet) communicate in VT100 mode.

WAIS (Wide Area Information Services): A program for keyword searching through libraries on the Internet.

WAN (wide area network): A network spanning large geographical distances, often consisting of interconnected LANs.

WebTV: A service for browsing the Web by using your TV monitor as the display. You must pay a monthly connect fee in addition to the cost of the equipment. A keyboard is optional.

whois: A TCP/IP protocol and service that requests information about network sites. The whois utility is well known for its former role, finding users at Internet sites. Recently, when the volume of Internet users became too large to manage, whois information became restricted to network sites rather than individual users. See also *finger.*

wide area network: See *WAN.*

WinSock (Windows Sockets): An API (application programming interface) for Microsoft Windows programs to communicate with TCP/IP. Based on the Berkeley UNIX socket specification.

World Wide Web: See *WWW.*

WWW (World Wide Web): A hypermedia information system on the Internet. Also known as "the Web" or "W3". See also *browser.*

X Window System: The graphical user interface (GUI) software developed at MIT. Uses TCP as its transport protocol.

X.500 Directory Service: An OSI-standard way to build an electronic directory of an organization's personnel. Using X.500, the organization's directory can be part of a global directory that's available on the Internet.

XML (eXtensible Markup Language): A language for creating Web pages that describes the data as well as how the data should look. The description makes Web searching more efficient.

XOR: Stands for the binary mathematical operation eXclusive OR. The result of XORing two bits is 1 if and only if the value of both bits is 1; otherwise the result is 0.

Yellow Pages: See *YP* and *NIS.*

YP (Yellow Pages): The original name for NIS. British Telecom owns the trademark for Yellow Pages but not the initials YP. See also *NIS.*

zone: The group of computer names for which a name server has authority.

Index

IDG BOOKS WORLDWIDE BOOK REGISTRATION

We want to hear from you!

Visit **http://my2cents.dummies.com** to register this book and tell us how you liked it!

- ✔ Get entered in our monthly prize giveaway.

- ✔ Give us feedback about this book — tell us what you like best, what you like least, or maybe what you'd like to ask the author and us to change!

- ✔ Let us know any other ...*For Dummies*® topics that interest you.

Your feedback helps us determine what books to publish, tells us what coverage to add as we revise our books, and lets us know whether we're meeting your needs as a ...*For Dummies* reader. You're our most valuable resource, and what you have to say is important to us!

Not on the Web yet? It's easy to get started with *Dummies 101*®: *The Internet For Windows*® *98* or *The Internet For Dummies*®, 6th Edition, at local retailers everywhere.

Or let us know what you think by sending us a letter at the following address:

...*For Dummies* Book Registration
Dummies Press
7260 Shadeland Station, Suite 100
Indianapolis, IN 46256-3917
Fax 317-596-5498

BESTSELLING
BOOK SERIES